Visionary republic

Visionary republic

Millennial themes in American thought, 1756–1800

Ruth H. Bloch

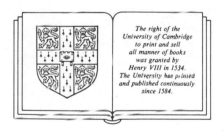

The right of the
University of Cambridge
to print and sell
all manner of books
was granted by
Henry VIII in 1534.
The University has printed
and published continuously
since 1584.

Cambridge University Press

Cambridge
London   New York   New Rochelle
Melbourne   Sydney

Published by the Press Syndicate of the University of Cambridge
The Pitt Building, Trumpington Street, Cambridge CB2 1RP
32 East 57th Street, New York, NY 10022, USA
10 Stamford Road, Oakleigh, Melbourne 3166, Australia

First published 1985

Printed in the United States of America

Frontispiece courtesy of the American Antiquarian Society

Library of Congress Cataloging in Publication Data
Bloch, Ruth H., 1949–
Visionary republic.
Includes index.
1. United States – History – Revolution, 1775–1783 –
Religious aspects. 2. United States – History – Revolution,
1775–1783 – Causes. 3. Millennialism – United States –
History – 18th century. 4 United States – Church history
– Colonial period, ca. 1600–1775. 5. United States –
Intellectual life – 18th century. I. Title.
E209.B58 1985   973.3   85–474
ISBN 0 521 26811 7

TO MY MOTHER, LORE BLOCH,
AND THE MEMORY OF MY FATHER, FELIX BLOCH

It is, in fact, at such moments of collective ferment that are born the great ideals upon which civilizations rest. . . . Such were the Reformation and Renaissance, the revolutionary epoch and the Socialist upheavals of the nineteenth century. At such times the ideal tends to become one with the real, and for this reason men have the impression that the time is close when the ideal will in fact be realized and the Kingdom of God established on earth.

Emile Durkheim, "Judgments of Value and Judgments of Reality" (1911)

Contents

Acknowledgments

This book began with a suggestion by Robert Middlekauff in an introductory graduate seminar many years ago. Thanks largely to his confidence and encouragement, I returned to the subject for my dissertation. As chair of my thesis committee, he gave me both the independence and the advice necessary to develop the topic as my own, while at the same time displaying in his own life and scholarship an inspiring commitment to good history. I was also fortunate to have the intellectual benefit and pleasure of working with Henry May. I was always stimulated by his keen interest in my work, and his careful attention to matters of style improved the quality of my prose. I am, in addition, indebted to several other teachers, friends, and colleagues who commented upon all or part of the manuscript at various stages, including Robert Bellah, Daniel Howe, Wayne Carp, Mark Gould, Joyce Appleby, and Steven Novak. The UCLA Academic Senate and the American Council of Learned Societies, with support from the National Endowment for the Humanities, gave me research grants that facilitated the transformation of the thesis into a book. The women and men at Central Word Processing at UCLA did a splendid job typing and retyping the manuscript through its many revisions. Martin Dinitz supervised the fine copy-editing of Nancy Landau. Frank Smith at Cambridge University Press did what initially seemed the disservice of asking me to cut it down, but he eased the task by offering helpful suggestions and I eventually became convinced that he was right. My husband, Jeffrey Alexander, has read this work over and over again, providing me with loving support as well as the type of invaluable criticism possible only from a sympathetic reader outside the field. Somehow he managed to sustain his enthusiasm for the project over the years. I hope that his unfailing conviction that I have something significant to say here will prove at least partly true.

ix

Acknowledgments

As Jewish immigrants, scientists, and devotees of the "high" culture of classical music and art, my parents were always somewhat perplexed about my decision to study early American religious history. This volume is, however, dedicated to them with the deepest gratitude, for they instilled in me the basic love of learning without which it would never have been begun. Their cheerful willingness to read the long dissertation from cover to cover gave me a lift at a time when my academic fortunes were down. I am only sorry that my father did not live to see this book.

Introduction

The belief in the millennium is one of the oldest and most enduring patterns of thought in Western civilization. The idea that human history is divinely ordained and will lead to a period of heavenly perfection on earth can be dated at least as far back as the prophecies of Isaiah in the eighth century B.C. Since then the idea has received extensive and diverse elaboration within the providential religions of Judaism, Islam, and Christianity and, in combination with other mythologies about the future, has spread throughout the world.

How much the basic millennial belief in a future age of perfection is a specifically biblical one is a matter of debate among historians, folklorists, and anthropologists. What does seem clear is that the Judaic belief in a universal and transcendent God known primarily through his people's experiences on earth served to produce a particularly keen sense of the sacred significance of secular history. Time was conceived by the ancient Israelites as possessing a linear structure with a clear beginning and an end. History was expected to culminate in the glorious triumph of God's people across the world. The earth would then become a paradise for the righteous; sickness, deprivation, war, and oppression would cease to exist. This Old Testament vision of the future has repeatedly been challenged, reinterpreted, and rendered anew, from the age of the Hebrew prophets to the present day. It has formed the core of a remarkably persistent millennial tradition that has deeply affected the historical consciousness of the modern world.[1]

The history of this tradition has been the object of an enormous secondary literature characterized by vigorous interpretative debate and empirical controversy. Historical interpretations of millennialism are, indeed, almost as diverse as those of religion itself, usually proceeding along much the same lines. Millennialism has been interpreted as a spur to action, as a source of comfort, and as a rationale for passivity. It has been described as a feature of fanatical sects or messianic cults and as the belief of an entire society or age. Ideologically it has been judged inherently radical, "progressive," and conservative. It has also been viewed as merely bending with the intellectual wind, attaching itself to the prevailing mode of thought without providing direction of its own.[2]

Only insofar as these various positions are susceptible to factual refutation or confirmation can such debates be resolved. Dissimilar cases obviously call for different interpretations. The disagreements often hinge, however, not merely on the discovery of disparate facts but also on less tangible differences in theoretical and ideological orientations. Historians' preconceptions about the relationship of religion to society, value judgments about the desirability of social movements with utopian goals, assumptions about the disjunction (or conjunction) of popular and elite cultures – all have deeply affected thinking on the subject.

Just as students of millennialism have disagreed about its historical role, American historians have been engaged in a more specific debate about the relationship of religion to the American Revolution. On the one hand, most twentieth-century scholars have stressed the importance of the political philosophy of the Enlightenment and English constitutional theory over that of revealed Christianity. They have portrayed American revolutionaries as supremely rational, sober, and pragmatic, as avoiding the utopian zeal of so many other revolutionary movements in history.[3] Even recent historians concentrating on the highly emotional revolutionary polemics influenced by the English "radical whigs" have assigned religion at most a secondary role, one defined by radical whig ideological imperatives.[4] On the other hand, some scholars have presented religion itself as a major force leading to the American Revolution. Important revolutionary values and ideas have been traced to the popular evangelism of the religious revivals of the mid-eighteenth century, and beyond that to the wider background of seventeenth-century Puritanism and Reformation Protestantism. The idea of America as an elect nation under God, the distrust of elevated institutional hierarchies, the organization of patriot rituals, the pervasive moral asceticism of the American revolutionary mentality – all have been interpreted as derived largely from Protestant religious origins.[5]

No small part of this scholarly debate over the role of religion in the American Revolution has focused on the subject of millennialism. Some historians have stressed the importance of the visionary idea that the Revolution was itself a step towards the millennium. These scholars have, however, so narrowly associated revolutionary millennialism with specific "postmillennial" doctrine and revivalist religious groups that they have failed to make a compelling case for its wider significance.[6] Indeed, their particular arguments have been largely discredited by critics who have gone on to conclude that millennialism (and, by implication, religion in general) played no important autonomous or creative role in the shaping of American revolutionary thought.[7]

The following study of millennial themes in late eighteenth-century America cannot hope to yield definitive answers to the many open questions about millennialism and the role of religion in the American Revolution. By examining the subject anew, however, it can suggest additional ways in which the millennial tradition contributed to the formation of revolutionary consciousness. The form and the intensity of the millennial ideas varied considerably, both over time and among different religious and political groups. The basic millennial vision of future worldly perfection was, however, malleable only to a point. Far from merely reflecting or transmitting other components of revolutionary ideology, millennialism provided the main structure of meaning through which contemporary events were linked to an exalted image of an ideal world.

It is my contention that the existence of this general cultural pattern was basic to the formation of American revolutionary ideology in the late eighteenth century. By this I do not mean that millennialism "caused" the American Revolution in any deterministic sense or that millennial "religious" ideas, as opposed to "secular" liberal or civic republican ideas, provided the "real" ideological basis for the American Revolution. The Revolution is inconceivable without the constitutional and social theories that developed out of the Renaissance and the early Enlightenment. But if millennialism cannot explain the grievances against the Stamp Act or the structure of the United States Constitution, it can illuminate how many Americans understood the ultimate meaning of the revolutionary crisis and the birth of the American nation. The American Revolution involved more than constitutional grievances and institutional change. A large and impassioned popular movement mounted resistance, fought a war, suffered through economic difficulties, and finally bound its fate to that of the American nation. The conviction that history was drawing to its glorious conclusion, when the world would be transformed into a paradise for the righteous, predisposed large numbers of American Protestants to throw themselves behind the revolutionary cause with a fervency that is otherwise hard to explain.

Although it is impossible to know how many Americans were millennialists, the extent and diversity of printed millennial literature suggests that a broad spectrum of American society entertained millennial ideas.[8] Judging from the clerical authors of most millennial publications, perhaps the best way to generalize about the kinds of people who were millennialists is by religious denomination. Congregationalists, Presbyterians, and Baptists seem to have been the most overtly and consistently millennialist groups, and Quakers, Anglicans, Lutherans, and Methodists the least. The smaller Reformed German and Dutch denominations and pietist sects apparently fell somewhere in-between.

Not incidentally, the most millennialist denominations were also those that most solidly backed the American Revolution and tended to take a millennial view of the patriot cause and the new republican nation. They all also had their roots in seventeenth-century British revolutionary Calvinism, each inheriting the originally Calvinist attitude towards the world, which was at once critical and activistic. This attitude, related by Max Weber to the emergence of capitalism, was also indirectly associated with the growth of millennial desires to remake the world during and after the Protestant Reformation.

By the late eighteenth century the distinctively Calvinist characteristics of revolutionary millennialism had largely receded from sight. Millennial ideas were held by people with various social backgrounds and fundamentally different theological beliefs, ranging from strict Calvinism to moderately Enlightened liberalism. The seventeenth-century origins of the American millennial tradition were still visible only as they became institutionalized in the denominational pattern of millennial thought.

Individuals affiliated with one of the more millennialist denominations were, of course, not automatically millennialists themselves. Some people were always intellectually or temperamentally incapable of millennial thinking. The general denominational pattern does, however, suggest certain possibilities about the social base of late eighteenth-century millennialism. Although there is no way of determining what proportion of the Congregationalists, Presbyterians, and Baptists shared the millennial tendencies of the published clergy and laity, it is nonetheless striking that these denominations, taken together, represented close to half of the white population in America in the latter half of the eighteenth century.[9] Regionally, these denominations were most concentrated in New England, where the Congregationalists and the Baptists claimed the vast majority of the population. In the middle and southern regions the picture is more mixed, but even there Baptist and Presbyterian churches comprised almost half the total number of churches.[10] As far as social class is concerned, the more millennialist denominations included virtually all the largest economic groups in the white social hierarchy.

Only a few distinct classes in American society appear from their denominational affiliations to have been notably disinclined towards millennial thought: large southern planters, who were still predominantly Anglican; urban merchants, many of whom were Quaker or Anglican; and, probably, at the bottom of the social scale, christianized free blacks and slaves, who were still disproportionately Anglican or Methodist. The meager published record of merchant and planter millennialism probably reflects the general disinclination of such people to expose themselves in print as much as it reflects the strength of the Quaker and Anglican religions in elite culture. Similarly, the virtual absence of millennialism in the published literature by and about blacks may have been only partly due to the disproportionately strong Quaker, Anglican, and Methodist influence within the antislavery movement and the free black religious community. Perhaps there was also an understandable desire to impress upon white readers the practicality and moderation of black social and religious goals. Given our growing recognition of nineteenth-century black millennialism and the fact that at least a few known white Baptist, Presbyterian, and other millennialists were preaching to blacks in the late eighteenth century, it seems unlikely that so little black millennialism actually existed in America before the year 1800.

Any study based on printed source material cannot avoid overrepresenting the literate. Literacy was comparatively high in late eighteenth-century America, but it was far from universal. It has been estimated that about 75 percent of the adult white males could read (more in New England and fewer in the South). Among women literacy was substantially lower, and among slaves it was virtually negligible. Within a given area literacy correlated highly with wealth.[11] Not all published literature, however, was written for those with a classical education. There was plenty of millennial literature addressed to the unsophisticated. Many printed works such as sermons, orations, and songs were initially designed for oral rather than written presentation. There also remain some nonverbal graphic images and secondhand accounts of sermons, speeches, and visual symbolism used during popular political gatherings. Then as now, moreover, publishers for the most part printed with an eye to the market. The genre of a piece of literature, the relative complexity or simplicity of its language, the region where it appeared, the number of editions printed – all provide clues about the nature and extent of its audience.

In assessing the significance of millennialism in late eighteenth-century America, I have attempted to gauge the popularity and social appeal of millennial literature, to describe its thematic variations, and to examine its relationship to other patterns of thought. To do so has required a consistent definition of what constitutes millennialism, particularly because the boundaries between millennialism, civic republicanism, and the secular utopianism of the Enlightenment were often vague. On the one hand, "millennialism" can be defined very narrowly, as referring only to the literal belief in the supernatural, imminent, and total transformation of the world as foretold in the twentieth chapter of the Book of Revelation. On the other hand, it can be defined very broadly, to mean any vision of a future golden age. Both of these definitions present interpretative difficulties. As for the first, it is frequently impossible to know if the author of a millennial statement meant it literally or not. Moreover, many of the most fervent believers in the millennium expected it to arrive sometime in the more or less distant future, to appear gradually, to be ushered in by human means, or to retain certain valued features of the present world. Yet visionary ideas in this period were still predominantly biblical ones, and an excessively broad definition of "millennialism" would tend to obscure this point. However blurred the line dividing the "religious" from the "secular" – the "millennial" from the "utopian" – may have been, any attempt to clarify the relationship between the Protestant tradition and the new secular utopianism of the Enlightenment must distinguish between them. For the purposes of the present study, it has thus seemed best to restrict the use of the term "millennialism" to statements directly referring to the visionary prophecies of the Bible.

I

The development of a millennial tradition in colonial America

1

Millennialism and the origins of Anglo-American radicalism

> ...and they lived and reigned with Christ a thousand years.
>
> Revelation 20:4

Historians of American revolutionary thought now generally trace the origins of eighteenth-century Anglo-American radicalism to the civic republican tradition imported from the English radical whigs.[1] Although much attention has been given to the transmission of eighteenth-century English republican literature to the colonies in the decades before the American Revolution, there has been a tendency to overlook the religious context in which civic republican ideas first arose in England and which continued to supply much of their meaning in America. It can scarcely be overemphasized that radical whig ideology grew out of the experience of the English Revolution and Commonwealth of the 1640's and 1650's. Remembered with mixed feelings in both England and America, this event was nonetheless the source of many of the cherished political principles supposedly confirmed by the more openly celebrated and moderate Glorious Revolution of 1688–9. Far more than the 1680's, the 1640's and 1650's in England were also years of millennial expectation. Millennialism and civic republicanism gained ascendency together in revolutionary England, and together they also gave rise to American revolutionary ideology during the next century.

THE PURITAN REVOLUTION AND EIGHTEENTH-CENTURY ENGLISH RADICALISM

Although eighteenth-century English political dissent included a few Jacobites who mourned the end of the Stuart reign, the whig opposition always drew more conspicuously on seventeenth-century

Puritan revolutionary thought. Among the intellectual heroes of such radical whig polemicists as John Trenchard and Thomas Gordon were John Milton, James Harrington, and Algernon Sidney. Most of the radical whigs themselves were religious Dissenters, a fact most evident in their stinging denunciations of Anglican bishops. Despite the largely secular, political orientation of their polemical literature, many of their basic premises remained imbedded in an essentially Puritan cast of mind. The assumption that unchecked power would automatically be corrupt drew conviction from the belief in the depravity of unredeemed human nature. The very words "corruption," "virtue," and "vice," which so infused radical whig rhetoric, were laden with religious connotations. Even the qualities thought to be inherent in the civic virtue of the body politic – self-sufficiency, industriousness, frugality, public responsibility – were cornerstones of the Puritan ethic. The civic humanist tradition conceived of this virtue as having a material basis in the wide distribution of land among independent citizen farmers, but it was usually attributed as well to Protestant religious morality. Conversely, along with luxury and economic dependence, a key symptom of the corruption of public virtue was the ignorant acceptance of superstitious and despotic religion. By this, the radical whigs, like several generations of American Protestants, meant Catholicism and high-church Anglicanism.

The historical and symbolic convergence of Dissenting Protestantism and radical whig ideology points to the difficulty of defining one as purely religious and the other simply as secular. Just as Max Weber wrote of the Protestant ethic that lay beneath "the spirit of capitalism," it may be argued that a secularized religious impulse infused oppositionist whig ideology in the eighteenth century. Of course, Reformation theology did not necessarily breed political rebellion, much less dictate specific constitutional arrangements. But such fundamental doctrines as the priesthood of all believers, the corruption of unredeemed human nature, and the need to activate faith in this world had a radical political potential that carried into the eighteenth-century whig opposition.

Not that radical whig ideology can be understood merely as a product of the radical Reformation. What most clearly distinguished it from the Protestant religious tradition were the elements it borrowed instead from classical republican thought. The distance between the civic republican tradition and seventeenth-century English and American Calvinism is particularly evident in their

4

conflicting conceptions of history. Whereas radical whig ideology derived its historical theory from classical and Renaissance thought, the Anglo-American revolutionary religious tradition inherited the endemic millennialism of English Puritanism.

The radical whigs generally assumed a cyclical perspective on history. According to this originally classical view, the history of human society showed continuous circular movement among various forms of government, of which the "republican" mixture of monarchical, aristocratic, and democratic parts was by far the most preferable. Because republics were established on the fragile basis of liberty and public virtue, however, they were particularly vulnerable to internal corruption, external invasion, and eventual overthrow by despotic power. The basic question that had long confronted theorists of republican government was how to maintain republics against these formidable odds. The traditional answer was to divide power against itself, particularly by limiting the nonrepresentative monarchical branch and by guaranteeing the political expression of public virtue in the representative legislature. According to the radical whigs this was the very solution enacted in England during the previous century by the constitutional settlement of the Glorious Revolution. But in the eighteenth century they worried that the self-interested machinations of executive power had begun seriously to weaken the legislature. They warned that corrupt ministers of the Georgian monarchs had undermined the autonomy of the House of Commons and, in league with dishonest financial speculators and popish Anglican bishops, were threatening to destroy the entire fabric of British liberty. Unless virtue and balance could be rapidly restored, the radical whigs repeatedly warned, the future promised unmitigated despotism. Dominated by an idealization of the past and a fear of change, their perspective on history was fundamentally conservative. Its object was the protection of a preexisting political, social, and moral order against the continuous threat of degeneration.[9]

This fearful, pessimistic vision of the future drawn from civic republicanism was fundamentally in conflict with millennialism. Millennialists foretold not the probable demise of liberty but the creation of a heavenly paradise on earth. They conceived of history not as an endless series of cycles but as an essentially progressive movement towards an inevitably happy conclusion. Viewing this movement in Manichaean terms as a cosmic conflict between good and evil, they recognized that the Antichrist might seem to be

5

winning in the short run but held that his days were fatefully numbered. His final defeat would usher in a new dispensation realizing the Edenic possibility of human virtue, physical comfort, and spiritual grace. There would then be no more tyranny or oppression, no more war or animosity, no more greed or want, no more ignorance or false belief.

The millennial tradition in colonial America, like the ideas of the radical whigs, can largely be traced back to revolutionary England of the seventeenth century and, beyond that, to the Protestant Reformation. Prior to the Reformation the orthodox Catholic position of Augustine had been that the millennial prophecies be read figuratively, as referring to the perennial perfection of the City of God but not to the future of the City of Man. Thus deemed heretical by the medieval church, the millennial ideas of ancient Judaism and early Christianity nonetheless persisted underground. They had already gained strength by the late Middle Ages and then rose to the surface within the left wing of the Protestant movement, first in Northern Europe and then in England and the American colonies.[3]

Luther and Calvin themselves had sought to establish a Protestant eschatology in keeping with Augustine. But despite their efforts the critical rallying cry of the Reformation invited the dismantling of the orthodox Catholic position on this as on other matters of doctrine. For against the authority of ecclesiastical tradition, the reformers upheld the biblical word as spoken to the individual conscience before God. This central teaching inevitably gave rise to the proliferation of individuals and sects who claimed their own understanding of Scripture. It was in this more fluid situation, in which bare biblical text commanded the highest respect, that a more literal reading of the millennial prophecies in the books of Daniel and Revelation acquired a legitimacy long lost in the traditional church.

Protestantism also gave rise to millennial aspirations by intensifying the ambiguity towards the world that had always been a source of tension within Christianity. On the one hand, the reformers, like Augustine, concentrated on the fallibility of humanity and the corruption of earthly existence. In their view even fully moral people were unworthy of salvation. Grace came only as the free gift of an utterly inscrutable God. But the Protestant abolition of traditional devotional works, monasteries, and the sacred priesthood at the same time made the world the only possible arena for the expression of grace. Even predestinarian Calvinists admitted there was a connection between behavior and redemption, for activity in the world was a sign (if not a source) of grace. In collapsing the Catholic duality between lay and priestly, sacred and profane, mainstream Protestantism left less room for either extreme acceptance or extreme rejection of the things of this life. Protestants were called to activate their faith in righteous and productive work in the world. Weber saw in this conception of the calling an incentive for the hard work and frugality at the basis of entrepreneurial capitalism. The same constellation of attitudes towards the world – at once critical and activistic – also indirectly encouraged the development of a millennial outlook on history. For in the work of transforming the world from the dominion of Satan to the Kingdom of Christ, the faithful could see themselves directly manifesting the glory of God. In Protestantism as in medieval Catholicism, this perspective was always particularly attractive to sectarians who set themselves in opposition to the rest of society. The sectlike features of Calvinism, with its doctrine of the predestined Elect, also pulled strongly in a millennial direction.

England provided a fertile environment for the growth of Protestant millennial thought. By the time of the Reformation there already was a strong indigenous tradition of prophetic folklore and theology. In the fourteenth century John Wyclif had taught specifically that the destruction of the Beasts in the Book of Revelation prophesied the end of the Roman Antichrist, a judgment that passed into popular Lollardism in the following century. Not surprisingly, with the Reformation this view of the papal adversaries became far more compelling in England as well as in Northern Europe. Especially after Queen Mary's harsh repression of the Protestants and the outbreak of continuing Tudor wars with Spain, the identification of the Pope as the Antichrist became an integral part of English Protestant doctrine.[4]

Several prominent reformers in the late sixteenth century interpreted the Book of Revelation as prophesying contemporary events. By far the most influential was the Marian exile John Foxe, whose epic *Actes and Monuments* chronicled the Antichrist's persecution of righteous English Protestants. Under the Protestant Elizabethan and early Stuart crowns the notion that the Catholic powers represented the Beast of the Revelation was in itself far from being a subversive doctrine. Such a reading of prophecy tied the fortunes of true Christianity closely to the Church of England and monarchy. Gradually, however, dissident Puritans loosened this connection, stretching the definition of the Antichrist to include what they regarded as the papist features of the established ecclesiastical order. Sensitive to the implications of this development, the church hierarchy began toning down its apocalyptical rhetoric, and under Archbishop Laud and Charles I altogether ceased to identify even the Pope as the Antichrist. In 1637, Laud forbade the printing of a new edition of Foxe.

During this period of increased tension in the early seventeenth century, many Puritans moved beyond the mere identification of the Pope as the Antichrist to full-blown millennial expectations. Until then, Foxe and other reformed exegetes in England – much as Luther himself – had interpreted the Book of Revelation as foretelling the Protestants' victorious struggle against the Catholics without pointing to a specifically millennial conclusion. By the late sixteenth century, however, some English Calvinists had added the prediction that as the end of the world approached, Jews would be converted and return to Israel and the true church would experience a tremendous revival. The definitive break with Augustine's and Luther's nonmillennial eschatology was made in the biblical commentaries published by the German Calvinist Johannes Alsted in 1627 and, following Alsted, by the Cambridge Platonist Joseph Mede (himself neither Puritan nor Laudian) in 1632. These writers held specifically that the thousand years of Revelation 20:4 was a distinctive historical age that had yet to begin. Mede, in addition, maintained that Christ need not visibly descend to inaugurate this felicitous period but would work through his spirit within the saints.[5]

This doctrine of the future millennium was eagerly embraced by English revolutionaries in the 1640's.[6] In 1643 a committee of the revolutionary House of Commons ordered the translation of Mede's Latin treatise into the English vernacular (complete with a "compendium" of world history for the less educated), and the protomillennialist works of Foxe and other earlier Puritans also appeared in numerous new editions. Although Mede himself envisioned the millennium in purely religious terms as the consummation of Protestantism, in the context of the revolutionary turmoil the ideas about the arrival and character of the millennial state took a decidedly political turn. Revolutionaries of many shades now associated the Antichrist not only with popery and Laudism but with the secular power of the monarchy. And whereas only a small number of radical sectaries like the Diggers strove towards a millennium of social equality, many republicans of the Commonwealth period entertained millennial ideas. The Fifth Monarchist movement, consisting of London artisans who turned against Cromwell in the early 1650's, combined a belief in saintly rule during the millennium with such strong republican sentiments that one member of the sect actually advocated a holy alliance with the Catholic republicans of Venice.[7] John Milton emphatically dissociated himself from the Fifth Monarchists' worldly conception of the Kingdom of God – eventually concluding in *Paradise Regained* that the fulfillment of millennial prophecy must await God's good time – but in the early 1650's he, too, still identified Christ's rule with republican principles of government.[8] Even the utopian vision of James Harrington was, for all its greater materialism, only one step removed from revolutionary Puritan apocalypticism.[9]

Over the course of the revolutionary period, however, English millennialism became associated with increasingly narrow and sectarian forms of radical extremism. By the time of Cromwell and the Rump Parliament the intense millennial hopes of most revolutionaries of the 1640's had already faded in disillusionment. With the Restoration the few remaining radical millennialists were effectively suppressed. The Glorious Revolution of 1688–9 stimulated the publication of several pamphlets interpreting William's invasion as a step towards the defeat of Antichrist, but these were aimed primarily at James's Catholicism rather than at the structure of government.[10] In the place of revolutionary millennialism there arose more quietistic, esoteric, and moderate interpretations of prophecy, which posed little threat to the state.

Most of the English prophetic writing of the late seventeenth and early eighteenth centuries was by Nonconformists and Anglican latitudinarians who were politically whiggish and theologically liberal. The most influential exegetes of this period were part of a circle of low-church theologians and lesser Newtonian scientists who sought to synchronize sacred and natural history according to the principles of the new science. Only occasionally, in times of unusual crisis, did their apocalyptical speculations include commentary on political affairs. Sensitive to the lingering public associations of millennialism with the radicalism of the Puritan Revolution, they seldom aired their specifically millennial ideas either in sermons or in vernacular print. The apocalyptical process was for them primarily the unfolding of natural law. This conception left little room for revolutionary upheaval by the people of God, but it did at least deny

9

the need for miraculous intervention by God. These latitudinarians usually took the view that Christians would prepare themselves for the millennium by accumulating scientific knowledge and by spreading the faith.[11]

Other commentaries upon prophecy written in the first half of the eighteenth century also described the coming of the millennium in nonmiraculous and activistic, if essentially apolitical, terms. For example, Daniel Whitby, another liberal churchman, argued against the literalist view that the dead saints would be supernaturally resurrected for the millennium. Instead, he more simply envisioned a universal revival of the Protestant faith that would result in millennial peace and prosperity. Moses Lowman, a Nonconformist minister influenced by Whitby, likewise advanced a figurative interpretation of the latter-day raising of the saints and the coming of Christ. Both Whitby and Lowman saw human history as gradually, if not altogether smoothly, progressing to the millennium. Their works became standard academic references on biblical prophecy throughout the Anglo-American world.[12]

Although interest in prophetic speculation continued among these scientists and theologians, millennial thought in England became an almost exclusively academic and theoretical concern. Since the Puritan Revolution millennialism had been on the wane, declining from the stature of a popular public ideology to a rare item of technical theological debate. There is some sign of a surviving tradition of millennial radicalism in the following that gathered behind the French Protestant "prophets" of the Camisard Rebellion who found refuge in England in 1706, but it was only at the end of the eighteenth century, during the economic and political crisis engendered by the French Revolution, that popular millennialism again rose to the surface in England. Significantly, neither the radical whigs in the political opposition nor the preachers of the Methodist revival gained a reputation for millennial thought.[13]

EARLY AMERICAN MILLENNIALISM AND THE GREAT AWAKENING

Millennialism in the American colonies took an entirely different course. Although our knowledge of early American millennialism is unfortunately far from complete, what emerges from the fragments is a picture of diverse millennial traditions maintaining a great deal of vitality throughout the eighteenth century. The most compelling evidence of a powerful and continuing millennial tradition in colonial America comes, of course, from Puritan New England. Puritans in America as well as in England were at the forefront of early seventeenth-century millennial thought. And in New England, unlike in other parts of the colonies, religious ideas found their way into print and therefore have more easily survived the passage of time. Although historians have been slow to recognize the eschatological element of American Puritanism, several recent studies have demonstrated that many, perhaps most, of the leaders of the 1630's thought about their migration to New England in the terms of millennial prophecy.[14] During the revolutionary decades of the 1640's and 1650's, John Cotton and John Eliot, under Fifth Monarchy auspices, published inflammatory works that proclaimed the imminent dissolution of all earthly monarchies and the ascendance of rule by the saints. Two other New Englanders, William Aspinwall and Thomas Venner, both of whom were influenced by Cotton, returned to England and in the 1650's threw themselves into Fifth Monarchy agitation.

Yet within New England, millennialism never took the radical forms it had in revolutionary England. This relative moderation was partly because of the more successful repression and banishment of dissidents like Anne Hutchinson (herself a millennialist) and partly because the existing colonial government came closer to realizing a theocratic ideal. Moreover, first-generation New England Puritans saw themselves primarily as exiles and still viewed England, not America, as the spearhead of apocalyptical developments. When John Winthrop explained why immigration to New England had fallen off in the 1640's, he stressed that the revolution had made "all men to stay in England in expectation of a new world."[15]

Although less radical than English revolutionary millennialism, American Puritan millennialism proved the more culturally persistent. New Englanders did not, as their English counterparts had done, generally abandon a prophetic outlook on history after the Puritan Revolution in England was over. To be sure, when the political situation in England stabilized in the late seventeenth century, the earlier sense of apocalyptical crisis abated. New England Puritans began instead to develop the more provincial mythology of the new American Israel. If less expectant and less English in its orientation than that of the previous generation, millennialism remained far more firmly intact in the colonies in the late seventeenth century than in England itself. As Increase Mather observed in 1710, a belief in the coming of the millennium "has ever been received as a Truth in the

Churches of *New-England*."[16] It has even been argued that Cotton Mather, the leading Puritan of the early eighteenth century, moved eschatology for the first time to the very center of New England theology, displacing even the doctrines of Calvin as the key to the meaning of God's sovereignty.[17]

This is not to say that all New Englanders agreed about how the millennium would come. Both Increase and Cotton Mather came to reject the commonly held idea that New England would usher in the millennium while growing ever more convinced of the imminent, literal, and cataclysmic advent of Christ. Other religious figures of the early eighteenth century denied that the millennium would come soon or that Christ would appear in the flesh.[18] Yet these substantive debates actually confirm the view that millennialism was, in itself, still very much a part of New England orthodoxy.

This prophetic speculation was far from merely a rarefied theological concern. Such popular works as Joseph Morgan's *History of the Kingdom of Barasuah* (1715), based on the allegorical model of John Bunyan, held out the promise of Christ's Kingdom in the New World.[19] Millennial theory also received much practical application in colonial New England. On the front of the continuing imperial wars with France, for example, patriotic exhortations repeatedly associated the Catholic enemy with the Beast of Revelation.[20] The Church of England also continued to be a victim of New Englanders' polemical readings of prophecy. Cotton Mather not only watched expectantly for signs of the French papists' defeat but followed the lead of his forefathers in viewing the English ecclesiastical system as dangerously contaminated by the Antichrist.

Politically, these New England interpretations of prophecy were at once patriotically British and tinged with nascent American nationalism. As in sixteenth-century England, it was the Papacy, not any system of government, that appeared as the main enemy. It would be a mistake to conclude, however, that late seventeenth- and early eighteenth-century American millennialism altogether lacked political significance. The idea of the Elect Nation – as applied to the British Empire and, in particular, to America – was as much political as religious from its very inception. Moreover, the revolutionary ideology of the seventeenth century, now in loyal whiggish form, still periodically cropped up in American apocalyptical rhetoric. Benjamin Colman, for example, worried that the New England earthquake of 1727 might be a bad omen of the end times for British civil liberties as well as for the Protestant faith.[21] Jonathan Edwards wrote in 1724 that when the millennium came "the absolute and despotic power of the kings of the earth shall be taken away, and liberty shall reign throughout the earth."[22] In the context of the early eighteenth century there was, of course, nothing particularly revolutionary or republican about these libertarian ideas. That millennialism still carried the old associations to popular radicalism, however, is suggested by an article that appeared in the *New England Courant* in 1721. Probably written in criticism of one of the expectant sermons by Cotton Mather, the piece warned that millennial proclamations by European prophetic pretenders had in the past stirred "whole Hords of the Vulgar."[23] The anxiety expressed in this statement would later find repeated expression among the opponents of the great American millennial movement of the mid-eighteenth century – the religious revivals known as the Great Awakening.

It was the Great Awakening that spread the millennial tradition of New England Puritanism into the rest of the colonies. Prior to its eruption in the 1740's, the evidence of millennialism outside New England comes primarily from the small Dutch and German pietist sects, groups like the Labadists on the northern shores of Chesapeake Bay, the Society of the Woman in the Wilderness in Germantown, the Ephrata community, and the Moravians, all of whom formed communistic (and usually celibate) communities in Pennsylvania and Maryland to await the onset of the latter-day glory.[24] Refugees from religious persecution in Central and Northern Europe, these scattered groups were among the few surviving remnants of the great revolutionary millennialist uprisings that occurred there in the fifteenth and sixteenth centuries. Whether or not the mainstream English and other, nonsectarian ethnic immigrants in the middle and southern colonies also brought with them a strong millennial tradition has yet to be determined (if it is possible to do so at all). It is known that there were millennial overtones in the literature promoting Virginia in the early seventeenth century – a fact that should not be surprising given the prophetic tenor of English nationalism at the time – but it is uncertain whether these ideas persisted after the Puritan Revolution.[25] In New York as late as 1724 the Anglican governor William Burnet anonymously published a treatise on the Book of Daniel predicting the oncoming fall of the Antichrist.[26] It is quite possible that there were other American Anglicans in the middle and southern colonies who also still thought in these terms, much like the English liberal latitudinarians, but one cannot tell merely from the meager published record of their thought. It is even more likely, although still uncertain, that the numerous Calvinists among the minority ethnic immigrant groups – the Presbyterian Scotch-Irish and Scots, the Germans and Dutch in the Reformed churches, the French Huguenots – retained some of the millennial inclinations of their sixteenth and seventeenth-century forebears.

Surely one reason the religious revivals of the mid-eighteenth century spread so rapidly throughout the American colonies was this vast reservoir of ethnic immigrant Calvinism; the Congregationalist, Presbyterian, Baptist, and Reformed colonists who constituted the great majority of American revivalists were, unlike the English Methodists, almost all Calvinist in their theology. The Great Awakening was the first real mass movement in American history, enlisting the fervent participation of colonists from New England to Georgia, of many Dutch, German, and Scotch-Irish settlers as well as the English, of theologians of the stature of Jonathan Edwards along with illiterate backwoodsmen and even some slaves. Never before had so many Americans been mobilized behind so deeply compelling a common cause. Whereas the spiritual outpourings of the Awakening had numerous forerunners in colonial religious experience, none had occurred on so tremendous a scale. Contributing to the success of the evangelical preaching were long-range social changes common to many parts of the colonies – growing economic inequalities, increasing demographic pressures, the rise of a commercial and secular culture – that helped to produce widespread spiritual and psychological malaise. A scarcity of ministers in many places, moreover, meant that new settlements were often left unchurched. And growing numbers of clergymen (whether out of genuine intellectual commitment or simple incompetence) preached formal and rational creeds that failed to address the emotional needs of the ordinary laity. In this environment, the dynamic and heartfelt Calvinism of George Whitefield and the other revivalists rapidly swelled the strong undercurrent of American pietism into a flood.

The revivals at times assumed a pronounced populist tone. Especially in the seaboard cities and in the southern plantation colonies, where society was most highly stratified, wealthy merchants, planters, and clergymen of the established Congregationalist and Anglican churches tended not to support the Awakening. As Jonathan Edwards noted with dismay in 1742, "There is commonly a certain unhappy shyness in great men with respect to religion, as though they were ashamed of it, or at least ashamed to do very much at it."[27] Small farmers, traders, artisans, servants, and laborers – in short, the middle and lower classes of white colonial society – seem to have constituted, by contrast, the vast majority of the population swept by revival enthusiasm. Many New Light preachers directed scathing attacks not only against the privileges of the "unconverted" established clergy but against the luxurious pleasures of the well-to-do. The Great Awakening powerfully reaffirmed the radical and democratic elements of Reformation Protestantism in its insistence on the fundamental equality and solidarity of the faithful and the higher virtues of the simple, ascetic life.

Not that the revivals aimed at a goal of social or political equality. The anti-authoritarian contempt for the intellectual pretensions of the rationalist clergy and the pride and luxury of the rich were criticisms of worldly values, not of social structure or of government. There was plenty of room left in the revivalists' scheme of things for righteous wealth and righteous kings. Yet this type of moral argument did serve in the long run to corrode the legitimacy of established sources of prestige and power. The Awakening, like many other episodes in the history of Christianity, encouraged ordinary people to disparage worldly standards of greatness, to insist upon the real superiority of the regenerate saints and their own collective equality before God. The same volatile religious issues of spiritual equality, human depravity, worldly asceticism, and the righteousness of the Elect that had rocked England in the seventeenth century now rose once again in America in the mid-eighteenth century. Even the numerous detractors of the Awakening were forced to defend themselves in terms largely set by the revivalists – to deny their own worldliness, for example, or to argue their own greater virtue.

As the great wave of religious enthusiasm subsided in the 1750's it left in its wake a sensitivity to those very moral issues that formed the religious dimension of radical whig ideology. The rapid importation of radical whig ideas to America in the 1720's and 1730's may already have owed as much to Calvinist religious dispositions as to the structure of colonial politics. By the time the American Revolution began in the 1760's, the Great Awakening had made Americans even more receptive to these ideas. The revolutionary appeals to a virtuous citizenry, the ethic of self-sufficiency and frugality, the suspicion of institutionalized authority, the characterization of the royal ministers as greedy, self-interested, dissolute, and even Catholic at heart – all these fundamental features of American revolutionary rhetoric drew sustenance from popular religion as well as from whig constitutional theories.

The Great Awakening also raised and diffused intense millennial expectations. Since the principal medium of communication in the revivals was oral preaching and personal testimony, it is impossible to determine from the remaining literary evidence precisely how often New Lights understood the conversions in millennial terms. But the writings of the Awakening that do survive strongly suggest that millennial ideas were widespread among American evangelicals. A widely reprinted sermon about George Whitefield by the South Carolina Congregationalist Josiah Smith suggested in 1740 that revivals were a harbinger of the new age.[28] In Pennsylvania the New Side Presbyterian Samuel Finley published a sermon in 1741 interpreting the effusions of grace as proof that "the Kingdom of God is come unto us at this Day."[29] The weekly reports publicizing the progress of the revivals in Thomas Prince's *Christian History*, the Boston evangelical magazine printed between 1743 and 1745, were likewise periodically punctuated with millennial exclamations.[30]

It was Jonathan Edwards, however, deemed by Perry Miller the "greatest artist of the apocalypse," who furnished by far the most authoritative and articulate millennial interpretation of revivalism.[31] Edwards's fascination with millennial prophecy did not originate in the Awakening. In 1723 he had begun his private "Notes on the Apocalypse," in which he recorded exegetical theories about the Book of Revelation and his periodic thoughts on the signs of the times. In public, however, Edwards avoided all direct reference to the millennium before the Awakening, perhaps because, as one Edwards scholar has suggested, he wished "to escape the taint of fanaticism and radicalism associated with the idea."[32] Even during the Northampton revival of 1734–5 he merely alluded in his preaching to the possibility of glorious consequences without assigning to the wave of conversions any explicitly millennial role. He still confined millennial speculation to his notebook despite the fact that other ministers commenting on his news were quick to publicize their millennial conclusions.[33]

After the 1734–5 revival was over, however, in the spiritually "dead" interlude before Whitefield's arrival, Edwards preached a series of sermons that pointed directly to the glorious consummation of history. Posthumously published in 1774 under the title *A History of the Work of Redemption*, these sermons provided a narrative of the workings of Providence from the time of the Creation to the end of the world. Edwards was seeking to rekindle the spark of revivalism by looking beyond the darkness of the immediate present to the grandeur of the whole of the historical process and the promise of social redemption in the millennium and the new heavens and earth. Although he abstained from speculation as to precisely when the Antichrist would fall and the millennium begin, there were many hopeful ingredients in his vision. He endorsed the theory of the English exegete Moses Lowman, who interpreted the Protestant Reformation as the "fifth vial" of the Book of Revelation and present history as the sixth, the vial that was immediately to precede the final destruction of the Antichrist. Edwards regarded recent religious revivals in Germany as well as New England as major portents of the approaching new age.[34]

When in 1740 God's spirit again burst forth under the charismatic preaching of Whitefield, Edwards was eager to announce the millennial significance of the event. His letter that February inviting Whitefield to Northampton already expressed heightened millennial hopes.[35] Edwards's boldest and most optimistic assertion appeared in print in his major polemic on behalf of the revivals, *Some Thoughts Concerning the Present Revival of Religion in New-England*, published in Boston in 1742. He interpreted the Awakening as a sign that the millennium would come soon, and he declared, in addition, that it would probably begin in America.[36] This speculation, entirely unlike Edwards's earlier, far more cautious statements about prophecy, rephrased older Puritan ideas about the Elect Nation in exceptionally extravagant terms. The passage rapidly became notorious among opponents of the revivals, who viewed it as the consummate expression of unbridled enthusiasm.[37] Several years later, after the Awakening in New England had died down, Edwards again aired his lingering – although less provincially American – millennial hopes in a 1747 pamphlet endorsing a transatlantic "concert of prayer" proposed by fellow evangelical ministers in Scotland. As Edwards explained the purpose of their program, the prayers would lead to more religious revivals that would in turn bring on the final fulfillment of prophecy. Again he voiced his opinion that the world was currently under the sixth vial and that, with the aid of further effusions of grace, the Antichrist would soon fall. He pointed to the recent New England military victory over the antichristian French Catholics at Cape Breton and to the continuing religious revivals in Protestant Europe, Britain, and America as auspicious signs that the latter days were nigh.[38]

The social and political implications of the millennial ideas of Jonathan Edwards and other leaders of the Great Awakening are of special historical interest because of the subsequent coming of the American Revolution.[39] But New Light millennialism during the Great Awakening certainly did not contain a critique of the British government or call for any institutional social or political reforms. It invested its hopes for the world first and foremost in widespread spiritual regeneration. The activity it promoted as "means" to the millennium was strictly evangelical – preaching, missionary work, and prayer. Even Edwards's idea about the inaugural role of America, however expressive of a kind of protonationalism, was couched in this evangelical framework and scarcely provided either a program or the incentive for political revolution.

Yet various features of New Light millennialism did contribute to the development of revolutionary ideology. This contribution consisted not so much of specific political arguments as of a general orientation towards the meaning of human action. One important characteristic of New Light millennialism was its assumption that purposeful endeavor was instrumental in achieving millennial happiness. This emphasis on the redemptive possibilities of human behavior has been related by some religious historians to the spread of "postmillennialism," the theory that Christ's presence in the millennium would be spiritual and his miraculous physical coming would occur only afterwards.[40] Jonathan Edwards and his closest disciples were indeed postmillennialists. Other revivalists, however, were not. The activism inherent in New Light millennialism was clearly independent of either postmillennial or premillennial exegetical theory.[41]

As good Calvinists the revivalists, of course, never claimed that God gave grace as a reward for good behavior. They did, however, seek to promote the work of the spirit through the activities of preaching and prayer. They also believed (in accordance with the classic loophole of Calvinism) that faith would become sanctified in works. Although the action they advocated in the 1740's was mostly evangelical, Edwards and other New Light clergymen were also quite capable in the same decade of celebrating the Cape Breton victory over the Catholic French in millennial terms.[42] Their belief that the Kingdom of God would advance primarily through effusions of grace by no means denied that the saints might also employ violence to defeat the Antichrist.

The militant attitude encouraged by such a perspective arose not only from New Light confidence in the efficacy of human action but from their marked propensity to divide the world between the forces of Christ and those of the Antichrist. God's purpose in history, as Edwards explained it, was "to put all enemies under his feet,[so] that the goodness of God should finally appear triumphing over all evil."[43] When considering who constituted the satanic alliance, moreover, Edwards did not stop at the standard papal Antichrist, or even at the Turks and the heathens, but also perceived other enemies closer at hand. The Anglican Church was little better than the Roman Catholic, Edwards believed, reiterating the Puritan charges, and he added a host of other sinful deviations that threatened American Protestantism from within, including Old Light Arminianism.[44] He once even cited the English radical whig James Burgh on the general corruption of the mother country, warning in the manner of a jeremiad that the colonies were equally bad.[45] Luxury, selfishness, and pervasive disregard of religion were among the most common charges. The impulse to purge such corruptions as well as to destroy all foreign legions of the Antichrist formed an integral part of New Light millennial consciousness. If not defined in political terms, this constellation of desires – purist, aggressive, and visionary – contained the makings of later revolutionary ideology.

Occasionally, moreover, the millennialism of the Great Awakening did incorporate more explicitly political statements. When Edwards discussed the nature of government in the millennium, for example, he emphasized the godliness of the rulers and the love between them and the ruled.[46] Although he never suggested that the institution of the monarchy would collapse, he relished the saints' future reprisals against unrighteous kings. Using the language of Psalms, he described the coming of Christ's Kingdom as a time of holy vengeance upon "such rulers as oppose him, or won't bow to him; a day wherein he shall 'strike through kings,' and 'fill the places with the dead bodies,' and 'wound the heads over many countries.'"[47] He criticized the Massachusetts government for not encouraging the revivals, threatening, "The days are coming, so often spoken of, when the saints shall reign on earth, and all dominion and authority shall be given into their hands."[48]

There are also notable passages in Edwards's eschatological writings, beginning as early as 1724, that describe the millennium as a time of civil and religious liberty for the saints. Sermons of the late 1730's portrayed the early progress of Christianity toward "a state of liberty from persecution" as foreshadowing the "advancement of the church into that state of the glorious prevalence of truth, liberty, peace, and joy, that we so often read of in the prophetical parts of

Scripture." Edwards also indicted the papal Antichrist for robbing the people of both their civil and ecclesiastical liberties.[49] The millennium, he reiterated in his *Humble Attempt* of 1747, would be a time of "glorious liberty," of "liberty and glory."[50]

In these passages Edwards did not always specify whether such liberty was a quality of civil as well as of ecclesiastical and spiritual life. The word "liberty" was used in a similarly inclusive sense by other revivalists as well. At times it referred to the ecstatic feeling of release from sin that came with religious conversion, but it also often meant freedom from state laws discriminating against nonestablished and itinerant preachers and, beyond that, liberation from all forms of civil tyranny.[51] This identification of political liberty with righteousness was in itself, however, scarcely radical. It was quite conventionally Protestant whig. The radicalism of New Light millennialism had less to do with the content of these scattered political reflections than with the immediacy of the expectations and their context within the popular revival movement.

During the Great Awakening visionary ideas were diffused among an exceptionally large and committed population of colonists. And, as is usually true of millennial aspirations, evangelical religion could not in the long run satisfy all the expectations it fostered. However exaggerated the fears of the leading opponents of the Awakening, it is still indicative of the temper of the revivals that they reminded so many people of the revolutionary Protestant sects of previous centuries.[52]

The millennial hopes stirred by Edwards and the other evangelists were significant above all because they were so intense and widespread. The Great Awakening itself did not introduce a millennial theory of history to American Protestantism. Millennialism already had deep roots in Anglo-American culture, roots that primarily extended back to the Puritan movement in the early seventeenth century but that also drew nourishment from other forms of Calvinism, latitudinarian Anglicanism, and English Dissent. Indeed, for all the publicity given to New Light millennialism, even in mid-eighteenth-century America a millennial outlook was never altogether confined to revivalist pietists. The more rationalist millennialism that characterized English latitudinarianism and liberal Nonconformity also had its representatives in the colonies, especially among those New England Congregationalists who moved away from the traditional Puritan emphasis upon free grace. If temporarily drowned out by the revivals, their voices would be heard more in the following decades – at times converging with those of post-Awakening evangelicals – in pursuit of now common American causes. The Great Awakening, for all its divisiveness, unquestionably broadened the audience for these subsequent appeals, imbuing them with an emotional fervor that carried over into the issues ahead.

Colonial millennialism on the eve of the revolutionary crisis

This know also, that in the last days perilous times shall come.

2 Timothy 3:1

The 1750's, like the 1740's, were years of great eschatological expectation. Not even during the high tide of the Great Awakening did colonial presses issue as much millennial literature as they did in the following decade. If, in this relatively literate society, the sheer numbers of publications on the subject can be taken as a rough index to cultural preoccupations, more Americans thought about the Last Days in the late 1750's than ever before. Unlike the evangelical Calvinist millennialism of the Great Awakening, moreover, the millennialism of the 1750's cut across the religious divisions created by the revivals. Now Old Lights as well as New Lights embraced a millennial view of the future, and rarely did prophetic pronouncements address the emotional, theological, and ecclesiastical issues that had divided them previously. Much of the millennial literature published in the 1750's was aimed at a more general audience than any particular religious group, and no longer were most of the works written by leaders of the New England clergy, such as Edwards and Prince. Many authors were obscure or anonymous. A few of them were distant historical, even legendary, figures whose reputations as millennial prophets had been passed down in religious folklore through the generations.

Both the volume and the content of the millennial literature printed in the 1750's attests to the general reduction of religious antagonism as the Great Awakening, at least in the northern colonies, petered out. In part the burgeoning interest in millennial speculation can be explained by events that had nothing to do with revivalism at all. A worldwide series of earthquakes and the onset of the French and Indian War sparked thoughts of the Last Days among a wide range of colonists, revivalists and nonrevivalists alike. Yet, indirectly, the influence of the Great Awakening on American millennial thought was still deeply felt. The religious enthusiasm of the 1740's had spread millennial hopes throughout the colonies and had drawn attention to a general perspective on history that did not necessarily depend for its appeal on participation in the evangelical movement. Many moderate Calvinist or liberal clergymen who in the 1740's had not partaken in the millennial euphoria of the New Lights nevertheless felt more free, even eager, to express their own millennial ideas after the revivals subsided than they had been before the revivals began. There were, moreover, lingering differences between the revivalists and the nonrevivalists that were reflected in their millennial outlooks. Although neither group espoused its own coherent exegetical theory, such as premillennialism or postmillennialism, there were still significant contrasts in their social and political sensibilities, as well as in the timing and mood of their eschatological pronouncements. In the long run, however, the main impact of the Great Awakening lay not in these divisions but in the general upsurge of millennial expectations, expectations that by the late 1750's took an impressive variety of forms and were no longer distinctively evangelical Calvinist in their appeal.[1]

PROPHETIC SENSATIONALISM

One of the most widely printed publications of late colonial America, appearing in Philadelphia, Boston, and Charleston, South Carolina, in 1759, was a short millennial treatise entitled *The Prophetic Numbers of Daniel and John Calculated*. The author of this unusually popular work was Richard Clarke, a former rector of the leading parish of the established Church of England in Charleston. Clarke was a native Englishman who had been sent to the colonies in 1753 by the evangelical Society for the Propagation of the Gospel (SPG). Although an Anglican, Clarke can be seen as a representative of the moderate wing of the wider British evangelical movement that encompassed missionary endeavors like the SPG, the popular Methodist revivals in England, and what would later be called the Evangelical Party within the Church of England. During the six years he lived in South Carolina as an SPG missionary, he enjoyed a reputation as an unusually tolerant and eloquent Anglican clergyman. He also maintained exceptionally good relations with local revivalists, even occasionally sharing his pulpit with Calvinist evangelical preachers despite the general opposition of the Church of England to the Awakening. It is quite likely that Clarke's interest in prophecy was first stimulated by the preaching of Calvinist New Lights in the southern American colonies in the 1750's. All Clarke's many works on prophecy were initially conceived while he was still in America, even though they were published only after his return to England. According to the contemporary South Carolinian historian David Ramsay, "the substance of a considerable part of them was preached in Charleston."[2]

Like many of the popular millennial publications that appeared in America in the 1750's, Clarke's *Prophetic Numbers* made sensationalist historical predictions. He manipulated various dates and numbers from Scripture in an effort to reveal the time of prophetic fulfillment when horrible supernatural judgments would occur and the millennium begin. His calculations repeatedly yielded the years 1758 to 1766. In typical evangelical fashion he pointed to the excessive worldliness of the present age as evidence that it would soon be destroyed to make way for the new. It is left ambiguous in his account whether or not Christ would actually descend in the flesh to deliver judgment and inaugurate the millennium, but it is clear that the process would first be set off by a wave of religious revivals. He expected a dramatic infusion of the gospel, one particularly awakening the souls of the "the humble and lowly at heart," to prepare for the new gospel age.[3]

Clarke attempted to bolster the credibility of his dramatic conclusions by noting the close correspondence between his proposed dates and the prophecies contained in another work, entitled *The Strange and Wonderful Predictions of Mr. Christopher Love*. Also well known in the American colonies, this work appeared as a broadside in 1759 in Boston, Newport, and New York. Later in the century it would be printed again in both England and America in updated form. As did the belief in numerology upon which Clarke's predictions were based, the appeal of Love's prophecies came from deep within popular religious tradition. Christopher Love was a seventeenth-century English Presbyterian minister and revolutionary supporter of Parliament who was executed by Cromwell shortly before the Restoration. There is no evidence that he actually made the predictions attributed to him. According to popular folklore, however, Love received a divine revelation disclosing the events of the future just before his execution. His hallowed reputation as a pious martyr to the Parliamentary cause appears to have been responsible for the development of this myth.[4] Another legendary feature of Love's predictions was their supposed agreement with the Book of Enoch, an ancient text that had long possessed a sacred aura in popular Christianity despite its official exclusion from the Old Testament.[5] Such unorthodox sources as apocryphal texts, divine revelations, and numerological calculations clearly contributed to the popularity of these sensationalist prophecies even in the highly biblical culture of eighteenth-century American Protestantism.

In the version of Love's prophecies that appeared in the colonies in 1759 and was cited by Clarke, the events of the Last Days were all scheduled to occur between 1756 and 1763. Under the heading "Short Work of the Lord's in the latter Ages of the World" appeared the following timetable:

Great Earthquakes and Commotions by Sea and Land, in the Year of our Lord,	1756
Great Wars in Germany and America, in	1757
Destruction of Popery, or Babylons fall, in	1758
The Anger of God against the Wicked, in	1759
God will be known, in	1760
This will produce a great Man; the Stars will wander, and the Moon appear as Blood, in	1761
Africa, Asia, and America will tremble, in	1762
A great Earthquake over all the World, in	1763

God will be universally known by all in general, and a Reformation and Peace forever, when People shall learn War no more.
Happy is the Man that liveth to see this Day.[6]

In 1759 Richard Clarke did not need to tell his readers that Love's predictions were, so far at least, eerily close to the mark. Earthquakes and wars had, in fact, rocked Europe and America in the 1750's. In 1755 a large tremor was felt in the Boston area, followed shortly by the devastating earthquake in Spain and Portugal that flattened the city of Lisbon. There were also still more recent reports of earthquakes in other places, such as the Caribbean and Peru. As for Love's vision of wars in Europe and America, the intermittent eighteenth-century imperial conflict between France and England had expanded into a major war among all the great European powers and was just coming to a head on the colonial front in the French and Indian War. For those who would seek apocalyptical signs of the times, the late 1750's offered ample opportunity for reflection. The widespread publication of such works broadcasting the arrival of the millennium within a few years suggests that the dramatic events of the earthquakes and the war, coming on the heels of the popular religious revivals, raised millennial expectations among a large number of American colonists.

Still another sensationalist millennial prophecy, printed in 1756 in both Boston and Philadelphia (in German as well as in English), was that of David Imrie, a little-known Presbyterian minister in Scotland. Imrie's brief *Letter* proclaimed that the world could look forward to the fulfillment of the many scriptural prophecies pertaining to the Last Days – the conversion and restoration of the Jews, the destruction of the Roman Antichrist, the conversion of gentiles, and the commencement of the millennium – all in the next forty years. More ominously, Imrie also announced the immediate coming of a series of judgments that would spare the faithful but destroy two-thirds of the earth. To help avert the impending disaster, he advised the renewal of the Concert of Prayer, the transatlantic program of coordinated prayer that had earlier enlisted the support of Jonathan Edwards. This strategy suggests that Imrie, like Clarke, spoke at least partly to an evangelical audience. And, like Love's predictions, Imrie's were at the same time related to the recent earthquakes and war. Apparently influenced by the apocalyptical geophysical theories of the seventeenth-century English latitudinarian scientist Thomas Burnet, Imrie believed the earth was about to change its axis back in line with where it had been before the Fall. If the occurrence of the earthquakes seemed to validate this theory, so did the French and Indian War. The anonymous American editor added this postscript: "And Mr. Imrie further thinks, 'The *present Commotions* between *Us* and the *French* are a *Beginning* of the Judgments spoke of in his printed Letter.'"[7]

Imrie's *Letter* was based at once on the authority of the Bible and on a personal gift of divination. The events it foretold were supposedly those of the Book of Revelation, but the ability to predict when they would happen was a matter of magic, not exegesis. According to the legend promoted in the *Letter*, David Imrie, like Christopher Love, was miraculously blessed with the supernatural power of prophecy. The boundary between biblical exegesis and popular religious folklore was, here again, quite thin.

Other examples of prophetic literature in this period strayed even farther from a biblical base. One curious publication, printed in Philadelphia in 1760 after reportedly being discovered in "an ancient Latin manuscript," predicted the decline of the French clergy, the outbreak of war in Europe, and the triumph of the Prussian state in language that employed the eccentric symbolism of the unorthodox

26

pseudo-Joachite and Sibylline millennialism popular in Europe in the Middle Ages.[8] Although written in English, its emphasis on Prussia suggests some relationship to the Pennsylvania German community, which would, in 1762, also have available a German edition of Sibylline and pseudo-Joachite writings printed by the Moravians.[9] The theme of the emergence of a "northern Hero" in another nonbiblical prophecy about war that was printed in Philadelphia also may well have referred to a Sibylline precedent.[10] Still less biblically grounded was a piece entitled "A Warning-Piece to *Europe* and *America*" that appeared in a New York almanac in 1761. Supposedly a prophecy told to an English farmer by an angel on March 12, 1760, it foretold the defeat of the French after a period of terrible bloodshed, the bountiful production of crops and flourishing of trade as never before, and, finally, the beginning of real "happiness" in Europe and America.[11]

Clarke's *Prophetic Numbers* thus arose within a general cultural context virtually teeming with fantastic predictions. Imported from overseas or printed anonymously, forecasting events with a confidence bordering upon the magical, these sensationalist prophecies of the late 1750's were probably not all taken seriously. Yet even the wild predictions of Clarke, according to which the millennium would begin by 1766, were deemed worth the effort of earnest rebuttals by two readers in Boston and Charleston. These pieces attacked both Clarke and Christopher Love for their claims that the millennium was about to begin and expounded alternative versions of the Last Days. The Boston critic stressed the error of setting the decisive date so close to the present and argued that the final downfall of the Antichrist and the commencement of the millennium would occur only in the mid-twentieth century. In the meantime, perhaps with the current war between the Protestant English and the French Catholics in mind, he offered the consolation that the faithful would make continuing advances over the Beast of the Book of Revelation, the Church of Rome.[12] Clarke's Charleston critic was more hostile. Evidently a former parishioner in Clarke's church, he claimed that the minister's millennial theory was based on an implicit belief in the unorthodox doctrine of universal salvation. Clarke's piece never actually drew this connection, but his prophecy of a day of judgment before the millennium did leave room for yet another judgment day, after the millennium, when the previously damned might be saved. Amassing scriptural quotations to prove the permanence of damnation, his critic complained that Clarke gave unwarranted hope to sinners, not only by suggesting that eventually all would be saved but by his very belief in the millennium. Besides, the argument continued, Clarke never presented adequate justification for his chronological calculations: "Nothing appears clear to me from Mr. C's performance, but that he was determined all his prophetic calculations should terminate between 1758 and 1766."[13] The prophecies by Love that Clarke cited were equally invalid because they also were based on the apocryphal Book of Enoch and because some of the dates projected in them had already been proved wrong: The earthquakes had really occurred in 1755, not 1756; the war had begun in 1756, not 1757; and (writing from the vantage point of 1759), the Pope had not fallen in 1758.[14] Hoping this exposé would dispel the illusion that the end of the present dispensation was at hand, the author deplored the great impression made by Clarke's bogus predictions on the "many" who naively believed them without having seriously "considered the matter."[15]

If this critic could scoff at the ignorance and credulity of the numerous believers of Clarke, he would not find all American millennialists such easy targets for his literal-minded antimillennial criticism. For the penetration of millennial ideas into American culture did not stop with the risky if dramatic announcement of particular dates in the manner of Clarke, David Imrie, and Christopher Love, or with the dubious use of apocryphal sources like the Book of Enoch or pseudo-Joachite prophecies. Numerous less flamboyant and more reputable prophecies, often by well-known clergymen working strictly within the Protestant biblical tradition, were issued in the late 1750's as well. These relatively sober and judicious eschatological reflections further illuminate the cultural context in which the wild predictions of these years were read and appreciated. Surely one reason for the alarm of Richard Clarke's critics was that heightened millennial expectations had gained so much legitimacy in the years following the enthusiasm of the Great Awakening.

POST-AWAKENING SCRIPTURAL COMMENTARY

The millennialism of the Great Awakening was kept alive in the 1750's not only in the excited pronouncements about the earthquakes and the French and Indian War but in numerous evangelical publications that propagated a millennial theory of history without reference to contemporary events. As the evangelical fervor in the north subsided, revivalists in New England, especially, felt the need to disengage their millennialism from their earlier hopes for an indefinitely continuing effusion of grace. The decline of revivalism left them with the problem of how to sustain their belief in the millennium while living in a less promising time. Increasingly they sought to achieve a broader and more detached perspective on biblical prophecy. They disregarded contemporary events and concentrated instead on textual analyses of scriptural prophecy. Prophetic speculation began to take a more sober and scholarly turn. This development, much like the fantastic predictions of popular religious folklore, shows both the continuation and the breadth of American millennial ideas in the decade between the Great Awakening and the Revolution.

There were essentially two different types of New Light millennial literature in the 1750's. On the one hand, prophetic statements about contemporary "signs of the times" like the earthquakes and the French and Indian War took the form of spontaneous exclamations similar to those made during the halcyon days of the revivals. These assumed, rather than defended, a millennial understanding of Scripture. But alongside these repeated exclamatory statements arose a second type of literature, a series of analytical and expository works that presented the case for fairly traditional millennial readings of prophecy. Rather than attribute millennial significance to the revivals, the war with the French, or any other recent development, these more scholarly works usually adhered closely to the language of the biblical word. Inasmuch as they considered the present course of human history at all, they usually did so only in the most general terms. Some drew conclusions about the timing of the latter-day glory from the obscure prophetic chronology; others dwelt instead on the manner of its coming and the nature of the millennial kingdom. A number of these works came directly from the New Light ministry, and they apparently all circulated primarily within evangelical religious circles. Taken as a whole, the exegetical publications of the 1750's were part of the continuing fallout of the religious excitement of the previous two decades, excitement now increasingly translated into the more detached and authoritative language of textual argument.

Probably the most important New Light work on prophecy to appear in these years was Joseph Bellamy's sermon entitled simply *The Millennium*. It entirely disregarded such current events as the war. Bellamy, a leading disciple of Edwards's, advanced the same basic argument contained in his mentor's still unpublished *History of the*

Work of Redemption, about which he undoubtedly knew. Above all, he sought to demonstrate God's controlling providence and ultimate purpose in history by a detailed rendition of the meaning of Scripture. He explicitly aimed to counteract currents of historical pessimism that had arisen since the end of the revivals by reminding the faithful that the final goal of history was the perfection of the millennium.[16]

In his interpretation of the Revelation, Bellamy, like Edwards, was decidedly postmillennialist, believing that Christ's reign in the millennium would take spiritual rather than physical form. But he was ambiguous about whether the millennium would come gradually through progressive amelioration or suddenly by means of destructive upheaval. On the one hand, he noted that "the State of the World and of the Church appears so exceeding gloomy and dark, and still darker Times are by many expected."[17] On the other hand, he concentrated not on this state of decline but on the hopeful prospect of the destruction of the Antichrist. Using fairly conventional Protestant ideas of periodization, he explained that the Beast's reign of 1,260 years began with the gradual ascendency of the Papacy in the early Middle Ages and had started to decline with the Reformation. As for the exact time when the Antichrist would collapse and the millennium would begin, Bellamy refused to speculate. Perhaps with Edwards's earlier rash predictions about the revivals in mind, he insisted that the exact timing of prophetic events could not be known to human understanding. Yet, like many other millennialists who disclaimed the ability to predict with precision, he strongly intimated, along with Edwards, that the Antichrist was presently approaching his final demise.

Lest the righteous lose sight of the glorious promise of history, Bellamy furnished a vivid description of the impending millennial kingdom. Just as he avoided reference to specific current events, he never mentioned any particular American role, dwelling instead on the vast, universal dimensions of the millennium. All humanity would embrace true Christianity; God would remove his various historical judgments such as famine and war; and the people of the earth would live together in harmony and abundance. Bellamy offered an arithmetical proof that human population would so multiply under the healthful conditions of the millennium that at the Last Judgment the millennial saints would greatly outnumber the sinners who had predominated in earlier times. In the *Humble Attempt* Edwards had made a similar observation, but Bellamy now furnished far more elaborate computations, according to which "above 17000 would be saved to one lost."[18]

Clearly defensive about Calvinism's traditional insistence upon the small number of the Elect, Bellamy was also partaking in a common eighteenth-century exaltation over demographic expansion. Not only had Edwards indulged in such speculation about the millennium, but Benjamin Franklin, whom Bellamy cited, had recently published figures proudly demonstrating the phenomenal rate of population increase in the American colonies. In addition to orthodox Calvinists, other American millennialists in the late eighteenth century similarly pointed to demographic growth as a major index to social and material well-being.[19] In Bellamy's case these computations were designed to show not only the extraordinary physical happiness that would prevail in the millennium, but the nonmiraculous basis of this achievement. There was need of supernatural grace to achieve universal conversion, to be sure, but otherwise Providence would work through natural human means. Bellamy urged continuing struggle on behalf of Christ's Kingdom by the church militant, "this glorious Army, which has been in the Wars above these five Thousand Years."[20] He reminded the saints that assurance of individual salvation was not enough "without a clear View and fair Prospect of Christ's final Victory over all his Enemies."[21]

Other detailed expositions of the prophetic Bible passages emanated from New England presses in the late 1750's, and they too seemed to have come mostly from the ranks of former revivalists. Two were previously unpublished treatises on prophecy by earlier Puritans, *A Brief Discourse Concerning Futurities or Things to Come* by the seventeenth-century divine William Torrey and *Scripture Prophecies Explained* by Ezekiel Cheever, a much revered schoolmaster of late seventeenth-century Boston. Torrey's work had been procured in manuscript by the Boston New Light minister Thomas Prince, who edited the first and only edition in 1757. The belated unearthing of Cheever's manuscript the same year probably also stemmed from New Light desires to draw upon the authority of the earlier Calvinist precedent.[22]

Both these resurrected works of Puritan eschatology sought primarily to piece together the sequence of events that were prophesied for the latter days. Cheever's treatise, in particular, shorter and easier to read than Torrey's, must have served New England Calvinist circles well as a simple introduction to millennial theory.[23] Both works adhered closely to the language of the scriptural text and drew no relationships to past or present human history. Nor does there seem to have been anything particularly controversial about their apocalyptic scenarios. Both these Puritan commentators, unlike later Edwardsians, took the premillennialist view that Christ's return at the beginning of the millennium would be physical. But in the 1750's this interpretative disagreement was apparently subsumed by a common Calvinist commitment to a basic millennialism. In the preface to Torrey's work Thomas Prince entirely overlooked its premillennialist conception of Christ's literal descent, choosing instead to debate a small point about the appearance of the enigmatic figures Gog and Magog. Premillennialism and post-millennialism could evidently coexist quite peacefully even within evangelical Calvinist circles.[24]

If there was any interpretative consensus in the prophetic commentary that appeared in America in the 1750's, it had less to do with such technical points than with a general expectation that things would get worse just before the millennial dawn. Scarcely a new theme in Christian eschatology – in fact, one featured in the Book of Revelation itself – this perspective was more pronounced in the millennial literature of the 1750's than it had been during the Great Awakening.[25] Just as Bellamy saw the world as declining on the threshold of the new age, the newly published Puritans Cheever and Torrey expected the Second Coming to occur unexpectedly at a time of great wickedness. Another exegetical work published within evangelical circles in New England, sermons by the English Baptist John Gill, also held that the faithful would be severely persecuted before the final defeat of the Antichrist before the millennium.[26]

The view that dark days would precede the new dawn understandably received more attention in colonial revivalist circles after the initial enthusiasm of the Great Awakening could no longer sustain millennial hopes. The series of earthquakes and the early reversals in the French and Indian War also undoubtedly contributed to this altered perspective. Yet these various works of biblical commentary were scarcely pessimistic in their broad historical outlook. If they foresaw the prospect of temporary decline, their focus remained on the millennial promise itself. For all their differences in style and interpretation, they together described the glorious establishment of God's kingdom on earth in vivid and compelling detail. It was in the propagation of this general millennial perspective, rather than in any specific historical or exegetical application, that they reinforced the widespread millennial expectations in America in the decades after the Great Awakening.

OLD LIGHTS, NEW LIGHTS, EARTHQUAKES, AND WAR

By the time millennial publications reached their numerical peak in the late 1750's, much of the influence of the Great Awakening had already been filtered through other developments. Earthquakes, the French and Indian War, and the very demise of revival enthusiasm had shifted the focus of millennial thought. Several Old Light antirevivalists now were professing millennial views in much the same terms as the revivalists. In the long run the impact of the Awakening upon American millennialism was not confined to evangelical Calvinist circles. The Great Awakening not only spread millennial expectations among its widespread enthusiasts, but aroused interest in biblical prophecy within the religious culture at large.[27]

Because of its close association with the Great Awakening, millennialism had for a few years appealed almost exclusively to revivalists. The evangelicals never really, however, had a monopoly on millennial thought. In New England especially, evangelical New Lights, Old Light Calvinists, and "liberal" Arminian Congregationalists were, despite their differences, all part of a post-Puritan culture that conceived of the future partly in millennial terms. Although many of the divisions between Old Lights and New Lights certainly persisted into the 1750's, the differences between them became less sharply defined once the great wave of conversions subsided. When the decline in revivalism divested millennialism of some of its earlier sectarian coloring, colonial Protestants of various persuasions were all the more primed to apply a millennial perspective to subsequent events.

Initially the millennial expectations stirred by the Awakening had celebrated the outbreak of revivalism itself. The frequently extravagant quality of New Light prophetic conjecture understandably aroused Old Light antagonism. In his major polemic against the revivals, the liberal Congregationalist Charles Chauncy described Jonathan Edwards's heady predictions about the impending commencement of the millennium as the dangerous, even potentially revolutionary, deceptions of "vain Imagination."[28] In time, however, the association between the Great Awakening and millennialism was gradually loosened. In response to the less divisive events of the earthquakes and war, even the former critics of the Awakening, including Chauncy himself, turned to the subject of prophecy and proclaimed the glorious destiny of history.

The articulation of a millennial outlook outside revivalist ranks in the 1750's reflected a significant decline in religious polarization as American Protestants were once again influenced by common experiences. The first major catalyst of eschatological speculation after the Awakening was the global series of earthquakes that shook New England along with other parts of the world in 1755. Scientific theories about earthquakes were in this period still closely tied to religious cosmology. Particularly in New England, strange occurrences in nature inevitably gave rise to sermons about the controlling power of Providence. Like a number of other lesser natural spectacles that occurred in this period – comets, shooting stars, lightning, and fire – the earthquakes stimulated thoughts about the final conflagration.[29] Earthquakes were featured in the Book of Revelation and elsewhere in the Bible as a sign of God's anger before the Last Judgment. As in 1727 when New England had experienced a more isolated tremor, several sermons were delivered in 1755 and 1756 that interpreted the tremors as a threatening preview of the apocalypse. Evoking terrifying images of divine wrath, these earthquakes, like other natural disasters, understandably raised the spectre of the Last Judgment more often than that of the millennium. The heightened emphasis placed upon fear and judgment on this occasion did not, however, preclude millennial hopes. By framing observations of nature within the context of apocalyptic history, even catastrophic interpretations reinforced the general mythology of the future in which millennial beliefs found their place.[30]

The earthquakes inspired sermons about Judgment Day not only by Thomas Prince and other New Light ministers but by their major liberal Congregationalist opponents. Charles Chauncy and Jonathan Mayhew both turned to biblical prophecy upon this disturbing occasion. Chauncy, still reacting against the millennial enthusiasm of the evangelicals, used the earthquakes to illustrate the inevitability of human suffering in this hopelessly fallen world. He too warned that the tremors were a divine command to heed the coming of Judgment when the earth would completely break asunder. In direct opposition to the postmillennialism of Jonathan Edwards, he argued that only after the literal Second Coming, the resurrection of the dead, the Last Judgment, and the physical reconstitution of the universe – events that would be accomplished solely by miraculous divine intervention – would a paradise be created for the saints. Technically, Chauncy's scenario was not millennialist at all, since he did not believe that this future paradise would take place in the existing universe. Yet even his strong note of pessimism about the fate of the world gave way to an extravagantly hopeful eschatological vision as he contemplated the delights that would come with the new heavens and earth. Death would be turned to life, pain into pleasure; the world would be free of both toil and sorrow. "There shall be," he promised, "no more sighing or tears, but unmixed joys ever flowing from the right hand of God."[31]

For all Chauncy's manifold differences with the evangelical millennialists, he spread the hope for the speedy culmination of history to his nonrevivalist audience. He used the opportunity presented by the earthquakes to expound his own euphoric version of the future glory, perhaps hoping to rescue prophetic speculation from the revivalists' domain. Later he would take still another step in this direction when he developed an anti-Calvinist but more fully millennial eschatology in support of his liberal doctrine of universal salvation.[32]

Jonathan Mayhew, next to Chauncy the leading liberal minister in Boston, delivered more than a dozen sermons on earthquakes in late 1755 and 1756. He too related them in various ways to the subject of biblical prophecy. Like Chauncy, Prince, and others, he at first warned his frightened congregation of the terrifying "dissolution of all things" that would occur at the Last Judgment.[33] A month later he preached on the less alarming theme of God's providential role in both natural and human history. In the course of this discussion he more hopefully pointed to the prophecies of Babylon's downfall and the saints' future glory that still remained to be fulfilled. Unlike Chauncy, he adhered to a technically millennial outlook, expecting this fulfillment to take place within history and on earth.[34] Neither of these sermons by Mayhew, however, both published within weeks of the tremor, suggested that any of these future events were imminent. But towards the end of another, longer sequence of sermons delivered in 1756 and published only in 1760, Mayhew returned more expectantly to the prophetic implications of the earthquake. Noting that there had recently been other strange "appearances" in the sky and sea, he observed a close likeness to the various natural phenomena that would, according to prophecy, occur before the Second Coming. "There has probably been no age or period of the world, wherein events have more nearly corresponded to this prophetic description, than the present."[35]

While disclaiming the ability to tell for sure when the millennium would begin, Mayhew nonetheless expected in the near future a fundamental transformation of the world. Despite the fact that the earthquakes themselves were purely natural phenomena entirely outside human control, Mayhew extrapolated from them to impending social upheavals. In effect dismissing the whole question of whether the millennium would come by supernatural, natural, or human means, he assumed there was a general "correspondence, between the natural, civil and moral world." Soon there would be "great revolutions" producing "some very remarkable changes in the political and religious state of the world."[36] He gave no indication of what kind of "revolutions" these would be – in fact he deliberately left it open whether the outcome would be good or bad. His undefined premonition of tremendous human upheaval, however, like the revivalists' heady forecasts of an imminent new age, helped clear the way for the more avowedly revolutionary millennialism that would emerge later on.

Both of these liberal, nonrevivalist Boston clergymen seized upon the occasion of the earthquakes in the mid-1750's to elaborate ideas about the fulfillment of prophecy. Each did so with one eye on the millennialism of the revivalists, seeking to make his own, competing claims about the glorious destiny of history. Chauncy painstakingly couched his alluring vision of the future within a highly conservative, nonmillennial framework. Mayhew, however, aware of how much he sounded like the New Lights he opposed, felt compelled to deny that his millennial vision contained "any tincture of superstition or enthusiasm."[37]

The earthquakes, coming directly after the Awakening, provided a nonsectarian stimulus for the belief that history was moving towards a glorious conclusion. It was variously suggested by ministers that Providence could work through miracles or through natural or human agency. There would be horrifying judgments as well as blissful rewards. But whatever the process, history would at the end bring happiness to the saints. It was this highly general perspective on the future, articulated widely in the colonies during the Great Awakening, that now received further reinforcement through a broad spectrum of New England religious opinion.

Adding greatly to the apocalyptic significance of the earthquakes was their concurrence with the French and Indian War. Works interpreting the signs of the times often cited these two recent developments in conjunction, as together the basis for millennial expectations. If the Great Awakening provided a general background for the rise of millennial expectations and the earthquakes began to bring Old Lights back into the eschatological fold, the French and

Indian War was clearly the event most responsible for the numerous millennial works published in the 1750's. It was viewed as a great turning point in world history, one that might well lead to the establishment of the latter-day kingdom on earth.

The French and Indian War was the largest and most costly of a series of British imperial wars with France waged intermittently throughout the eighteenth century. At stake were vast amounts of territory both within the British and French colonial settlements and far to the west. Unlike the previous wars, the battlefront in the 1750's extended all the way from Quebec in the north to the backcountry of the middle and southern colonies, uniting most of the British colonies in support of the royal and local-militia troops. Casualties among both soldiers and civilians were heavy and widely publicized, economic hardships were widespread, and for years American colonists lived with the serious prospect of British military defeat at the hands of the French and their Indian allies. Only in 1759, after five years of fruitless fighting in the colonies, did the tide turn towards the British side. Even long after the celebrated fall of Quebec the American economy was still slumped in a postwar depression. In this context of increased poverty, death, and fear of invasion, the millennial promise of a future era of happiness understandably gained in appeal.

It is clear that the experience of the war, even more than that of the earthquakes, sustained and generalized the eschatological interests raised by the revivals. Just as the Great Awakening had carried the millennialism of American Puritanism throughout the colonies, the millennial interpretation of the imperial conflict spread millennial expectations well beyond the New England clergy. Like the apocalyptic ideas stimulated by the earthquakes, moreover, these wartime visions were relatively nonsectarian, appealing to nonrevivalist as well as revivalist patriotic Protestants. There were, however, notable differences between their interpretations. The liberal nonrevivalists as a group tended to be more vague and cautious in their millennial predictions than the evangelical Calvinists. They were also more optimistic about America's future within the British Empire. The evangelicals, to the contrary, were quicker to reach millennial conclusions and more strident in their denunciation of the antichristian enemy. Their millennial prophecies rarely focused on the cultural and material advantages of the imperial connection. In the decades to follow, American revolutionary millennialism would incorporate many of the themes that appeared in both liberal and evangelical millennialism in the late 1750's. The more daring and combative elements of the patriot millennial vision were, however, clearly owed more to the New Light millennial legacy.

Most of the millennial statements by liberal Congregationalist and Anglican clergymen came in the form of ambiguous rhetorical flourishes, couched in the allusive language of scriptural metaphor rather than in the form of discernable predictions. Even those who did present an overtly millennial interpretation of the war believed the millennium to be in the yet distant future. As the Pennsylvania Anglican William Smith explained, "both in the Natural and Moral world, the advances to Perfection are gradual and progressive."[38] Numerous New England Arminian Congregationalists likewise foresaw incremental improvements leading slowly but surely to the millennium. History was described as a "progressive Scheme of Happiness," one in which all events were somehow "preparatory to, and introductive of . . . that most perfect and glorious State" that itself was "not for Ages to commence."[39]

According to this typical liberal view of the future, the millennium would come through a gradual process of diffusion rather than through a climactic struggle with the Antichrist. The Boston liberal Samuel Cooper concluded his election sermon of 1759 with the hope that God would continue to favor the British cause indefinitely, "till every Nation shall be happy under the Government of the Prince of Peace."[40] In 1763 the Anglican East Apthorp interpreted the British victory as evidence that God had appointed the English nation to use its "influence and example" to spread "the blessings of humanity, freedom, and religion" throughout the world.[41] Not surprisingly, the liberal millennialist perspective on the war, with its conception of smooth historical progress into the future, usually waited for its expression until the years between 1759 and 1763, when the British victory had been effectively decided. Prior to these years, when the outcome was less certain, scarcely any liberals ventured to make millennial predictions. The strident and expectant apocalyptical statements between 1756 and 1759 generally came instead from the evangelical camp.

It was the revivalist Calvinists, primarily Congregationalists and Presbyterians, who throughout the war voiced the keenest enthusiasm and the most literal hope for the destruction of the French Catholic Antichrist and the dawning of the millennial age. Often announcing their prophetic predictions well before the fall of Quebec, their sermons communicated a sense of acute eschatological crisis. Although they did not necessarily assume in fearful moments that the Antichrist would collapse as a result of the war, they held on to the conviction that history was approaching the Last Days. Just a few months before the conquest of Quebec, Ebenezer Prime, the New Light minister in Huntington, Long Island, conceded that he could not tell "what shall be the Issue of particular Struggles of the Protestant and Antichristian Powers," but at the same time he reminded his parishioners of the millennial promise that the Powers of Darkness would fall.[42] The wartime threat posed by the legions of the Antichrist, like the cosmic fears aroused by the earthquakes, occasionally raised for New Lights the immediate prospect of tribulation and judgment rather than millennial happiness. As late as 1762 an obscure New England Separatist named Joseph Fisk issued such a warning. He cited the examples of the war and earthquakes to substantiate his belief that God was pouring vials of wrath upon established Protestant as well as Catholic churches. He criticized clergymen for failing to "preach up the Coming of Christ to Judgment; neither do they alarm the Consciences of Sinners, neither do they behold the Signs of the Times, to give warning of approaching Judgments."[43]

This kind of doomsdaying arose most dramatically on the sectarian fringe of the evangelical movement.[44] The revivalists' typically Manichaean view of a universe polarized between satanic and divine forces usually produced more hopeful millennial expectations. During the gloomiest time of the war, in 1756, when the British were suffering repeated defeats, the Pennsylvania and New Hampshire evangelical ministers Gilbert Tennent and Jonathan Parsons both published sermons interpreting the war and the earthquakes as signs of "some extraordinary event" or "some extraordinary Revolution" near at hand.[45] Preaching a militant sermon against Quaker pacifism in 1757, the New Light Samuel Finley of Nottingham, Pennsylvania, warned of the approach of Judgment Day if colonists did not mobilize to fight for God against the French Antichrist. Yet Finley juxtaposed this threat with the promise of divine favor once the challenge was dutifully met. Employing reassuring imagery from the Book of Revelation, he switched the theme of his sermon from the threat of destruction to the manifold blessings promised in prophecy to "the Instruments of [God's] Vengeance on spiritual *Babylon, the Mother of Harlots, and Abominations of the Earth.*"[46]

Other New Light preachers offering a more explicit prophetic analysis likewise associated the war with an imminent apocalyptic upheaval destined to bring on the millennial age. With considerable dramatic flare they pointed to the great clashes prophesied to occur between the forces of sin and righteousness at the End. A sermon preached by the prominent New Jersey New Light minister Aaron Burr before the Presbyterian synod in New York in 1756, subsequently printed in New York, Philadelphia, and Boston, took the position that the biblical prophecy of the slaying of the righteous witnesses was currently being fulfilled. Respectfully disagreeing with Edwards's earlier, more optimistic view in the *Humble Attempt* that this dreadful period of suffering was long past, Burr interpreted the passage of the Revelation to mean that it would occur at the very end of the present dispensation. As he analyzed current affairs, the recent British military defeat by antichristian papists at Oswego as well as the decline in revivalism conformed closely to the description of this great prophetic event. The faithful should prepare for even worse times ahead, but also take heart in the knowledge that out of the darkness "the Morning cometh." Despite the blows to Protestants delivered by the Catholic Beast, "the Destruction of *Antichrist*, and the End of this Night of *Popish* Darkness, is near at hand." God would suddenly send forth "a *plentiful, outpouring* of the Spirit of all Grace," all the world would convert to the true faith, and Christ's millennial reign of "universal Harmony and Peace" would begin.[47]

Similarly expecting the imminent and swift destruction of the Antichrist in 1756, the New Light Presbyterian Samuel Davies in Virginia allowed himself higher hopes for the war itself despite recent British losses. "Now who can tell," he asked in a fast-day sermon preached in Hanover, "but the present war is the commencement of this grand decisive conflict between the Lamb and the beast, i.e. between the protestant and the popish powers?"[48] Either a French victory would fulfill the prophecy of the slaying of the witnesses, as Burr had suggested, or British victory would substantiate Edwards's more optimistic view that the slaying was already over and Babylon was about to collapse. "However bloody and desolating this last conflict may be," he reassured his fellow Virginia evangelicals, "it will bring about the most glorious and happy revolution that ever was in the world."[49] This acceptance of bloodshed as the means to the millennium gave New Light sermons a fiercely militant cast. Even after the tide of the war had turned toward the British in 1759, Robert Smith, a New Light Presbyterian in Lancaster, Pennsylvania, expected the wheels of Providence soon to turn with even more "dreadful Vengeance, to tumble Antichrist from his usurped Seat and give the *Whore of Babylon her Double Cup!*"[50]

The sense of immediacy and intensified conflict so characteristic of evangelical millennialism during the war was shared as well by a few nonrevivalist ministers. The Reverend Samuel Langdon of Portsmouth, New Hampshire, later president of Harvard, was a moderate Old Light Calvinist who steered a middle course through the period's doctrinal controversies. Yet his millennial perspective on war, offered in a victory sermon of 1760, similarly stressed the need for struggle with the Antichrist and held out the possibility of imminent millennial transformation.[51] In the same year of victory Jonathan Mayhew, echoing his earlier earthquake sermon, also delivered two sets of sermons that were virtually indistinguishable in their keen sense of expectancy from those of the millennial evangelicals. Significantly, however, he once again felt compelled to remark that to entertain millennial expectations was not "enthusiasm," as though he himself recognized how close he was coming to the revivalists.[52]

The differences in the millennial outlook of evangelical Calvinists and liberals during the war were related only loosely to underlying theological divisions. The evangelicals' acute sense of the individual's struggle with sin and their belief in an instantly transforming conversion experience were generally reflected in their combative and keenly expectant millennialism. Conversely, the liberals' greater confidence in human nature and their emphasis upon the individual's incremental moral improvement found expression in their eschatology. Yet whereas each group's conception of the process of collective redemption tended to parallel its most general ideas about individual redemption, neither developed an actual doctrinal position on the interpretation of prophetic text. Their respective cataclysmic and progressive views of history did not, in particular, correspond to the premillennialist-postmillennialist exegetical distinction that historians of early American millennialism have until recently stressed. Scarcely any of the ministers who saw the French and Indian War as the fulfillment of prophetic text bothered to consider such details as whether Christ would come before or after the millennium. As far as it is possible to ascertain, the variations among millennial perspectives almost all took place within a postmillennial framework. Equally significantly, the ministers composing these sermons, like many eighteenth-century exegetes, placed little emphasis on this technical point.[53]

The differences between evangelical Calvinist and liberal millennial perspectives on the French and Indian War were as much ideological as doctrinal, reflecting varying degrees of identification with the British imperial victory. The Arminian liberals who waited until victory was secure to issue millennial statements and who looked forward to the smooth and gradual unfolding of the millennium were generally those who placed the most confidence in the empire as an agent of millennial change. Significantly, many of these ministers, including the liberal Congregationalist millennialists Thomas Barnard and John Mellen and the prominent northern Anglicans East Apthorp and William Smith, later refused to support the American revolutionary movement. Their expansive visions of the long-range effects of the imperial victory arose from a cosmopolitan attraction to British civilization that would later incline them away from the patriot cause. Conversely, virtually all of those who conceived of the millennium coming by means of a climactic struggle with the Antichrist, and who took an apocalyptic view of the war early on, later supported the American cause. This group consisted mostly of evangelical Calvinists but also included the exceptional Old Lights Jonathan Mayhew, a liberal, and Samuel Langdon, a moderate Calvinist. These two New Englanders were still very much a part of the post-Puritan religious tradition even though they rejected the extreme Calvinism of the revivalists. They, for example, unlike more Anglophilic liberal Congregationalists, remained decidedly hostile to the Church of England. Their combative and expectant millennialism during the war with France was consistent with the fact that they, like the evangelicals, found victory in itself unsatisfying. The war was won, but the Antichrist was not vanquished. Sin still prevailed, even in the English ecclesiastical establishment.

THE POLITICS OF MILLENNIAL VISIONS IN THE 1750'S

Looking backwards from the American Revolution, it is striking how often the political terms "liberty" and "tyranny" appear in the religious pronouncements about the French and Indian War. But however political in comparison with the evangelical millennialism of the Great Awakening, the millennialism of the 1750's was still a far cry from the revolutionary millennialism that would emerge later on.[54] When clergymen during the imperial war described the enemy as antichristian and tyrannical, their traditional Protestant hatred of Catholicism was still at least as important as their hatred of repressive systems of government. Indeed, for most of them, regardless of

42

whether they were evangelical or liberal, these two threats posed by the French were inseparable. Ministers encouraged militancy by presenting the horrible alternative of conquest by "papists, Tyrants, and Slaves," "*popish Bigotry* and *lawless Tyranny*," "French Tyranny, Romish Idolatry and Superstition."[55] One New Light explained that it was "the bloody power of Popery" that was ultimately responsible for the world's "ignorance, idolatry, and slavery."[56] Even Samuel Langdon, who otherwise displayed great pride in British civil liberty, interpreted the millennial significance of the war primarily in terms of the victory of Protestant over Catholic powers: Catholicism was in his view "spiritual tyranny."[57] Jonathan Mayhew, too, described the Catholic Church, not the French monarchy, as having "tyrannized" over its people.[58]

The idea that Britain was waging a decisive battle against popery was what gave the French and Indian War its specifically eschatological meaning. When the war was interpreted in the terms of biblical prophecy, it was the Catholic religion that was identified as the Beast in the Book of Revelation. Nathaniel Appleton, the Old Light Calvinist minister in Cambridge, Massachusetts, quite simply explained that the French were "of the Church of Rome; which we Protestants maintain to be Antichrist."[59] Some of the most powerful and overtly millennial sermons about the conflict, including those by Aaron Burr, Samuel Davies, and Jonathan Mayhew, conceived of the significance of the war solely in terms of the Protestant confrontation with the Catholic Antichrist and scarcely mentioned secular tyranny or liberty at all. As Mayhew put it, the real providential purpose of the war was to weaken the "roman pontiff."[60]

Nor was the identification of the French with the papal Antichrist merely a clerical concern. A song called "Canada Subjected," printed as a broadside somewhere in the colonies probably in 1759, celebrated the fall of Quebec with the following verse:

> The Time will come, when Pope and Fry'r
> Shall both be roasted in the Fire;
> When the proud *Antichristian* Whore
> Will sink, and never arise more.[61]

New England's annual Pope's Day of November 5, during which the association between the Pope and the devil was ritualized by rowdy mobs who hung and burned effigies of the two figures together, also seems to have become firmly established as a distinctive popular holiday in the 1740's and 1750's, in the context of the virulent anti-Catholicism of the war with France.[62]

Far from constituting a break with eschatological tradition, this identification of the Papacy as the Antichrist was the oldest and least controversial feature of Protestant millennial thought. Luther, King James I, and eighteenth-century English latitudinarians all agreed about this interpretation of the Book of Revelation. If the association of Protestantism with liberty and of Catholicism with tyranny possessed greater political implications, these were not especially radical – particularly by the standards of the Anglo-American world in the mid-eighteenth century. The Antichrist had always been a symbol of tyranny, as well as of sin. As the British in the seventeenth and eighteenth centuries consolidated their national identity on the basis of constitutional liberty, the characterization of their anti-christian Catholic foes as tyrannical was virtually automatic, indeed, even conservative. In seventeenth-century England the revolutionary break in Puritan eschatology occurred when the identity of the tyrannical Antichrist shifted from the Pope to the King. The reversion to an emphasis on the Catholicism of the Antichrist after the Restoration and the Glorious Revolution – an emphasis encouraged by the series of eighteenth-century British wars with France – was thus a return to a politically secure and socially acceptable tradition. In the American colonies, where Puritanism kept millennialism more alive than it was in postrevolutionary England, the designation of the Catholic French as the Antichrist already had been a common rhetorical feature of the imperial wars earlier in the eighteenth century. Similarly, the general association of Protestantism and liberty, so pronounced in the sermons about the French and Indian War, extended back to seventeenth-century England.[63]

By the mid-eighteenth century the word "liberty" had assumed a more specifically whig connotation, evoking the various rights guaranteed by the Glorious Revolution. But scarcely any American ministers in the late 1750's drew this constitutional connection. Most of their references to British liberty were vague and perfunctory. The religious association with Protestantism remained far stronger than the political association with the Glorious Revolution. Indeed, even that historic event was described by patriotic clergymen as "the great revolution by which Great-Britain was happily secured from popish kings and pretenders."[64] There was also an implication in sermons about the French and Indian War that "liberty" simply meant the freedom of the British from French domination regardless of their respective political systems.

As the term typically appeared in conjunction with Protestantism, "liberty" connoted not only national independence and British constitutional rights but spiritual freedom, "the liberty wherewith Christ has made you free" of Galatians 5:1. In 1758, William Hobby, a New Light minister who saw the war as a sign of the oncoming fall of the Catholic Beast, cited Scripture to this effect.[65] A victory sermon by Samuel Haven, a New Hampshire Congregationalist with Arminian tendencies, similarly recounted how God had begun to pour the prophesied vials of wrath on the Antichrist when he led Luther and Calvin "to declare that pure gospel of Jesus, and to assert that liberty which believers enjoy in Christ their only Lord."[66] Aaron Burr in 1756 conveyed the same religious meaning of liberty when he contrasted French "*popish Bigotry* and lawless *Tyranny*" to American "*Gospel Light and Liberty*."[67] Samuel Langdon, who on other occasions used the word "liberty" in a strictly political sense, also referred, in identical language, to the "light and liberty of the gospel" in his millennial sermon on the war.[68]

Perhaps the best example of the multivalent meaning of the word "liberty," however, was a sermon printed in 1757 by Joshua Tufts, a minister with pronounced evangelical leanings who lived in a remote region of Maine. Preaching on the text "If the Son therefore shall make you free, ye shall be free indeed," Tufts stressed that "it is the new birth that makes them [sinners] free; a new nature, and a new principle is infused into them, a free spirit is implanted into them."[69] Tufts's decision to focus on the meaning of "liberty" was probably due to the patriotic rhetoric about British liberty surrounding the war. The frontier preacher acknowledged the threat of the French and "heavy yoke of popish ceremonies," but for him true liberty was essentially the product of spiritual grace.[70] Earlier revivalists had also periodically stressed the value of "liberty," by which they variously meant the emotional effect of grace, the right to religious dissent, and a feature of good civil government.[71] A purely religious, even evangelical, conception of liberty thus continued to overlap with the political, whig definition.

Even when "liberty" was meant politically, it is significant, in comparison with later revolutionary ideology, that there was nothing about this usage to identify it with the "radical whigs" of the British opposition. The patriotic religious supporters of the French and Indian War, unlike the revolutionary clergy a decade later, entirely abstained from making criticisms of the British government. The few American clergymen who specifically described the millennium in terms of political liberty tended to be Old Lights and liberals. Samuel

Langdon, a nonrevivalist Calvinist, envisioned the millennium as a time when God would bless not only Great Britain but all nations with liberty in addition to peace.[72] Victory sermons by the Anglicans William Smith and East Apthorp and the Boston liberal Congregationalist Samuel Cooper similarly proclaimed the British millennial mission to carry "Liberty" or "Civil Freedom" as well as "pure Religion" to the rest of the world.[73] But such an emphasis on the political dimension of the war was rare in the millennialism of these years. When clergymen viewed the French and Indian War as a contest between English liberty and French tyranny, their statements usually did not take a specifically millennial form. Of the few who combined millennialism with a celebration of civil liberty, the two New England Congregationalists, Langdon and Cooper, became patriots later on, but Apthorp and Smith were notably unsympathetic to the American revolutionary cause. Both in its spokesmen and in its central themes, the millennialism of the French and Indian War bore little relationship to the revolutionary millennialism of the following decade.

It is only in the most immediate comparison with the relatively apolitical millennialism of the Great Awakening that the millennialism of the French and Indian War appears as a major break with the past that anticipated the American Revolution. Moreover, in the long run, what might be called the implicit political message of the Great Awakening – its call to rebellion, equality, and mass participation – laid an ideological groundwork for the American Revolution that was quite independent of the whig confirmation of liberty that occurred during the French and Indian War. These qualities of the Great Awakening can be found in some of the millennial literature of the 1750's as well. The former South Carolinian Richard Clarke's popular millennial prophecy of 1759 criticized the present world for its infatuation with wealth and drew attention to the exalted station that the lowly would enjoy next to Christ in the millennium.[74] Joseph Bellamy's Connecticut election sermon in 1762 highlighted the pivotal role of righteous rulers advancing Christ's Kingdom and looked forward to the mutual love, charity, and cooperation that would prevail in the millennium. The number of the poor would be "but small" because people would be rewarded for their industriousness and frugality with material prosperity, and their generosity would be such that even the needy would be "really Happy."[75] Bellamy attributed Connecticut's present failure to attain this ideal to the influence of luxury, idleness, debauchery, and

46

financial dishonesty – which were responsible for lawsuits, poverty, and partisan strife.[76]

Without elaborating any constitutional theory or in any way referring to the structure of government, the millennial literature written and read in America in the late 1750's perpetuated the expectations of forthcoming social perfection so prevalent during the revivals. The strident and intense quality of the evangelical prophetic statements about the war, as compared to those by liberal Protestants, attests to the enduring strength of the revivals' millennial legacy. As two major events in the background of the Revolution, the Great Awakening and the French and Indian War reinforced each other by generating an acute sense of American religious mission phrased in the inspirational terms of millennial prophecy. Many New Lights sustained their earlier millennial expectations by taking up the banner of the anti-Catholic war after the revivals had subsided. And now antirevivalists could safely stretch their millennial imaginations as well, for the conflict presented a united Protestant struggle against the traditional, external forces of the papal Antichrist.

One characteristic that the millennialism of the French and Indian War shared with that of the Great Awakening and the Revolution, for all of their differences, was a strong element of provincial American patriotism. Jonathan Edwards during the heady days of the revivals had extravagantly proclaimed that the millennium would probably "begin in America."[77] The idea that America had a special role to play in apocalyptic history had deep roots in seventeenth-century Puritan thought, and the Awakening had brought it back to the surface and transmitted it widely across the colonies. In the late 1750's and early 1760's numerous ministers preaching about the war celebrated the millennial implications of American expansion into the western territories. The prospect of colonial civilization expanding into previously uncultivated, "heathen" lands was often described in the millennial language of the prophet Isaiah, as the wilderness and solitary place becoming glad or the desert blossoming like a rose.[78] Old Light moderate Calvinist and liberal clergymen expressed particularly grandiose ambitions for American greatness – including not only continental expansion but material enrichment and cultural prowess. Even the Anglican William Smith, who later refused to support the patriot movement, echoed Bishop Berkeley's poetic theme of civilization traveling from east to west.[79] Another Anglophilic liberal Protestant, the Salem minister Thomas Barnard, voiced his expectation that "till Time shall be no more" America

47

would be the seat of peace and freedom, the abode of arts and sciences, and the "perennial Source of [Great Britain's] Strength and Riches."[80] Such a vision of future colonial wealth and power also captured the imagination of Jonathan Mayhew towards the end of the war. As he speculated on the effects of British victory over the Catholic Beast, he envisioned a splendid American "kingdom" replete with "mighty cities," "commodious ports," "mighty fleets," "happy fields and villages," "pastures cloathed with flocks," and "vallies cover'd with corn."[81] Moderate Calvinists like Ezra Stiles and Eli Forbes too saw "Towns enlarged, Settlements increased," populations expanding "like the sand of the sea" into millennial times.[82]

On occasion these visions of American grandeur featured the expansion of civil liberty, but on the whole they were dominated by very worldly images of territorial growth, cultural achievement, rising population, and material prosperity. What tended to give them religious legitimation was, of course, the belief that the gospel would spread along with the rest of American civilization. In particular, liberal sermons commenting upon the promise of victory almost always turned to the theme of Indian conversion. It was this missionary hope – however inconsequential it may have been as an actual source of motivation during the war – that usually provided the specifically millennial coloring to these scenes of the American future. If British victory in the French and Indian War presented the glorious prospect of expanding American civilization across the continent, of rising cities, sophisticated culture, prosperous commerce and agriculture, it would also lead to the prophesied conversion of the heathen. Almost as though they sought an alternative to religious revivalism as the means of spreading the gospel, it was the few millennial Anglicans and the liberal Congregationalists, not the New Lights, who after the war were most taken with the idea of converting the Indians as a way to bring on the millennium.[83]

The picture of American civilization progressively advancing into the wilderness pulled together a constellation of images that appealed mostly to liberal Protestants. Evangelical Calvinists, to the contrary, did not generally welcome the British imperial victory in these terms. Their earlier apocalyptical interpretation of the war had instead featured a climactic struggle with the forces of the Antichrist, and once British victory was secure they usually lost their millennial perspective on the conflict. Although they, too, periodically urged missionary endeavor among the Indians, and similarly conceived of their conversion in millennial terms, only rarely did they seem to expect this as a consequence of the war.[84] For them, however desirable the conversion of the Indians, sin remained endemic among many nominal American Protestants. The establishment of the millennial Kingdom of God, with all its acknowledged blessings of liberty and opulence, awaited the internal renewal of society more than its physical extension into the west. Joseph Bellamy's Connecticut election sermon of 1762, for example, scarcely mentioned the war, conceiving of Connecticut's millennial potential primarily in terms of the need to overcome pervasive worldly sins. He envisioned the millennium as a time when general prosperity would be secured by the collective piety, industry, frugality, and charity of the regenerated saints. Unlike the liberals, who essentially assumed religious morality among American Protestants, Bellamy called for internal reform rather than for external growth or the conversion of others.[85]

For liberal Protestants, the prospect of successful Indian missions, like the defeat of the Catholic French, raised millennial possibilities for the American future in terms of relatively uncontroversial religious goals. But it is revealing that even this symbolism of the converted heathen could be used to divisive effect as tensions began to develop between New England Anglicans and Congregationalists in the wake of the war. Jonathan Mayhew twice pointedly suggested that the English Society for the Propagation of the Gospel – then focusing its efforts on New England Congregationalists and raising the spectre of an Anglican Bishop in America – redirect its proselytizing energies towards the Indians so as to contribute to the higher goal of establishing the millennium.[86] Even this seemingly apolitical millennial vision could thus be turned to a kind of political use. In itself, however, the liberal Protestant hope for the propagation of the gospel was no more political than the revivalists' idea of the millennium coming through an effusion of grace.

The large reservoir of American millennial hopes and apocalyptic fears that spilled into print on the eve of the Revolution had little to do with politics in the usual sense of the word. What gave the rise in eschatological publications its latent political signficance was less the endorsement of particular values and goals than the basic millennial promise of future happiness on earth. An ideal human order would be established in the world, this literature contended, and some authors even announced that it would come within a few years. Many New Lights in the late 1750's, a time of dwindling revivals and wartime anxieties, saw the millennium coming through a crisis bringing great adversity to the saints. Later, after the British victory in Quebec in 1759, the theme of gradual advancement towards the millennium became more pronounced, as it had been during the Awakening, only this time it arose mostly in sermons by nonrevivalist liberal Protestants. Still, whether the path seemed smooth or ridden with obstacles, the millennium loomed on the American horizon. The successive experiences of the rise and decline in revivalism, the shock of the earthquakes, and the setbacks and victory in the French and Indian War together had the effect of broadly disseminating a millennial perspective on the eve of the revolutionary period.

Each of these events quickened the currents of millennial expectation that had long run within American Protestantism and kept millennial ideas in the forefront of popular imagination for almost a generation. It was this process of mutual reinforcement, rather than any single one of these developments, that by the late 1750's had created an environment unusually receptive to prophetic speculation. The numerous publications of these years encompassed a range of millennial outlooks: Some writers expected the immediate dawn of a new age, others its distant unfolding; some stressed the prospect of bliss, others the dangers of judgment; some spoke to spiritual concerns, others to imperial ones. Some demonstrated greater intellectual sophistication than others. Whatever the variations, the significance of the millennial thought of the 1750's lies mostly in its wide range and intensity. Millennial ideas gained great currency in America in the late colonial period, their value successively bolstered by revivals, natural disasters, and war. When the crisis that led to the American Revolution erupted in the 1760's and 1770's, these themes were in a position to wield formidable interpretative power.

II

The rise and decline of millennialism in the revolutionary era

3

Whig resistance and
apocalyptical Manichaeanism

The wicked plotteth against the just and gnasheth upon
  him with his teeth.
The Lord shall laugh at him: for he seeth that his day is
  coming.

Psalm 37:12, 13

During the course of the revolutionary crisis the preexisting millennial tradition developed a reciprocal, dynamic relationship with
secular political thought. The two came fully together only in the
mid-1770's, as the patriot movement moved from resistance to
revolution. Long before the full expression of revolutionary millennialism, however, an apocalyptical perspective on the struggle with
Britain had already emerged. When the British government in the
mid-1760's sought to impose tighter controls over America, the
colonial opposition moved rapidly to interpret the emerging imperial crisis as an apocalyptical event. Eschatological imagery from
the beginning intermixed with constitutional arguments, contributing a cosmic dimension to patriot political understanding. Not all
patriots shared this perspective – many adhered to the measured
reasoning of the law and political philosophy or else vented their
emotions purely through radical whig political rhetoric. In the actual
arena of public debate, however, these various outlooks did not exist
in isolation, and even the more narrowly political arguments often
took on an eschatological coloring. On the level of popular culture,
especially, religion deeply informed political ideology.

ANTICHRISTIAN TYRANNY AND DIVINE LIBERTY

In Boston on February 14, 1766, the Sons of Liberty assembled near
Liberty Tree to hear an address. Subsequently printed in Providence

under the pseudonym "Pro-Patria," it was designed to stimulate New England patriots into continued resistance against the Stamp Act. The Sons of Liberty, who had already been for months in the forefront of popular agitation against the new British taxes, conducted much of their propagandistic activity through public assemblies such as this. The oration did not, however, discuss strategy; nor did it delve into constitutional arguments. Its structure was sermonic, based on the explication of the prophetic symbols of the two terrible Beasts in the Book of Revelation.

The orator began by observing that the colonists' objections to the British government had thus far been too limited. The enemies they faced were much more vast than mere "wicked men and wicked measures." The sacred word, containing "the best admonitions" about temporal as well as spiritual concerns, "foretold the great waste that would be committed in the world by monsters in the shape of men, who under a pretence of governing and protecting mankind, have enslaved them."[1] These monsters, described as the two Beasts in John's Revelation, had recently appeared in Britain under the guise of the royal ministers Bute and Grenville. Like the first Beast of the prophecy, with seven heads and ten horns, which rose from the sea and remained in power for forty-two months, the Earl of Bute, with "so many capital posts or offices," rose from the Isle of Scotland and had by then held office for precisely forty-two months.[2] Similarly, the second Beast which had two horns like a lamb, spoke like a dragon, and permitted men to buy or sell only upon receiving his mark, was George Grenville forcing the colonists to receive stamps. "I beseech you then to beware as good christians and lovers of your country," the orator exhorted his audience, "lest by touching any paper with this impression, you receive the mark of the *beast*, and become infamous in your country throughout all generations."[3] Attacking American merchants who were willing to cheat their compatriots by accommodating to the Stamp Act, he concluded by recommending the patriot policy of nonimportation and self-reliance: "Industry is our best barrier against slavery."[4]

This early patriot identification of the British ministry with the symbol of the Antichrist marked the first step towards an eschatological understanding of the revolutionary conflict. Although the use of this symbolism was not yet combined with millennial hopes for the dawning of a new republican age, it is striking how quickly American colonists in the forefront of the rebellion saw their struggle with Britain in terms of a conflict between the forces of righteousness and those of the devil. During the first phase of rebellion against the Stamp Act, colonists often employed demonic images to portray the British ministry. Patriot poems and songs printed in 1765 and 1766 in Boston, New York, and Philadelphia presented Bute, Grenville, and North as the minions of Satan, conspiring by means of the taxes to bring England and America into his eternal domain.[5] A widely circulated pictorial pun that originated in Boston at the time of the August 1765 riots showed Satan's face peering out of a boot (Bute), and effigies displayed in political processions and hung from Liberty Trees throughout the colonies – a ritual borrowed from the earlier Pope's Day parades – represented the ministers, American stamp-men, and the devil, all in league.[6] In Connecticut a patriot orator described the stamp distributor Jared Ingersoll in the words of the Revelation as "the Beast . . . set up in this Colony to be worshipped," and the Tory historian Samuel Peters later recalled that the repeal of the Stamp Act was celebrated as a victory "over the beast, and over his mark."[7] Another hostile observer, the Massachusetts Loyalist Peter Oliver, regarded the patriots' frequent depiction of the Stamp Act "with Horns, Tails, & cloven Feet" as a prime example of their demagogic manipulation of the weak and uneducated.[8]

As Oliver painfully remembered, once the pattern of symbolic association between British policy and the devil was established during the Stamp Act crisis, it remained a standard feature of patriot propaganda. Political cartoons printed in Boston in late 1760's and early 1770's depicted Satan securing the souls of several Americans deemed traitors to the American cause.[9] Effigies of the devil continued to be hung alongside those of British ministers and loyalists in well-publicized political rituals as far south as South Carolina.[10] Various kinds of patriot literature, including pamphlets, printed speeches, songs, poems, broadside leaflets, and even newspaper articles that appeared in the years before Independence similarly depicted the devil at work in the imperial administration.[11] The quasi-biblical "Books" of the popular *American Chronicles*, at once a parody and an example of patriot propaganda, contained a description of Bute, William Mansfield, Francis Bernard, and Thomas Hutchinson as "four great beasts," and declared with reference to biblical prophecy, "these are the four beasts . . . in whom is the spirit of the evil one."[12]

As the revolutionary movement gained momentum, the King himself also increasingly fell victim to these symbolic assaults. The outraged Philadelphia stamp commissioner John Hughes complained to his London superiors that "lower-class" Presbyterians were exclaiming, "No King But King Jesus," as early as 1765.[13] The explicit designation of the King as the Antichrist, however, proceeded somewhat more slowly than that of the royal ministry. In 1773 it was suggested in an illustration that appeared on the title page of *Freebetter's Connecticut Almanack* depicting the profile of the monarch with a hole in his wig shaped like the horns of the Beast or the devil.[14] By 1775 a popular revolutionary polemic printed throughout the American colonies was still more forthrightly addressed, "To his Tyrannic Majesty – the Devil."[15] When the Continental Congress finally declared American independence, the *Maryland Journal* reported that a group of soldiers in New York celebrated the news by throwing down and decapitating "the IMAGE of the BEAST" representing George the Third.[16] The identification of the King with the symbol of the Antichrist in biblical prophecy shortly thereafter received its most complete explication in an anonymous pamphlet by an American numerologist who demonstrated that the Hebrew and Greek words for "*Royal Supremacy* in *Great Britain*" possessed the hidden value 666, the "number of the beast" in Revelation:13.[17]

The idea that imperial officials were the henchmen of the devil took the struggle between America and the London government far outside the context of British constitutional debate and into the realm of sacred history. The new policy of taxation without representation seemed to threaten not only civil "slavery" – itself terrible – but subjugation to the most absolute, all-encompassing evil. The rapidity with which the colonial resistance movement seized upon this extreme symbolism illuminates the extent to which large numbers of Americans were predisposed to think about the world in these Manichaean terms. The idea that the universe was divided into opposing forces of good and evil, saintliness and sin, Christ and the Antichrist, was already a salient feature of American popular religious consciousness, one recently reinforced by the struggles of the Great Awakening and the French and Indian War.

In those previous times of crisis it was the clergy, particularly the New Light clergy, that most forcefully articulated this perspective. In the early years of the revolutionary movement, however, few patriot ministers published sermons that explicitly identified the British government with the devil. Colonial clergymen, like most of the more respectable defenders of the American cause, were still relatively cautious in the initial phase of resistance, regardless of whether they were Old Lights or New Lights.[18] Later, in the mid-1770's, revivalist

and liberal patriot ministers would both join in the public denunciation of Britain as the Antichrist, but in the early years of the
revolutionary movement this diabolical imagery was used first in the
street rituals of the Sons of Liberty and in usually anonymous
popular patriot literature. The fact that in the 1760's and early 1770's
influential clergymen did not take a conspicuous lead in developing
this perspective by no means indicates that religion was incidental to
the shaping of American revolutionary consciousness – rather, it
suggests quite the reverse. Especially in New England, the cutting
edge of the revolutionary movement, Manichaean religious assumptions were so deep among ordinary colonists that the objectional
imperial measures were almost immediately presented by patriot
publicists not merely as unconstitutional but as demonic. If the
patriot clergy was reluctant to draw such an extreme conclusion early
on, the radical laity was not. By the mid-1770's this perception of
British policy had become deeply ingrained in the popular culture of
the American revolutionary movement.

The horror of the Antichrist and the determination to expunge
antichristian agents from the world were integral components of the
prophetic outlook on history long familiar to most American
Protestants. According to the traditional religious perspective on
history, the forces of sin and righteousness were engaged in a
continuous warfare that had begun with the Fall and would end with
the concrete as well as spiritual defeat of the Antichrist. This was
already the historical understanding of many American colonists
when they were confronted with what seemed a fundamental threat to
their political rights. According to the standard Protestant reading of
prophecy, however, it was above all the Papacy, not secular power,
that was the Antichrist. In America links between tyranny and
Catholicism had recently been drawn during the French and Indian
War. The rhetorical power of this constellation of images persisted
into the revolutionary period. Not surprisingly, as the conflict with
Britain intensified, American patriots came to portray the Pope
conspiring with Satan behind the screen of the new imperial policy.
The perception of the British government as popish, joined to the
traditional view of Antichrist as a tyrant, lent even greater legitimacy
to the emerging symbolic connection between the conflict with
Britain and the struggles foretold in biblical prophecy.

Before the colonial resistance to the Stamp Act, the theme of
creeping Catholicism had already permeated American protests
against the Church of England's efforts to strengthen its American

base. In Virginia in 1759 the controversy known as the Parsons Cause inflamed the opinion of the lay gentry against the Anglican ecclesiastical hierarchy. When local clergymen protested against an attempt by the House of Burgesses to cut their recently inflated salaries, they were accused by the anticlerical polemicist Richard Bland of being like "Romish Inquisitors."[19] Drawing directly upon the language of biblical prophecy, Bland compared the royal prerogative disallowing the colonial legislation to "the King of Babylon's Decree," for it seemed designed to "almost force the People of the Plantations to fall down and worship any Image it shall please to set up."[20] In New England, where the association of the Church of England with the Roman Antichrist was an enduring part of the Puritan heritage, tensions between Congregationalists and Anglicans exploded between 1763 and 1765 in the pamphlet war over the possibility of an American episcopate. "Popery is now making great strides in England," warned Jonathan Mayhew in a discourse on Catholic idolatry in early 1765, "as great, perhaps as it did in the reign either of Charles or James the second."[21] Especially since Anglicans in the northern colonies tended to remain loyal to the crown, New England patriots continued to level charges of antichristian popery at the Church of England well into the 1770's.[22]

Because the Church of England was legally established by the English state, such accusations were never entirely nonpolitical. But it was still a further step for American patriots to connect the secular British government directly with the Church of Rome. Only rarely did they hint at such a connection before the autumn of 1774. Then, however, when news reached the colonies of the Quebec Act granting toleration to Catholicism in French Canada, Americans rushed to interpret the legislation as evidence of a Catholic menace in the London government. During the two years that passed between its passage and the Declaration of Independence, sermons, patriot newspapers, pamphlets, and even the official proceedings of the Continental Congress drew attention to the danger that the royal government was conspiring with Catholic Quebec to destroy the Protestant colonies.

These suspicions were yet another variant of the fear that the British ministers were engaged in a satanic conspiracy of universal proportions, a fear that had already been widely expressed and that now seemed confirmed by hard fact. It was at this juncture that the patriot clergy, both Old Light and New Light, joined the laity in publically condemning Great Britain as an agent of the Antichrist.

The Quebec Act revealed the British oppressors' "associations with the Man of Sin," declared the Congregationalist minister Joseph Lyman in western Massachusetts.[23] The Canadian Catholics were described in the *American Chronicles* as "devils with seven heads and ten horns," and as "the scarlet whore" of biblical prophecy in a poem by the young Philip Freneau.[24] Even so worldly a revolutionary as Alexander Hamilton expressed outrage at Britain's acceptance of Canadian Catholicism: "If they [the members of Parliament] had been friends to the protestant cause, they would never have provided such a nursery for its great enemy: They would not have given such encouragement to popery."[25]

Once the passage of the Quebec Act had duly established the connection, patriot imagery after the summer of 1774 repeatedly presented the British in league with the Pope as well as the devil. The *South Carolina Gazette* reported from Charleston that on Guy Fawkes Day that autumn "an incredible Number of Spectators" assembled to witness "a MAGNIFICENT EXHIBITION of EFFIGIES, designed to represent Lord North, Gov. Hutchinson, the Pope, and the DEVIL."[26] Hymns composed by Elhanan Winchester, then a popular Baptist preacher in rural South Carolina, described the British measures as a plot by "Rome and Hell."[27] Harvard president Samuel Langdon, who had recently argued in quite orthodox fashion that the Beasts in the Book of Revelation symbolized the Papacy, asked in 1775, "Have we not great reason to suspect that all the late measures respecting the colonies have originated from popish schemes of men who would gladly restore the race of Stuarts and who look on Popery as a religion most favorable to arbitrary power?"[28] As George III himself increasingly fell under attack, revolutionary polemicists denied there was a difference between the "Devil, Bishops, Pope, and such a King." Was he not "set at the head of the Romish Church in *Canada*," the "KING of TYRANNY, CONFUSION and POPERY, DEFENDER of the ROMISH FAITH, &c?"[29]

Further consolidating the symbolic association of the British government with the Antichrist was the traditional view that both the Pope and Satan were, in essence, tyrannical powers. The meanings of tyranny and Catholicism had long been conflated in Anglo-American Protestant thought. For colonial patriots the Quebec Act seemed a further step towards tyranny, just as tyranny promised to lead, in turn, to Catholicism. The royal ministers were "spreading the tyrant hand of popish power"; imperial policy was "a plot of popish tyranny."[30] Behind the association of tyranny with popery was the related association of tyranny with the Beasts, Babylon, "mother of harlots," and the other symbols for the Antichrist in biblical prophecy – symbols that had traditionally been understood to refer to the Catholic Church.[31] A 1744 printer's illustration that reappeared in 1770 and 1772 in a nonpolitical moral tract by the New Jersey Presbyterian clergyman Jacob Green showed the many-headed beast and other diabolical figures under the caption "Tirant Sin."[32] Throughout the years of mounting resistance to the British government, ministers who preached on the need for religious salvation exhorted against the spiritual "tyranny of Satan" and the "slavery of sin."[33] Just as the Antichrist was commonly described as tyrannical, these words could continue to be used in a purely spiritual sense to refer to the intangible power of evil. But the vocabulary always drew upon a political analogy. Once the actual abuse of state power became a serious political issue, the age-old view of the Antichrist as tyrannical easily translated into a perception of civil tyranny as the Antichrist.

Even when they did not explicitly identify the British government with the Antichrist, colonial patriots frequently pointed to this established connection between Satan and political tyranny. John Adams's 1765 *Dissertation on the Canon and Feudal Law*, which was printed in the *Boston Gazette* as part of the opposition to the Stamp Act, claimed that unchecked power "would soon become the man of sin, the whore of Babylon, the mystery of iniquity."[34] To Jonathan Mayhew the Stamp Act had similarly threatened to leave "that ugly Hag Slavery, the deformed child of Satan" in place of "celestial" liberty.[35] By the mid-1770's the association between civil tyranny and the Antichrist was a standard feature of American rhetoric. New England patriot ministers taught their congregations that the symbols of the dragons, the Beasts, and the Beast's image in biblical prophecy referred to "all the tyrants of the earth," to "every species of tyranny."[36] A contributor to the *New York Journal* in 1775 warned George III that "an arbitrary cruel spirit of tyranny" makes "kings like unto 'the great dragon, which is the devil and satan,' the grand tyrant of hell."[37]

In the context of the colonists' developing arguments about the constitutional limits of legitimate authority, the image of the Antichrist as a tyrant took on a force it had not possessed since the days of revolutionary Puritanism. Americans relied on political theory and constitutional precedent for their conclusions about what particular British acts could be described as tyrannical, but the symbolic association between tyranny and the Antichrist added another – and to many a deeper – layer of meaning to the crisis. The repeated radical whig statements that the royal government was "venal," "corrupt," "wicked," "diabolical," or "infernal" were received and understood by a still largely orthodox (even largely Calvinist) Protestant population. American patriots often went beyond the loose imputations of moral evil characteristic of radical whig ideology to more systematic Manichaean conclusions. British tyranny was viewed not only as evil but as part of the devil's continuing quest for cosmic power. The universe was divided into opposing forces of Christ and the Antichrist, sin and righteousness, and all of human history – including the imperial conflict – was fundamentally the struggle between them.

The association of tyranny with sin and the forces of the Antichrist was always juxtaposed in patriot literature to the association of liberty with righteousness and the forces of Christ. Thus, just as British tyranny was tied to the machinations of Satan, the colonial quest for political rights was also imbued with transcendent significance. The assertion that liberty was God-given or God's cause was a standard refrain in American revolutionary argument. The precedent for this view went back to the seventeenth century and had recently been widely reaffirmed in the sermons of the French and Indian War. In eighteenth-century England, especially, the mythic understanding of the Puritans as having fled Stuart tyranny to establish liberty under God in America tailored this perspective to a provincial colonial audience.[38] What was meant by the term "liberty" often extended beyond the political definitions of popular legislative representation and the protection of individual rights. Not only had the older Puritan ideas of America as an Elect Nation gradually come to take on a whig libertarian coloring, but the very idea of liberty was laden with religious connotations. Just as tyranny was closely identified with sin, so liberty was closely identified with grace. Even the commonplace radical whig idea that liberty depended on disinterested "virtue" or "public spirit," a perspective usually associated with the secular theories of civic republicanism, was essentially another variation on the same theme – for American Protestants usually assumed that true virtue was impossible to achieve without Christian faith.[39]

The "blessing of freedom," explained the Baptist preacher John Allen, was received "from Heaven, as the breath of life, and essence of our existence."[40] His *Oration upon the Beauties of Liberty*, first delivered in Boston in 1772, became one of the most widely reprinted pamphlets of the revolutionary era, appearing not only in several New England editions but even in Wilmington, Delaware. For Allen, liberty clearly possessed transcendent qualities, and he, like many other patriot spokesmen, drew an analogy between liberty and religious redemption. In the *Boston Gazette*, "Cato of Utica" joined him in exclaiming, "Liberty is inspiration, it is . . . 'the divinity that stirs within us,' 'tis the very principle of self valuation."[41] "Liberty is salvation in politics, as slavery is reprobation," *The Crisis* further developed the metaphor; "neither is there any other distinction but that of saint and devil, between the champion of the one and of the other."[42] So interlocked were the meanings of liberty and grace that both religious and secular publications in various parts of the colonies implored Americans in the words of Galatians "to stand fast in the freedom wherewith Christ hath made you free."[43]

If patriot publicists associated liberty with Christ in order to highlight the sacred character of their cause, so did preachers interested in saving souls exploit the intensely positive feelings about liberty that emerged in the early revolutionary movement. Several clergymen drew upon the phraseology in the Book of James to define the Christian gospel as the "law of liberty."[44] Christ's liberty, the Anglican Jacob Duché told rebel troops in Philadelphia in 1775 before he switched to the loyalist side, is "an enlargement of the soul by the efficacy of divine grace."[45] "The whole plan of Redemption," as the Connecticut New Light Levi Hart described it, "is comprised in procuring, preaching and bestowing liberty to the captives, and the opening of the prison to the bound."[46] For some ministers, particularly evangelical Calvinists in the early phase of resistance, the common comparison between civil liberty and the liberty of the gospel afforded a means not only to endorse whig political principles but to stress the higher value of spiritual salvation. The "slavery of sin" is far worse than "civil slavery," they reminded their parishioners; the most "perfect liberty" is reserved for "the free and happy subjects of the Prince of Peace."[47] The most extreme position was taken by the New England evangelical Baptist Isaac Backus, who, still alienated from what he regarded as primarily a Congregationalist struggle with Britain, in 1767 altogether disparaged the worldly goals of the patriot movement:

We have lately been upon the borders of a civil war, for LIBERTY: hanging and burning were not too bad for the enemies of LIBERTY! Ah! little do many see what they are doing; for after all this noise: *Whosoever committeth sin is the servant of sin.* . . . Such harbour the worst enemies to liberty in their own bosoms.[48]

The use of the term "liberty" to describe spiritual salvation, like the use of tyranny to describe the Antichrist, was not new in the revolutionary period. The New Testament itself usually gave the term this spiritual meaning, and in mid-eighteenth-century America revivalist preachers, in particular, had freely employed this vocabulary. Yet well before the outbreak of conflict with Britain, the word already carried positive whig connotations as well. Once colonists began to protest the infringement of their constitutional rights in the 1760's and 1770's, this double meaning even further enriched its rhetorical power. The high evaluation of liberty enhanced religious exhortations by drawing upon the political excitement of the patriot cause and, simultaneously, infused political debate with the sacred meaning that inhered in the religious vocabulary. If religion was politicized, so was politics sacralized. Not only did ministers respond to the imperial crisis by preaching about liberty and tyranny in the language of the radical whigs, but the very terms "liberty" and "tyranny" were deeply infused with religious, even spiritual, meaning.

THE COMING CONFLAGRATION AND DESTRUCTION OF BABYLON

The conflation of "tyranny" with the Antichrist and "liberty" with redemption had outlined critical elements of a prophetic understanding of the American Revolution very early in the imperial conflict. But American patriots only gradually arrived at the full-blown millennial conviction that their struggle with Britain would lead to the coming of the Kingdom of Christ. In the early years of the American revolutionary movement, their interpretation of the imperial crisis reflected more uncertainty about the outcome. They presented the legions of Christ and the Antichrist as nearly equally matched, and raised the horrifying spectres of defeat, catastrophe, and judgment more than the prospect of millennial bliss.

Scriptural prophecy not only described a Manichaean world divided between forces of good and evil. It also provided an apocalyptical theory of history according to which these contending forces would engage in a climactic confrontation. The idea that the American struggle for liberty marked a decisive turning point in history pervaded patriot literature. The common notion that the future could still turn either way, towards misery or happiness, was ridden with the threat of potential disaster and judgment. As seen within the framework of radical whig ideology, failure would result in tyranny driving liberty from the earth; the citizens who lacked sufficient virtue to arise in defense of their rights would find themselves enslaved and reduced to the most abject moral and physical condition. The same basic historical scenario was also symbolized in religious terms. The New England jeremiad, a sermonic form repeatedly used by the revolutionary clergy, conformed closely to this radical whig understanding of history. Just as the radical whigs called for the defense of traditional liberty against the threat posed by corrupt and tyrannical power, so these ministers enjoined Americans to preserve their divine covenant by the righteous repudiation of vice. Both views conveyed an essentially moral theory of historical change, according to which virtue led to renewal, vice to decline. And both in addition saw the present as morally degenerate and upon the threshold of ruin. In these respects classical republican and biblical traditions converged, the one reinforcing the other.[49]

With the approach of American independence, the covenant theology would extend to incorporate millennial themes, thereby more clearly departing from the radical whig vision of decline and ruin. In the early years of colonial resistance, however, the spectre of fallen virtue and divine judgment generally prevailed instead. Only if Americans would take the necessary steps to recover their ancestral holiness through prayer, repentance, and reformation, the jeremiads conventionally warned, would God spare them this rod of oppression. As the aged minister of Cambridge Nathaniel Appleton ominously invoked this tradition in 1770, "we are under the rebukes of Divine Providence, and dark and threatening clouds hang over our nation, and over these colonies in America."[50]

If the future was feared, the past was idealized. Characteristically, the Reverend Timothy Hilliard compared "this day of darkness and gloominess, of clouds and thick darkness," with the "halcyon days" of the past.[51] In the 1760's and early 1770's, as relations with Britain disintegrated, an idyllic picture of colonial history repeatedly graced patriot literature. The poem "America" by the North Carolina attorney and judge Alexander Martin, which was published in Philadelphia around 1769, dwelt on the felicity enjoyed by Americans before the recent taxation policies.[52] An image of America as previously happy, prosperous, and free appeared most frequently, however, in New England, where the long tradition of ancestor worship supplied a ready mythological framework. Using biblical metaphors to suggest the perfections of paradise, New England patriots described America as "a land flowing with milk and honey," and where "the wilderness blossoms as the rose."[53] Only when "the *locusts leave the land*," the physician Benjamin Church concluded in an oration commemorating the Boston Massacre in 1773, would the colonies return to their earlier state of pristine happiness.[54]

Even though this idealized image of the past was used by patriots to attack the new imperial measures, it reflected a deep-seated conservatism, a backward-looking orientation shared with radical whig ideology. Whereas English radical whigs tended to idealize the Saxons or the Commonwealthmen, American patriots, particularly New Englanders, more often idealized their own provincial history. The hope of both was to preserve what they regarded as their venerable heritage rather than to initiate any fundamental change. Within this ideological context, change only aroused suspicion as a sign of decline and ruin. What was deemed valuable was projected not into the future but, however imaginatively, into the past.

From the perspectives of both the jeremiad and radical whig ideology, the past seemed idyllic particularly in relation to the present prospect of doom. American patriots throughout the first decade of the imperial controversy portrayed themselves not only as defending a tradition of purity but as keeping the forces of utter devastation at bay. Upon the repeal of the Stamp Act, Charles Chauncy, for example, stressed how narrowly America had escaped "total ruin."[55] The fear that British policy represented a threat of cataclysmic proportions often extended beyond the jeremiads' repeated warnings of judgment to the more extreme dread of the approaching apocalypse. Whereas the crisis envisaged in the jeremiad was not necessarily described in an eschatological framework, this explicitly apocalyptical perception was expressed directly in terms of the language and imagery of biblical prophecy.

During the first decade of colonial resistance, several publications appeared in the American colonies that warned of the final conflagration and Last Judgment. A seventeenth-century English work that contained a detailed description of the end times, including the Second Coming of Christ in the clouds, the resurrection of the dead, and the horrors of everlasting punishment, went into four New England editions between 1766 and 1773, far more than ever before.[56] Contemporary American writers, particularly in New

England, also dwelt on apocalyptical themes. The Presbyterian minister John Murray's sermon *The Last Solemn Scene*, and the obscure poet John Peck's *Description of the Last Judgment*, each of which were printed twice between 1768 and 1773, likewise provided vivid accounts of the fearful events to occur at the End.[57] In Philadelphia in 1765 a broadside reported the prophetic vision of a dying girl who was commissioned by an angel "to warn all *America*" of the bloody purge of sinners about to ensue.[58] A comet that appeared in New England in 1769 also inspired thoughts of the terrors of the approaching conflagration, as did a widely reprinted account of a dream by a New Light layman in Gloucester, Massachusetts, named Samuel Clarke, who envisioned the imminent pouring of "the first vials of God's Wrath."[59]

Some of these publications were essentially apocalyptical versions of the jeremiad, castigating Americans for their sins and demanding repentance in order to avert the awful judgments of the Last Day. The child prophet in Philadelphia likened the city to "Sodom" and cited apparent instances of infanticide as the primary cause of God's wrath. Samuel Clarke interpreted his prophetic dream as the judgments brought on the world by the sins of the unregenerate rich, who "wrong the distressed to such a degree that they are brought to suffer Hunger and Cold." "Now you can brag and boast, and use Authority," he rebuked the wealthy and powerful, "but know that for all these things God will will you to Judgment."[60] If for Clarke the comet and the recent "troubles" from England presaged divine vengeance on the worldly elite, others concentrated more specifically on the political conflict with England. Using language taken directly from biblical prophecy, the Baptist John Allen proclaimed "the day of the watchmen of America" had come. "Consider," he warned America's oppressors, "that we must all appear before the judgment seat of Christ."[61] The Presbyterian William Tennent in South Carolina interpreted the threat of British tyranny as divine chastisement for America's irreligion and vice and, observing that the "Day of Vengeance" may be near, expected the British also shortly to receive severe judgments from God.[62]

Of course, some of the apocalyptical writings of the late 1760's and early 1770's made no reference to the emerging revoutionary crisis and represented an older religious tradition of doomsdaying. But as the conflict over British imperial policy intensified and the royal government was increasingly identified by American patriots as Antichrist, the political situation gave greater immediacy to even the nonpolitical warnings about the final conflagration and Last Judgment. Visions of approaching destruction were particularly widespread during the first decade of the imperial crisis, just as they had been during the mid-1750's before the British had defeated the French. In the 1760's and early 1770's, as Americans mobilized to resist the imposition of new imperial regulations, this cataclysmic outlook on the future coincided in patriot literature with an idealized image of the past. The apocalyptical thought of the early revolutionary movement generally regarded the future in terms of horrors, not bliss. The emphasis was upon doomsday, not the millennial age.

MILLENNIAL FORESHADOWINGS

Even in the 1760's and early 1770's, however, a thin line separated catastrophic from millennial eschatologies. Each of these visions of the End had long been a part of American religious tradition, and upon several occasions the two had arisen in tandem. In the reactions to the earthquakes of 1727 and 1755 and to the French and Indian War, for example, hopeful and fearful apocalyptical perspectives were profoundly intermixed. The relationship between apocalyptical doomsdaying and hopeful millennial prophesying continued to be close in the following decades. Although colonists resisting the new imperial measures tended at first to idealize the past and to associate change with destruction, the millennialism endemic to American religious culture always remained close at hand.

Just as the apocalyptical warnings of conflagration and the Last Judgment took nonpolitical as well as political form, so millennial speculation persisted into this period without any apparent reference to the imperial controversy. In language reminiscent of the Great Awakening, for example, evangelical ministers in New England whose congregations were swept by minor revivals in the mid 1760's interpreted the conversions as a hopeful sign that the millennium would come soon.[63] Others, primarily liberal Congregationalist clergymen, continued to publish sermons on the well-worn theme that the papal Antichrist had been declining ever since the Reformation and would soon, according to prophecy, make way for true Christianity to prevail.[64] In Philadelphia a falling star was reported in 1765 as a portent of the latter-day glory.[65]

Although none of these prophetic forecasts were issued with the imperial crisis in mind, an atmosphere of millennial expectation quite clearly carried over from the 1740's and 1750's into the period of colonial resistance. Only rarely before the mid-1770's, however, did millennial visions appear in political discourse alongside the more common spectres of cataclysm and judgment. An exception was the group of Philadelphia Presbyterians who, according to John Hughes, cried, "No King But King Jesus," with clear reference to the millennial reign of Christ, as early as the Stamp Act controversy. For the most part the extension of political apocalypticism to full-blown revolutionary millennialism occurred relatively slowly and was completed only as resistance was transformed into rebellion and war.

Just as the patriot clergy, unlike the radical laity, hesitated to identify Great Britain with the Antichrist in the early years of the imperial conflict, so too most colonial clergymen in the 1760's also stopped short of airing millennial hopes in the course of their political commentary. Upon the rare occasions when they did so, it was usually in the context of purely religious exhortations tacked on to their political arguments. During the Stamp Act crisis, for example, the moderate Calvinist Joseph Emerson of Massachusetts concluded his sermon defending the American cause by calling for a revitalization of piety both as a means to secure divine protection of civil rights and, beyond that, as the way to bring on the full glory of the millennial dawn.[66] In Georgia, the Swiss Presbyterian minister John Joachim Zubly, who later came out as a Tory, preached in a similar but more conservative vein, urging prayer for the millennium while insisting that real freedom comes only with faith.[67] Another, anonymous minister in South Carolina in 1769 urged a society of planters to support the nonimportation agreements as part of the moral and religious reformation that would both save America from sinful luxury and oppression and eventually lead to the millennial triumph of the Kingdom of Christ.[68] None of these ministers presented political action as a means to, or as a sign of, the approaching millennium; nor did they conceive of the millennium in political terms. Rather, the restoration of American constitutional rights appeared at most as a kind of residual reward that God would grant to the faithful on the way to the religious redemption of the world.

Another way in which millennial themes permeated patriot rhetoric in the 1760's was by recapitulating the visions of Anglo-American imperial glory that had so recently been used to celebrate the British victory in the French and Indian War. Such visions, at once patriotically British and imbued with nascent American nationalism, would in the long run help to inspire rebellion against Britain. Throughout the first decade of the imperial conflict, however, they did not imply independence or revolution. Indeed, the millennial hopes of the early revolutionary movement, much like its idyllic view of the past, were often pinned to peaceful reconciliation with Britain rather than to the perpetuation of the current hostilities. Compared to the apocalyptical imagery of Great Britain as the Antichrist, which although defensive still had a radical and militant tone, these scattered examples of early patriot millennialism were still quite mild and traditional in form.

When, in 1764, James Otis wrote the first important pamphlet protesting infringements upon colonial rights, for example, he described the British Empire as the potential redeemer of the world in terms very similar to the victory sermons delivered the previous year after the French and Indian War. The critical difference was that Britain's glorious destiny had now become contingent on the continuing preservation of colonial liberties. If only the London government would show "the same moderation of government" that America had enjoyed since the Glorious Revolution, then the colonists would demonstrate "perpetual lawful and willing subjection, obedience, and love to Great Britain." Under these happy circumstances, the monarchy would continue to thrive until the millennial age, when all the tyranny on earth would be vanquished. "Rescued human nature must and will be from the general slavery that have so long triumphed over the species," he proclaimed, "Great Britain has done much towards it: what a glory will it be for her to complete the work throughout the world!" This image of Great Britain bringing glorious liberty to the world was couched in terms of a clear political threat: If the London government continued to violate traditional rights, the English would abdicate their exalted role as millennial agent. Yet, for Otis, America's future happiness was still linked to the "sound health and full vigor" of the monarchy.[69]

The specific emphasis upon the glories of British imperial power became less pronounced within the patriot movement over the course of the following decade. Several New England ministers who preached jeremiads blaming the political controversy on America's sins, however, still raised the possibility that religious reformation would lead to both imperial reconciliation and the fulfillment of millennial prophecy. Once God removed his judgments, "harmony

69

and affection shall be restored between Great-Britain and her colonies."[70] Then America would enjoy full liberty, peace, commercial prosperity, and territorial expansion: "We shall sit quietly under our vines and fig-trees . . . and have none to make us afraid," the standard biblical phrases proclaimed; "the wilderness shall become a fruitful field, and the desert shall blossom as the rose."[71] These were not, however, leading patriot voices. By the late 1760's the idyllic view of America as part of the British Empire was more commonly taken by those unsympathetic to the American cause. The liberal Massachusetts Congregationalist minister Daniel Shute, for example, later described as having "stood aside and watched the Revolution run its course," preached an election sermon in 1768 in which he tied millennial prospects to lawful obedience to government.[72]

If colonial patriots came to place less emphasis upon the millennial promise of the British Empire, they continued to stress America's own redemptive mission in world history. Of course, the notion that America would be the seat of the millennial kingdom long antedated the growing crisis in British imperial relations. In New England, especially, the idea had long been associated with provincial covenant theology. Like the identification of the colonists with the Chosen People of God, this millennial vision reflected a kind of provincial nationalism, but it did not necessarily depend for its fulfillment on any decisive break with the English past. The belief that America would inaugurate the millennial kingdom had traditionally been perfectly compatible with patriotic loyalty to the crown, a combination of sentiments that was characteristic of the sermons delivered in the early 1760's upon victory in the French and Indian War. As late as 1773 the Philadelphia college provost William Smith, never a supporter of the revolutionary cause, could still envision the future grandeur of the American colonies in essentially the same terms as he had in 1763. Smith described "the Progress of the Arts, like that of the Sun, from East to West," and looked forward to "that glorious Period . . . when the Regions on this Side of the Atlantic, as well as those on the other, shall enjoy their Day of Freedom, Light and Polished Life!"[73] For Smith, and perhaps for other American loyalists as well, the millennial missions of America and British civilization were still one and the same. Gradually, however, the patriot movement appropriated for itself these grandiose ideas about America's future.

What had in 1763 sounded like loyal tributes to the western branch of the empire took on a more threatening edge in the context of the new imperial conflict. As early as the Stamp Act crisis John Adams pointedly described the original settlement of the colonies as "the opening of a grand scene and design in Providence for the illumination of the ignorant, and the emancipation of the slavish part of mankind all over the earth."[74] This traditional idea of a special American destiny was phrased in distinctively millennial terms by an increasing number of ardent American patriots in the early 1770's. Among the first literary efforts of the budding young writers Timothy Dwight, Philip Freneau, and Hugh Henry Brackenridge were patriotic poems about the rising glory of America composed at college in Connecticut and New Jersey in 1770 and 1771. Recounting the familiar tale of America's material and cultural progress since the original flight from oppression into the wilderness, Freneau and Brackenridge looked ahead from present achievements in the arts, sciences, agriculture, and commerce into a still more magnificent millennial future:

> And when a train of rolling years are past
> (So sang the exil'd seer in Patmos isle,)
> A new Jerusalem sent down from heav'n
> Shall grace our happy earth, perhaps this land,
> Whose virgin bosom shall then receive, tho late,
> Myriads of saints with their almighty king,
> To live and reign on earth a thousand years
> Thence called Millennium. Paradise a new
> Shall flourish, by no second Adam lost.[75]

Verses prophesying American millennial grandeur appeared as well in John Tobler's *Georgia and South-Carolina Almanack* for 1774, which reprinted Bishop Berkeley's visionary poem "On the Prospect of Arts and Sciences in America."[76] Berkeley also foretold the future triumph of civilization as it progressed from the Old to the New World, and this work, originally written in the 1720's and already well known in the colonies, probably served as a model for the poems by Dwight, Freneau, and Brackenridge. Alluding to the millennial reign as the fifth monarchy, Berkeley's concluding lines about America as the fifth and last empire, "Time's Noblest Offspring," must have fired patriot imagination in the early 1770's.

In the poems by Berkeley, Dwight, Freneau, and Brackenridge, as in the victory sermons at the end of the French and Indian War, the prospect of cultural and economic achievements vastly overshadowed the promise of liberty. But by the early 1770's millennial ideas about

71

American destiny were beginning to be woven into the fabric of patriot political ideology. When in 1773 Samuel Mather cited the prophecy that America was destined to be the "great Seat of Empire and Religion and the Theatre of considerable Events before the End of the World," he, like Warren, noted in addition that America was intended to be God's asylum for the oppressed. In his view, the colonists' recent defense of their rights showed that things were "tending apace" towards that glorious era.[77] At commencement exercises at Nassau Hall in 1774 Hugh Henry Brackenridge delivered yet another poem that recapitulated the familiar theme of America's rise to millennial grandeur. This time, however, in contrast to the complacent verses he had composed earlier with Freneau, Brackenridge inserted a discordant political note. He warned that despite all America's manifold blessings the Kingdom of God would not flourish as long as the soil was flooded by "persecution, in malignant streams."[78]

The thematic incorporation of millennial expectations into American revolutionary argument was, however, still far from complete. Both the evangelical idea that religious regeneration would lead to the millennium and the nationalist idea of America as the future seat of the millennial kingdom drew upon established millennial traditions without proclaiming a millennial goal for the patriot movement. Significantly, the militant revolutionary millennialism that would emerge later on was foreshadowed most clearly not in the mainstream of patriot resistance but in the overtly rebellious North Carolina Regulation. This movement of backcountry farmers, opposed not to royal but to eastern and local administrative power, objected particularly to the corrupt management of the local court system by privileged officeholders, lawyers, and merchants and to the collection of tithes for the Church of England, to which few westerners belonged. Their protest through the 1760's sporadically erupted into armed confrontation until they were effectively suppressed by the provincial governor's troops in the Battle of Alamance in 1771. As a group the North Carolina Regulators appear to have later divided over the American Revolution.[79]

In 1770 a leading supporter of the Regulation named Herman Husband, a planter from the settlement of Sandy Creek then running for reelection to the colonial assembly, wrote the only pamphlet published in defense of the movement. His plea on behalf of the Regulators was partially couched in the inflammatory rhetoric of biblical prophecy, raising briefly the possibility of a millennial conclusion to the conflict. To overcome the oppression of the backcountry, he advocated the popular election of juries and, of course, the careful selection of reform-minded assemblymen such as himself. Turning to his most lofty hopes for the future, he confided, "Methinks when a Reformation can be brought about in our Constitution by a legal and constitutional manner, then will commence that Thousand Years Reign with Christ, and utter downfall of Mystery *Babylon*."[80]

Elsewhere, Husband compared the Regulators to the chosen people of Israel, endowed by Providence with a spirit akin to religious enthusiasm. He concentrated heavily on the injustices of the Anglican religious establishment as well as the selfish greed of land speculators, lawyers, officials, and merchants "whose interests jar with the interest of the publick good."[81] Both his religious and his political message were surely roundly approved by the Scotch-Irish Presbyterian freeholders who for the most part formed the ranks of the Regulation. Husband's own religion was closer to the less structured and more spontaneous spirituality of the Quakers – he had been only recently disowned by the Friends for objecting to the hierarchical organization of the Monthly and Quarterly Meetings – but as a Maryland youth he had been converted to New Light Presbyterianism under the preaching of George Whitefield and Gilbert Tennent. He later recounted that he became convinced during the Great Awakening that the apocalyptical prophecies of the Bible would be fulfilled during his lifetime, and in the early 1740's he began to preach a millennial message to neighbors and even to fieldworkers. He held on to this millennial conviction after he joined the Quakers, believing them to be the best approximation of the true church that would bring on the new age, although as a group the Quakers had long since abandoned the intense millennialism of their seventeenth-century origins. Husband's hopes for the millennial reign of Christ during the Regulation, as well as his analogies to the Old Testament, were not Quaker but evangelical Calvinist in both substance and tone.[82]

Husband was evidently not a participant in the early anti-imperial agitation, although he went on to become an active member of the radical Constitutionalist Party in western Pennsylvania during the Revolution. Some years later he recalled that "when the Opposition to the Stamp Act began, I was Early Convinced that the Authors who Wrote in favour of Liberty Was Generally Inspired by the Same Spirrit that we Regeleous Professors Called Christ."[83] This sentiment, already much stronger in the 1760's in the mainstream of the patriot movement along the northeastern seaboard, soon gave rise to radical millennial visions there on a much larger scale. But before the mid-1770's, when the American colonists at last moved from defensive resistance to outright revolution, Herman Husband's argument on behalf of the North Carolina Regulation represents one of the first examples of radical millennialism in the revolutionary period – and it significantly came from outside the patriot ranks.

As yet, few patriot spokesmen had moved beyond apocalyptical predictions of destruction and judgment to the declaration of a millennial goal for their actions. The few millennial statements issued by patriots before the mid-1770's were not especially militant in tone. Compared to the frightening possibilities of disaster and ruin, the more reassuring prospects of millennial happiness seemed farther removed and less ridden with urgency. The apocalyptical thought of the early revolutionary movement, like the radical whig ideology with which it was fused, was highly combative but still essentially fearful and defensive. Much like the conservative Protestants at the time of the Reformation, or English Puritans in the early seventeenth century, American patriots in the 1760's and 1770's most often used prophecy negatively, to denounce Babylon rather than to proclaim the imminent dawn of a new day. During the first decade of colonial resistance, millennialism appeared only on the periphery of political debate, and, with the partial exception of the North Carolina Regulation, it did not yet take an explicitly rebellious form.

As a more general outlook on the meaning of history, however, millennial theory remained conspicuously evident on the sidelines of radical politics. It coexisted with the patriot imagery of Great Britain as the Antichrist and with the colonists' widespread conviction that the imperial conflict signified a great historical crisis. If American whigs were slow to apply a fully millennial perspective to their constitutional struggle, this hesitancy merely reflected their halting progress from resistance to full-scale rebellion. All the ingredients of a revolutionary millennial vision were already there. The view that British tyranny was the Antichrist, the view that America was intended to usher in the Kingdom of God, the view that the latter days were near at hand, all were ideas that had in various forms taken hold by the early 1770's. They only awaited the decisive confrontations of the mid-1770's to be fully combined.

4

The revolutionary millennialism
of the 1770's

To drive out nations before thee greater and mightier than
thou art, to bring thee in, to give thee their land for an
inheritance, as it is this day.

Deuteronomy 4: 38

Between 1773 and 1776 a fully millennial interpretation of the
imperial crisis rose to the fore as American patriots finally moved
from resistance to revolution. Sermons now often described the trials
and tribulations of the conflicts with Great Britain as the last "Cup of
Affliction" before the elect would be "crowned with Glory," as the
debacle that would lead to "a new and more perfect system," as
"Calamities . . . preparing the Way" for the millennium.[1] In 1775 a
loyalist satire portraying the colonists as lawless fanatics pointed
precisely to their wild hope that "the glorious reign of Independency
shall begin in America – the long wished-for Millennium of the
Saints."[2] With varying degrees of biblical literalism, millennial
aspirations became a prominent feature of American revolutionary
consciousness. Such secular statements as the declarations of the
newly formed Continental Congress actually alluded to biblical
prophecy in their visions of "the golden period, when liberty, with all
the gentle arts of peace and humanity, shall establish her mild
dominion," "that latest period, when the streams of time shall be
absorbed in the abyss of eternity."[3] Newspapers looked ahead to the
prospect of America shining "brighter and brighter," becoming
"more and more free," until, under the protection of God, "she may
bid defiance to every oppressor throughout the world" and approach
the "*perfect* freedom and happiness" of the heavenly kingdom.[4] Even
the ringing phrases of Thomas Paine's *Common Sense* must be read
against this background of eschatological thinking: "We have it in
our power to begin the world over again. A situation, similar to the

75

present, hath not happened since the days of Noah until now. The birthday of a new world is at hand.''[5]

The outburst of millennial excitement in the mid-1770's reflected a fundamental shift in the American revolutionary movement. Between the time of the Boston Tea Party and the Declaration of Independence, the British government demonstrated an increased determination to enforce its controversial imperial policies, and colonial patriots were pushed beyond hopes for further parliamentary repeals and peaceful reconciliation with the mother country. What had earlier been rather naively viewed as the conspiracy of a few ministers essentially at odds with Parliament and the crown, now appeared as the overriding position of the entire British state. Of course, in the classical terms of radical whig ideology Americans had entertained the possibility of unmitigated despotism all along. They had repeatedly expressed the fear that ministerial corruption would spread like a cancer throughout British government and destroy the delicate constitution of liberty. But previously this particular scenario had been entirely catastrophic. The only hopeful alternative lay in the return to tradition, in the recovery of an earlier virtue and constitutional balance. Insofar as the dire perspective was phrased by American patriots in the terms of biblical prophecy, it was fearful and apocalyptical. The colonial past was idealized, and the prospect of change signaled a future of utter devastation and doom.

The events that transpired between the Tea Party and the Battle of Lexington in effect burned all the imaginary bridges to this idealized past. After a lull in patriot activism between 1770 and 1773, Americans reacted swiftly to the institution of the Coercive Acts in 1774. They mobilized through the recently formed revolutionary committees of correspondence, organized the new Continental Congress within months, and the following year met British troops in armed confrontation. Under the pressure of these new developments, the political crisis magnified beyond all previous proportions. Isolated regions of the colonies were for the first time drawn into the patriot movement. Colonists mobilized not only to resist but to create new, alternative structures of government. As they moved towards the conclusive indictments of the King and the system of monarchy itself, a process completed with the Declaration of Independence, they finally had to face the prospect of a future divorced from the past. Not that Americans – particularly filiopietistic New Englanders – did not continue to idealize their own past, but it was a past with a difference, a past simultaneously projected

76

ahead into a vision of a new order. American victory in these years was still far from secure, but once the colonial patriots came to the dreaded conclusion that British tyranny had gone beyond the point of return, their earlier fears of disaster gave way to even more extravagant hopes.

The basis for this ideological transformation did not lie in radical whig political thought, with its fear of change, nor, for most Americans, in Enlightenment ideas of progress. The main connecting link that afforded this remarkably easy transition was rather the religious tradition of millennial prophecy. By the mid-1770's this tradition had, to be sure, absorbed many whig and Enlightenment ideas. It was its own basic vision of future felicity that, however, largely defined the utopian dimension of American revolutionary ideology.

INDEPENDENCE AND THE LATTER-DAY GLORY

The revolutionary millennialism that emerged in the mid-1770's incorporated many elements of the apocalypticism of the previous decade. The image of British tyranny as the Antichrist, for example, which had first appeared in the anonymous literature of the Stamp Act crisis, received even more elaboration after the conflict with Britain broke into war. Earlier an expression of popular radicalism, this association of Great Britain with the devil had already gained increased respectability among colonial Protestants with the Quebec Act of 1774, which firmly identified the London government with the popish Beast. Once the bloodshed began, the influence of Rome no longer remained crucial to this symbolic connection: The British alone became the target of extreme vilification as the agents of the Antichrist. The patriot clergy and laity of varying degrees of religious orthodoxy repeatedly described the American patriot forces as the soldiers of Christ doing heroic battle against "*all the powers of Hell,*" "the prince of darkness," "the serpent," "the dragon," "the antichristian beast" of biblical prophecy.[6]

This further elaboration of the Manichaean perspective of the 1760's and early 1770's intensified the pervasive feeling of crisis surrounding the war. The idea that history was currently reaching a dramatic climax became even more predominant. Revolutionary literature repeatedly claimed that history stood at a critical juncture: on one side lay the possibility of American defeat, with ensuing "slavery," "despotism," "fraud," and "misery," while on the other side lay victory, with the promise of "liberty," "virtue," and "happiness."[7] As John Joachim Zubly succinctly assessed the alternatives before the Georgia legislature while he was still a believer in the patriot cause, "the ALL of the present and future generations lies at stake."[8] The moral categories of the 1760's became even more sharply defined; both humanity and history were divided into the polar extremes of good and evil, future misery and future happiness.

What changed in the mid-1770's was that the earlier mood of fear and foreboding was overridden by an expectation of impending glory and happiness. Images of the final conflagration and Last Judgment now only rarely appeared. The afflictions of the present were seen less as the foreshadowing of ultimate doom than as the temporary period of darkness before the new dawn. Even the widely reprinted prophetic dreams of the Massachusetts layman Samuel Clarke, which had previously told only of impending "vials of wrath," were now revised to predict the imminent coming of the Kingdom of God. As Clarke laid out the events of the future, the antichristian "Spirit of Persecution" had only one brief "Draught of the Blood of the Saints" remaining. Then the Lord would "raise up the Powers of the Earth to . . . deliver his Servant," declare the rule of the gospel, and make all "Opression cease from among his chosen People."[9]

Other such popular prophecies about the Revolution and war similarly foretold a happy conclusion. Citing evidence from both scripture and folklore, a lead article in the *Maryland Journal* in early 1777 stressed the prophetic significance of the number 7, concluding that the "year 1777 will be the grand Jubilee of AMERICAN FREEDOM and INDEPENDENCY."[10] In David Rittenhouse's *Continental Almanac* and William Goddard's *Maryland, Delaware, Virginia and North-Carolina Almanack* appeared a series of enigmatic prophecies interspersing biblical and astrological imagery, including, in the millennial language of Isaiah, the transformation of bayonets into plowshares.[11] Described by the author as the visions of a reclusive red-bearded, gray-haired man who lived in a cave, these almanac prophecies were most likely the work of Herman Husband, now an active patriot in western Pennsylvania.[12]

Conventional religious literature also sounded a much more optimistic note by the mid-1770's. Both lay and clerical publications now couched the fearful image of the British Antichrist within a vision of the future that highlighted Satan's capitulation before the forces of Christ. As the moderate Calvinist minister Elisha Fish forcefully reminded the Worcester Committee of Correspondence shortly after the Battle of Lexington, "although men or devils, earth or hell, Antichrist or the dragon rages, the people of God may still triumph in Christ, the Captain of their salvation."[13] In patriot sermons and poetry Britain was cast in the role of the persecuting dragon of the Book of Revelation, and America portrayed as the "woman in the wilderness" who escapes and gives birth to a heroic son.[14] An unusually detailed exegetical essay on biblical prophecy by "M. W." of Lewes, Delaware, that appeared in the Philadelphia *United States Magazine* suggested that the symbol of the "man child" represented America's "faithful *and pious freemen*; preserved in infancy from the devouring *dragon of arbitrary power*."[15]

No longer looking back towards an idealized past, American patriots were turning to consider still more splendid possibilities lying ahead. Official fast and thanksgiving proclamations issued by New England state governments during the war often expressed the wish that God would ordain an American victory and then proceed to inaugurate the millennial Kingdom of Christ.[16] Going beyond the castigations of the jeremiad to highlight future millennial possibilities, *A Solemn Warning* printed in 1778 by the Associated Presbytery in Pennsylvania blamed the hardships of the war on America's sins but also held out the exhilarating prospect of divine deliverance, future American glory, and "the more eminent glory of the latter days."[17] Patriot polemical literature resounded with exclamations about "the great ends" of Providence in bringing about the Revolution, the "new" and "illustrious" era about to unfold when temporal things would progress towards "perfection" and God would fulfill his ancient promises to the Jews.[18] Flowery verses about America's destiny by Elhanan Winchester, a largely self-educated Baptist, and Joel Barlow, the young poet recently graduated from Yale, culminated with descriptions of Christ's "long and glorious reign" with the saints upon earth.[19]

So intense were these millennial expectations during the early years of the revolutionary war that numerous patriots foresaw the final destruction of Antichrist and the establishment of the Kingdom of God within the immediate future. While accepting the conventional periodization of scriptural prophecy according to which the millennium itself would not arrive for another two hundred years, the Connecticut Congregationalist Ebenezer Baldwin nonetheless offered the "conjecture" that the American patriots were already "preparing the Way for this glorious Event."[20] The exegetical writers "M. W." in Delaware and Thomas Bray in Guilford, Connecticut, more specifically maintained that the sixth vial of the Book of Revelation was either already poured or else now being poured in America, and that the Revolution was a sign that the millennium was presently drawing near.[21] More commonly, the suggestion that the culminating events of prophecy were about to occur was phrased in less precise if still highly evocative language. The tyrannical Antichrist would fall in "a short space of time," predicted the Presbyterian lay army chaplain Hugh Henry Brackenridge.[22] Samuel Magaw, an unusual Anglican millennialist patriot, also told a meeting of Delaware freemasons in 1779, "I am inclined to think, the happy aera is not exceeding distant."[23]

In New England this sense of imminent expectation was so widely diffused that Congregationalist clergymen across the theological spectrum issued excited pronouncements about the impending new dawn. "The time is coming and hastening on, when Babylon the great shall fall to rise no more," exclaimed the Connecticut evangelical Calvinist Samuel Sherwood in 1776.[24] According to Chauncey Whittelsey, an elderly New Haven Old Light with Arminian inclinations, the events to introduce the latter-day glory were "high at hand, and perhaps, at this very day beginning to take place."[25] Samuel West, a liberal minister from New Hampshire who had joined Washington's army after the Battle of Bunker Hill, composed a sermon interpreting the Revolution as the fulfillment of the millennial prophecies of Isaiah, which he circulated to fellow clergymen with a letter explaining that the "present Times in America" were also foretold in Ezekiel, Daniel, Micah, and Revelation.[26] To substantiate his prophetic theories, West observed in 1778 that "many judicious persons" had predicted that "some grand events would soon take place, and a new and remarkable aera commence from this period."[27]

Despite the pervasiveness of these keen millennial hopes, there was little effort to consider, much less to agree upon, the concrete form the millennium would take. Millennial scenarios were rarely tied to specific programs for change. One writer for the *New-England Chronicle* who argued in 1776 for a unicameral legislature and an elected executive, on the principle that "THE VOICE OF THE PEOPLE IS THE VOICE OF GOD always," presented this form of republican government as the means to the millennium.[28] In nonbiblical terms, both Thomas Paine and John Adams suggested that their otherwise very different proposals for government would enable America to become "the glory of the earth," another "Arcadia or Elysium."[29] Usually, however, debates over the merits of alternative structures of government took place on a level of political discourse altogether different from such visionary speculation. Thoughts about future perfection did not easily lend themselves to immediate, practical application.

Yet the failure of American revolutionary millennialism to provide a workable blueprint for the future era of happiness in no way undercut its ideological power. Indeed, such a failure has characterized most modern revolutionary thought, including as effective an ideology as Marxism. It was not that the millennial visions of the American revolutionary movement had no content whatsoever. Rather their descriptions of the forthcoming millennium served to define and affirm general values – the highest and most widely held millennial aspirations of the American Revolution – instead of engaging in the more limited advocacy of specific courses of action.

Liberty, of course, more than ever before, appeared to American patriots in the middle and late 1770's as a striking feature of the coming new age. The millennium was viewed repeatedly as a time of "perfect freedom and liberty," "Light and Liberty," "peace, liberty, and righteousness," "truth, liberty, and happiness," "Peace, Liberty, and Virtue."[30] Abraham Keteltas, a Long Island revolutionary leader and former Presbyterian clergyman, described the millennium as "the happy period when tyranny, oppression, and wretchedness shall be banished from the earth; when universal love and liberty, peace and righteousness, shall prevail."[31] Even newspaper columns upheld visions of a future era of liberty that suggested the fulfillment of biblical prophecy even though they were not explicitly millennial. Articles in the *Boston Gazette* described America rising to that "happy period" when "virtue and liberty [shall] reign here without a Foe, until rolling Years shall measure time no more."[32] The *New York Journal* printed a resolution from Monmouth, New Jersey, urging perseverance in the revolutionary cause until "true freedom and liberty shall reign triumphant over the whole globe," and a writer for the *Virginia Gazette* similarly envisioned liberty heroically bursting forth to "destroy all before it."[33] The common theme that God had intended America to be a refuge for the oppressed of all nations, the last "seat" or "asylum" of liberty, also often had strong millennial overtones.[34]

The concept of "liberty" generally continued to resonate with religious meaning, and most revolutionary millennialists, especially within the New England clergy, still linked the fates of political liberty and true religion together. The rise of revolutionary millennialism in the 1770's did not mark a departure from an earlier purely religious millennialism, for American millennialism had often incorporated general political values before.[35] In the context of the struggle with Britain, however, various elements of earlier American millennial thought took on a far more radical meaning. Not only did the word "liberty" come to imply independence and republicanism whereas earlier it had expressed a conventional whig affirmation of the English system of government, but traditional political values other than liberty also became overtly revolutionary. The theme of national mission, for example, was applied with increasing intensity to an independent American state. Like the idea of millennial liberty, the idea of the United States as the principal seat of the millennial kingdom integrated the biblical symbolism of the Anglo-American Protestant tradition with a new revolutionary nationalist creed. Revolutionary millennialists now anticipated the day when the triumphant American nation – not merely New England or the British-American colonies – would become "Immanuel's land," "the principal seat of that new, that peculiar kingdom, which shall be given to the Saints of the Most High."[36]

Although in general agreement, these references to the exalted American future differed on various details. The most literal millennialists, particularly among the evangelical clergy, placed somewhat more emphasis upon the religious and emotional qualities of the American nation than did the liberals and moderates. David Avery, a New Light Congregationalist Calvinist from western Massachusetts who served as an army chaplain through most of the war, looked forward to the millennial day when America would become "a Mountain of Holiness, a Habitation of Righteousness! The LORD's spiritual Empire of Love, Joy, and Peace."[37] The evangelical Baptist Elhanan Winchester similarly portrayed the American saints in the millennium joining "heart and hand" and crying, "Frcc gracc, free grace, . . . Throughout this happy Land!"[38] While revolutionary millennialists of varying theological persuasions wrote with unmeasured ecstasy of the "joy," "gladness," and, especially, "happiness" that would come to pervade the American nation, not all of them did so in distinctively spiritual terms.[39] The conception of religion in the millennium held by moderate Calvinist

and liberal millennialists, generally New England Congregationalists, was simply that it would be "pure and undefiled," that the
impending age of American glory would bring "christian light and
knowledge," "piety and virtue," "uncorrupted faith."[40] The emphasis on the diffuse love, holiness, and grace of God's Kingdom was
characteristically evangelical instead.

Just as at the end of the French and Indian War, the liberals'
millennial visions also more frequently featured images of thriving
agriculture and trade.[41] At times evangelical Calvinist millennialists
too looked forward to an era of material abundance, but they were
geared less towards the expansion of commerce and more towards
the provision of gifts from on high. The evangelical Congregationalist David Avery preached about God's creation of a new paradise
"like EDEN . . . the Garden of the Lord."[42] The Baptist Winchester,
then in the midst of conducting religious revivals among both whites
and black slaves in Welch Neck, South Carolina, proclaimed that in
the millennium an apparently spontaneous profusion of resources
would guarantee that "No more the labour'r pines and grieves, For
want of plenty round."[43]

In line with this emphasis on the satisfaction of material needs,
numerous revolutionary millennialists envisioned America multiply-
ing in population and expanding across the continent to the west. A
major theme already in the liberal victory sermons at the end of the
French and Indian War, this forecast of American growth, if not
commercial expansion, now permeated evangelical patriot statements as well. As "the principal Seat" of the millennial kingdom,
America would become "a great and mighty Empire; the largest the
World ever saw," the Connecticut New Light Ebenezer Baldwin
proclaimed.[44] "It appears," the Presbyterian minister William Foster
told a company of recruits at Fags Manor, Pennsylvania, in 1776,
"that the church is not yet arrived to its perfection in America, but
will extend wider and wider, until it has reached to the Pacific
ocean."[45] In addition to achieving perfection through physical
growth, the Kingdom of God in America would, according to these
patriots, attain great intellectual and cultural eminence. Citing the
precedents of native geniuses like Franklin and Rittenhouse in his
millennial poem of 1778, Joel Barlow, recently graduated from
Congregationalist Yale, felt sure that in America knowledge would
reach "her meridian height."[46] Like the vision of national expansion,
this anticipation of intellectual prowess characterized Old Light and
New Light revolutionary millennialism alike.[47] Variations between

liberal and Calvinist millennialists that had been so pronounced at the end of the French and Indian War were now only matters of degree, producing no focused disagreement about national goals. At the high tide of American revolutionary enthusiasm, patriots of various theological and intellectual persuasions proclaimed nearly identical views of American destiny.

Of course, not all such descriptions of future American greatness took an overtly millennial form. Clergymen frequently speculated about a Providential plan to raise America to the "highest pitch of glory, honour, opulence, and renown," "to lay a firm foundation for the lasting future peace, tranquility and liberty," without explicitly citing the millennial passages in biblical prophecy.[48] In a public oration delivered in 1778 the South Carolina Presbyterian patriot David Ramsay acknowledged the "special interposition of Providence on our behalf" but otherwise presented his utopian hopes for America in purely secular terms:

> Is it not to be hoped, that Human Nature will here receive her most finished touches? That the arts and sciences will be extended and improved? That Religion, Learning, and Liberty will be diffused over this continent? And in short, that the American editions of the human mind will be more perfect than any that have yet appeared?[49]

Poems by John Trumbull and Philip Freneau similarly looked forward to the "dawning age" of American greatness, to "a Paradise," a "golden reign" as the "glorious empire rises bright and new"; and "A Prophecy of the Future Glory of America" that appeared in the *Lancaster Almanack* for 1779 presented a scene in which "for ages without end, the glories of the Western World ascend!"[50] Such statements, whether or not they included scriptural references, inevitably carried millennial overtones. Even in the absence of literal millennial predictions, numerous revolutionary spokesmen used millennial images metaphorically to articulate their exalted conceptions of America's promise.[51]

These ideas about American liberty, religion, material prosperity, physical expansion, and intellectual achievement transferred older ideas about the colonies' future within the British Empire into a newfound American nationalism. Not all such visionary speculation was, however, so narrowly nationalistic in its scope. American revolutionary radicalism also found expression in a more universalistic millennial vision. According to this still wider perspective, the glory of the Revolution inhered not only in America's own special promise but in its larger role in world history. Already before independence, American patriots had increasingly regarded the colonies as the only potential saviors of English liberty. As the revolutionary crisis intensified in the mid-1770's, the imagined arena of American influence rapidly extended beyond the British empire to the entire globe. The theme that America was struggling on behalf of "all mankind" pervaded revolutionary rhetoric. Liberty "is God's own cause: It is the grand cause of the whole human race," preached the New York Presbyterian Abraham Keteltas, looking ahead to the millennial day when the universal application of American revolutionary principles would transform the world from "a vale of tears, into a paradise of God."[52] Sermons by New England clergymen and state proclamations for fast and thanksgiving days often suggested that the millennium would first come to America and then spread to the ends of the earth.[53] Joel Barlow described America as the stone in the Book of Daniel that smote "the image of the beast," became "a great mountain," and "filled the whole earth:"

> Then Love shall rule, and Innocence adore,
> Discord shall cease, and Tyrants be no more;
> 'Till yon bright orb, and those celestial spheres,
> In radiant circles, mark a thousand years; ...[54]

In the revolutionary period, numerous American Protestants highlighted the global dimensions of the millennium even when they did not particularly stress the redemptive role of the American nation. They envisioned the gospel itself spreading through the world, converting heathen and Jew, and establishing the basis for the universal Kingdom of Christ.[55] Largely because of this common universalism, the distance between biblical religion and Enlightenment ideas about natural rights was often exceedingly small. In 1776 the young Connecticut Congregationalist Timothy Dwight enlarged upon the millennial possibilities of the American Revolution in universalistic language almost identical to that used by Thomas Paine a few months before. "Never were the rights of man so generally, so thoroughly understood, or more bravely defended," he told the students at Yale. "You are to act, not like inhabitants of a village, nor like beings of an hour, but like citizens of a world, and like candidates for a name that shall survive the conflagration."[56]

According to Dwight, as well as to Paine, the American patriots were propagating a principle that applied equally to all nations of the earth. The value of the American Revolution lay not in what it promised to America alone but in what it promised to the human race. Simply by providing an asylum for the oppressed and setting an example to the world, the American nation would prove the means of advancing the cause of freedom and righteousness across the earth. Elements of nationalism and universalism thus were drawn together in a kind of passive political messianism, according to which American principles, not power, would ultimately prevail through the globe. In later decades this vision would begin to come apart, but in the intensely idealistic years of the mid-1770's nationalism and universalism were compatible parts of the new revolutionary millennial creed.

The heightened attention to civil liberty, American nationalism, and universal rights certainly distinguished American revolutionary millennial thought from the colonial millennialism that preceded it. Even though each of these values had been expressed at least partly before, never had they been so emphasized and combined. In articulating these general ideals, the millennialism of the American Revolution was at once absorbing contemporary political ideas and forging them into its distinctive religious pattern. Behind the references to civil liberty, American nationalism, and universal rights there still lurked the inescapable biblical shadows: the liberty of the gospel; the chosen people of God; the universal Kingdom of Christ. By interpreting the ultimate meaning of the American Revolution in the sacred terms of biblical tradition, revolutionary millennialism infused the highest political ideas of the patriot movement with transcendent religious significance and gave contemporary actions a pivotal place in the cosmic scheme of history.

The grandiosity of this vision encouraged confidence in the newborn American republic despite all the uncertainties of the continuing struggle with Britain. In contrast to the French and Indian War, when many triumphant millennial proclamations were made only upon victory, the revolutionary war was accompanied by these exuberant statements from the start. In the fall of 1775, shortly before he joined the militia, Ebenezer Baldwin prefaced a millennial sermon with the hope that "it might have some Tendency to keep the Spirits of People in the important and dangerous Struggle in which we are now engaged."[57] Identifying the pouring of the "sixth vial" of the Book of Revelation with the destruction of spiritual and civil tyranny, another New England Congregationalist minister, Thomas Bray, also intended his treatise on prophecy "to support and animate a christian people [to] stand up in defense of the precious rights of an injured country against the lawless oppressors."[58] The inflated optimism of the revolutionary rhetoric clearly aimed to galvanize active support for the cause, not merely to offer consolation or to teach the passive forbearance of divine will. Although God was still regarded as the primary mover of history, the American struggle for liberty was now viewed as one of his chosen instruments or "means." As the *New-York Journal* explained the need for militancy after the outbreak of war, "That which the great monarch of the universe requires of us, is to burst the bands, break the chains, and throw off the iron yoke of sin, satan and the world's thraldom."[59] "Zion is founded; yet means must be us'd," a popular volume of revolutionary poetry proclaimed in 1778, "'*Cursed be he that keeps his sword from blood.*'"[60] The belief that sacred prophecy foreordained the defeat of their enemies, especially when joined to expansive visions of forthcoming glory and happiness, inspired passionate commitment to the American cause despite all the risks and hardships of war.

As these visionary patriots foretold the future, America's Christian soldiers would first crush the British Beast in fulfillment of biblical prophecy and then watch their superior religion and republican system of government establish the basis of the universal Kingdom of Christ. Occasional voices, which would become louder in the late 1770's and 1780's, sounded a more critical note, calling for various social and political reforms. Even these complaints were, however, fully compatible with an enthusiastic endorsement of the American cause. Only a handful of Americans in the 1770's turned a millennial perspective into a radical condemnation of American society and these, significantly, were entirely outside the revolutionary movement. Not militant but pacifist, neither universalistic nor nationalistic but sectarian, these individuals would soon gather themselves into isolated communities of the Elect designed to inaugurate the millennial age.

REVOLUTIONARY MILLENNIALISM AND RADICAL SECTARIANISM

Despite their small size, the radical millennialist sects that emerged in the 1770's pose an illuminating contrast to the widespread revolutionary millennialism of the period, for they were formed in reaction against virtually every feature of the prevailing political environment. The fact that they were so exceptional also highlights basic differences between the millennialism of the American Revolution and the earlier millennialism of the Puritan Revolution and the English Civil War. Unlike revolutionary England, where radical millennialist sects proliferated on the fringe of political life in the 1640's and 1650's, revolutionary America produced few new sects. One reason for the relative dearth of sectarian movements was surely the integrative effects of the shared political focus of the Revolution itself. And it is significant that in revolutionary America, unlike in seventeenth-century England, the exceptional radical millennialist sects that did arise were apolitical – indeed, usually even antipolitical – in their outlook.

There were revivalist groups with sectlike features that had originated in the decades before – for example, the Separate Baptists and the Methodists – but they did not grow appreciably during the Revolution and they soon became mainstream denominations. Most other deviant religious figures and ideas of the period did not generate the formation of distinctive groups. The few exceptional sects to emerge in the 1770's drew their members primarily from the recently settled hinterlands of New England, where a religious revival called the New Light Stir took hold in the years 1778 to 1782. Several inspirational leaders arose who preached a millennial message that elevated spiritual over temporal preparation. Although they all rejected the Calvinism of their forebears and espoused more egalitarian doctrines of salvation, perhaps indirectly expressing the revolutionary temper of the age, none of them assumed active political roles. Their millennialism was typically combined with pacifism even in the immediate context of the continuing war with Great Britain. At least two of these groups, the Universalists and the Freewill Baptists, would by the end of the century establish themselves as sizable and increasingly respectable religious denominations. At the time of the Revolution itself, however, the new sects that were both the most coherent and the most fully imbued with their own sense of millennial mission were the Shakers and the Universal Friends.[61]

Despite little evidence of mutual influence, the Shakers and the Universal Friends were remarkably similar. Both were heavily influenced by the Quakers, with whom they shared a firm commitment to pacifism and to the abolition of slavery. They also perhaps received from the Quakers their strong belief in the religious equality of women. Unlike most Quakers, however, the Shakers and the Universal Friends were ardent millennialists, and like many American millennialists, these radical sectaries owed some of their ideas to earlier outbreaks of millennial religious enthusiasm. In Manchester in the late 1750's followers of the Camisard prophets who had preached a fervent millennial message in England at the turn of the century inspired Ann Lee, the "Mother" of the Shakers. In early 1776 the Society of Friends in Cumberland, Rhode Island, expelled Jemima Wilkinson, "the Publick Universal Friend," because she had joined a group of New Light revivalists. But it was only later, after Ann Lee had immigrated to America and the revolutionary war was well under way, that each of these women proclaimed her own messianic mission and began to recruit an American following.[62]

Ann Lee and her small band of original English disciples had already lived for several years in New York before they attracted an appreciable number of converts. Many of the salient features of the sect had been established from the beginning. The Shakers had always, for example, practiced strict sexual abstinence and participated in ecstatic religious experiences. But the first clear expression of Ann Lee's messianic pretensions came only in 1780. Upon learning that a recent revival in the nearby town of New Lebanon had been interpreted (in typical New Light manner) as a harbinger of the millennium, she announced that the Second Coming had occurred in her own spiritual rebirth.[63] Explaining that the millennium had already begun within the fold, the Shakers began to make headway among some disillusioned revivalists. Soon the sect spread beyond New Lebanon into several communities in Massachusetts, with the ground similarly prepared by earlier revivals and the widespread millennial expectations of the period.

Jemima Wilkinson began her ministry as the Publick Universal Friend in late 1776, just as the revolutionary war struck her native Rhode Island. In the midst of an illness she felt that she had died and been resurrected from the dead with a new spirit. Like Ann Lee she drew parallels between her own divine mission and Christ's, strongly conveying the impression (although never forthrightly claiming) that she thought the Messiah had been born the second time in her. She preached to British and American soldiers, Tories and patriots alike, presenting herself, in the words of a follower, as "the Messenger of Peace . . . Travelling far & wide to spread the glad tidings & news of Salvation to a lost and perishing & dying World who have all gone astray like Lost Sheep."[64] She gained a number of converts, among them the family of a wealthy Narragansett judge and several former Quakers, as well as (reported a hostile critic) "many simple Women" and "ignorant and illiterate People."[65] In 1779 and 1780 she, much like Lee, prophesied that the millennium was about to begin. She announced that the great day would occur sometime in April 1780, and after the month passed uneventfully she managed to salvage her reputation among the faithful by interpreting a strange atmospheric clouding of the sun in May as the partial fulfillment of her prophecy. A follower who had defected wrote an exposé of the Universal Friends in 1783 stressing Wilkinson's heretical ideas about her role in the coming millennium.[66]

In many ways the millennialism of the Shakers and the Universal Friends was diametrically opposed to that of the American revolutionary movement. In both sects the message was strictly pacifist, to the point of arousing accusations of hidden Toryism from American patriots (Ann Lee was even briefly jailed on such charges). The groups were small and sectarian, based not upon a diffuse cultural tradition but upon the personal charisma of two individuals. They founded their hopes neither on historical observations nor on the biblical word but on the belief that Ann Lee and Jemima Wilkinson were themselves reincarnations of Christ. In obvious contrast to the revolutionary movement, moreover, both sects were led by women rather than men (although the Universal Friend made it her custom to wear masculine dress). Both, to varying degrees, concentrated much of their animus against the private institution of the family – especially against matrimony and sexual relations. Later the Shakers, in particular, would work out living arrangements based upon the collectivization of property that posed a striking alternative to both the American family and the economy. Each of these groups conceived of itself as a spiritual vanguard establishing a perfect community on earth in preparation for the day when the millennial kingdom would spread throughout the world. They felt no allegiance to either the secular state or the wider society beyond their sects. Far from believing the republican principle of popular sovereignty, they not only shunned the rest of American society but distributed power within their own sects in a highly authoritarian manner.

For all of these contrasts to the American revolutionary movement, however, it is significant that these millennialist sects emerged in the cultural context of burgeoning revolutionary millennialism. Like the English Quakers in the 1650's, they can be understood, in part, as reacting against the heightened politicization of millennial thought. Their repudiation of violence, their elevation of women to authority, their hierarchical distribution of power, their preoccupation with personal domestic life, were all directly opposed to the prevailing political ethos. Yet, at the same time, they partook of the widespread millennial excitement of the revolutionary period. The revivals that helped to catalyze these movements were instances of the same millennial fervor that underlay so much of the popular revolutionary enthusiasm. Even among Quakers, who for the most part by the eighteenth century were no longer millennialists, one of Jemima Wilkinson's main sympathizers in Philadelphia was the "fighting Quaker" Christopher Marshall, who had himself earlier expressed keen millennial hopes for the Revolution.[67] Perhaps it is also significant that both Lee and Wilkinson applied to themselves the same prophetic text about the persecuted woman in the wilderness that was so often used by revolutionary millennialists to refer to the American nation.[68]

Another example of the thin boundary that existed between revolutionary millennialism and the millennialism of these sects was the way various figures interpreted the "Dark Day" that occurred in southern New England on May 19, 1780. Both Jemima Wilkinson and Ann Lee explained the mysterious blockage of the sun, caused by large quantities of smoke from fires set to clear forests in New Hampshire and Vermont, as supernatural testimony to their messianic missions.[69] For other New Englanders, however, the Dark Day gave legitimacy to millennial prophecies about the Revolution. Samuel Gatchel, for example, a New Light deacon in Marblehead, published a work called *The Signs of the Times* that interpreted both the Dark Day and the war against the British Antichrist as signs of the imminent fulfillment of prophecy.[70] As Gatchel himself pointed out, the more sophisticated "Wise Men and Astrologers" had overlooked the prophetic significance of the uncanny atmospheric condition. He and other obscure New Englanders, however, in addition to the followers of Lee and Wilkinson, still believed strongly in the interpenetration of natural and supernatural agencies.[71] Other ideas of the Shakers and the Universal Friends, including elements of messianism and millennial pacifism, were also shared by scattered individuals who were not themselves part of any sectarian organization.[72]

Given the numerous forms that millennial thought had previously taken in American history, it is scarcely surprising that the revolutionary movement did not contain within itself all the millennial excitement generated during the years of the war. What is more noteworthy is the extent to which American revolutionary millennialism, unlike seventeenth-century English millennialism, remained part of the ideological mainstream rather than splintering into radical sectarianism. Even when the widespread millennial enthusiasm about the American Revolution started to decline in intensity after its peak in the mid-1770's, it never became confined to radical extremists but continued to hold sway over many both ordinary and highly respectable patriots into the 1780's. One reason for the limited appeal of radical sectarianism was that by the time of the American Revolution, particularly as a consequence of the Great Awakening and the French and Indian War, highly generalized millennial expectations had become widely diffused among the American populace. These expectations had rarely been tied to particular groups or sets of predictions. Few millennialists, moreover, were inclined to worry over the details of prophetic exegesis. It had often been quite simply proclaimed, usually in response to some dramatic occurrence, that perhaps the millennium would come soon. To share in the millennial excitement it was enough to know from prophecy that God had ordained the coming of a glorious age of peace, freedom, and rule by the saints standing at the right hand of Christ. Beyond this general understanding of millennial theory, events were left to speak for themselves. Just as in earlier millennial responses to the Great Awakening and the French and Indian War, the focus during the Revolution was on the immediate crisis at hand.

The fact that revolutionary millennialism was typically conceived in such general terms discouraged the formation of millennialist sects. The broad and sweeping perspective allowed it to absorb a wide range of more specific ideas, some of them even contradictory. Samuel Gatchel's idea of God directly intervening in nature is difficult to reconcile with a belief in the human agency of the revolutionary army, or with hopes for the transforming effects of science. But such apparent disagreements never came to a head. Some revolutionary millennialists presented the struggle for civil liberty as the main avenue to millennial glory; others, the attainment of religious morality; still others, the reception of grace.

Even secular utopian statements about the Revolution bore a complementary rather than an antagonistic relationship to the biblical millennialism of the period. In fact, the distinction between secular and religious utopianism is difficult to make. Since most biblical millennialists did not engage in sustained biblical exegesis, the boundary between the literal and the metaphorical usage of prophetic symbolism often remained suggestively vague. Secular visions of enduring happiness, liberty, virtue, knowledge, plenty, and peace, whether on a national or a universal scale, contained many of the same elements as biblical millennial interpretations of the Revolution. At a time when Thomas Paine still quoted extensively from scriptural texts and when Thomas Jefferson's draft of the Declaration of Independence emerged from Congress with references to the power of Providence, revolutionary millennialism quite comfortably straddled traditional Protestant and Enlightened world views.

Among those who paused to expound upon the ultimate meaning of the crisis, millennial ideas were expressed by a remarkable variety of American patriots. In New England, where the established Congregationalist churches vigorously promoted a millennial under-standing of the conflict with Britain, visions of the approaching Kingdom of God clearly appealed to an especially wide audience. Elsewhere, Presbyterian, Baptist, and even a few exceptional Angli-can clergymen also publicized this perspective, and revolutionary millennial ideas periodically appeared in secular and popular lay literature. Some Americans conceived of the millennial future precisely within the framework outlined in biblical prophecy. Others were more elastic in their formulations, using Scripture largely as metaphor. Taken together, however, these were variations on a common theme. They articulated for a diverse population the visionary dimension of American revolutionary ideology.

Without this visionary dimension it is difficult – perhaps even impossible – to imagine the development of an American revolu-tionary ideology at all. The leaders of the American Revolution have, to a point, deserved their traditional reputation for lucid principles, sober realism, and whiggish conservativism. In themselves, however, these qualities were not sufficient ideological basis for a large social movement pushing towards a fundamental political transformation. However restrained or pragmatic the American Revolution may seem in comparison to other major revolutions in world history, it stirred up intense popular emotions and created a new republican order. An animating ideal of the future was necessary to propel American colonists to make their decisive break from tradition, an ideal supplied neither by the backward-looking radical whigs nor by the still relatively moderate and Anglophilic Enlightenment of the mid-eighteenth century. In America in the 1770's most of this ideological leverage was provided by the millennial tradition within American Protestantism.

5

Visions of progress and ruin
in the Critical Period

Fear not, O Land; be glad and rejoice: for the Lord will do
great things.

Joel 2:21

Upon the triumph of American arms and the settlement of peace,
American revolutionary millennialism rose to its last fever pitch in
the early 1780's. Numerous clergymen who printed sermons celebrating the victory described the Revolution as establishing the basis
for the future Kingdom of God. God had secured the American
republic in order "to prepare the way for the promised land of the
latter days," observed the exultant Scotch-Irish Presbyterian Robert
Smith.[1] The Revolution appeared to David Tappan, a Congregationalist minister in Connecticut, to be "a principal link – a chain,
which is gradually drawing after it the most glorious consequences to
mankind, . . . hastening on the accomplishment of the scripture-
prophecies relative to the *Millenial State*."[2] Such statements were
frequently expressed by the laity as well. The physician Thomas
Welsh of Boston, chosen in 1783 to give the last oration in
commemoration of the Boston Massacre, told the town that soon all
nations would "beat their swords into ploughshares and their spears
into pruning hooks," and in Baltimore a college commencement
speaker likewise anticipated "that Happy Period" when war would
be no more.[3] A gathering of "respectable" citizens in 1782 in
Richmond, Virginia, a social group not normally given to millennial
declarations, toasted the wish that "universal liberty soon fulfill the
design of Heaven in promoting universal happiness."[4] Even as
typically sober- and secular-minded a revolutionary as John Adams
was so moved by the news of victory at Yorktown that he referred to
millennial prophecy in expressing his high hopes for the future:
"The great designs of Providence must be accomplished. Great
indeed! The progress of society will be accelerated by centuries by this

94

revolution. . . . Light spreads from the day spring in the west, and may it shine more and more until the perfect day."[5]

These grandiose predictions by American patriots in the early 1780's invoked the revolutionary millennial symbolism of the mid-1770's in the service of both less obvious and less consensual national goals. Victory over Great Britain was the final occasion for the expression of an undiluted revolutionary millennial euphoria. Beginning already in the late 1770's and continuing into the 1780's, Americans were experiencing growing doubts about the meaning and destiny of the new republican nation.

HOPEFUL NATIONALISM AND THE MODERATION OF MILLENNIAL FERVOR

The millennial vision repeatedly brought to view after Yorktown was above all one of material prosperity and national growth. America would abound in riches, multiply in population, spawn great works of art and science, and expand to the Pacific. The nation would thus become a "large and glorious empire," bound to "exceed all empires of the world," according to the standard clerical predictions, while at the same time serving as the happy abode of the "Scholar, the Philosopher and all the Sons of science and genius."[6] As the popular poet David Humphreys expressed these nationalistic sentiments, "All human greatness shall in us be found, / For grandeur, wealth, and honor far renown'd."[7]

Such descriptions of the future glory of America appeared both inside and outside an explicitly millennial framework. Combining extravagant speculations about future American wealth, power, and culture, the particular constellation of images was in itself, however, not new in the early 1780's. It had already crystallized in the prerevolutionary period as part of British imperial patriotism. By the mid-1770's this glorious vision of American destiny had become a common feature of emerging American nationalism.

But in the 1780's, the hopes for a strong and prosperous nation took on a new urgency. Independence had been successfully won, yet the republic was nonetheless ridden with economic and political problems. Wartime inflation was followed by postwar overconsumption and depression; the national credit was foundering; American ships and settlements remained vulnerable to North African pirates and the British still occupied the frontier. Under these circumstances, the belief that America was destined to become economically affluent, powerful, and secure addressed both the fears and the

95

wishes of ardent American nationalists in an especially compelling way.

A few patriots celebrating the recent victory still pointed to the universal as well as the national implications of the Revolution. The "sacred flame" of liberty promised to spread from America through the world, the Congregationalist minister Levi Frisbie of Ipswich, Massachusetts, told his congregation upon the news of the peace: "Happy indeed would be the effects of the American Revolution, should it be the means of communicating liberty and happiness to millions of mankind.!"[8] Political protests in Ireland and the extension of legal toleration to French Protestants were cited by several other New England clergymen as examples of America's beneficent influence on the rest of the world.[9] One writer for the *Virginia Gazette* who signed himself simply "A Countryman" looked forward to the day when the world would unite in a universal millennial confederation of freedom and Christianity.[10]

In comparison to the intense universalism of the 1770's, however, the global perspective of the 1780's was much more limited and restrained. Rather than highlighting the American republic's role at the vanguard of world revolution, hopeful visions of the future tended to concentrate more on the internal potential of the American nation. George Duffield, minister of Philadelphia's Third Presbyterian Church, stressed the benefits of America's geographical isolation "from the noise and tumult of contending kingdoms and empires."[11] The vision of America providing "a safe retreat from the cruel fangs of tyranny and oppression," "an asylum for the injured and oppressed, in all parts of the globe," received more emphasis in sermons than did hopes for the universal downfall of tyranny.[12] In general, patriotic writers of the 1780's expressed less concern with the meaning of the Revolution for world history than with the future prospects of the new republic. Whereas in the 1770's nationalist and universalist themes combined, in the 1780's nationalism overrode the earlier identification with universal humanity. Visions of the future contracted, focusing more exclusively on America and, specifically, on the happy prospects of internal economic and physical growth.

Significantly, inasmuch as visionaries of the 1780's did express hopes for the future of the world as a whole, they usually stressed the promise of commercial expansion rather than worldwide revolution. In accord with the liberal economic theories of the day, patriotic writers of the 1780's repeatedly emphasized the ameliorative effects of international free trade.[13] In New England millennialist Congregationalist clergymen preached that a thriving commerce between nations not only would lead to "an inexhaustible source of wealth and opulence" but would "expand the human mind," "humanize the heart, soften the spirit of bigotry and superstition," and "carry forward mankind to greater perfection and happiness than have yet been attained."[14] The poet Joel Barlow suggested in his epic *Vision of Columbus* that the rising "spirit of commerce" was the best means to the end of millennial happiness.[15] This widespread enthusiasm for commercial growth in effect replaced the earlier confidence in revolutionary political change.

The burgeoning faith in commercial development, earlier associated more with liberal than with evangelical Protestantism, now cut across these different religious groups. Through most of the 1780's, however, particularly among the New England clergy, those projecting an image of future national greatness did so without taking a distinctively partisan religious or political stance. The tensions between commercial and agrarian interests that had emerged in several regions during the war, for example, and that would be reflected in the debate over the Constitution, rarely appeared in the visionary literature. Commerce and agriculture were usually expected to prosper together. Thus the spectre of America's "streams floating with merchandise uninterrupted," "populous towns and cities rising to view," merged in millennial sermons with the more bucolic image of "the wilderness changing into a fruitful field," and "the desert blossoming as the rose."[16] Timothy Matlack, the Philadelphia revolutionary leader, delivered an oration before the American Philosophical Society in which he insisted that agriculture was essential to the support of trade. "Husbandmen compose the great Majority of Citizens," he told his urban audience, "Their Industry and Skill in Agriculture will determine the Value and Extent of our Commerce." For him the millennium represented the perfection of agriculture based on this harmonious fusion of interests:

Mankind have talked of a Milennium – a Thousand Years of perfect Peace and Happiness – and some have looked for it to happen about this Time. Whenever the Prophecies of this great Event shall be fulfilled, and the whole Earth become one fruitful *Eden*, the benign Sun of that happy Day will rise upon a perfect Knowledge of Agriculture, a sober persevering Industry, and a virtuous, chaste Enjoyment of the Fruits of the Field.[17]

Such predictions of unprecedented abundance could clearly appeal to all groups alike. Some American visionaries, however, went further towards defining a social ideal, insisting that the dream of material well-being was tied to justice for the poor and the otherwise oppressed. In this respect millennialism moved beyond the sacrali-

97

zation of widespread desires for wealth and performed a more critical, prophetic function. The millennial call for internal social reform had been pronounced already in the late 1770's, as the hardships of the war and economic inflation began to corrode the generally high spirits of the mid-1770's. Several Protestant patriots in those years had delivered scathing attacks on exploitative economic practices – on greed and covetousness, the "spirit of Avarice, oppression and Monopolizing."[18] As the Presbyterian minister John Murray described the machinations of satan in 1779, "the grand enemy of mankind has put off the skin of the roaring lion – and in the tamer habit of *selfishness* and *extortion* now stalks about undisturbed."[19] Scattered voices, almost all those of New England evangelical Calvinists, called for the end of extortion and for mercy to the poor as necessary conditions of the millennium.[20] In 1778 the liberal minister Samuel West qualified his revolutionary millennial message with similar reservations. He warned those engaged in economic exploitation that they, along with the British, would not survive the conflagration to enjoy the millennial reign along with the rest of America's saints.[21]

In the 1780's evangelical Calvinists were no longer so unusual in inclining towards such specifically egalitarian visions of a future social ideal. In the wake of the war, as more Americans addressed the concrete social prospects before them, several more secular and liberal Protestant commentators expressed a similar wish that America be a haven for the humble and poor. At times such conceptions of a future egalitarian order were framed in terms of a specifically agrarian ideal. Thomas Jefferson's famous characterization of tillers of the soil as "the chosen people of God," for example, exemplified an investment of hopes in the class of independent farmers.[22] In South Carolina an anonymous author of a secular utopian treatise called for the more equal distribution of farmlands in order to establish in America a perfect state of nature.[23] Expressing more specifically millennial aspirations, the English liberal Dissenter Richard Price, a leading spokesman for the Revolution who was widely read in America, similarly maintained that future happiness depended on the preservation of a citizenry of "hardy YEOMANRY, all nearly on a level" with "the rich and poor, the haughty grandee and the creeping sycophant, equally unknown."[24] The millennial vision of the Philadelphia evangelical Presbyterian clergyman George Duffield did not glorify agrarian life, but he too described a condition of "happy equality" prevailing in the glorious era.[25]

A millennial tract printed anonymously by Herman Husband introjected a still more socially divisive note. Husband, now a large farmer in Bedford County in western Pennsylvania, where he had been twice elected to the state assembly as a partisan of the radical Pennsylvania Constitution of 1776, complained that too many wealthy merchants and lawyers were elected to political office. His pamphlet advocated a more decentralized system of government ruled by the common people and defended the inflated paper currency as a kind of progressive tax on money, idleness, and luxury. He recommended that the paper money be tied to a fixed rate of depreciation in order to curb fluctuations in value, and he proposed a land tax to discourage speculators from engrossing large pieces of unsettled property. In his view it was "this very Plan" of government that was sketched in the millennial texts of Ezekiel, Daniel, and Revelation, all of which "hint at the Perfection of our Protestant Constitution of Government erected in *North-America*."[26] The pamphlet ended with a call for subscribers to a massive ten- to twelve-volume "Explanations on the Prophecies" that would, presumably, pursue this radical interpretation of scripture.

Occasionally millennial writings of the 1770's and 1780's featured concrete proposals for institutional change. An oration printed in William Goddard's *Maryland Journal* in 1783 urged the end of imprisonment for debt as a step towards the latter-day glory.[27] Beginning already in the mid-1770's, a few millennial writers, mostly American Baptists who were fighting against the legal privileges of the American Anglican and Congregational churches, characterized ecclesiastical establishments as the Antichrist and envisioned the millennium as a time of full religious equality.[28] Elisha Rich, a Baptist preacher and gunsmith recently ordained as minister in Chelmsford, Massachusetts, published a treatise in 1775 entitled *The Number of the Beast* in which he identified the Beast of Revelation with Protestant churches tied to the state.[29] The leading Baptist crusader for religious disestablishment in Virginia, John Leland, expressed his conviction that "Jesus will first remove all the hinderances of religious establishments" before inaugurating the millennial reign.[30] In the 1770's and early 1780's the influential New England Baptist Isaac Backus likewise often referred to the established churches as "the mystery of iniquity," "the powers of darkness," insisting that the millennium could not come without disestablishment.[31] Outside of Baptist circles, such millennial arguments for full religious liberty were seldom made. An exception was the Pennsylvania liberal Presbyterian Benjamin Rush, who in 1784 objected to the test law discriminating against Quakers in much the same terms, claiming that America could not aspire to millennial perfection until complete religious freedom had been achieved.[32]

Sometimes similar kinds of prophetic arguments were used against the institution of black slavery, usually by northern evangelical Baptists, Calvinists, and Presbyterians. For Rush the Quakers were playing a particularly important role in the fulfillment of prophecy because of their opposition to black slavery.[33] Already in the mid-1770's slaveholding and the slave trade both were identified with the symbol of the Antichrist. In one of the most important antislavery tracts of the period, the strict Calvinist minister Samuel Hopkins of Newport referred to the figure of the Beast in Revelation when he described slavery as "this seven-headed monster of iniquity."[34] Other ardent New England patriots, including Elisha Rich, David Avery, and Joel Barlow, presented millennial possibilities for the Revolution as depending upon the abolition of slavery.[35] An anonymous *Discourse on the Times*, which went into two editions in Norwich in 1776, urged Americans to help the poor, abolish religious establishments, and free "those vast numbers of *Africans*, . . . who have as good a right to Liberty as we have." Only when Americans "break every yoke, and every heavy burden, and let the oppressed go free," warned the author, using the millennial words of Isaiah, would God pour his grace upon American churches and accomplish the glorious fulfillment of prophecy.[36]

By the 1780's, however, comparatively few millennialists engaged in social criticism or invested their hopes for the American nation in fundamental institutional change. The antislavery movement, while still growing, produced virtually no millennial literature until the 1790's, and then only little.[37] The only concrete suggestions to arouse much millennial enthusiasm in the 1780's were those for educational reform. Rush, once again, overflowing with ideas to perfect the republic, concluded his celebrated essay on "the mode of Education proper in a Republic" with the speculation that the widespread establishment of his proposed system of learning would result in the coming of "the golden age."[38] In Massachusetts the Congregationalist minister Charles Turner of Duxbury called for a special tax on luxuries so that the state could better support schools to instruct its citizens in the principles of liberty. Much like Rush, he maintained that "if all the youth were educated, in the manner we recommend, *The Kingdom of God* would appear to have *come*, . . . the approach whereof, does perhaps at this time appear . . . to be in some degree probable."[39] Another proposal to the Massachusetts legislature by an obscure eccentric named David Hoar called for the establishment of an educational society that would, by its steadfast devotion to learning, rationally determine how best to realize the millennial order prophesied by Isaiah and John.[40]

If learning seemed to some to be a way to the millennium, more often visionaries of the 1780's simply called for virtue and faith. Both Calvinist and liberal New England Congregationalist clergymen, in particular, repeatedly argued that by spurning sinful luxuries, pride, indolence, and selfish ambition – and, above all, by manifesting "a sacred regard to the great Governour of the world" – America would "become an ample theatre for the last and most glorious displays of the divine benevolence to the human species."[41] The millennium was increasingly conceived in purely religious rather than political terms. Compared to the revolutionary millennialism of the 1770's, which typically merged the meanings of political liberty and grace, political tyranny and the Antichrist, millennial thought in the 1780's gravitated towards an exclusively moral and spiritual understanding of history. As early as 1781 the evangelical Calvinist Timothy Dwight preached a sermon on the victory of Yorktown in which he reminded his Northampton parishioners that the American Revolution was only a prelude to providential acts of much "higher importance." In the future God would "make an entire separation between civil and ecclesiastical things," and would destroy his enemies not by material power but by "an extensive diffusion of holiness, the work of his Spirit."[42] Yale president Ezra Stiles, a moderate Old Light Calvinist, rejoiced at length over America's new political order in his Connecticut election sermon of 1783. He grounded his specifically millennial expectation, however, not on the spread of republican government but on the triumph of primitive Christianity – best approximated, he proudly believed, in American Congregationalism and Presbyterianism. Stiles took heart in the prediction that with the free competition of ideas and the fast rate of natural increase in America, these denominations would achieve "a singular superiority, with the ultimate subserviency to the glory of God in converting the world."[43]

The view that the millennium would come by means of religious conversion rather than political change arose outside Congregationalist circles as well. In 1784 the Baptist Warren Association stressed that the American Revolution was designed not just to bring freedom, independence, and material gain but to "advance the cause of Christ in the world; or as one important step towards bringing the glory of the latter day."[44] The same shift away from a reliance upon worldly means to perfection can also be seen in more sectarian and deviant forms of millennial thought that raised the spectre of messianic deliverance. One anonymous tract published in Boston in 1784 announced the appearance of a messiah who would miraculously bestow "an infinite benediction upon men, their restoration to social happiness, and righteous unchangeable government."[45] The Shakers and the Universal Friends also both grew in the 1780's, and began to form separate communities that further accentuated their sectarian withdrawal from the affairs of this fallen world.[46]

Whereas in the 1770's the struggle against British tyranny seemed to be a way of ushering in the millennial kingdom, in the 1780's even the most patriotic millennialists lost most of their confidence in the transforming effects of liberty and republican government. America's route to the latter-day glory no longer appeared to lie in military or political activism. Instead, despite the frequent materialistic emphasis of the visions of American imperial growth and commercial expansion, millenialists tended to encourage more contemplative intellectual, moral, and spiritual pursuits. In the postwar period, after American independence had been successfully won and attention turned increasingly to internal problems, it became clear that the establishment of republican government was not itself a sufficient basis for American happiness. Only through education, the cultivation of private and public morality, and – the clergy in particular insisted – the regeneration of Christian faith, would the American republic realize its exalted millennial goal.

This altered conception of what would be required to bring about the millennium came along with a lessening of immediate expectations. A few millennialists still believed that the Revolution signaled the imminent coming of the final days, but compared to the heightened sense of expectancy that was so pervasive in the 1770's, the millennial statements of the 1780's took a much longer view of the future. Commentators of divergent religious persuasions drew upon the conservative calculations of standard exegetical works and predicted that the millennium would begin only around the year 2000.[47] Ezra Stiles, who had already very cautiously placed the date five hundred years in the future in an unpublished manuscript of 1774, now did not expect the glorious age to arrive "under seven or eight hundred years."[48] For all the wonders of the American Revolution, it was not "the ultimate object in the divine plan," clergymen repeatedly reminded their previously expectant congregations, for the millennium itself was "yet to begin."[49] In 1787 the poet Barlow accepted Richard Price's optimistic predictions "respecting the future progress and final perfection of human society" but thought that the human race was still only in its "infancy" and not yet, as Price had suggested, "approaching to manhood."[50]

The millennium, according to this long-range perspective, would come only gradually, not by means of a tremendous upheaval. "The world has hitherto been gradually improving," Richard Price explained the course of history to Americans in 1784. In his view "this progress must continue," for although occasionally "interrupted," it would eventually lead to the glorious fulfillment of "the old prophecies" of the Bible.[51] This confidence in the incremental, if not necessarily steady, improvement of human society was characteristic of American millennialism in the 1780's. "It is the tendency of human affairs, unless interrupted by extraordinary incidents, to be constantly progressive towards what may be termed natural perfection," claimed Timothy Dwight in Northampton in 1781, thus preparing the way for the moral perfection of the millennium.[52] Samuel Magaw, the Philadelphia Anglican clergyman, explained that Providence was bringing on the millennium very gradually, through "the revolution of numerous periods."[53]

Many of the dominant features of American millennial thought in the 1780's intersected closely with Enlightenment theories of history. The belief in gradual historical amelioration, the emphasis on the critical role of education, and the celebration of prospects of commercial development, for example, were shared by leading secular as well as religious thinkers. This had to an extent been true in earlier decades as well. Intellectual historians have pointed to the underlying affinities between Jonathan Edwards's millennial theories and liberal ideas of historical progress, and the same observation could equally well be made of many of his theological rivals such as Jonathan Mayhew. In the 1780's, however, millennial and Enlightenment theories came together on a much larger scale than before, both because secular ideas of progress had gained wider currency and because, after the end of the revolutionary war, millennial speculation tended to become less radical and more gradualistic in its predictions. Just as men like Jefferson and Franklin looked ahead in these years to the future triumph of reason and liberty, so did numerous millennialist Protestants. Several Calvinists within the New England Congregationalist establishment, both strict and moderate, articulated this position in the 1780's. The unfolding of scientific truth seemed to them perfectly consonant with biblical revelation.[54] Those who went the farthest in blending a faith in science with a belief in the prophetic texts of the Bible, however, were not Calvinists but liberal Protestants like the English Dissenters Richard Price and Joseph Priestley and the Philadelphia physician Benjamin Rush. Often tied closely in friendship to such secular thinkers as Jefferson, Franklin, and Paine, they formed a kind of international network of Enlightened Protestants.[55] Rush, a confirmed biblical millennialist, told the American Philosophical Society in 1786 that the scientific manipulation of the human senses could rid the world of "baneful vices" and change the human moral character into the "likeness of God himself."[56] In 1790 Princeton's Samuel Stanhope Smith, then also professing advanced liberal theological principles that he would later abandon, wrote Rush that there might be "no need of any other millennium than the general progress of science, & Civilization."[57]

Yet, although it expressed the continuing liberal optimism of some Americans about the destiny of the republic, the millennialism of the postwar period significantly rose in the context of increased anxiety. No longer did the millennial future seem as assured as it had during the high tide of revolutionary enthusiasm in the previous decade. Despite the fact that the 1780's were years of great institutional innovation, the best means to the millennium now seemed to be knowledge, science, faith, and morality rather than structural change. Far fewer millennial pronouncements of any kind were made, and their generally cautious stance show the extent to which millennialism, in general, had been put on the defensive by a rising tide of historical pessimism. The millennialism that survived did so in diluted form, largely devoid of its earlier revolutionary radicalism, and it competed with widespread fears of historical decline and failure. Large numbers of Americans now looked ahead with as much apprehension as confidence, throwing the revolutionary faith in a millennial future into serious doubt.

The ebbing of millennial fervor in the 1780's was largely due to the inevitable failure of the American Revolution to live up to the intense millennial expectations of the previous decade. There had been no massive religious revival establishing a new order on the basis of Christian love. The social changes brought about by the Revolution were on the whole rather modest and piecemeal. Although the political reforms were more far-reaching, even they were not very dramatic and were slow to mature. Most immediately and most concretely, the vicissitudes of the American economy in the late 1770's and 1780's defied any general conviction in a just and harmonious order. Swinging from inflation to depression, the economy capriciously elevated the fortunes of war profiteers and land speculators while endangering the livelihoods of ordinary artisans and farmers. There was both considerable scarcity and, once trade routes reopened, a preponderance of European luxuries for the well-to-do. All of these developments bred widespread feelings of instability and distrust. No wonder millennial visions so often featured plentiful harvests and thriving commerce throughout the American continent. If the millennial statements themselves became more moderate, narrowly nationalistic, and gradualistic in these years, they also often came couched in a framework that simultaneously emphasized the possibility of the decline and fall of the American republic.

PROSPECTS OF DEGENERATION AND FAILURE

"Great indeed is our felicity, and the prospect before us," exclaimed an anonymous Maryland orator, referring to the millennial promise of America in 1783, "but equally great is the danger." Scarcely had the Israelites escaped from Egypt, he warned, "when those very spoils they had recovered from their task-masters were formed in the place of that GOD, whose outstretched arm had wrought their deliverance." Drawing analogies to the rotation of seasons, the rising and setting sun, and the human life cycle, he wondered if America would continue to rise in greatness until the millennium or if, in accordance with classical historical theory, the present period of splendor would be followed by degeneration and ruin.[58] Also noting the precedents of Greece and Rome along with Israel, the Congregational minister Samuel MacClintock of Portsmouth offset his optimistic millennial vision in a similar way, fearing that the republic would succumb to "luxury, dissipation, and those other vices" that result in destruction.[59] Even Richard Price balanced his millennial euphoria over the American Revolution against a dire prediction of doom. If "false refinement, luxury, and impiety" should spread over the new republic, he concluded his otherwise hopeful address, the Revolution would fail to achieve its exalted promise and instead "prove only an opening to a new scene of human degeneracy and misery."[60]

Such sober warnings of impending ruin were certainly not new in the 1780's, least of all among the Congregationalist and Presbyterian clergy. Already in the 1770's the need to repent and reform in order to secure continuing favor had become the automatic refrains of the revolutionary clergy. The sins most frequently cited, aside from neglect of religion, had, moreover, always involved excessive worldliness: "pride," "intemperance," "extravagance," "foreign fash-

105

ion," "convivial mirth."[61] But in the 1770's most revolutionary jeremiads had assumed the continuation of divine favor, and had emphasized the possibility of divine reward for due repentance and faith more than the possibility of divine chastisement for sin. The perfunctory list of sins was often followed by heady visions of millennial glory.[62] By the 1780's, however, although jeremiads at times continued to serve as vehicles for millennial speculation, these expressions of hope became more qualified than they had been before. Now the threatening cutting edge of the jeremiad grew more pronounced and the spectre of failure gained greater vividness, frequently embellished by the historical analogies with the decline of classical Greece and Rome.[63]

This shift from extravagant optimism to a more guarded pessimism did not, of course, occur all at once. Beginning in the late 1770's, as the war dragged on and the economy foundered, the theme of retributive judgment began to compete with that of impending millennial glory.[64] In 1777 the New Hampshire Congregationalist minister Samuel West, for example, warned Americans engaged in extortion that they would be destroyed with the British before the new dawn.[65] Critics of black slavery, for whom the American republic was from the beginning failing to achieve its highest ideals, often struck the same apocalyptical note, raising the spectre of Judgment Day to frighten slaveholders into an awareness of their sin.[66] While acknowledging that "the cause of Britain is most unjust, and our contest with them is most righteous," the New Jersey Presbyterian Jacob Green added the frightening prediction that America would "have inward convulsions, contentions, oppressions, and various calamities, so that our liberty will be uncomfortable, till we wash our hands from the guilt of negro slavery."[67]

Understandably, antislavery spokesmen so attuned to the failings of American society usually abstained from full-fledged millennial exaltation of the Revolution.[68] As they invoked broader concepts of liberty and happiness – ones that went beyond the political goals of the Revolution – confidence in the millennial future seemed not to be grounded in historical fact. Significantly, the most steadfast critics of slavery in America were the Quakers Anthony Benezet and John Woolman, who were neither revolutionaries nor ardent millennialists. Highlighting the individualistic and quietistic Quaker approach to social redemption, Woolman once explained that the only way to achieve the "true harmony of mankind" was by the inner perfection of souls altogether separated from the violent powers of the world.[69]

106

In the 1780's, much as in the 1750's, even avowed millennialists often saw dark days preceding the new dawn. In 1783 an anonymous Virginian deploring recent lapses in piety warned that before America would fulfill its millennial destiny God might deem it necessary "to visit us with some severe stroke to rouse us to a sense of our duty and interest."[70] Congregationalist ministers suggested that the recent upsurge of luxury, avarice, and irreligion was evidence of the Antichrist's *"great wrath,"* for he knew "he was likely to have but a *short time"* before his final demise.[71] In Boston the historian Hannah Adams anonymously published an *Address To the Honourable Women of the United States* analyzing the prevalence of sin in America as a sign that the terrible slaying of the witness would occur in the United States before the millennium would begin. Now that the Revolution was over, and sin rather than Great Britain was the enemy, she argued, women should uphold the standards of Christianity on their own rather than depend on male religious leadership.[72]

Several apocalyptical prophecies issued in this period were exclusively catastrophic, overlooking millennial possibilities altogether. One piece published in 1788 in Hudson, New York, under the pseudonym "Prophet Nathan," interpreted crop damage caused by the Hessian fly as a sign that God was determined to punish Americans for their wicked greed, extortion, and religious and political divisiveness.[73] Religious dissidents like the Baptist Issac Backus and the recent convert to Universalism Elhanan Winchester inveighed against their ecclesiastical oppressors by issuing similar warnings of divine retribution and judgment.[74] This theme of divine wrath had already appeared in the late 1770's, especially in response to inflation and slavery, but in the 1780's, as intense millennial expectations for the Revolution faded away, it became much more widespread. Works of prophetic exegesis published in the decade began a trend towards "premillennialist" interpretation that would continue into the 1790's. Primarily written by Baptists and laymen, these works advanced the view that the millennium would await Christ's physical coming, thereby implicitly challenging the "postmillennialist" interpretation of most leading New England clergymen, who held that the millennium would precede the Messiah's return. Since the Second Coming was usually associated with the Biblical prophecies of the terrifying conflagration and Last Judgment, there was an apocalyptical tenor to most of these premillenialist interpretations. According to their predictions, times would get far worse before Christ's miraculous intervention would bring history to its happy culmination. Although they generally avoided contemporary social or political commentary, and for the most part suggested that the final conflagration was still far in the future, a few of them made ominous predictions of imminent upheavals and wars that were more directly in keeping with the growing historical pessimism of the 1780's.[75]

Writers reflecting upon the uncertainties of the future at times even openly disparaged millennial dreams. In 1782 the *Virginia Gazette* reprinted an article from the *London Courant* that cynically observed that if the world ever really achieved the millennial ideal – becoming peaceful, righteous, healthy, and harmonious – this would directly oppose the interests of three-quarters of the population, who earned their livings from military, spiritual, medical, and legal suffering.[76] Still more telling than this satirical humor were the doubts expressed by members of the New England Congregationalist clergy, a group that had so long been at the forefront of millennial speculation. "Let us not flatter ourselves too much with an idea of the future prosperity and glory of these United States," Yale divinity professor Samuel Wales cautioned the Connecticut General Assembly in 1785. Underscoring the precariousness of America's destiny, he took issue with the nationalistic millennial visions so confidently proclaimed upon victory:

It has lately become very fashionable to prophesy about the future greatness of this country; its astonishing progress in science, in wealth, in population and grandeur. . . . But although the foundation is laid, the superstructure is not yet finished, nor ever will be, unless we use the proper means. And whether we shall use such means or not, is a matter of great uncertainty.[77]

In 1788 the Congregationalist minister Charles Backus of western Massachusetts offered an extensive analysis of the growing sense of moral decline. Not only were Americans succumbing to the temptations of vice, he warned, reiterating the standard charges of the jeremiad, but in the excitement of the Revolution "we raised our expectations of happiness from the world, beyond what it can afford." Given these excessive hopes, disillusionment was inevitable. "How vain it is for us in a world like this, to look for a paradise?" he asked rhetorically, criticizing the revolutionary millennial visions. Such earthly aspirations were futile, even sinful. Only when the spirit of God spread through the world would the promise of the millennial New Jerusalem finally be fulfilled.[78]

As millennial expectations eroded with the decline of revolutionary euphoria, cyclical and organic theories of history supplied more important modes of analysis. Rather than conceiving of history as approaching a glorious culmination, American writers began to think more in terms of a pattern of rise and fall. Much as in the early years of the revolutionary movement, when American patriots so frequently idealized their colonial past, change came to be associated as much with deterioration as with progress. The frequent analogies drawn in political literature between America and the classical republics of Greece and Rome dwelt above all upon the theme of preserving the republic against forces of corruption and decline. This classical perspective corresponded closely to that of the traditional Protestant jeremiad, with its similar stress on prospects of ruin, and in the 1780's these two modes of expression were often combined.[79]

How exactly to guard against the fall of the American republic was the subject of extended discussion throughout the 1780's. Prior to the debate over the Constitution, concrete proposals ranged from proto-Federalist arguments for stronger currency and government to pleas for the abolition of slavery, full religious liberty, and the preservation of an agricultural economy. By far the most dominant cry, however, heard along the entire social and political spectrum, was for the need to curb luxury and restore the public virtues of benevolence, productivity, and self-sacrifice deemed vital to the preservation of republican government.

The word "virtue" in American political discourse contained many different shades of meaning throughout the revolutionary period, drawing at once upon secular republican theory and Protestant ideas about righteousness.[80] The classical republican definition of virtue always overlapped with Anglo-American Protestant values – not suprisingly, since the sixteenth- and seventeenth-century civic humanist theory had itself emerged out of religious reform movements in Renaissance Florence and England. The personal virtues of industry and frugality deemed essential to a good citizen were essentially the same as those prescribed by Protestant morality. The belief that the individual should sacrifice for the common good was also integral to Protestant, and particularly to Puritan, ideas of saintly community. But the American religious definition of virtue also diverged from the classical republican one in its strong emphasis on Christian belief.[81] In the 1780's, as anxiety about the future of the republic rose, it became commonplace to link the perceived failure in virtue to a "general neglect of religion" and to call for faith as the mainstay of public spirit.[82]

The clergy's denunciations of selfishness in the revolutionary period did not require a fundamental shift from a religious to a political framework. Nor was its insistence in the 1780's that religion lay at the basis of virtue in itself anything new. The confluence of classical republican theories and traditional Protestant values had long enabled the concept of virtue to draw upon a rich combination of spiritual as well as secular associations. What had changed by the 1780's was that the virtue of the American republic seemed more than ever in doubt. The political and economic difficulties confronting the new nation cast a shadow over earlier assumptions of America's superior righteousness. The persistent anxieties about money, the conspicuous consumption of foreign goods, the failure of the states to unite behind the impost necessary to pay federal debts, all seemed signs of flagging public spirit and Christian faith. The rising anxiety about American virtue in the 1780's, phrased in both civic republican and religious terms, not surprisingly came alongside a marked decline in millennial faith.

SHAYS'S REBELLION AND THE CONSTITUTION

The major events of the late 1780's, Shays's Rebellion and the drafting of the United States Constitution, crystallized many of the widespread anxieties about the national future while at the same time shifting the argument from moral exhortation to institutional and legal debate. Shays's Rebellion, the uprising in western Massachusetts in protest against scarce currency, high taxes, and the high cost of judicial administration, was defended by its supporters as an antidote to the decline of the republic since the Revolution. The abusive power wielded in Boston threatened the security of the hard-won liberty, so the Shaysite argument ran, creating factionalism and undermining the strength of the commonwealth. The rebellion aimed to reverse these destructive tendencies, to put the Revolution back on its proper course. An address from Worcester County in November 1786, for example, objected to the rebels' armed obstruction of the courts but upheld the right of the people to censure their rulers and justified the rebellion as a means of restoring harmony to the commonwealth.[83] One anonymous piece appearing in the *Hampshire Gazette* at the height of the insurrection in October 1786, signed "a Regulator," expressed bitter disillusionment with the false promises made by the revolutionary leadership. Asking, "how did we know in the year 1774 it would be best to revolt from Great Britain?" he then answered, "we did not; but there was many clever things said of our future glory and we were induced to put to sea without a compass." Now, like the Israelites who were asked to return to "the leeks and onions of Egypt, when the quails filled their camps, and manna rained down from heaven to support them," we are unnecessarily "pressed hard for our debts and taxes." Arguing for a reenactment of the Revolution, the "Regulator" claimed the rebels had little to lose and that the upheaval might prove "much to our advantage."[84]

This allusion to the manna and quails of the promised land is exceptional among the printed statements by the Shaysites. However, according to one historian of the rebellion who has read through the archival sources, there were some other occasions in which religious ritual and biblical language were employed. The county conventions of the insurgents commonly opened with prayer; the leader, Luke Day, according to his minister, Joseph Lyman, once defended the uprising by drawing a parallel to the condition of the oppressed in Ecclesiastes 4:1; and Daniel Shays himself likened the convictions against the rebels to the captivity of Zion.[85] Yet such efforts to enlist religion on the side of the rebellion were apparently rare. Indeed, compared to earlier popular disturbances in western Massachusetts in which ministers had played a prominent role – Joseph Lyman, David Avery, and other patriot clergymen in the Revolution; Thomas Allen in the Berkshire Constitutionalist movement; and Samuel Ely in more recent rioting against debt collection in 1782 – Shays's Rebellion elicited virtually no clerical support.[86] Moreover, when religious language was used by the rebels, it tended not to be millennial in tone. The "Regulator" notwithstanding, Shays's Rebellion for the most part did not give rise either to revolutionary aspirations or to desires to remake the world anew.

It was more in the reaction against the uprising than in the printed statements by the rebels themselves that ideas about Shays's Rebellion were framed in a sweeping historical perspective. The most common interpretation of the rebellion viewed it as an alarming demonstration of the fallen virtue of the republic. Rather than a corrective action designed to reverse the course of decline, as the rebels described their movement, critics saw the rebellion as the embodiment of subversive anarchy or selfish, materialistic factionalism that threatened to lead the republic to "misery and ruin," "confusion and slavery."[87] Ironically, even though the rebels themselves tended to stick to fairly narrow demands for reform, they were often accused by opponents of having utopian aims. A newspaper column headed "Salem, Nov. 11 [1786]," which was printed as far away as Pittsburgh, portrayed the rebels as fanatics trying "to totally annihilate the evils which have, till this aurora of the Millenium, been tacked to human life!"[88] During and after Shays's Rebellion, several of the poets known as the "Connecticut Wits," including the authors of earlier millennial verses written to celebrate the American Revolution, now collaborated on an extended satire called "American Antiquities," which was purportedly based on a recently discovered book of prophecy entitled *Anarchiad*. This work was meant to ridicule not only the political protests but the entire genre of optimistic millennial prophecy.[89]

The reaction against Shays's Rebellion was an important part of the background to the Constitutional debate. Both Federalists and Anti-Federalists recapitulated in their arguments many of the same hopes and worries that had been stirred by the unrest in Massachusetts. The Federalists typically presented the government of the Confederation as feeble, embarrassed, and anarchical. "Anarchy, with her haggard cheeks and extended jaws, stands ready," "confusion" prevails, "order and honor [lie] every where prostrate in the dust," complained the polemics in defense of the Constitution.[90] "Where no permanent security is given to the property and privileges of the citizens," wrote Charles Pinckney of South Carolina, "the progress has been regular, from order to licentiousness, from licentiousness to anarchy, and from thence to despotism."[91] Anti-Federalists, to the contrary, insisted that it was the Constitution that threatened to deliver the death blow to the American republic. The new government would commence "in a moderate aristocracy," George Mason predicted, and would soon produce either "a monarchy, or a corrupt oppressive aristocracy."[92] As William Findley, a leading Pennnsylvania Anti-Federalist, warned his fellow patriots in 1787, "You are on the brink of a dreadful precipice. . . . One step more, and perhaps the scene of freedom is closed forever in America."[93]

In turn, each side balanced their prophecies of doom with alternative visions of national happiness. Federalists repeatedly expressed their conviction that under the Constitution America would become "a great and boundless empire," flourishing in the arts, science, commerce, and agriculture.[94] A newspaper column signed "Ezekiel" lambasted the Anti-Federalists for their "distrust," maintaining that in America – a land of peace, plenty, and "virtuous freedom" surrounded by "the beneficent smiles of the KING ETERNAL" – it was impossible for hopes to rise too high.[95] Anti-Federalists responded by insisting upon the advantages of the status quo. They disparaged the ambitious Federalist dreams of national grandeur, arguing that instead of seeking to "be great amongst the nations," America should recognize that "quiet is happiness."[96] The Anti-Federalist pamphleteer the "Federal Farmer" objected to the

Federalist characterization of the American republic as in a state of crisis at all. "When we want a man to change his condition, we describe it as wretched, miserable, and despised; and draw a pleasing picture of what we would have him assume."[97] In fact, the present condition of the American states was perfectly acceptable, even commendable. Employing the language of biblical prophecy, the polemicist "Brutus" asked, "Does not every man sit under his own vine and his own fig-tree, having none to make him afraid?"[98]

Ironically, both Federalists and Anti-Federalists accused one another of entertaining too high expectations and prided themselves on their own greater realism. One Anti-Federalist referred to the supporters of the Constitution as "the young visionary men."[99] Another derided Federalists who "promise us such extravagantly flattering advantages to arise from it [the Constitution] as if it was accompanied with such miraculous divine energy as divided the Red Sea, and spoke with thunder on Mount Sinai."[100] The Federalists objected to their opponents' complacency about the present in much the same way. In *The Federalist*, Number 6, Alexander Hamilton characterized those who failed to see the need for stronger government as being "far gone in Utopian speculations." "Is it not time to awake from the deceitful dream of a golden age and to adopt as a practical maxim for the direction of our political conduct that we, as well as the other inhabitants of the globe, are yet remote from the happy empire of perfect wisdom and perfect virtue?"[101] Federalists defended the Constitution as the best possible form of government in an imperfect world. Those who could not tolerate any potential flaw in the proposed system should, they contended, "be quiet and cease complaining." "'Tis not in the power of human wisdom to do more; 'tis the fate of human nature to be imperfect and to err."[102] "Perfection is not the lot of human institutions."[103] Only naive "visionaries" could expect Americans "to perpetuate their happiness and freedom, without the restraints of civil institutions, to the latest period of time."[104]

For all the hard pragmatism on the Federalist side, however, it was their grandiose hopes for the future that most often found expression in millennial terms. The Anti-Federalists, much like the American patriots of the early revolutionary movement, were oriented more towards the preservation of current conditions. Although Anti-Federalist rhetoric at times referred to the felicity of biblical paradise, opponents of the Constitution generally did not await realization of this ideal in a millennial future. A rare exception was Herman Husband from western Pennsylvania, the advocate of paper money

113

and critic of merchants, lawyers, and land speculators. In 1788 and 1789, Husband wrote pamphlets warning against the adoption of the Constitution on the typically Anti-Federalist grounds that it would tilt the balance of power away from the states and foster an aristocratic political system. Far from typical, however, was his conviction that the Bible revealed an alternative, far more decentralized structure of government that would establish the basis for the millennial New Jerusalem in America. Whereas in 1788 Husband envisioned this New Jerusalem as a confederation of four empires including all the new American states, after the passage of the Constitution in 1789 he lost faith in the rest of the nation and confined its boundaries to the region west of the Alleghenies.[105]

Herman Husband's extreme form of Anti-Federalism notwithstanding, most of the millennialism that surfaced in the debate over the Constitution came from the Federalist side. For whereas the Anti-Federalists generally feared the fundamental political transformation associated with the Constitution, the Federalists welcomed the prospect of change. The cool antibiblicism and skeptical conservatism of men like Hamilton were not entirely representative of the Federalist side. Federalist millennialism was never as intense or as radical as the revolutionary millennialism of the 1770's, but in the late 1780's the nationalistic hopes of supporters of the Constitution were expressed in decidedly millennial terms. "By adopting this system," proclaimed James Wilson at the Pennsylvania ratifying convention, "we shall probably lay a foundation for erecting temples of liberty in every part of the earth. . . . It will be subservient to the great designs of Providence, with regard to this globe – the multiplication of mankind, their improvement in knowledge, and their advancement in happiness."[106] The Constitution, Joel Barlow told the Connecticut Society of the Cincinnati in 1787, would lead to the fulfillment of the biblical prophecies of glory and peace.[107] A few New England Baptist and Congregationalist clergymen also preached that the Constitution helped to open the way to millennial glory.[108] John Woodhull, a Presbyterian minister from Freehold, New Jersey, went so far as to suggest that perhaps the millennium had "already" commenced with the ratification of the Constitution.[109]

In the midst of a rising tide of historical pessimism, the persistence of millennial hopes through the Critical Period kept certain visionary expectations of the American Revolution alive. The millennial optimism of the late 1780's, although less pervasive and more moderate than that of the 1770's, maintained the eschatological embers that would spark a major revival of American millennialism

114

in the 1790's. And whereas in the late 1780's millennialism was most conspicuously associated with conservative nationalism, in the 1790's it would once again spread among Americans of many religious and political persuasions.

III

The eschatological revival
of the 1790's

6

Exegesis

> Tell us, when shall these things be? and what shall be the
> sign of thy coming, and of the end of the world?
>
> Matthew 24:3

References to the prophetic texts of the Bible pervaded the visionary statements of the American Revolution. Yet, in the heat of political turmoil, few Americans concerned themselves with the sustained exegesis of Scripture. Probably the most important reinterpretation of biblical prophecy published in the 1770's was Jonathan Edwards's *History of the Work of Redemption*, originally written two decades before. Charles Chauncy's liberal reworking of eschatology in accord with his belief in universal salvation, conceived before the Revolution but published anonymously in London in 1784, probably reached only a limited number of American readers. Only one full-length published exposition of prophecy bore the imprint of revolutionary millennial thought, the Connecticut evangelical Congregationalist Thomas Bray's *Dissertation upon the Sixth Vial* of 1780.

Numerous patriot sermons, as well as political orations, pamphlets, and newspaper articles, drew specific parallels between biblical prophecies and current events, but American revolutionary millennialism of the 1770's and 1780's generally did not take the form of new biblical scholarship. Rather, revolutionary millennialism infused what were primarily political arguments, and, although the millennial theory of this period was by no means uniform or unchanging, its development occurred more within political than within theological debate. Despite the fact that key biblical passages were brought to bear in numerous ways in the printed millennial literature, the meaning of Scripture was usually not itself a major subject of inquiry.

In the late 1780's this pattern started to change. Exegetical treatises began to appear that offered detailed expositions and interpretations

119

of biblical prophecy. The three-volume *Dissertations on the Prophecies* by the English Bishop Thomas Newton, a complex and exhaustive study covering all of the major and minor prophecies that appear in the Bible, went into many American editions, beginning in 1787. It was first printed in Elizabethtown, New Jersey, by Samuel Kullock, an elder of the local Presbyterian church. The lengthy subscription list for this edition indicates that the *Dissertations* sold widely. Its readers included both Presbyterians and other American Protestants, who ranged in class position and prestige from the governor of New York to unknown farmers, tanners, and carpenters.[1] Written by Newton in the early 1750's in response to Deist attacks on Christianity, this voluminous treatise sought to demonstrate the truth of revelation by showing that most biblical prophecies had already been fulfilled. By his estimate, the present was in the midst of the sixth trumpet of the Book of Revelation, which would accomplish the defeat of the Turks. Soon the last, seventh trumpet would sound the death of the Catholic Beast.[2]

In the late 1780's several such exegetical works also originated in America. Although most were written by clergymen, two of the most expectant ones were by laymen. A piece entitled *Observations upon the Fall of Anti-Christ*, by Charles Crawford, a former Deist and minor poet from the West Indies living in Philadelphia, went into three editions in the second half of the decade. Comparing the earlier calculations of such authorities as Joseph Mede, Moses Lowman, and Isaac Newton, Crawford agreed with Mede that the numbers in the prophetic texts pointed to the downfall of the papal Antichrist as soon as 1806 or 1836.[3] In Connecticut the liberal Congregationalist physician Benjamin Gale offered a detailed chronological scheme linking the seals, vials, and trumpets of the Book of Revelation to major historical events from ancient times to the present. Like Newton and Crawford, Gale concluded that the present was fast approaching the new millennial age.[4]

American clergymen of various denominations also became engaged in close interpretations of prophetic texts in the late 1780's. Two prominent Baptist ministers, Benjamin Foster and Morgan Edwards, published detailed expositions of the books of Daniel and Revelation. Foster, a Yale graduate and the leading Baptist minister of Newport, Rhode Island, in 1787 issued his *Dissertation on the Seventy Weeks of Daniel*, a work that earned him an honorary degree at Brown College. Much like Thomas Newton's *Dissertations*, it aimed to prove the authenticity of scriptural prophecy by showing with minute computations that Daniel had exactly predicted the events leading up to the death and resurrection of Christ. He ended with the observation that the Book of Revelation must be comparably accurate in its promise of a future millennial kingdom, although he did not offer a date.[5] Neither did his Philadelphia colleague Morgan Edwards, an educated Welsh immigrant and founder of Brown, who nonetheless complained in his treatise on the millennium "that Christ's thousands years reign is not more thought of by modern Christians."[6] Edwards had earlier lost his influential pulpit in Philadelphia because of his disapproval of the American Revolution (an unusual position for a Baptist), but he evidently still retained considerable prestige in Baptist educational circles and was employed as a roving Lecturer of Divinity in Delaware, Pennsylvania, New Jersey, and New England in the 1780's. His treatise briefly betrayed his Tory sympathies by making the special point that Christ and his viceroys would institute monarchical rule in the millennium, but otherwise he stuck to a nonpolitical and fairly conventional rendition of the various events of the Last Days described in the Book of Revelation.[7]

These lay and Baptist publications of the late 1780's were followed by the much delayed appearance of Samuel Langdon's *Observations on the Revelation of Jesus Christ to St. John* in 1791. Langdon, former Harvard President and moderate Calvinist Congregationalist, had conceived this work as far back as 1774, when he had solicited subscriptions for a continuation of his *Rational Explication of St. John's Vision of the Two Beasts*. In the midst of the Revolutionary crisis, however, interest in purely exegetical issues was evidently insufficient to support Langdon's endeavor. The longer and more scholarly volume remained in gestation until 1791. Challenging the theories of the renowned English exegete Moses Lowman, Langdon contended that Revelation did not present events in strict chronological order. Instead Langdon divided the prophecy along thematic lines into five separate, overlapping sets of historical developments, all of which pointed to the imminent downfall of the Antichrist and the commencement of the millennium.[8]

If interest in the exposition of biblical prophecy was thus beginning to grow already in the late 1780's and early 1790's, it swelled to much larger proportions by the middle of the decade. Between 1793 and 1796 the number of works on eschatology printed in America multiplied, averaging between five and ten times more per year than during the period 1765 to 1792.[9] Clearly, the French Revolution and the outbreak of the European war catalyzed much of this increase in eschatological publication. Many of the millennial works focused on the meaning of the events then convulsing Europe. Even some of the older works on prophecy that were reprinted in America in the 1790's were often issued with this end in mind. Political events abroad were not, however, the exclusive source of inspiration for this great upsurge in prophetic speculation. Several of these works were clearly the fruits of long incubation, and many treated the French Revolution as at most an incidental event. Exegetical scholarship that made little or no reference to contemporary politics had already begun to appear in the late 1780's, before the French Revolution, and continued to be published alongside the more political interpretations of prophecy of the mid-1790's. Although by no means all Americans partook of this exegetical enthusiasm, a substantial number of millennial writers and readers had developed a taste for prophetic analysis that evidently remained independent of any immediate desire to understand current affairs. This growing interest in the details of biblical exposition – in the multitude of prophetic symbols and in their long-term historical and doctrinal meanings – simultaneously undercut and sustained the more political interpretations of prophecy.

In the 1790's many authors interested in prophetic analysis turned away from politics to more strictly religious issues and to the remote, relatively uncontroversial historical concerns of traditional eschatological analysis. Works published in this period often considered such technical matters as whether all the saints would be resurrected from the dead and whether Christ would be present in the millennium in the flesh or the spirit. In contrast to the nationalist millennialism of the 1780's, perspectives also widened to encompass the entire history of the church across the western world. The Romans, the Saracens, the Turks, the Jews, and the Pope once again became major figures on the millennial scene as writers became absorbed in the interpretation of the complex imagery of biblical prophecy.

This literature often had underlying social and political implications, but on the surface it steadfastly disregarded current affairs. The preoccupation with the meaning of the scriptural word comprised both a theological backlash against the earlier politicization of prophecy and a revitalization of the more universalistic, cosmic, and utopian elements in millennial symbolism that, ultimately, gave it its social and political as well as religious meaning. The increased concentration upon exegetical details may have stemmed in part from the increased leisure and opportunity to delve into such scholarly matters after the revolutionary crisis had passed. It also, however, was a response to the growing need to buttress millennial faith after the excitement generated by the American Revolution had begun to flag. Perhaps in the wake of the intense political involve-ment of the 1770's and 1780's, which had given rise to largely unexamined millennial assumptions as well as subsequent disil-lusionment, growing numbers of Americans felt the need to specify, consolidate, and systematize their millennial theories with reference to the sacred authority of scriptural text. The most eminent theo-logians involved in this exegetical endeavor were joined by pastoral clergymen, prominent laymen, and obscure, even unidentifiable, writers. The multiplication of the numbers of these publications also indicates a growing appetite for this literature among the reading public at large.

Two of the most widely distributed scriptural commentaries in which contemporary affairs assumed at most a marginal role were Thomas Newton's *Dissertation on the Prophecies* and Jonathan Edwards's *History of the Work of Redemption*. Both of these scholarly works went into new editions in the 1790's. Edwards's other major millennial work, "A Humble Attempt to Promote Union in Prayer," and Joseph Bellamy's "Millennium" of 1758, moreover, both reappeared in 1794 in a collection entitled *The Millennium*, edited by the New Jersey Presbyterian David Austin.[10] Austin, later to become notorious for his own, much wilder prophetic pronouncements, was then still a respectable minister whose editorial project won support from his Presbyterian and Congregationalist colleagues. In 1794 a new English translation of the Book of Isaiah also came out in Albany, New York, with an appended chapter-by-chapter "expla-nation" by the Scottish minister John Smith. It contained many cross-references to the Book of Revelation and showed that while most of the ancient prophecies had already come to pass, others – particularly that of the millennium – remained to be realized in the future.[11]

TWO PREVIEWS OF THE KINGDOM OF GOD

Among the most illuminating contemporary expositions of scrip-tural prophecy that appeared in the 1790's were Samuel Hopkins's *Treatise on the Millennium* and Elhanan Winchester's *Lectures on the Prophecies That Remain to Be Fulfilled*. Whereas for the most part late eighteenth-century millennial writers abstained from detailed specu-lation about what life would be like during the millennium – concentrating instead on the past and future events leading to it –

123

Hopkins and Winchester each provided a window through which could be seen the ideal world of the Kingdom of God.

In both books, millennial theories were integrated closely with more general theological arguments. Hopkins's *Treatise* was appended to his much larger *System of Doctrine*, which soon became the standard text for the post-Edwardsian "New Divinity" school of Congregationalist Calvinism. The former Baptist Winchester's *Lectures* were written in part to defend his new Universalist belief in the eventual salvation of all souls. Along the late eighteenth-century American theological spectrum, the Calvinist Hopkins and the Universalist Winchester could not have been farther apart. Socially as well as theologically the two men spoke to different segments of the American Protestant community. Both endorsed popular revivalism, but whereas Hopkins and other New Divinity ministers drew their support from established churches in New England's small towns and villages, Winchester had made his mark as an itinerant preacher in the southern and middle areas of the country, particularly in the city of Philadelphia.[12] Yet despite all these differences, their millennial visions were remarkably similar. Taken together, they show clearly how the movement towards detailed scriptural exegesis in the 1790's at once supplemented and displaced revolutionary political interpretations of prophecy.

Hopkins's New Divinity theology was a revised system of Calvinism developed by several New Light Congregationalist disciples of Jonathan Edwards beginning in the late 1750's. In opposition to antirevivalist and liberalizing tendencies within the Congregationalist churches, this group of ministers held tenaciously to an exceptionally strict interpretation of the Calvinist doctrines of predestination and original sin. Hopkins, Edwards's protégé and after 1770 a highly visible minister in Newport, Rhode Island, had from the beginning been a leader in the New Divinity movement. He became widely known for his extreme position that God had himself created sin to benefit the universe, and that the reprobate should rejoice in the prospect of eternal damnation because it served the glory of God. His ideas about the millennium, published in 1793 shortly before his death, conformed to this uncompromising belief in the absolute sovereignty of God and the inefficacy of human efforts to remake the world. Although he believed that evangelical religious activity could hasten the millennium by spreading the divine word, he did not think that other forms of human action played a constructive millennial role.

As Hopkins foresaw the future and interpreted John's Revelation, the world had yet to endure abut two hundred years of tribulation under the seventh vial before the millennium would begin around the year 2000. Neither the extended destruction during the Great Battle of God Almighty nor the subsequent thousand-year period of peace and happiness would be the work of human beings, he declared. Rather, all would be done by supernatural Providence. Hopkins conceded that Christ would use instruments such as angels, the church, and the wicked themselves, but he insisted that the battle would "not consist in the church of christians raising armies, and fighting and carrying on war with the antichristian party," but would be "commenced and carried on by Christ, while invisible in heaven."[13] Even this terrible time of tribulation would, moreover, prove insufficient to bring humanity to voluntary repentance for its sins. In the end Christ would save the world by a massive effusion of grace, showing definitively "that men are saved not by human might or power, but by the spirit of the Lord."[14]

In line with the New Divinity teaching about the glory of human damnation, Hopkins observed that true Christians should take pleasure in what he saw as recent signs of religious and moral decay, for "however undesirable and dreadful, in themselves," these developments were "necessary for the greatest good of the church of Christ, and to introduce the Millennium in the best manner."[15] The faithful who helplessly stood by while things became progressively worse (he predicted a fifty-year period of degeneracy beginning around 1800) could take heart in the scriptural promise of their ultimate vindication. Hopkins viewed the main purpose of millennial prophecy not as attempting to motivate worldly action but as providing spiritual consolation for the godly during hard times. Only once, briefly, did he observe that the recent "rapid spread of zeal" to promote religious and civil liberty served to hasten the demise of the papal Beast.[16] The only activities he actually recommended were purely devotional and evangelical: prayer, the spreading of the Word, and the maintenance of the church.[17] Not surprisingly, Hopkins deplored the "unscriptural and ridiculous notions" of the millennium entertained by "enthusiasts" during the English Revolution. He welcomed instead the more moderate, "rational, scriptural and important" opinions of Whitby, Lowman, Edwards, and other relatively nonpolitical eighteenth-century theologians.[18]

Elhanan Winchester similarly downplayed the importance of politics. Far from adhering to the strict Calvinism of Hopkins, however, he presented his view of the millennium as part of his

Universalist theory about the eventual redemption of saints and sinners alike. Born and raised in Brookline, Massachusetts, the son of a "respectable" mechanic, Winchester switched as a youth from the ancestral Congregationalism of his family to the Baptism then spreading over New England in the aftermath of the Great Awakening. He began his ministerial career in 1771 as a confirmed Calvinist, but after spending several years successfully preaching predestinarian Baptism in New England, South Carolina, Virginia, and Philadelphia, he decided by 1780 to reject the doctrine of election and to embrace Universalism. According to his own account, he was brought to this position partly by his sympathy for black slaves in South Carolina who were suspicious of Christianity and who refused to convert until told that "Jesus Christ loved them, and died for them, as well as for us white people, and that they might come and believe in him and welcome."[19] Winchester was also persuaded to abandon Calvinism by his readings in German pietist and Methodist literature. By the time of his conversion a few small Universalist groups had begun organizing in New England under the leadership of the former English Methodist John Murray, with whom Winchester soon started a correspondence, and the movement would grow rapidly in many parts of the country in the following decades. Winchester was quickly forced to resign from his position as the minister of the Baptist Church in Philadelphia despite the fact that he retained the support of the majority of the congregation. His Universalist preaching continued to attract large numbers in the early 1780's, however, and in 1787 he moved to England to continue propagating his new faith. He stayed abroad until 1794, when he returned to America briefly before his death in 1797.

It was in London that he preached and wrote his *Lectures on the Prophecies* and his *Three Woe Trumpets*, both of which were reprinted in the United States in the mid-1790's. Over the course of his active career the apparently charismatic Winchester attained impressively wide-ranging influence despite his chronically deviant religious affiliations. When still a Calvinist Baptist he conducted massive revivals among both whites and blacks, and he was chiefly responsible for the conversion of John Leland, one of the most successful Southern evangelists of his generation.[20] Already in his Baptist years Winchester's strong millennial beliefs had found expression in a book of hymns he published in 1776. Later, as a leading American Universalist, he not only contributed to an intense interest in the latter days among others in that denomination – an interest evident in publications by Universalist churches in Philadelphia and

126

Lexington, Kentucky, in the mid-1790's – but he also had an acknowledged impact on the eschatological thought of prominent liberal Protestants such as Joseph Priestley and Benjamin Rush.[21]

For Winchester, unlike for Hopkins, the primary significance of the millennium was that it provided a limited period of reward for the righteous alone, before the Last Judgment when all humanity would be saved. His Universalist eschatology closely resembled that of Charles Chauncy, whose own work on the subject had been published anonymously in London some years before.[22] Like Chauncy, Winchester held that the glories of the millennium only prefigured the far more magnificent "new earth" when the souls of sinners previously condemned to hell would join the saints in eternal union with God: "The Millenium is a kind of Middle State, between this present, and the final condition of the earth."[23] Damnation, which would continue in hell while the regenerate enjoyed the millennium on earth, was a temporary expedient designed to reform the otherwise intractable: "Judgment is a mean, but never an end."[24] The true end of the providential plan, to be realized after the millennium was over, was universal salvation and the creation of an entirely new and heavenly earth for all souls for all time.

Although in his Universalism Winchester differed dramatically from the predestinarian Hopkins, he too insisted that the fulfillment of prophecy would occur by supernatural rather than by human means. Much like Hopkins he deplored the mistaken interpretation of Scripture used to entitle subjects to rebel against kings and set up a Fifth Monarchy.[25] The millennium would be achieved by super-natural feats performed by the Prince of Peace, who would wage spectacular warfare against his enemies just before the sounding of the seventh trumpet. Aside from some brief speculation on recent earthquakes, Winchester's *Lectures on the Prophecies*, originally published in London in 1789, made little attempt to relate biblical passages to current events in the world. Even when his revised *Three Woe Trumpets* later interpreted the French Revolution as a sign of the Last Days, he emphatically denied any political intent: "I do not so much as enter into the matter in a political view, I mean to soar as far above that sphere as the heavens are above the earth, and only speak of these things as wonderfull illustrations and fulfillments of prophecy."[26]

Given this sublime refusal to see activity in this world as a means to the millennium, it is ironic that both Winchester and Hopkins were unusually concrete and expansive in their descriptions of the coming glorious order itself. Considerable portions of their treatises were devoted to rapturous accounts of what life would be like in the latter days. Drawing freely from imagination as well as from the relevant biblical texts, they each presented a compelling picture of universal love, joy, and plenitude. In the millennium all physical needs would be amply satisfied: The earth would abound with bountiful crops, and very little labor – according to Hopkins, "no more than two or three hours in a day" – would be required to produce the necessities and comforts of life.[27] Like Joseph Bellamy, Ezra Stiles, and others before them, they both foresaw a vast increase in population (Winchester estimated that there would be five hundred times more people than at present), still a consummate sign of social well-being.[28] All these people would, moreover, live together in absolute harmony. Not only would there be no more war and, as Hopkins stressed, no more lawsuits, but there would be no more petty squabbles among individuals and within families.[29] Furthermore, humanity would reach the pinnacles of learning, for, as Hopkins explained, "knowledge, mental light, and holiness are inseparable connected; and are, in some respects, the same."[30]

Both men emphasized that the comfort, peace, and knowledge that characterized the millennial order would extend throughout the earth. Following prophetic tradition, they especially stressed that the Jews would return to Israel and be converted to true Christianity along with the rest of the world. Different nations would not only be bound by a common faith, but would, as suggested in biblical text, speak the same tongue.[31] In accord with the pronounced universalism of their visions, as well as their relative lack of interest in politics, neither Hopkins nor Winchester (unlike Jonathan Edwards and others before them) assigned a special role to America in the millennial kingdom. At most Winchester expressed the fleeting hope that the Lord would recognize that the United States had tolerated Jews and therefore would spare Americans the worst punishment on the day of vengeance.[32]

Of the two visions, Winchester's depended more on supernatural events, not the least of which was Christ's literal descent from on high and his personal assumption of power over the millennial kingdom. Other, relatively minor, miracles that highlighted Winchester's description of the new age included the advent of painless childbirth, the end of infant mortality and other deaths before the age of one hundred years, the creation of new sources of water, and, as prophesied in Isaiah, the end of predatory killing within the animal kingdom.[33] Although Hopkins was generally more sparing in his prediction of miracles, he, too, occasionally looked forward to God's physical intervention in the millennial world: For example, the earth would become more fertile following a supernatural regularization of the seasons and draining away of parts of the sea.[34]

But by no means all the marvelous changes these millennialists anticipated necessitated such concrete supernatural intervention. Explaining the great rise in material comfort during the millennium, Hopkins argued that the end of warfare would in itself provide a tremendous savings of wealth. In a characteristically New England manner, he also insisted that people would become more properly ascetic in their tastes. In their "use of the things of this life" they would exercise "great prudence and economy" and nothing would be "sought or used to gratify pride inordinate, sensual appetite or lust."[35] They would become far more productive as well. With the increase in scientific knowledge and great improvements in industry and agriculture, Hopkins surmised, "all the necessary and con-venient articles of life . . . will be formed and made, in a better manner, and with much less labor, than they are now."[36] Winchester resorted more than Hopkins to the effects of supernatural power, but even he assumed the continuance of physical conditions of nature as he considered how the multiplied population of the millennium could survive on the earth's resources. He imagined the construction of vast cities on top of water, the settlement of newly discovered lands, the expanded consumption of plentiful seafood, the universal cultivation of South Sea Island breadfruit trees – and then added that people would have smaller appetites from working so much less.[37]

As they spun these fancies, neither Hopkins nor Winchester gave much attention to the social and political structure that would exist during the millennium. The few observations they did offer on this subject were, moreover, remarkably similar, despite the fact that Hopkins was a staunch Federalist in his politics and Winchester a confirmed Republican.[38] In a footnote Hopkins regretfully conceded that the church would not entirely replace the secular state in the millennium, but aside from specifying that government would consist of "wise men chosen and appointed," he said nothing about political function or organization.[39] For Winchester this particular problem largely resolved itself because Christ himself would become the absolute sovereign of the world. As far as human involvement was concerned, he proclaimed with Jesus that "the meek shall then inherit the earth," but he also accepted at face value the passage in Revelation that describes Christ's royal assistants administering justice to the poor.[40] Hopkins similarly foresaw a stratified social order in which everyone would behave in a manner appropriate to "station and connections," while he denied that anyone would be deprived of material comforts.[41] He went so far as to claim that "all worldly things will be a great degree, and in the best manner common; so as not to be withheld from any who may want them."[42] The baneful effects of private property would thus be eliminated, and a massive effusion of grace would enable everyone to "have pleasure and joy, in proportion to the degree of his benevolence."[43] In the final analysis, the alleviation of the miseries of the world would be accomplished not by any structural reorganization but by a generalized holiness – in Hopkins's vision, due to the pouring out of God's spirit; in Winchester's, to the direct rule by Christ.

For all their elaborate descriptions of the many wonders attending the millennial age, Hopkins and Winchester were careful to insist that the earthly perfection of the millennium still fell short of the ultimate perfection of heaven. Just as they both emphasized the great gap between present worldly realities and the millennium – a gap to be bridged by divine intervention alone – so too they foresaw a further step from the millennium, which was still on earth and within history, to the new creation that would appear only after the end of the world. Winchester was especially concerned to draw a distinction between the millennial period when the saints would live in Christ's Kingdom on earth, and the new heaven and earth when the damned would be saved and the entire world would be remade anew. Hopkins, too, explained that during the millennium, before the perfection of the new heaven and earth, "every one will be attended with a degree of sinful imperfection while in the body."[44]

Thus each of them qualified their millennialism with constant reminders about human imperfection and the folly of worldly ambitions. Indeed, their unusually elaborate visions of the millennial state were inseparable from their vehement denial that human beings would play a part in the establishment of the millennial kingdom. By rejecting the view that the saints themselves could bring on the millennium, they were free of the imaginative constraints of relating the goals of contemporary revolutionary politics to the promise of millennial bliss. In this respect they can be seen as salvaging the millennial dream from a too intimate association with republican politics – an association that so easily bred disillusionment with the grand eschatological scheme.

WHEN AND HOW CHRIST RETURNS

In their broadest outlines, Winchester's and Hopkins's portraits of the millennium were nearly identical. Although their chronological interpretations of the vials in Revelation differed in details, they fundamentally concurred in their identification of the Turkish and papal Beasts, their judgment that history was approaching the last days, their prediction that the glorious age would be preceded by a terrible time of tribulation, and their conviction that it would be introduced by supernatural rather than human agency.[45] Apart from their nearly opposite Calvinist and Universalist views of the Final Judgment and eternal damnation (positions that had little to do with the coming or nature of the millennium itself), there was only one pronounced exegetical difference between them: their timing of the Second Coming of Christ. Whereas Winchester took the premillennial position that Christ would descend in the flesh personally to inaugurate and rule over the millennial kingdom, Hopkins took the postmillennial view that Christ would be present in spirit during the millennium and would visibly appear only afterwards at the Last Judgment.

Beginning in the 1790's the difference between premillennialism and postmillennialism was becoming the major polarizing issue within exegetical debate. Gradually over the course of the following century the two sets of interpretations widely diverged and each became associated with broader eschatological and political outlooks. Postmillennialism came to signify an optimistic belief in progressive human action towards the millennium, according to which God's providential plan would be carried out by human means and the world would enjoy a period of social perfection before the supernatural intervention at the end of time. This millennial theory became part of most American liberal theology in the nineteenth century. Premillennialism, to the contrary, with its prediction of the physical descent of Christ before the millennium, became associated more generally with a passive reliance on divine miracles and a tendency to withdraw from the world in the expectation of the approaching conflagration. This was the dominant millennial view of Protestant fundamentalists in the nineteenth century and remains so to the present day.

Although some religious historians have maintained that these divisions extend back to the seventeenth century, it has recently been demonstrated that before the end of the eighteenth century there was little polarization along premillennial and postmillennial lines. Earlier premillennialist and postmillennialist interpretations were respectively linked with a seemingly infinite combination of magical, otherworldly, naturalistic, optimistic, and pessimistic points of view.[46] Even in the 1790's, differences between premillennialists and postmillennialists did not correspond clearly to wider progressive and fatalistic world-historical outlooks: There were still both activistic premillennialists and pessimistic postmillennialists. But beginning in the late 1780's, postmillennialists and premillennialists were becoming distinct, self-conscious groups, and this new exegetical alignment revealed an emerging antagonism between different parts of the American religious community. The conflict arose from social as well as theological origins, and may even have had underlying political significance.

Samuel Hopkins's postmillennialism came out of a long and fairly established exegetical tradition, including not only the works by Whitby and other earlier commentators, but the writings of Hopkins's own mentor Jonathan Edwards and other distinguished Edwardsians such as Aaron Burr, senior, and Joseph Bellamy. By the late eighteenth century this tradition had apparently become that of most Calvinist Congregationalist clerics, and probably, with the exception of Charles Chauncy, most liberal Congregationalist ones as well. The established New England ministers Ebenezer Baldwin, Thomas Bray, Levi Hart, and Samuel Langdon all, for example, took postmillennial positions in their millennial writings between the 1770's and the 1790's.[47] Although Baldwin and Hart were both, like Hopkins, New Divinity men, Bray and Langdon were not. In 1797 a work published by an obscure figure in Maine named Eliphaz Chapman was specifically designed to popularize orthodox eschatological doctrine, to help "the common people ... understand the scriptures where they most need it." In the course of explicating the prevailing clerical opinion on various matters of exegesis, Chapman laid particular stress on the point that Christ's rule in the millennium would be spiritual rather than physical.[48]

This effort to popularize postmillennial theory was evidently due to the failure of the works by Hopkins and others to reach and persuade many ordinary people. Like other tendencies within eighteenth-century theology, especially the New Divinity system, the belief in Christ's purely spiritual millennial reign drew upon an intellectual sophistication, a metaphorical imagination, and a belief in the concrete power of intangible grace. It also involved a somewhat Enlightened reluctance to rely too much, for the too near future, on miracles so beyond either natural or spiritual understanding as the physical descent of Christ from on high. Just as Hopkins refused to depend on worldly action for the fulfillment of prophecy, he preferred not to embody mysterious divine power in the flesh. God would inaugurate the millennium without enlisting Christian soldiers, but he would do so invisibly, by means of an effusion of grace and indirect modification of the natural environment.

Winchester, on the other hand, opened the second volume of his *Lectures on Prophecy* with a repudiation of postmillennial theories. Indeed, he held these interpretations responsible for the general failure of commentators to agree about the meaning of the prophecies.[49] He claimed that the postmillennial view that Christ would return for the millennium only in spirit involved a figurative, metaphorical reading of Scripture, whereas his own approach was simply "to take the whole Bible as canonical and authentic."[50] For him as for Chauncy before him, premillennialism was an integral part of Universalism, since, by situating Christ's Second Coming and Judgment at the beginning rather than at the end of the millennium, he could maintain that after the thousand-year period was over the previously damned would be saved.

But Universalists were by no means the only Americans who were gravitating towards the more literal, premillennial version of the Messiah's return. Beginning in the late 1780's, growing numbers of publications in America either tacitly assumed or aggressively advocated a premillennial position. Although by the middle and late 1790's premillennialism at times was interwoven with political reactions to the French Revolution, the European war, and domestic political conflict, it first arose in nonpolitical form.

Just as postmillennialism had a long history before it became a matter of doctrinal debate toward the end of the eighteenth century, premillennialism was in itself scarcely new. The premillennial scriptural exegesis of the late 1780's and 1790's drew sustenance from numerous pieces of popular religious literature, many of them written earlier, which described the coming of Christ as physical without engaging in explicit debate on the exegetical issue. The radical millennialist sects that formed in New England during the Revolutionary War were also notably premillennialist in their forecasts of the coming of Christ.[51] On the level of popular culture, the image of Christ appearing in the flesh had probably always dominated over the idea of a purely spiritual coming, both because of its greater dramatic power and because of its greater faithfulness to the literal biblical word. In the late eighteenth century many widely distributed religious publications conveyed such a tacitly premillennial view. Works of devotional poetry, many of them reprinted from England, contained vivid accounts of the Messiah's return to judge and to preside over the new heavenly kingdom. William Cowper's *Task*, a long, rambling ballad concluding with a flowery description of Christ's descent in his chariot, went into seven editions in different American cities between 1787 and 1796. Edward Young's *Last Day*, which presented a highly literal rendition of the events in Revelation, was reprinted five times between 1786 and 1797.[52] Books of popular hymns that referred both to the Second Coming and to millennial bliss frequently implied this order of sequence but abstained from such considerations as whether Christ would appear in flesh or spirit.[53] Other often reprinted religious publications, including a children's biography of Jesus and a playfully apocryphal work claiming to be the sequel to the Book of Revelation, also held out the prospect of a sudden, perhaps imminent, Second Advent.[54]

Such general works of popular piety forecasting the dramatic, physical appearance of Christ were joined in the late 1780's and 1790's by an increased volume of literature concentrating specifically on the theme of the Messiah's return. For the most part these pieces of apocalyptical writing focused on the Last Judgment rather than on the millennium. In announcing the possibility of Christ's imminent return, however, their predictions were consistent with premillennial eschatology. One writer for the Boston *Independent Chronicle* in 1786 urged his readers to make themselves ready for "Christ to *come immediately.*"[55] The New England Congregationalist minister John Smith similarly preached a sermon interpreting a recent strike of lightning as a warning foreshadowing Christ's sudden and spectacular descent.[56] Two anonymous publications bearing the titles *An Essay on the Signs of Christ's Second Appearance* and *Four Sermons, on the Second Coming of Christ* also appeared in New Hampshire and Philadelphia in the mid-1790's. The *Sermons* disparaged the present pursuit of happiness in this world and condemned the excessive preoccupation with political revolution, human judges, and earthly laws – like Winchester and Hopkins seeking to disassociate the history of redemption from the uncertain consequences of worldly affairs. Instead the author advised spiritual preparation for "the grand revolution of universal nature," the coming of Christ, the Judgment, and infinite reward and punishment.[57]

This emphasis on Judgment Day was not in itself millennial, for Christ's return could as well bring the end of the world as a heavenly kingdom on earth. The sermons and hymns of Methodists, for example, who issued few specifically millennial statements in the late eighteenth century, frequently stressed the themes of Christ's physical return, the Judgment, the end of the world, and the new heaven and earth.[58] Yet the distinction between a millennial and a nonmillennial eschatology was not always clear. At least a few Methodist preachers in the late eighteenth century evidently did believe in the millennium even though they almost never mentioned it in their printed literature. According to the diary of the circuit rider Ezekiel Cooper, a group of high-ranking American Methodists gathering in his Wilmington, Delaware, boardinghouse in 1797 argued for hours "whether Christ's reign would be personal or spiritual."[59] Curiously, none of the group seem to have adopted John Wesley's own unusual theory, borrowed from the German exegete Johann Albrecht Bengel, that Christ would rule spiritually in the first part of the millennium and physically in the rest. Cooper himself favored the spiritual or postmillennial position, but most of the others present that evening, including the Bishop Thomas Coke, developed the premillennialist case for Christ's literal appearance in the flesh.[60]

As this very debate suggests, the question of Christ's physical or spiritual presence in the millennium was gradually becoming a more explicit focal point of concern in the late 1780's and 1790's. Although the premillennialists undoubtedly drew upon the long tradition within popular religion that highlighted the prospect of a physical Second Coming, the horrors of Judgment Day, and Christ's personal reign, by the end of the century they grew more self-conscious, deliberately taking a polemical stance. If Methodists abstained from this public debate, conducting their disputes in private instead, others joined Elhanan Winchester in arguing against the postmillennial, figurative interpretations so common among leading American theologians like Edwards and Hopkins. Literature began to appear that presented the exegetical case for the literal premillennial coming of Christ. The figures most involved in issuing this doctrinal challenge to the Calvinist clerical establishment were usually Baptists and Congregationalist laymen removed from the intellectual center of American theological life. They were occasionally joined by a few deviant and alienated members of the Presbyterian and Congregationalist clergy itself. The various efforts to construct a premillennial interpretation of prophecy represented a kind of rebellion against religious intellectualism, which would eventually lead to the emergence of Protestant fundamentalism in the following century.[61]

In the late eighteenth century American Baptists rarely involved themselves in the intricacies of prophetic exegesis, but when they did they usually took the premillennial position on the appearance of Christ. In his treatise on the Book of Daniel the distinguished Rhode Island Baptist Benjamin Foster stressed the literal accuracy of the biblical promise that Christ would return in the clouds of heaven to judge and reign over the millennial kingdom, and Morgan Edwards, the Welsh immigrant Baptist clergyman, attacked "spiritualizing Millennarians" and insisted that Christ would descend in person for the millennium.[62] The premillennialism of Baptist leaders like Foster and Morgan evidently permeated through the denominational ranks. Printed minutes of Baptist Associations in Virginia, New York, and Connecticut in the 1790's all expressed belief in the physical coming of Christ.[63] An obscure New England Baptist preacher named Abraham Cummings also published an aggressively premillennialist tract positing a theory of three successive historical dispensations, each ending with a miraculous judgment and resurrection. He maintained that Christ's Second Coming was soon to occur, and cited Samuel Hopkins's *Treatise on the Millennium* as an example of the mistaken postmillennial belief that there should be "first a long thousand years, happy years" – a belief that was, in his view, one of the main signs of apostasy that signaled the approach of the Judgment Day.[64]

Lay writers without clear denominational preferences also added to the developing critique of postmillennialism towards the end of the century. In Philadelphia in 1785 the West Indian immigrant poet Charles Crawford wrote an exegetical work in which he highlighted the goriest sections of the Book of Revelation and pointedly objected to those "who conceive that Christ's reign of a thousand years on earth, is meant nothing more than the prevalence of the gospel in singular purity."[65] Another vocal premillennialist of the period was the New York lay biblical scholar Samuel Osgood, a former Continental congressman, commissioner of the federal treasury during the Confederation, and postmaster general in the Washington administration. Osgood had been a vigorous opponent of the financial program of Robert Morris and became an Anti-Federalist in the late 1780's. Later, he would be elected to the New York assembly on the Jeffersonian side. In the early 1790's he temporarily retired from his long career in government and wrote a book about prophecy published by the Republican printer Thomas Greenleaf in 1794. The main purpose of the work was to revise the standard historical interpretation of the kingdoms represented by the symbols of the kings and the Beasts (expanding their number from four to eight), but it also engaged in a detailed refutation of Lowman and Whitby's figurative conceptions of the first resurrection and the coming of Christ.[66] Perhaps reflecting Osgood's disillusionment with national politics under the Federalists, his premillennialism was combined with a firm denial of the power of human action. "Jesus Christ himself . . . will visibly close the present dispensation. We have therefore only to wait patiently for the event; as nothing we can do, will hasten or procrastinate it."[67] The Last Days would bring not merely Christ's visible descent and the raising of the dead but even, he insisted, "the end of all flesh."[68] Osgood also took an unorthodox position on the afterlife, arguing that the soul does not exist between death and the resurrection at the beginning of the millennium, a view that further underscored the importance of the miraculous events of the Second Coming.[69] His premillennialism was thus part of a deviant theological system that took him far afield from both New England orthodoxy and his earlier involvement in the course of republican government.

Despite the fact that postmillennialism was strongest among the established New England Congregationalist clergy, the lay challenge to it extended into the New England churches themselves. Dissenting voices often tinged with populist anti-intellectualism objected to the insubstantial figuratism of a spiritual Second Coming. They sought to challenge the dominant clergy with a literal interpretation presumably based on the authority of the Bible alone. Samuel Fish, an obscure layman from Lebanon, Connecticut, for example, outlined his prophetic scheme in a series of three published works contending that the millennium would come in two stages, in one of which Christ's reign would be spiritual, in the other, physical.[70] This position was more consistent with the views of the English Baptist John Gill and the Methodist John Wesley than with the perspective of the local Congregationalist ministry. Another Connecticut layman, the physician Benjamin Gale, ventured still more aggressively into the theological field by publishing his analysis of the outpouring of the vials through history. Much of his reading was fairly conventional, but his interpretation of the fifth vial was not. He considered it to be the Protestant Reformation – not in the conventional laudatory sense of a scourge on popery, but critically, as one of the seven last plagues on Christianity.[71] In particular he attacked the Calvinist doctrines of unconditional election and reprobation, apparently with New Divinity theologians like Hopkins in mind. Somewhat ostentatiously displaying his college knowledge of Greek, he went on to insist upon the literal meaning of "the (epiphaneia) *appearing* of Jesus Christ" at the time of the seventh vial. He ridiculed the metaphorical fancies of the postmillennialists by asking the rhetorical question "have not the Revelationists the strongest reason to expect, and the fullest grounds to hope [that] the Messiah will really *come*, not in some *unintelligible, spiritual,* or *mysterious* manner, not to be seen but thro' metaphysical optiks?"[72]

Even more extreme was the lay premillennialist in the western Massachusetts town of Stockbridge, Simon Hough, who was actually excommunicated from the Congregational Church in 1792 for his efforts to awaken the world to Christ's imminent return and judgment. In his published defense of himself, entitled *An Alarm to the World*, Hough amassed scriptural citations to refute the postmillennial view that Christ would appear only after the millennium at the Last Judgment. Fervently anticlerical, he reserved his harshest attacks for the learned and salaried ministers of the established church. He especially welcomed the thought that at the coming apocalypse the churches "built on the sandy foundations of worldly wisdom, traditions of men, money, and liberal education will fall, and great will be the fall."[73]

Although this combination of premillennialism and anti-establishment feeling was most characteristic of Baptist and lay writers on prophecy who took to the press in the late 1780's and 1790's, such sentiments even occasionally appeared within the Congregationalist and Presbyterian ministries themselves. Perhaps the most notorious example of a premillennialist with prophetic pretensions in the 1790's was the New Jersey Presbyterian clergyman David Austin. Austin, the son of a successful New Haven merchant, graduated from Yale in 1779 and then studied theology under the New Divinity postmillennialist Joseph Bellamy. After traveling in Europe and marrying the wealthy Lydia Lathrop of Norwich, Connecticut, Austin accepted a call from the First Presbyterian Church in Elizabethtown, New Jersey, in 1788. His congregation contained many influential members, including United States Senator Jonathan Dayton and Congressmen Abraham Clarke and Elias Boudinot. Austin soon became a prominent figure in the northeastern Congregationalist-Presbyterian clerical establishment. He undertook, for example, the editorship of a major four-volume collection of American sermons entitled *The American Preacher*, among whose sponsors were the governors of New York and New Jersey and the president of Columbia College. He also served as the president of a moderate antislavery organization, the Connecticut Society for the Promotion of Freedom, which listed as its other officers such leading New Englanders as Jonathan Edwards, Jr., John and Benjamin Trumbull, Noah Webster, and Theodore Dwight.

Gradually Austin's attention began to turn more towards eschatology. In 1794 he issued another edited collection called *The Millennium*, which contained earlier pieces on prophecy by Edwards and Bellamy and his own sermon "The Downfall of Mystical Babylon," originally preached in Elizabethtown and New York in early 1793. In it Austin already veered towards unorthodoxy by suggesting that the first stage of the millennium had begun with American independence, but he never discussed the descent of Christ and clearly saw himself as proceeding in the steps of Edwards and Bellamy.[74] The year after the publication of *The Millennium*, however, Austin fell victim to scarlet fever. Although there are already hints of a disordered imagination in the earlier sermon, a contemporary reported that the illness permanently damaged his mind.[75] Whatever the psychological genesis, in early 1796 he received a vision from God and announced to his congregation that Christ would visibly appear and start the millennium on the fourth Sunday that May.

Coming from such a respectable minister, the news created a local sensation. As the fateful day approached, Austin's church overflowed with people from neighboring parishes. "Weeping and mourning were heard in all parts of the assembly."[76] When nothing unusual happened, many of his followers fell away in disillusionment, and leading members of the church sought to persuade their troublesome minister that he was under a delusion. Austin, however, quickly found reasons for Christ's last-minute delay and only stepped up the pace of his preaching. He traveled through the countryside surrounding Elizabethtown, sometimes delivering as many as three sermons per day proclaiming the imminent (although apparently now undated) return of the Savior. He regarded himself as the modern equivalent of Joshua, who led the Jews into Israel, and of John the Baptist, the forerunner of Christ. Crowds followed him and, according to one account, many conversions occurred in response to his message.[77] Although newspaper coverage of these events was scanty, an article defending Austin signed "An Enquirer after Truth" appeared in the *New-York Gazette* and in the local *New-Jersey Journal* in early June.[78] Its author overlooked Austin's prophetic error the previous month and underscored the optimism of his vision: Austin was not prophesying the end of the world, as a writer in the New York *Minerva* had accused, but the glorious commencement of the millennium. The world was now at the end of the sixth trumpet of the Book of Revelation. The American and French revolutions, the destruction of the Papacy, the rise of Washington as the new Zerubbabel – all confirmed Austin's belief that the new dispensation was about to arrive, and would happily come first to America.

By the spring of 1797, however, Austin had lost all remaining support from members of his congregation, and the New York Presbytery approved their petition to dissolve his connection with their church. After his dismissal Austin returned to New Haven, where he busied himself preparing houses and a wharf for the use of the Jews when they embarked for the Holy Land at the commencement of the millennium.[79] He was once imprisoned for debt, but appears for the most part to have been able to live off his and his wife's family income. According to one contemporary description of his life, after he moved back to New Haven he lost the sincerity of his premillennial convictions: "In a manner more comic than otherwise, he still maintained that the personal reign of Christ on earth was soon to commence."[80] He himself evidently paid for the publication of several sermons he wrote on millennial themes that were printed around the turn of the century. None of these highlighted Christ's physical coming, but on occasion he did formally adhere to the premillennial account.[81] Whether "comic" or not, his language had become so highly metaphorical that it is impossible to determine the intended theological meaning of these passages.

Not surprisingly, like the excommunicated premillennialist Simon Hough, Austin heaped abuse upon the ministerial profession that had disowned him. He declared that the Protestants were displacing the Catholics in assuming the role of the Beast. Once he even identified leading pillars of the New England Congregationalist establishment – Timothy Dwight, Nathan Strong, and Jedidiah Morse – as "political croakers" who fulfilled the prophecy in Revelation of the three frogs or unclean spirits coming out of the mouth of the Beast.[82] Elsewhere, in defiance of Dwight and others who in the late 1790's warned of an international conspiracy of Freemasons subverting political order and true religion, Austin dubbed Masonry itself a superior form of Christianity surpassing the institutional church. "At the consummation of your order," he congratulated the Masons, "the scriptures may be fulfilled."[83] His diatribes against the Federalist ministry at the end of the decade sounded almost like Republican polemics, even though Austin himself had no strong party preferences.[84] He kept lambasting the clergy long after he stopped predicting the Second Coming. His moment of glory as a premillennial prophet had been brief, if spectacular, and the rest of his life proved anticlimactic and doubtlessly frustrating. There is some evidence that he still maintained his skill as an orator and on occasion even spoke to large audiences, but he never regained the influence he lost in 1796. Discredited by a false prediction and removed from his prestigious ministerial post, he failed to maintain a following. Perhaps he lacked the mental capacity to organize and sustain a sectarian movement. But whatever the reason for his ultimate failure, his initial success in the Elizabethtown area shows that even the most extreme form of premillennialism in the 1790's could strike a responsive popular chord.

The most determined premillennialist polemicist of the period, the Congregationalist minister Joshua Spaulding of Salem, took a more cautious and scholarly approach. A student of Edwards and Hopkins, he had received training similar to Austin's, and for many years he loyally adhered to orthodox postmillennial doctrine. Later confessing that he had "been held in errors . . . for a number of years of adult age," this otherwise undistinguished cleric changed his mind and launched a fulsome attack on the postmillennialism of his eminent teachers.[85] His one published work, a series of lectures entitled *Sentiments Concerning the Coming and Kingdom of Christ*, was printed in Salem in 1796. Appearing amidst the proliferation of premillennial statements by recognized scholars, popular religious writers, and amateur theologians, his was by far the most complete and systematic defense of the position. He began by drawing a clear distinction between the premillennial "millenarians" like himself, who adhered to the true "ancient doctrine," and the postmillennial "millenists" who had fabricated the false "modern doctrine." Over two hundred pages of his argument rendered his version of the events of the last days, with liberal extractions from Scripture and "millenarian" scholarship. The present was under the sixth trumpet, which had been sounded by a series of natural disasters and by the upheaval in Europe caused by the French Revolution. Soon Christ would appear in full sight of the world, the Jews would convert, the dead saints would come to life, and the Great Battle of God Almighty would destroy all sinners and finally burn up the entire world. Then the millennium would commence with the creation of New Jerusalem in the New Heavens and New Earth. After the millennium the evil Gog and Magog would attack from outside the walls of the heavenly city and there would be one more battle, ending with their decisive defeat. Finally, the remaining, unsaintly dead would then be resurrected for the Final Judgment.

Spaulding admitted that other premillennialists might not agree with every detail of his account but complained that the postmillennialists differed among themselves even more.[86] His main case against his opponents, however, was that they were dangerous innovators. Only by changing the meaning of biblical language could they defend their position: "This way of turning the Scriptures into tropes and figures is called explaining them; but it ought rather be called a way of contradicting the Scriptures." Scanning the New England landscape for signs of heresy, he ominously observed that "by such means chiefly universalism has been introduced, and old arianism has been revived."[87] In his appendix he reviewed the history of millennial interpretation and presented the early Christian fathers, the Reformers, and the New England Puritans as confirmed pre-millennialists. As he saw it, the "modern" deviation from this primitive purity had begun only recently, with Whitby and Lowman, and yet despite its clearly heretical implications it had rapidly come to prevail. Perhaps with his own education under Edwards and Hopkins in mind, Spaulding complained of a vast postmillenialist conspiracy: "All hands, learned and unlearned, have employed to propagate it, and very little has been done or said to oppose it."[88]

Like most other self-conscious premillennialists at the time, Spaulding remained well outside the center of New England orthodox Calvinism. Even taken together, these scattered figures scarcely formed a coherent doctrinal movement. Gradually, over the course of the nineteenth century, premillennialism would become more closely associated with conservative attitudes of passive resignation and apocalyptical doom, and postmillennialism with the more progressive belief in determination by human action and the possibility of social betterment. In the 1790's, however, this set of correlations still did not obtain. Spaulding himself somewhat grudgingly recognized that the "millenarians" themselves were internally divided, and they were, in fact, much more divided than he thought. If there were Calvinist Congregationalists such as himself among them, there were also Arminians, Universalists, Baptists, and even more extreme theological eccentrics as well. Some premillennialists emphasized the horrors of the conflagration; others, the promise of bliss. Some called for human endeavor; others stressed its futility. Not only did the premillennialists fall across this entire spectrum, but the most outstanding postmillennialist, Samuel Hopkins, altogether defies such generalizations. He, more than several of the premillennialists, denied the efficacy of human action and expected a period of utter desolation and judgment prior to the millennium.[89] If his terrifying vision stopped short of the burning of the world and the end of all flesh, it was more a matter of degree than of kind.

The choice between premillennialism and postmillennialism did not, then, have definite repercussions in attitude towards historical change. Still, the choice in itself was becoming a more important factor in eschatological debate. Spaulding's polemic on the subject, for all its contemporary obscurity, marks a notable departure in the history of American millennial thought. A generation later this virtually unknown and isolated pastor from Salem was rediscovered by the Millerites; indeed, he was "lauded" by them, writes a modern Seventh Day Adventist scholar.[90] The great antagonism Spaulding described between the premillennial "millennarians" and the post-millennial "millennists" was in fact just beginning the the 1790's. In its initial phases at least, this polarization seems to have had less to do with conflicts between political conservatives and progressives, pessimists and optimists, fatalists and activists, than with tensions between the New England theological elite and several forms of popular religious dissent. This conflict had a social dimension, which was essentially one of education and status. Although authors of premillennial works tended to be fairly well educated themselves, the Universalists and Baptist ministers spoke for relatively unlettered constituencies, and the popular religious literature that so often assumed a premillennial Second Coming similarly appealed to the ideas of an untutored public. Nor were the lay premillennialist writers particularly sophisticated about exegetical issues despite their often extensive education in other fields. As a group, premillennialists were critical of postmillennialists for indulging in creative, nonliteralistic interpretations of Scripture, a criticism heavily tinged with anti-intellectualism and conveying a deep resentment of the scholarly traditions of the clerical elite.

The rise of combative premillennialism in the late 1780's and the 1790's was thus a further sign of the declining theological hegemony of the established clergy, especially that of New England. Of course, this decline was itself a long drawn out process, beginning at least with the Great Awakening if not before. At the height of the earlier revivals, however, more immediate theological issues such as the demonstration of saving grace had dominated religious controversies. Then the subsequent political and military crisis of the Revolution interfered with the production of detailed interpretative treatises on prophecy. In the long run, however, the Revolution served to encourage dissident clergy and laity to challenge religious orthodoxy on eschatology as on other matters. Both the disestablishment of the churches outside New England and a general undermining of deferential values fostered the expression of deviant religious opinions. Undistinguished people took to print on a wide range of subjects, and biblical prophecy – a topic long on the minds

143

of many Americans – invited reinterpretation by various kinds of religious nonconformists.

The debate over the Second Coming arose from a newfound interest in the details of prophetic exegesis as well as from a mounting dissatisfaction with prominent New England theologians. It was, after all, a fairly technical controversy, one that presupposed both a belief in a coming millennium and a commitment to the discovery of its unfolding in the arcane language of the Book of Revelation. In this respect premillennialists and postmillennialists were agreed; they all sought to ground their millennial visions in some precise variant of biblical interpretation. Unlike the earlier revolutionary millennialists, who remained relatively vague about such exegetical matters and who were more concerned with the interpretation of immediate and continuing events, these commentators of the 1790's turned to the examination of specialized eschatological questions. The growing argument over the timing of the Messiah's return can be seen as part of a wider attempt to rationalize millennial faith in the wake of the Revolution by reconstructing it on the basis of the biblical word. Hopkins, Winchester, Osgood, Spaulding, and others similarly partook of this effort, whatever their disagreements about the coming of Christ and the nature of the millennial kingdom. The insistent literalism of the premillennialists constituted only an extreme version of a more general interpretative development.

POPE, TURKS, AND JEWS

Older technical questions also arose alongside this new premillennialist-postmillennialist dispute. Writers took up the traditional task of integrating the entire history of the church into analyses of the complex symbolism of the books of Daniel and Revelation. Which Beast or king represented which ancient state was, for example, the major interpretative issue for the New York lay millennialist Samuel Osgood, who decided that these symbols referred to the history of the Roman republic as well as to the Roman Empire, Babylon, Medo-Persia, and Greece.[91] Many exegetes also dwelt on the historical rise and decline of the papal Antichrist during the Middle Ages and the Protestant Reformation, a traditional preoccupation of Protestant millennialists that had, however, lost most of its intensity in America in the decades immediately following the French and Indian War. In the 1790's the Papacy became once again a focal point of concern. According to Samuel Langdon's major millennial treatise of 1791, the recent political upheavals promoting religious liberty in America and France, the dissolution of the Jesuit order, and the increased toleration of Protestants in many Catholic countries were all promising signs of the further deterioration of the power of the Papacy since 1760.[92]

This renewed eschatological interest in the downfall of the Pope often came along with similar predictions about the destruction of the Turkish Empire. Although the Islamic Turks had long been regarded as an antichristian power throughout the European world, and had been viewed as such in earlier English and American works of prophetic interpretation, it was only late in the eighteenth century that this became a major theme in American millennial literature. In the late 1780's both Charles Crawford and Benjamin Gale described the future demise of the Turks as an event almost equivalent to the collapse of the Papacy.[93] Samuel Osgood in 1794 insisted that one of the Beasts in Revelation represented the Turks alone, not a combination of Turkish and papal power. He expected the final defeat of the Turkish Empire to occur in 1890, after which would proceed the Second Advent and, finally, the beginning of the millennium in 1960.[94]

For Osgood, as for many of the exegetical writers of the period, the concentration on past and future events involving ancient empires, the Pope, and the Turks corresponded to their efforts to downplay the importance of contemporary political action. American millennialists of the late 1780's and 1790's often turned away from the highly politicized revolutionary millennialism of the 1770's and 1780's. The relatively detached analysis of events that were centuries and continents removed from the immediate context shifted the scene of the eschatological drama safely away.

Even a more striking example of this inclination to dwell on remote eschatological issues can be seen in a dramatic rise of interest in the conversion and restoration of the Jews. This was another old idea associated with the coming of the millennial kingdom, one drawn partly from Romans 11:26 and partly from the Jews' own messianic hopes and longings for the restoration of the dispersed Jewish people to Palestine. The belief that the conversion of the Jews to Christianity would lead to the millennium had already surfaced within English millennial Protestantism early in the seventeenth century, and the idea even induced Oliver Cromwell and other revolutionary millennial Puritans to look favorably on the admission of Jews to England in the mid-seventeenth century. In America, millennial hopes for Jewish conversion were strong among early New

England Puritans as well.[95] The Boston publication of four editions of Flavius Josephus's ancient history of the Jews testifies to continuing interest in the fate of the Jewish people into the early eighteenth century. By mid-century, however, concern about the conversion and restoration of the Jews was mild at best. During the height of American revolutionary millennial fervor in the 1770's the writings by Flavius Josephus were reprinted again; an account of the seventeenth-century Jewish messianic pretender Sabbatai Sevi appeared in a Philadelphia almanac; and several American revolutionary millennialists mentioned the Jews, if somewhat perfunctorily, in the course of describing the prophetic events that still remained to be fulfilled.[96] Apparently, however, the only American millennialist in the 1770's with an especially keen interest in the Jews was Ezra Stiles, the moderate Calvinist Congregationalist minister of Newport and later president of Yale College. Stiles established friendly relations with various members of the tiny Newport Jewish community and learned Hebrew largely in order to study Jewish apocalyptical literature. In 1774 he sought to convince a rabbinical correspondent that Jesus was the Messiah and that both Christians and Jews should expect the millennium to begin in 2300 A.D. Stiles never published his treatise on the subject, however, and his fascination with the Jews was not typical of American millennialists in the revolutionary period.[97]

Only in the late 1780's and 1790's did the conversion and restoration of the Jews again become a major theme within American millennial thought. In his *Treatise on the Millennium* Samuel Hopkins dated the conversion of the Jews before the millennium and predicted that they would first suffer greatly under the seventh vial.[98] A circular letter issued by the New York Baptist Association announced that millennial expectations were "considerably raised" by news that a convention of Jews in Amsterdam was considering whether Jesus was the true Messiah.[99] Elhanan Winchester believed that they would become Christians only during the millennium itself, when they would be restored to their exalted status as the Chosen People.[100] One American millennialist who regarded the return of the Jews to Israel as a major precondition of the millennium actually urged the Holy Roman Emperor Joseph II to grant them full toleration in order to avoid divine punishment as their oppressor.[101] David Austin went so far as to build shipping facilities to launch the exodus of the few American Jews when the right time came.

Another indication of this rising eschatological concern about the Jews in the 1790's was the appearance of several pieces of literature that dealt exclusively with the subject of the Jews. Eight more editions of Flavius Josephus appeared in the 1790's. An anonymous pamphlet entitled *A Divine Call to the Jews* was published twice in Annapolis, Maryland. It announced the beginning of a new dispensation marked by the universal spiritual presence of Christ and predicted that the Jews would accept Christianity and return to Jerusalem by the year 1836.[102] Other, similar works were reprinted from England, where there were considerably more Jews to evangelize. Joseph Priestley's *Letter to the Jews* and James Bicheno's *Friendly Address to the Jews*, arguments on behalf of Christianity in dialogue with the London Jew David Levi, were published in New York and Rhode Island in the mid-1790's.[103] Both Bicheno and Priestley were ardent millennialists, and Priestley explicitly concluded his appeal with the promise that once Jews embraced the true faith God would gather them, restore them to Palestine, and favor them once again.[104] Even more widely reprinted was a sermon that had been preached before a group of London Jews by the minister William Cooper. It recognized the Jews as the Chosen People of God, berated them for their stubborn refusal to accept Christ as the Messiah, and reminded them of their pivotal millennial role because "probably their conversion will be the great means of effecting the universal spread of the gospel."[105] A special preface appended for American readers reported that Cooper's sermon had met with such an encouraging response that a new society had been formed in London for the religious instruction of the Jews.[106]

Americans in this period also paid special attention to past instances of the supposed near conversion of the Jews. A seventeenth-century English account of a rabbinical council that met to consider the validity of the New Testament was reprinted three times in New England in the mid-1790's.[107] Its Protestant author blamed the corrupt idolatry of the Catholic Church for the fact that these rabbis refused to accept the divine mission of Christ.[108] Two editions of this piece also contained a brief narrative describing the great Jewish messianic movement of the seventeenth century inspired by Sabbatai Sevi. The extract on Sevi was drawn from another seventeenth-century English work, Paul Rycaut's *Counterfeit Messiah*, which was also reprinted in New Hampshire as a separate book in 1795. Rycaut, who had been the British consul in Sevi's native town in Turkey, attributed the success of the false messiah to a concerted and cynical campaign by rabbis convinced that if they produced no messiah of their own, Jews would shortly "embrace the christian's Messiah for the true Messiah."[109] Rycaut's wishful thinking undoubtedly remained suggestive to late eighteenth-century American millennialists again watching for signs of the conversion of the Jews.

This interest in the Jews, like that in the Turks and the Pope, transferred the main events of the Last Days a great distance away. This occurred at the same time as writers on prophecy in the 1790's increasingly turned to remote exegetical questions. Langdon's reordering of the sequences of the seals, trumpets, and vials, Osgood's expansion of the number of beastly kingdoms, Hopkins's description of the actual features of the millennial kingdom – all this involved a preoccupation with textual detail that had little if any bearing upon the interpretation of contemporary events. Similarly, the mounting debate between premillennialists and postmillennialists was basically a technical controversy, one partly motivated by resentment of the theological virtuosity of the clerical elite, but nonetheless in itself without clear or consistent social or political implications. Prophetic exposition also served as a secondary vehicle for arguments over other doctrinal issues, such as universal salvation or the immortality of souls. Several commentators of the 1790's actually disparaged political involvement in defense of higher religious concerns and denied altogether that human action could aid in the establishment of the new millennial order.

This withdrawal from politics apparently stemmed in part from disenchantment with the course of the American Revolution. Samuel Osgood, the Anti-Federalist leader who abandoned a post in the Washington administration in order to develop his views on prophecy, most clearly suggests this motivation. Yet far from discussing such grievances, these writers appear to have been more concerned to refocus American millennial aspirations on a broader, providential, and world-historical plane. Their exegetical treatises can thus be seen as efforts to generalize, systematize, and even consolidate eschatological expectations by integrating them more closely with authoritative biblical text and the concerns of traditional scholarship. Many of these authors, even those most hostile to political activism, at least briefly acknowledged the American and French revolutions as positive signs of the approaching millennium. Hopkins noted that the zealous pursuit of liberty was undermining the power of the Beast (although he never mentioned any revolution by name); Winchester, Langdon, and Osgood interpreted revolutionary upheaval as part of the pouring of the last vials; and the New England laymen Samuel Fish and Simon Hough were notably positive in their appraisals of the American republic.[110] Even though these writers all directed their attention more towards the nonpolitical ends and means of Providence, they nonetheless tended to concede some relevance to contemporary political affairs.

In the 1790's few Americans watching for signs of the times could altogether ignore the French Revolution. By the end of the decade it had overturned the French monarchy, challenged the Papacy, increased toleration for the Jews, and triggered a general European war. It had also helped to catalyze the formation of American political parties. Indeed, the very disparagement of politics in some of the prophetic writings needs partially to be understood as a reaction against the increasing politicization of the period. Many millennialists withdrew into the intricacies of prophetic exegesis and theological debate, even expressing disillusionment with the false promises of worldly action. Others, however, did not. Instead, they invested revitalized millennial expectations in the worldwide triumph of republican government.

7

Francophilic millennialism and partisan Republican ideology

> . . . the stone that smote the image became a great
> mountain, and filled the whole earth.
>
> Daniel 2:35

The nonpolitical scriptural exegesis that emerged in the late 1780's
and 1790's arose in conjunction with, and partly in reaction against,
a resurgence of highly political millennial expectations. In contrast
to the millennial scholarship that revolved around such issues as
Christ's presence during the millennium, the conversion of the Jews,
and the identification of John's trumpets and vials with long-past
historical events, many contemporary observers articulated a more
directly political message. Even the exegetes who disparaged political
action usually reserved some small place for contemporary republican revolutions in their cosmic schemes. And, whether they liked it or
not, there were always political implications imbedded in their
common prediction of forthcoming social perfection. Samuel Hopkins, for all his caution and supernatural-mindedness, still expected
a millennium of shared property, universal benevolence, and spiritual enlightenment to begin within two hundred years. Other
interpreters of prophecy, celebrating the success of the American
Revolution and watching events then transpiring in France, assumed
a more expectant, activistic, and partisan stance.

These two tendencies within the millennial publications of the
1790's were at once conflicting and mutually reinforcing. The
exegetical writing that downplayed the immediate importance of
contemporary political events nonetheless provided a more systematic and self-conscious description of the sacred, universal, and
transhistorical context that gave these events their ultimate eschatological meaning. Moreover, for all their contempt for worldly
preoccupations, these expositors' interest in such seemingly nonpolitical issues as the millennial presence of Christ and the conver-

sion of the Jews often indirectly expressed social and political concerns. The rise of aggressive premillennialism signified a mounting and emboldened resistance on the part of disaffected laity and dissenting clergy to the theological claims of the more educated and higher-status Congregationalist and Presbyterian ministries. And the curiosity about the Jews, like the tendency to incorporate the Turks and the history of ancient kingdoms into prophetic analysis, reflected a growing interest in the world outside American national boundaries during the years of revolutionary upheaval abroad.

Especially before 1798, when the Federalist clergy began to publicize a more conservative millennial message, much of the millennialism of the 1790's both revived the millennialism of the American Revolution and carried it to a farther extreme. The same designation of tyranny and monarchy as the Antichrist, the same belief that liberty and republican government foreshadowed the millennial age, the same sense that history was in the throes of great providential events, pervaded millennial statements of the early and middle 1790's. Less moderate and nationalistic than the millennialism of the 1780's, the political millennialism of the following decade set its sights on the fundamental republican transformation of the entire world and projected an even more universalistic perspective on the future than the earlier revolutionary millennialism of the 1770's. It was also more specifically egalitarian than the millennialism of the American Revolution, often incorporating an emphasis on equal rights similar to the thought of Thomas Paine and other figures of the radical Enlightenment. Stimulated by the promise of the French Revolution and further sustained by domestic partisan strife, the political millennialism of the 1790's was, until late in the decade, far more compatible with Republican than with Federalist politics.

The political millennialism of the 1790's, like that of the 1770's, rarely took the form of detailed scriptural exegesis. One example does, however, stand out as an unusually impressive effort to infuse a systematic exposition of biblical prophecy with advanced Republican thought. The liberal Congregationalist James Winthrop, Harvard librarian and son of the natural philosopher John Winthrop, published two books in Boston in the mid-1790's that were intended to rationalize the ambiguous symbolism of biblical prophecy by revealing its true ideological meaning. Winthrop approached the Book of Revelation as though it were written in hieroglyphic code, aiming, as he put it, "to divest the language of the Apocalypse of the strong metaphors, which conceals its intent, and to reduce it to the

151

more simple style of conversation."[1] The glossary of terms that preceded his double-columned verse-by-verse "translation" of the text reflected Winthrop's thoroughly political understanding of John. He defined the term "devil," for example, as a "human force not regulated by religious principles, whether in legal Governours or seditious leaders." The phrase "sea of glass," according to him, meant "the Christian Republic founded in truth, in defense, and in common rights of mankind."[2] Obviously keeping America closely in mind, he believed the reign of the Beast to have ended in 1620, "when the church found a resting place in America," and described the millennial kingdom as a federation of states under constitutional law.[3]

The most original contribution of his second volume, which contained extensive historical analysis, was its emphasis on the millennial promise of contemporary republican revolutions. In the millennium, "all oppressive distinctions will be done away, and the government committed to the genuine lovers of equal right, to the people of the saints of the Most High." An enthusiastic admirer of the Jacobins, Winthrop now dated the end of the antichristian reign not at the founding of Plymouth Colony but at the outbreak of the French Revolution.[4]

Winthrop's unique mixture of extreme rationalism, radical political sympathies, and labored biblical exegesis understandably failed to enlist the support of the wider religious community.[5] His was precisely the kind of speculation that, in the minds of theologians like Winchester and Hopkins, gave political readings of prophecy a bad name. Yet, however objectionable such a brazen attempt to politicize Scripture may have been, many American millennialists watching the French Revolution were thinking along much the same lines. Winthrop had simply exaggerated what were fairly common prophecies of a millennium of equal rights and Christian republican government, prophecies that blended well with the ideology of the developing Republican Party. His writings were distinguished from other Republican millennialist publications not so much by their political values as by their liberal rationalism and their highly detailed "translation" of Scripture. Republican millennialists in the 1790's typically drew upon a more general and impressionistic understanding of biblical prophecy, celebrating the millennial possibilities of the French Revolution without sharing Winthrop's wholesale reinterpretation of biblical text.

The French Revolution and the European war clearly provided the greatest single stimulus for the growth of eschatological speculation.

Even nonpolitical works of scriptural exegesis often referred to the disorder in Europe, and whether or not they would have been written in any case, the sense of immediate crisis certainly added to the relevancy of their predictions. Also in response to these European developments, millennial ideas rose back to the surface in England in the 1790's after being largely submerged for over a century. Many popular English prophetic publications advanced a millennial interpretation of the French Revolution and were rapidly reprinted in America, which further encouraged American millennialists to look overseas.

Not all of the favorable response of American millennialists to the French Revolution in the early 1790's was Republican. In the beginning of the decade, several northeastern clergymen viewed the French Revolution as the spearhead of the millennium and then later became Federalist critics of France. Beginning already in 1793 and 1794, however, the millennial interpretation of the French Revolution was becoming associated far more with emerging Republican ideology. Especially before the XYZ Affair of 1798 shattered the already declining reputation of the Directory, the French Revolution provided the most coherent ideological focus for the critics of Federalist policy. By appealing to its example, and by drawing a connection to the supposed precedent of the American Revolution, Republicans saw themselves in terms of an ongoing struggle of liberty and republicanism against tyrannical (above all British) monarchy. During these initial years of political party polarization, the political attitudes of most biblical millennialists who commented on the French Revolution ranged from ardent to qualified support for the French as allies in holy warfare against both tyranny and Catholicism. Only in the final years of the decade did the most confirmed and vocal Federalist clergymen, such as Timothy Dwight and Jedidiah Morse, publicize their completely negative apocalyptical view of the French as the soldiers of the Antichrist. In the mid-1790's American millennial ideas about the French Revolution were usually positive, even enthusiastic, still expressing typically Republican rather than Federalist political sentiments.

The political significance of this francophilic millennialism has been overlooked, for historians have generally analyzed Republican ideology as an expression of the liberal Enlightenment or the secular civic republican tradition.[6] Inasmuch as Jefferson himself, a Deist and friend of the French philosophes, has been regarded as the chief spokesman for the Republican Party, it is no wonder that the religious dimension of Republican thought has usually been missed.

Millennial hopes for the French Revolution were always more a part of popular culture than of explicit political party debate. Most of the authors of the francophilic millennial literature were foreign, anonymous, or fairly obscure. The ones that can be identified were, however, generally Baptists and Presbyterians, denominations that contributed heavily to Republican ranks. There were, in addition, a few Anglicans and Methodists – also largely Republican, if not typically millennialist, denominations – who also expressed positive millennial hopes for the French Revolution.[7] The millennial celebration of the French Revolution probably appealed to many religious Protestants affiliated with the Republican Party.

REVOLUTIONARY SIGNS OF THE TIMES

There was widespread agreement in the 1790's among American millennialists of varying religious and political persuasions that the outbreak of the French Revolution portended the imminence of the Last Days. Already in 1791, Samuel Langdon, a moderate Congregationalist and later Federalist, noted contemporary events in France, along with recent blows to Catholicism and the success of the American Revolution, as signs of the forthcoming collapse of the Beast.[8] This sense of expectancy grew still more pronounced in the following years after the declaration of the French Republic, the Jacobin attacks on the Catholic Church, and the outbreak of the European war. In newspapers, sermons, and speeches numerous Americans across a wide regional and religious spectrum proclaimed that events in Europe would soon bring the fulfillment of millennial prophecy. These pervasive millennial expectations were, moreover, bolstered by the impressive revival of English millennialism at the same time. Both seventeenth-century and contemporary English millennial writings about France were given extensive publicity in America. Although the political ideology underlying such works was not always clear, their typically enthusiastic support for the French Revolution gave religious reinforcement to the francophilic sentiments of the newly formed Republican opposition.

With a few exceptions, Federalist millennialists did not publish their francophobic millennial theories until 1798. Evidently the only writer in America in the first half of the decade who did intermix an interpretation of prophecy with a hostile outlook on France was the little-known West Indian poet and abolitionist Charles Crawford, who had already developed his essentially nonpolitical eschatological theories prior to the outbreak of the French Revolution. Crawford had come to America from England, and, inasmuch as he had political views, they were loyally British. In his *Observations upon the Revolution in France* of 1793 he denounced French republicanism and hoped the French would restore the Constitution of 1789, which he thought best approximated the English constitutional monarchy. He defended the existence of the aristocracy and the House of Lords, although he conceded to the Americans that it was unwise to create a nobility from scratch. He was more in phase with American opinion in his attack on ecclesiastical establishments, and, taking a middle ground between Paine and Burke, concluded that the French Revolution's attack on Catholicism proved that religiously – if not politically – it was a positive step towards the millennium.[9]

However moderate for an Englishman, Crawford's anti-Jacobin millennialism evidently fell on deaf ears in America in 1793. No other writer then considering the millennial significance of the French Revolution took a comparably critical stance. In the United States in the mid-1790's the symbolism of biblical prophecy was still too closely associated with republican revolution to serve as a vehicle for antirevolutionary ideology. At the most, theological commentators like Hopkins and Winchester sought to devalue the millennial significance of politics altogether. The vast majority of those who did apply the prophecies to worldly affairs identified with the French republican cause and, in their exultations over the collapse of the monarchy, revived and expanded upon the revolutionary millennial outlook of the 1770's.

From New England as far south as South Carolina, scattered articles appeared in the American press that applauded the French Revolution in millennial terms. Millennial extracts from private letters by English correspondents jubilant over the French Revolution were printed verbatim. "All is working in Europe for the freedom of men [and] the downfall of Antichrist," reported one such letter in the *Boston Gazette*.[10] Another printed in the *New-Jersey Journal* described "the annihilation of anti-Christian hierarchy" in France as "the events of the latter days . . . preparatory to the commence [sic] of the kingdom of Christ in its glory."[11] The same spirit of millennial enthusiasm for the French Revolution also possessed American newspaper writers from various parts of the country. One column bearing the title "Millennium" printed in the Boston *Columbian Centinel* in 1793 concluded that the French struggle against the forces of "slavery, bigotry and superstition" meant the "glorious period foretold in sacred writ appears to be not far distant." The anonymous author even suggested a date: "about the 20th year of the nineteenth century."[12] Thomas Greenleaf's partisan Republican *New York Journal* likewise rejoiced that the French Revolution was hastening the day when all kings, "like *Babylon* the great," would fall, and a millennial state of "universal freedom from sin and slavery" would begin.[13] In the *State Gazette of South-Carolina* a piece signed "A Hater of Tyrants" quoted from biblical passages condemning kings and predicted, in the rhetoric of the French Revolution, that the "universal fraternity" of "tolerance, liberty, and equality" foretold in the gospel would inevitably prevail despite strenuous monarchical opposition.[14]

The idea that the French Revolution was moving towards the establishment of the millennial kingdom was still more widely disseminated in numerous published sermons and public orations. Especially in the years 1793 and 1794, despite the fact that many leading New England clergymen were already withholding endorsements of the Jacobin government, several Congregationalist ministers who later supported the Federalist Party were still capable of celebrating the French republican cause as a positive step towards millennial "truth, liberty, and peace."[15] The Boston Baptist clergyman Samuel Stillman, who deviated from the majority of his denomination in also developing Federalist sympathies, likewise still borrowed the words of Thomas Paine to praise the French Revolution as leading to "the universal establishment of the rights of man, and the peaceful kingdom of Jesus Christ."[16] Only as party lines became more clearly drawn in the second half of the decade would these New England ministers come to criticize the religion and politics of the French Revolution as part of their more fully articulated Federalist creed.

If several Protestant ministers did switch from vocal support to public condemnation of the French, most millennialists who rejoiced over the French Revolution in the 1790's, especially after 1795, were more closely identified with the Republicans than the Federalists. In New England several figures in addition to the eccentric James Winthrop challenged the reigning Federalism of the region and interpreted the French Revolution in millennial terms. The aged Samuel Adams, who parted company with most of his revolutionary followers in his Republicanism, delivered a speech to the Massachusetts legislature in 1794 expressing the hope that the liberty and equality pursued by the French Revolution would result in "that state of peace and prosperity, which antient prophets and sages have foretold."[17] In Ridgfield, Connecticut, a Baptist preacher named Elias Lee divulged his equally ardent Republican and francophilic convictions in a sermon entitled *The Dissolution of Earthly Monarchies*. He pointedly defended the French regicides against criticism and insisted that by fighting for liberty and republicanism, the Jacobins, like the American colonists before them, were striving to "pursue the spirit of monarchy to its very last recess; and completely demolish the empire and kingdom of Antichrist."[18] Despite the fact that even committed Republicans generally lost their initial ardor for France over the course of the decade, Simon Hough, the anticlerical premillennialist of Stockbridge, Massachusetts, took issue with the rising francophobia of Federalist New England as late as 1799. Hough actually advanced a more political, francophilic, and Republican analysis of the Book of Revelation than the one he had developed in 1792. He now rejoiced that the "fire of Liberty" started by the American Revolution was "caught by the French . . . and burnt in Europe," destroying the titles and privileges of the nobility in preparation for the millennial day.[19]

In New England millennial statements favorable to the French were always less common than in the middle and southern states, where there were many more Presbyterians, Baptists, Anglicans, and members of other Protestant denominations who gravitated towards the Republican Party. Only a few influential clergymen south of New England switched from francophilic millennialism in the middle of the decade to francophobic Federalism at the end.[20] Far more typical throughout the 1790's were expressions of millennial hope for France, hopes proclaimed by laymen and ministers of numerous denominations.

The northern cities of New York and Philadelphia, both the scenes of strident party conflict in the 1790's, produced ardently Republican millennial interpretations of the French Revolution. Probably the most prominent francophilic millennialist in America was the influential Presbyterian clergyman Samuel Miller. His printed sermon of 1793 to the democratic Tammany Society declared that the "wonderful" French Revolution, however "sullied by irreligion and vice," was fundamentally Christian and "a great link in the chain, that is drawing on the reign of universal harmony and peace."[21] His perspective on France was evidently shared not only by such other Republican Presbyterian clergymen as John McKnight and John Rodgers but by many rank-and-file New York Republicans as well. In 1796, by which time the French Revolution had become a heated political issue, the Republican *New York Journal* reported that an assembly of the Tammany Society and the Society of Mechanics toasted the French as well as the American Revolution and sang an ode rejoicing over the present progress of liberty and knowledge through the European world as a step towards "Immanuel's Reign."[22] This popular Republican political gathering also featured a sermon by Joseph Pilmore – a former Methodist minister who had by then become a leader of the "evangelical" movement within the Church of England – which was based on a millennial text from Isaiah.[23] And in Philadelphia as late as 1798, while New England Federalist pulpits were shaking with denuciations of France, the Baptist minister William Staughton preached a sermon dating the end of the reign of the Antichrist in 1789, "when the Assembly in France asserted civil and religious liberty."[24] While acknowledging the blemish of French infidelity, he nonetheless interpreted the spread of natural rights through the French Revolution as one of the main preconditions of the millennium.

Such millennial hopes for the French Revolution evidently extended into Protestant Republican circles in more sparsely settled western regions as well. Among the most francophilic millennialists of the period was a Welsh Baptist immigrant named Morgan John Rhees who settled in western Pennsylvania. Rhees was described by a biographer as a popular preacher "followed by admiring crowds wherever he spoke," a friend of Benjamin Rush and Joseph Priestley, and, despite his rejection of liberal religion, an ardent and steadfast supporter of Jefferson and "democratic principles."[25] In a printed sermon originally delivered to soldiers at a western military outpost near the Ohio River on the Fourth of July, 1795, Rhees deplored the "excesses" of the Terror but expected that "the energy of the [French] nation" would soon wash away the irresponsible "sons of faction." Mixing a paean to republicanism with the millennial imagery of the Book of Daniel, he envisioned the revolution spreading "the perfect law of liberty" through the whole earth.[26] Similar sentiments were expressed in upstate New York by John Blair Smith, the Presbyterian president of Union College at Schenectady. In 1797 Smith told members of a missionary society assembled at a Dutch Reformed church that the French Revolution was sounding the seventh trumpet of the Book of Revelation, which announced the "boundless prospect of universal liberty, universal reformation, and universal peace."[27] In the more remote location of Troy, New York, the anonymous "husbandman" author of a religious pamphlet entitled *A Northern Light; or New Index to the Bible* conveyed a surprisingly radical francophilic vision as late as 1800. Offering a simple, commonsense exposition of various doctrinal mysteries of Christianity, it maintained that the seven thunders of the Book of

Revelation represented the republics that "have arisen up out of the ruins of papal and arbitrary government, and have for their basis that great principles of nature – All men are born equal and free." The heroic two witnesses were designated as "the equal rights of man," and the demonic unclean spirits as the combined powers of Europe at war with France. Comparing Jefferson's Declaration of Independence, Article I of the Constitution of the French Republic, and Christ's declaration of the Golden Rule in Luke 6:31, the author concluded that "the modern doctrine of the rights of man" was "the same doctrine taught by our Savior when on earth." Although he regarded the recent assumption of power by the Directory as the prophesied death of the witnesses, this obscure farmer and radical biblical millennialist predicted their resurrection in 1801 and the worldwide commencement of the millennium in the late nineteenth century.[28]

In the southern states, where little religious literature ever found its way into print, the evidence of francophilic millennialism is sparse but impressive nevertheless. On Bastille Day, 1794, for example, the Presbyterian James Malcomson delivered a sermon in Charleston, South Carolina, that resounded with millennial expectation. Although he briefly criticized the Jacobins, he urged his listeners to "rejoice in the prospect" afforded by the French Revolution, which he saw as foreshadowing "that happy period, when the demon of tyranny will cease to oppress and afflict mankind."[29] The next year in Virginia the steadfast Jeffersonian Republican and Anglican Bishop James Madison likewise struck a millennial chord as he described God spreading the same "great and glorious revolution" to France that had already begun in America. Citing the words of Isaiah, he insisted that tyrants "shall be chased as the chaff of the mountain before the wind," that "the complete restoration of the human race to their inherent rights would be accomplished, throughout the globe."[30] Probably the most intriguing example of southern francophilic millennialism was, however, an anonymous work published in Virginia in 1796 under the elaborate title *Twilight's Orations, or Revelations of Politics, in XVII Chapters, or The Revelation of Politics and New Moral Liberty, or Temple of Jesus Christ, in The Historic Page of Jews and Christians.* The author, apparently a Baptist, was primarily concerned to show that "the Kingdom of Christ and new moral government of the World" would come once political democracy fully transcended mere "animal nature" and assumed the truly selfless and Christian "new human will."[31] Primarily an exhortation to faith, the argument was continuously interwoven with egalitarian

political values and included an explicit endorsement of the revolutionary French unicameral system of government.[32]

Not only was literature that rejoiced over the French Revolution
published by American Republican millennialists of various denominations and regions, but throughout the 1790's millennial writings
that lent support to their arguments were imported from abroad.
The most explicitly political of these foreign publications was the
English Baptist James Bicheno's *Explanation of Scriptural Prophecy*,
originally written between 1793 and 1795 and rapidly reprinted in
many parts of the United States between 1794 and 1797.[33] Bicheno
was a radical defender of the French Revolution, and by the second
half of the decade his highly ideological and intensely francophilic
reading of Scripture could only have been read sympathetically
in America by Republicans. According to his interpretation, the
prophecy in Revelation 11:13 of the falling of the tenth part of the
city was currently being fulfilled in the French Revolution; the second
Beast with two horns stood for the Capet dynasty; and the mysterious
number of the Beast, 666, corresponded to the numerical value of the
letters of Louis XVI's name written in Latin.[34] Bicheno concluded
that Satan would be bound and the millennium begin in 1819. In
Boston his fellow Baptist Samuel Stillman referred to Bicheno when
he, too, still welcomed the French Revolution as the falling of the
tenth part of the city in his thanksgiving sermon of 1794.[35] The view
that the tenth part of the city fell in the French Revolution continued
to find endorsement as late as 1800 in a prophetic tract by the
Connecticut school inspector Benjamin Farnham. Farnham predicted and welcomed French victory over the English and, as did
Bicheno, looked forward to the final demise of the Beast within the
next twenty years.[36]

Those supporters of France who saw the tenth part of the city
falling with the ancien régime drew legitimation from earlier
readings of the Book of Revelation by English Puritans and French
Huguenots. Understandably these seventeenth-century Protestants
had often viewed the French Catholic kingdom as a personification
of the Beast and, in what later seemed as marvelously prescient
visions, foretold its destruction by the forces of God just before the
millennium. In the 1790's many prophetic works by these earlier foes
of the French monarchy were cited and reprinted in both England
and America, bolstering contemporary millennial interpretations of
the French Revolution. Both Bicheno and Stillman, for example,
referred to the writings of the Puritan leader Thomas Goodwin and

the French Calvinist preacher Pierre Jurieu. Both of these radical Protestants of the seventeenth century had specifically singled out the French state as the tenth part of the city destined for doom.

From the perspective of the 1790's other authoritative figures of the past had also apparently foreseen the French Revolution and considered it as one of the final fulfillments of prophecy. The most impressive of the seventeenth-century predictions was attributed to the revolutionary martyr and Presbyterian clergyman Christopher Love, whose supposed prophecies had already been revived once before in New England during the French and Indian War. Whereas in the 1750's the apocalyptical events Love was said to have foreseen were all slated to take place between 1756 and 1763, in the 1790's the dates were revised: The earthquakes were to occur in 1779; the wars in Germany and America, in 1780; the destruction of the Pope and Babylon, in 1790; increased faith and the appearance of "a great man," in 1795; and – after more earthquakes and the reddening of the moon described in Revelation – the dawning of the millennium in 1805. Once again, these predictions seemed so uncannily close to the truth that they received a great deal of attention in both England and America. In case the connection to contemporary events was not clear enough, one editor pointed out that Germans had fought in the American Revolutionary War, thereby confirming the vision of both German and American wars in the year 1780.[37] Between 1793 and 1795 Love's *Prophecies* went through at least fifteen independent editions in New England alone. It was also extracted as a special item of human interest in several almanacs, probably the most popular genre of American literature at the time, distributed throughout the northern United States.[38] At least one newspaper article on Love's predictions even appeared in what was then the far west, in the Lexington *Kentucky Gazette*.[39]

Another earlier English millennialist who aroused considerable interest in England and the United States was Robert Fleming, a late seventeenty-century follower of William of Orange who had been influenced by the anti-French preaching of Pierre Juricu. What made Fleming's interpretation of the Book of Revelation particularly alluring to this later generation was his choice of the date 1794 as the time of the humbling of the French monarchy. The salient part of Fleming's predictions appeared in 1793 in the *New York Magazine*, one of the few successful American periodicals of the period, in "Father Hutchins's" almanac of New York, and in a more extended edition in Boston in 1794.[40] A widely reprinted critique of Paine's *Age*

161

of Reason used Fleming as well as Jurieu to argue that the Book of Revelation had accurately "predicted the French revolution . . . at the very period in which it happened."[41]

The prophecies of Fleming, Jurieu, Goodwin, and Love achieved even wider circulation as part of an edited volume entitled *Prophetic Conjectures on the French Revolution*. An English collection of visionary proclamations concerning the downfall of France and the subsequent coming of the millennial kingdom, this book was reprinted in Northampton, Philadelphia, and Baltimore, appearing even in German translation.[42] The English editor compiled extracts from numerous authors who had supposedly predicted the French Revolution, including an impressive range of English, French, Irish, Scottish, Swedish, Calvinist, Anglican, Baptist, and sectarian figures living between the mid-sixteenth and mid-eighteenth centuries. This great pile of evidence was clearly aimed to curb suspicions that these predictions had been merely haphazard or coincidental. Rather, the editor insisted in his extensive commentary on the compiled material, each of these students of prophecy had independently arrived at the correct interpretation of biblical millennial prophecy.[43]

Despite the fact that in England these rediscovered seventeenth-century prophecies were apparently read as critical of both the French monarchy and the French revolutionary state, in America they seem to have been given an enthusiastically prorevolutionary reading.[44] The editor of the often reprinted *Prophetic Conjectures*, although denying that he was an uncritical apologist for the Jacobins and deploring the infidelity and Terror in France, insisted that the republic would inevitably soon overcome these flaws. In a warning to the English that must have sounded sweet to American Republican ears he declared, "If the voice from heaven cry, 'REVOLUTION!' in vain would all the powers on earth attempt to arrest the motions of these wheels."[45]

The widespread fascination with prophetic luminaries of the past at times found expression in even more extreme kinds of sensationalism. For example, one entirely fabricated publication of the mid-1790's, entitled *A Remarkable Prophecy*, purported to be a text found on a stone inlaid in gold Hebrew letters that had been buried in France for six hundred years. Much like the prophecy of Christopher Love, it told of a rebellion in France against the king in 1790, the building up of a general European war, the appearance of Gog and Magog waging war against all nations in 1797, general destruction in 1798, the defeat of Gog and Magog by a descendant of David in 1799, and the establishment of the millennium in 1800. Its radical political perspective was revealed in a footnote defining Gog and Magog as the opponents of "liberty and equality or genuine Christianity."[46] The millennium was likewise to be an era of "friendship, equality, and . . . love."[47] Also an originally English production, the *Remarkable Prophecy* was extensively reprinted in American both as a separate publication and in almanacs and newspapers that reached into most regions of the country.[48] It is doubtful that many people took it seriously. Perhaps it was even intended as a spoof on contemporary credulity. However, at least one millennial writer in New England gave it the benefit of his doubt, citing "the Quarry-stone (if any such there be)" along with Love's prophecy as evidence that the Antichrist was about to collapse.[49] Whether or not it was actually widely believed, the repeated appearance and apparently common knowledge of this apocryphal prophecy reflected a burgeoning popular interest in millennial speculations about the French Revolution.

PROPHETIC PRETENDERS AND RADICAL SECTS

Among the many English prophetic curiosities that attracted widespread attention in America, by far the most sensational was the messianic mission of Richard Brothers.[50] A retired naval lieutenant who had fought for the British in the American Revolutionary War, Brothers created a minor disturbance in London in 1790 when he refused to swear a loyalty oath in order to receive his pension. Payment was stopped and Brothers was removed to a workhouse. Increasingly destitute and deranged, he received numerous divine visions. In response to these revelations he espoused pacifism, believed first that God would destroy London in the year 1791 and then that his own intervention had averted the disaster, and in 1792 became convinced of the sacred purpose of the French Revolution. He evolved a conception of himself as "the Revealed Prophet of the Hebrews," chosen by God to gather the Jews (including "hidden" Jews such as himself) and lead them to Palestine as antichristian monarchical governments fell throughout Europe. Perhaps because of a temporary imprisonment due to his repeated failure to pay his rent, he grew highly antagonistic to the English state. During these years he worked on the streets of London as a faith healer, even at times drawing large crowds. But it was only in 1794 that Brothers began to attract a real following.

The general political and economical crisis in England caused by the war with France suddenly gave Brothers's pacifist and antimonarchical message new meaning. Among his first disciples were the engraver William Sharp, one of the founding members of the radical London Corresponding Society, and two confirmed millennialist artisans, the carpenter John Wright and the printer William Bryan, who had embraced the prophetic ideas of French Mystical Freemasonry in the late 1780's. At the instigation of his early followers, a book of writings by Brothers called *A Revealed Knowledge of the Prophecies and Times* first appeared in print early in 1794. In it Brothers told of his various visions and quoted at length from supportive scriptural text. He announced his mission to the Jews, recounted warnings he had made to the King and William Pitt to keep out of the war with the French – "a people that have the judgment of God in their favor" – characterized George III and other monarchs as the four Beasts of the Book of Revelation destined for doom, and foretold a tremendous earthquake that would swallow up Parliament, most of London, and parts of the rest of the world in June 1795.[51] Between the time of its first appearance and the summer of 1795, the *Revealed Knowledge* attracted an enormous amount of attention in London. It went through several editions, inspired the conversion of Brothers's most prominent disciple, distinguished oriental scholar and member of Parliament Nathaniel Brassey Halhed, and provoked extensive criticism and ridicule in the British press. Brothers received flocks of visitors at his home. The government was sufficiently worried to arrest him on charges of treason in March 1795, after which he was declared legally insane and kept in an asylum until 1806. Despite his incarceration (which Brothers himself interpreted as a fulfillment of his prophecies) there is evidence that many Londoners continued to believe that some catastrophe would occur there in June 1795.

Because Brothers's London following never congregated, it is impossible to determine its actual size. The amount of publicity given his prophecies, as well as his timely arrest before the fateful month of June, suggests that he wielded considerable influence. In London, then under wartime conditions and undergoing a severe economic decline, his extravagant attacks on the Crown and prediction of the destruction of the city understandably made an impression. It is more puzzling why Brothers aroused so much interest in America. His *Revealed Knowledge* ranks as one of the best sellers of the 1790's: It went through at least seven complete editions in the peak year of 1795 alone, including one in German, and after the excitement had begun to die down in London it continued through three more in 1796 and 1797. Philadelphia printed the largest number, but places of publication ranged from Delaware to Massachusetts and even included such remote locations as Harrisburg, Pennsylvania.[52] Works defending Brothers's eschatology by his scholarly disciple Halhed also appeared in several American editions.[53] These were supplemented by one of the major orthodox critiques, the English Calvinist Thomas Williams's *Age of Credulity*, which characterized Brothers as one of the false prophets of Revelation and presented a detailed refutation of Halhed's biblical scholarship.[54] Like the prophecy attributed to Christopher Love, selections from Brothers and Halhead also appeared in many of the popular almanacs of the mid-1790's.[55]

As in the case of the *Remarkable Prophecy* and the widely disseminated predictions by Christopher Love, there is no indication that Americans accepted the fantastic visions of Brothers at face value. In the almanacs, at least, they seem to have been offered casually, as conversation pieces. Nor did Brothers inspire a tangible following in the United States, as he did in London. Yet many people were evidently intrigued enough to purchase the entire volume of his writings, and it is striking that for all the publicity given his visions, they never aroused the pervasive ridicule that they did in England. Partly this was because he never posed an equivalent threat, but it was probably also because more Americans found his message congenial. When brief extracts from the *Revealed Knowledge* were selected for almanacs, it was usually one of the passages that designated George III as a Beast.[56] And, in the mid-1790's, his glorification of the French republic as God's weapon against the monarchical forces of the Antichrist expressed strong francophilic sentiments similar to those of the budding Republican Party.

Brothers was simply the most bizarre of several eschatological oddities that aroused widespread fascination – if not committed belief – among Americans sympathetic to France expectantly watching events overseas. The only comparable prophet to emerge in America, however, was the New Jersey Presbyterian clergyman David Austin. Although equally colorful in his own way, he failed to attract a following close to the size of Brothers's and certainly never posed a danger to the stability of the American state. Inasmuch as he preached a political message at all, it was simply enthusiastic support of the American nation. Virtually all of his writings, both before and after his disastrous false prophecy of 1796, amplified the originally Edwardsian theme that America would be the seat of the millennium. In 1794, already betraying a psychological instability in the eccentricity of his views, he announced that the Kingdom of Christ had "begun on the Fourth of July, 1776, when the birth of MAN-Child – hero of civil and religious liberty took place in these United States."[57] At the end of the decade, after he had faded into obscurity, he lambasted the clergy for its political attack on the French Revolution and Freemasonry, but he was neither an ardent francophile nor a committed Republican critic of the Federalist Party. On the one hand, Austin saw the French Revolution as an extension of the American Revolution, likewise establishing civil and religious liberty that would open the way for spiritual regeneration and the millennium.[58] He welcomed the French attack on Catholicism, and once enthusiastically predicted the downfall of "mystical Babylon" in 1810.[59] On the other hand, he denied that the French revolutionary state was, like the American, a Christian power. In 1794 he actually took a much more hostile view of the French Revolution than most of his clerical colleagues, describing the Jacobins as "a lawless banditti – a race of infidels – men, who profess to 'know no God but Liberty, and no Gospel but their Constitution.'"[60]

Later, after his mind was clearly unhinged, he fluctuated between farther extremes in his assessment of France: He hailed Napoleon as a millennial agent who was spreading the glories of the American Revolution; he objected to his contemporaries who would cast France rather than the Pope in the role of the Beast; and yet he still described revolutionary France as a kind of antimillennium sabotaging the real one.[61] Throughout the period, despite these vacillations in his perspective on France, he formally adhered to the view that the millennium would come in two stages, first through a political revolution, then a spiritual revolution, and he maintained that the American national government was leading the way.[62] In the terms of his often extravagant imagery – which can be read either literally or metaphorically – Washington, D.C., was the New Jerusalem, George Washington the political equivalent of the Messiah, and he himself the new Joshua.[63]

Because Austin published so much and wrote in an evocative symbolic style, historians of eighteenth-century millennialism have tended to exaggerate his importance and misconstrue his political message. He has been viewed both as a radical and influential Jeffersonian Republican who kept American Revolutionary millennialism alive, and as representative of the more conservative republican millennialism of the Federalist New England clergy.[64] Actually he was always much more a simple nationalist than a committed republican of either Federalist or Republican persuasion. He often glorified the Federalist President Adams while upbraiding the

Federalist ministry for its political views. Although he transferred his allegiance to Jefferson in 1800 (evidently hurt that Adams refused to confer with him), he denied that it made much of a difference who won.[65] After 1797 it is, in any case, questionable whether he represented anyone other than himself.

Other self-proclaimed prophets in America recruited more dedicated followings than Austin did, but without casting their millennial message in a directly political framework. In rural New England in the late 1770's, the leaders of Freewill Baptism and backcountry Universalism received revelations from God that convinced them of the imminence of the Second Coming of Christ. By the 1790's, however, these groups were beginning to develop institutional structures that would propel them beyond their early charismatic sectarianism and establish them as more conventional religious denominations. Other millennialist sects established in the 1770's that were more tenaciously sectarian and explicitly messianic, the Shakers and the Universal Friends, also stood steadfastly aloof from the secular political world.[66] It is not surprising that they, too, failed to find inspiration in the radical republicanism generated by the French Revolution, although in 1795 Jemima Wilkinson, the leader of the Universal Friends, did give the visitor La Rochefoucauld-Liancourt a copy of *Christopher Love's Prophecies*.[67] The millennial strategy of these communitarian sects was perfectionistic withdrawal, not revolutionary change. The Universal Friends living in their small "New Jerusalem" on the New York frontier, the much more numerous Shakers living in several settlements according to their "Millennial Laws," both laid what they saw as the groundwork of the Kingdom of God on earth. For them the establishment of the millennial order by the loyal apostles of the new faith would presumably serve as an example to the rest of the world.

Although drawing from a different constituency and seeking the millennium on a more purely spiritual plane, another sectarian group that had begun to proclaim the beginning of the new dispensation was the Swedenborgians.[68] In the late 1780's and 1790's Swedenborgians started to attract converts in the Philadelphia area, Baltimore, and farther south – especially among German and English immigrants, and ex-Episcopalians, Baptists, and Methodists. From the complex theological system formulated by Emanuel Swedenborg in Sweden some years before, these apparently quite educated (and often wealthy) Americans drew a mixture of biblical religion, mysticism, and eccentric science that closely resembled other European post-Enlightenment intellectual movements such as mes-

167

merism and spiritualism that would later cross the Atlantic as well.[69]
According to Swedenborg's elaborate eschatology, the Last Judgment had taken place in the "spiritual world" of the afterlife in 1757, the Second Coming had assumed the form of the divine revelations to Swedenborg, and the New Jerusalem was the Swedenborgian New Church that had been founded in the spiritual world in 1770 but would make slow progress on earth. The heart of Swedenborg's doctrine was the idea of the "correspondences," which taught that all items in the natural world, including every word of the Bible, had a hidden double meaning, spiritual as well as literal. Aside from an opposition to slavery and a tendency to excuse adultery in marriages that lacked spiritual communion, there were no directly social or political teachings. Orthodox Christian anti-Jacobins charged Swedenborg with being one of the infidels who caused the French Revolution, an accusation Swedenborgians emphatically denied.[70] Indeed, the Swedenborgians' numbers included such staunch conservatives as the American Loyalist Jacob Duché. Swedenborg's vivid description of heavenly paradise evidently inspired some later socialists, but the one semicooperative Swedenborgian society attempted by the former plantation owner Robert Carter in the 1790's failed after one year. In England there was an indirect historical connection between Swedenborgianism and the early disciples of Richard Brothers by the way of French Mystical Freemasonry, but American Swedenborgians evidently steered clear of the millennial enthusiasm over the French Revolution.[71]

REPUBLICAN UNIVERSALISM AND ANTI-CATHOLICISM

Throughout the 1790's those who endorsed the French Revolution as a step towards millennial perfection typically conceived of it as the extension of an originally American republican ideal. As patriots they congratulated their fellow citizens that the American Revolution was the source of inspiration for the monumental changes occurring overseas. Much of the millennial rhetoric of the 1790's did, indeed, have precedence in the American Revolutionary movement. The radical republican equations of monarchy with the Antichrist and liberty with Christianity, as well as the notion that the American republic was at the vanguard of a world transformation, were older revolutionary millennial themes that were simply revived in their application to France. The millennial language of the 1790's was not, however, entirely the same as that of the 1770's. The words of the radical Enlightenment, "equality" and "the rights of man," were much more pervasive than they had been earlier. In the middle and late 1790's these had, moreover, a partisan as much as a patriotic ring. The frequent reminders about America's vital example to the French Revolution not only flattered American national pride but contributed to the growth of a new and divisive Republican ideology.

The egalitarian thrust of this francophilic millennialism high-lighted values at the ideological center of American political radical-ism in the mid-1790's. In the context of emerging party conflict, biblical millennialism added to the development of what was a decidedly left-wing Republican social ideal. In addition to being more egalitarian than the earlier American revolutionary millennial thought of the 1770's, the francophilic millennialism of the 1790's was also increasingly universalistic. In its universalism as well as its egalitarianism it resonated with the francophilic Republican radical-ism of the period. For all the appeals to American nationalism, millennial writers set their sights not just on America, or even on Europe, but on the entire globe. The French Revolution seemed to demonstrate beyond doubt what only the most audacious patriots in the 1770's had dared to suppose, that the liberty and republicanism established in America would immediately spread to the rest of the world.

In its universalism, especially, the political millennialism of this period not only revived features of American revolutionary millen-nialism but also closely integrated it with the concerns of traditional Protestant eschatology. Indeed, the worldwide scenario of the francophilic millennialists took directly into account the orthodox eschatological milestones elaborated by nonpolitical scriptural com-mentary. As the minister Joseph Lyman of Hatfield, Massachusetts, traced the sequence of future events, the later glory would "take its rise" in America, radiate through the hitherto "enslaved nations of the eastern continent," and then spread to the more standard objects of prophetic concern: Jews, Mohammedans, papists, and other infidels throughout the world. "Liberty and truth and grace shall return and dwell on earth, again, and all shall know the Lord, from the least, even, unto the greatest."[72] As remote as the connection may appear on the surface, many millennialists in the 1790's saw the conversion of the Jews and the downfall of the Turks following ineluctably on the heels of the French Revolution.[73]

The connecting link that drew these together was, above all, the French attack on the Catholic Church. The Revolution seemed to possess universal significance not only because it promised the spread of American liberty and republicanism to the rest of the world, but also because it directly challenged the traditional archenemy of Protestant Christianity, the Pope. In its concern with the Papacy, the Turks, and the Jews, the universalism of the republican millennialism of the 1790's intersected with that of the nonpolitical prophetic exegesis of the same period. In both cases, visions expanded far beyond the American continent to encompass the world, and both sought to relate their millennial speculations to traditional eschatological issues. In these respects the two major tendencies in American millennial thought were mutually reinforcing. For the radical republican millennialists, however, the collapse of the Catholic Church had political as well as religious significance. The Pope was viewed not only as the chief propagator of false religious beliefs but as the major source of civil tyranny in the Western world.

By the 1790's the identification of the Papacy and tyranny had had, of course, a long history within Anglo-American Protestantism. The symbol of the Catholic Antichrist was one of the core conceptions of the English Reformation. During the conflicts of the seventeenth century, Puritans, sectarians, Parliamentarians, and republicans had in various ways collapsed distinctions between the Pope and the English state, perceiving the Anglican hierarchy, the King, and finally Cromwell himself as the Beast of false religion and tyranny.[74] A century later the same symbolic fusion of the Pope, political tyranny, and the Antichrist heightened the American colonists' fear of the French during the French and Indian War. In the 1760's and early 1770's it also led American revolutionaries to search for signs of Catholicism behind British imperial policy. In the case of the French Revolution the association was much more powerful because the connection was ready-made. The French republicans aimed simultaneously to dismantle the monarchical political system and the Catholic ecclesiastical apparatus. For American Protestants exulting over the French Revolution, these were one and the same cause. When Napoleon finally marched into the Vatican in 1798, the revolution seemed to have fulfilled its ultimate promise.

Not surprisingly, given the seventeenth-century origin of this pattern of thought, the older prophecies by Thomas Goodwin, Pierre Jurieu, Robert Fleming, and others whose works were revived in the 1790's generally associated the collapse of the French monarchy with that of the Pope.[75] The connection was more explicitly drawn by contemporary supporters of the Revolution. The article, entitled "Millennium," that appeared in the *Columbian Centinel* in the spring of 1793, for example, rejoiced that the overthrow of the French monarchy signaled the end of papal Antichrist: "The great and extensive kingdom of France, seated in the heart of papal influence and power, whose kings have heretofore bowed with implicit and consummate reverence at the papal chair, now burst the iron bands of slavery, bigotry and superstition."[76] A *New York Journal* column entitled "The Last Book of Kings," which recounted the events of the French Revolution in parodied biblical language, presented the godly revolutionaries at once at war with Babylon and the Dragon, the King and the Pope.[77] Ministers of various regions and denominations also drew sustenance for their millennial expectations from the French combined assault on papal and secular tyranny. Many sermons delivered in the mid-1790's described the Pope as the center of the antichristian conspiracy with the royal heads of state as his henchmen. As the New England Congregationalist Joseph Lyman defined the relationship between secular monarchy and papal power, mystical Babylon was "nothing more or less, than that union and coalition of civil and ecclesiastical Power... The head of this dreadful beast is the court of Rome; its members are most of the European Kingdoms, both Popish and Protestant."[78] Once the Pope fell the monarchs would lose the basis of their power and crumble helplessly in turn. "The Popish beast has nearly numbered *his* days," announced the Baptist frontier preacher Morgan John Rhees in 1795, "The vassal kings, emperors, and princes, who have deluged the earth with blood, under his malign influence, shall soon take their exit with him."[79]

The simple fact that Britain had joined forces with the Pope against France seemed in itself to discredit the counterrevolutionary cause and to confirm the true godliness of the French republican cause. A letter from an unidentified English clergyman printed in the *State Gazette of South-Carolina* in 1793 interpreted the war between France and England as a fulfillment of the eleventh chapter of John's Revelation. Pointing out that the British monarchy had sided with Rome, he arrived at the ominous conclusion that "either tyranny must be on the eve of being destroyed in Europe or that Europe itself is on the eve of being once more sunk into the abyss of Gothic ignorance, barbarity, and bondage."[80] Isaac Backus, the leader of the Baptist struggle for ecclesiastical disestablishment in New England, saw the war as a graphic illustration of his view that Protestant state churches represented the Beast as much as the Papacy. Just as the English ecclesiastical establishment had already shown its satanic colors in opposing American independence, so now it had actually joined with the papists "in bloody attempts against liberty and religion in France."[81]

As late as 1800 the New England schoolmaster Benjamin Farnham declared his qualified support for France on the grounds that "for some time past the Terrible Republic has been destroying the terrible beast, and man of sin, and his associates."[82] The radical husbandman of Troy, New York, similarly identified the Pope as the Beast originally responsible for taking away religious and civil liberty and presented the French Revolution as the logical extension of the Protestant Reformation. He dated the end of the reign of the Beast at 1798, the year the French drove the Pope from Rome, and expected a millennium of equal rights and true Christianity to begin in 1872, after the conversion of the Jews.[83]

In celebrating the revolutionary attack on the Papacy, many francophilic millennialists of the period expressed the view that the French leaders themselves must be at least latently Protestant, however much they professed to reject Christianity. According to this view, it was only a matter of time before the French would abandon infidelity and embrace the true Reformed Christian faith. The editor of *Prophetic Conjectures on the French Revolution*, for example, found hope in the fact that revolutionary Deism had eliminated the superstitions of Catholicism and had reduced French beliefs "to a degree of primitive simplicity." Having thus prepared the way, the same God "that raised up Luther and Calvin to emancipate half Europe from the chains and darkness of popery; will revive the pure Spirit of religion in France."[84] Even Joseph Priestley, generally more critical of French infidelity and Jacobin politics, blamed the corruptions of Catholicism and described the revolutionaries as unintentionally preparing the way for the triumph of "genuine unadulterated Christianity."[85] James Bicheno, another English dissenter widely read in America, went so far as to liken contemporary France to the primitive church of Christ and the apostles. He pointed out that the Jacobins, for all their faults, had already implemented many of the very reforms proposed by Baptists and other dissenting Protestants in England and America: They had abolished religious tithes, undermined ecclesiastical hierarchy, reorganized the clergy on an electoral basis, and placed the different sects on an equal footing. Conservative English Protestants who opposed the Revolution were merely betraying the fact that "they had rather that all the absurdities and oppressions of the old Papal establishment should be restored, than such a dangerous example be set up in the heart of Europe."[86]

Americans who saw France inaugurating the millennial kingdom generally concurred in the judgment that revolutionary Deism would soon give way to true, Protestant Christianity. Even conservative Charles Crawford of Philadelphia, whose *Observations on the French Revolution* of 1793 was otherwise critical of the French republic, hailed its assault on the papal Antichrist and vigorously denied Burke's contention that the French revolutionaries were all deists and atheists. Citing statistics from several authorities, including Condorcet, he emphasized that the Protestant population in France was much larger than generally believed.[87] Through the middle of the decade several Federalist clergymen, including even the subsequent leader of attacks on France and Jefferson, Jedidiah Morse, also still saw grounds for hope in the possibility of France eventually turning to the Protestant faith.[88] Those who went the farthest in predicting the triumph of French Protestantism tended, however, to be more ardent and consistent friends of the Revolution. In the New York *Columbian Centinel* the francophilic article "Millennium" noted the improved condition of French Protestants and confidently proclaimed that "the protestant religion bids fair soon to become general in that country."[89] A contributor to the Republican *New York Journal* insisted that the revolutionary attacks on Christianity amounted to little more than the wiping of a soiled religious slate clean. "France, by throwing off all pretensions to religion, and giving up that bigotry which priests inculcated, will lie open, at [God's] good pleasure, to receive the truth."[90]

Clergymen seeking to reconcile their support of France with their religious convictions were especially taken with the vision of a Protestant France. The Presbyterian Republican Samuel Miller bolstered his argument that the French Revolution was based upon true Christian principles with a lengthy footnote contending that French Protestantism, while numerically small, had recently grown disproportionately powerful.[91] The Boston Baptist Samuel Stillman and the New Jersey Dutch Reformed minister William Linn, though later, like Morse, to become Federalist opponents of France, delivered sermons in the mid-1790's in which they still sought to justify the revolution on religious grounds. According to Stillman even the new calendar abolishing the sabbath might serve the cause of true Christianity, for it would at least "obliterate . . . every idea of saints days, feasts and fasts, &c."[92] Like the editor of the *Prophetic Conjectures*, Linn foresaw the day when "another Luther and another Calvin shall arise, to carry the banner of the cross triumphant round the globe" and in the meantime pointed to the positive sides of the religious decree of the National Convention of 1794. Since the French Deists recognized the existence of a Supreme Being and the immortality of the soul, he argued, they were obviously "unwilling to be reputed atheists; . . . there is more religion among the people of France than her enemies allow." Like Bicheno, Linn accused religious critics of France of desiring only to preserve their own religious establishments: "The nation which they abuse, are no greater infidels than themselves, save that they wear no mask, but openly appear what they are."[93]

On occasion this tendency to downplay the dangers of French infidelity corresponded with a surprisingly positive view of the revolutionary Enlightenment. Despite the fact that Timothy Dwight had already much earlier attacked Enlightenment philosophy as a cause of modern infidelity – a theme he and other Federalist clergymen were to take up with renewed vigor in the late 1790's – the religious friends of France in the mid-1790's still displayed the strong conviction that Enlightenment and Protestantism necessarily went hand in hand.[94] Not only did Paine's catchwords "the rights of man" reverberate through millennial statements about the French Revolution, but other standard words and phrases of the revolutionary Enlightenment were also absorbed into their predominantly biblical framework. Before Paine's Deist *Age of Reason* had given the word "reason" a bad name, numerous millennial statements about the French Revolution hailed the triumph of reason over Catholic superstition, fusing "reason and religion" and welcoming the "dawn of philosophy" as a step towards the fulfillment of biblical prophecy.[95] According to Samuel Adams, reason was the foundation of those basic principles of government, liberty and equality, which would be "rightly understood" as the world approached millennial perfection.[96] Two of the most radical millennial writings of the decade, the "republican Baptist" Elias Lee's *Dissolution of Earthly Monarchies* and the anonymous *Northern Light* of Troy, New York, closely integrated a radical Lockeanism much like Paine's into their otherwise biblical theory of history. In the state of nature that existed before the Fall, they each maintained, perfect liberty and equality had prevailed. Although civil and religious monarchies soon usurped these natural rights, "revolutionary light will," as Lee phrased it, "like the rising sun, dispel the monarchical mist of blindness and ignorance from the face of universal nature."[97] In such pieces the boundary between francophilic biblical millennialism and what historian Henry F. May has called the "secular millennialism" of the revolutionary Enlightenment virtually disappears.[98]

Emphasizing that Catholic superstition and political tyranny were equally the work of the Antichrist, most francophilic millennialists avoided consideration of the causal relationship between religion and politics, between ideas and institutions. For them, liberty, republicanism, reason, and Protestantism were all interdependent "means" to the millennium. God, in their view, could work through various secondary human agencies such as the Protestant churches and republican states as well as through the more direct effusion of grace. Even scientific discoveries, agricultural improvements, and achievements in literature and art were sometimes cited alongside the French Revolution as promising steps towards the millennium.[99] Only rarely did these political millennialists of the 1790's untangle the causal sequence and contend that revolution took precedence over religious change in the coming of the millennium, that the transition from monarchical to republican government set the primary preconditions for religious regeneration and the Kingdom of Christ.[100] More frequently those who highlighted the millennial role of French republicanism also underscored the revolutionary attack on Catholicism as part of a general effort to show both the political and the religious value of the revolution. In this respect, for all the greater radicalism of the francophilic millennial vision, it was actually less thoroughly politicized and more closely tied to traditional Protestant eschatological concerns than the earlier millennialism of the American Revolution. By concentrating on the demise of the Papacy as well as on the triumph of republicanism, commentators of the mid-1790's saw the revolution in France as the culmination both of the American Revolution and the Reformation.

Generally, those few who thought to distinguish at all between the political and religious foundations of the millennium did so not to stress the necessary political preconditions but to emphasize the insufficiency of political change unaccompanied by true Christian faith. The pervasive joy among admirers of France over the prospective downfall of Catholicism was based on the assumption that Protestantism would prevail once the forces of obscurantism were cleared out of the way. Samuel Miller actually maintained that Protestant religious principles were already the source of political liberty in France – more than laws, constitutions, or systems of government – even though the French themselves might deny it.[101] Others combined their millennial enthusiasm for republican government with urgent calls to propagate the faith. In 1794 William Linn, for example, saw the establishment of civil liberty in France as providing a special opportunity to righteous Protestants to be "the first in disarming infidels, by exhibiting Christianity pure and undefiled to the view of men."[102] The formerly Methodist evangelical Anglican Joseph Pilmore, preaching before a pro-French assembly in New York, similarly hailed the potential of the French Revolution but concentrated his sermon on the evangelical theme that the millennium would come only when all believed in Christ.[103] "Twilight" from Virginia also endorsed the republican political experiment in France but pointedly criticized those "Devotees to the supremacy and independence of the animal nature and rights of a Democratical Government" who were "decoyed by the Devil and old human will to deny Jesus Christ." For all their seemingly high motives, this author warned, such unregenerate democrats actually "have no other objects to pursue or wished to accomplish, but self-preservation and gratification." True general happiness, cooperation, and freedom from oppression would only arrive when Christ emerged as "the Shepard and Political Head" of the "new moral government of the World."[104]

One piece that appeared in the Boston *Columbian Centinel* in 1793 compared Christian and Enlightenment theories of history in order to demonstrate the superior revolutionary value of biblical faith. The article endorsed the political goals of the French Revolution but expressed the hope that the French would soon learn that true Christianity, "instead of tending to *retard*, will be the means of accelerating the progress of real freeedom." Complaining that secular theories of progress constituted mere wishful thinking in contrast to the certainties of biblical prophecy, the author contended that only devout Christians could confidently look ahead to the universal blessings of "rational liberty":

It is the privilege of *others* merely to *suppose*, that the state of human society may in future meliorate and improve. It is the privilege of good Christians, without the least *wavering* or *doubt*, to anticipate the scene, when agreeably to the intention of the gospel system, the iron-rod of oppression shall be broken into pieces, and liberty proclaimed to those who are in thraldom – when songs of melody shall be heard instead of the dire clamour of the instruments of war, and there shall be abundance of peace so long as the sun and moon endure.[105]

Thus, even those American Protestants who conceived of the French Revolution as the harbinger of the millennium did not completely politicize their perspective. The fate of the Papacy and of French infidelity were always salient issues to even the most francophilic American millennial Protestants. Many effectively rationalized their support for the revolution by minimizing the threat of French infidelity and maximizing the attack on Catholicism. The French, they claimed, were really Protestants at heart; irreligion was merely a temporary, transitional phase in the battle against superstition, which would eventuate in the triumph of true religion. And several of these figures even more pointedly maintained that republican government was not in itself a sufficient basis for the millennium, that politics need to be supplemented by faith.

For a time the very fact that the French republic was attacking the Papacy gave it sufficient credit to compensate for its internal religious deficits. Ardent supporters of France throughout the decade, speaking largely to Republican audiences, frequently maintained that French infidelity was itself a divine weapon against the papal Beast, that God in his benevolence had spared real Christians the onerous task of physically destroying political and ecclesiastical despotism.[106] Other millennialists who abstained from making a conclusive political judgment about the revolution likewise emphasized the essentially positive role of the French in defeating the papal Antichrist. This favorable but entirely religious perspective on the French Revolution appealed especially to members of the growing popular evangelical denominations, the Baptists and the Methodists, who were also generally Republican in their party affiliations but for whom the end of the Papacy entirely eclipsed purely political considerations. In 1796 the General Conference of American Methodists actually moved to reassure their worried British counterparts about the rise of infidelity, pointing out that the French, despite their false religion, were defeating the Pope and thereby ushering in the millennium.[107] Similarly, Joseph Priestley, a friend of Jefferson's and a confirmed Republican upon his immigration to America in 1794, had already grown critical of the Jacobins "as politicians" and "men," but nonetheless held that God was the real force behind the revolution and that true Christianity would replace French infidelity once the Pope was overthrown.[108] In the years 1793 and 1794 even some of those who later became staunch Federalists invested millennial hopes in the French attack on Catholicism while refraining from the celebration of French republican politics.[109]

The widespread millennial expectations set off by the French Revolution thus combined a variety of political and religious points of view, ranging from enthusiastic endorsement of the revolutionary politics of the Jacobins to the Protestant celebration of the downfall of the papal Beast. Although there were several francophilic millennialists who became Federalists, many did not. In the midst of the euphoria over France in the mid-1790's, the application of biblical prophecy to the French Revolution clearly served the Republican more than the Federalist cause. The Republicans, despite their subsequent reputation among Federalists as the party of Deists, always drew heavily on support from Protestants outside the New England ecclesiastical establishments, and from the beginning the French Revolution was perhaps the main organizing symbol of their partisan ideology. Since the generally Republican but highly pietistic Methodist and Baptist ministers rarely published at all in this period, least of all on general political subjects, the Republicanism of these groups has been understood in terms of their individualism, their antipathy to state control, their modest social origins, and their regional concentration in the otherwise Republican south and west. The fact that the typically Republican values of liberty, equality, and universal rights were so often articulated in biblical millennial terms, however, suggests that their commitment to the Republican cause was based in part on this religious understanding of contemporary events. Several Baptists, some southern and middle-state Presbyterians, a few Methodists and Anglicans, and even scattered New England Congregationalists promoted this positive millennial vision of the French Revolution in the 1790's. In such nondenominational publications as the biblical commentary *Northern Light* by the unknown farmer from Troy, New York, or *Twilight's Orations* by the anonymous Virginian, newspaper articles, and reprints of English prophetic writings (many of which also appeared in almanacs), this eschatological perspective on events overseas received even more widespread circulation in primarily Republican regions of the United States.

The revival of revolutionary millennialism in the 1790's at once reflected and reinforced the popular ideology of the emerging Republican Party. The link between millennialism and the Republican opposition has generally been overlooked by historians because the most conspicuous biblical millennialists, the New England Congregationalist clergy, were staunch Federalists by the end of the decade.[110] Beginning in 1798 New England Federalist millennial literature denounced the French as agents of the Antichrist, overshadowing and effectively obscuring the importance of the earlier francophilic, largely Republican millennialism. Even confirmed Republicans – especially religious ones – were no longer euphoric about the French Revolution by the time Jefferson successfully challenged Adams in the election of 1800, and the radical millennialism of their message had generally, although not entirely,

178

disappeared. Not only were the leading New England ministers themselves only to emerge as aggressively anti-French after the middle of the decade, but many who hailed the millennial promise of the French Revolution never followed them into the Federalist Party. Particularly during the period of the most intense radicalism in the mid-1790's, when the Republican Party actually took root, millennialists often phrased its basic values in terms of a culturally resonant and inspirational biblical symbolism.

MILLENNIALISM AND DOMESTIC SOCIAL CRITICISM

Although the French Revolution served as the focal point of most political millennial writings of the 1790's, some American radicals drew millennial inspiration from sources other than France and applied their perspective to a critique of domestic inequalities. Jedidiah Peck, for example, an artisan-farmer and lay Baptist preacher who became a leader of Republican politics in western New York, never endorsed the French Revolution but nonetheless drew abundantly upon the imagery of Daniel and Revelation in his fiery campaign journalism in the mid-1790's. Peck actually began his political career as a populist critic within the locally prevailing Federalist Party, and only joined the Republicans late in the decade after being elected to the state legislature. In a series of newspaper articles he wrote for the *Otsego Herald* and published separately in 1796, he vigorously disassociated himself from the "Jacobins, or Anarchites," whom he characterized as "libertine whigs and revengeful and avaricious tories" who together "make up a beast with, to be sure, seven heads, and ten horns."[111] Yet the major thrust of his polemic was aimed against the elitism of his Federalist antagonists, especially in their reluctance to support the abolition of slavery. Peck, a champion not only of abolition but of debtors' relief and public education, used the language of millennial prophecy to distinguish his egalitarian republicanism from the "monarchical" Federalism of his opponents: "Monarchical Government is the literal kingdom of Satan, and the antichrist or the Image of the beast – Representative government is the literal and peaceable kingdom of the Messiah." He warned his conservative American foes that his brand of "representative government" would, like the stone in the Book of Daniel, "chace [*sic*], break and destroy Monarchical Government and spread itself over the earth."[112] Other scattered and more obscure voices of the 1790's also used an eschatological perspective to inveigh against indigenous elitism, associating all "aristocratical" social privileges

179

with the Antichrist, for example, and calling for a more equal distribution of wealth.[113]

Within the domestic politics of the 1790's by far the most radical and dramatic protest against government policy was the Whiskey Rebellion in western Pennsylvania in 1794. As with Shays's Rebellion eight years earlier, the available sources make it virtually impossible to penetrate the thought of the participants in the rebellion. Most of the surviving evidence consists of the sparse official resolutions of the rebels, hostile accounts by their antagonists, or recollections by major Republican politicans in the area who had been lukewarm in their support of the rebellion and who later sought to downplay or discredit its radical tendencies in order to prove their own moderation. Despite our limited information about the aspirations of the insurgents, however, the Whiskey Rebellion appears to have given rise to a more avowedly revolutionary sentiment than Shays's Rebellion. Grievances against the federal government in western Pennsylvania were, to begin with, more general, extending beyond the matter of the excise taxes to poor transportation across the Alleghenies, the lack of a treaty with Spain opening up the Mississippi, and insufficient military assistance against Indians. Some rebels seemed even to have considered the possibility of separating from the United States and forming a new western government.[114]

Participants in the Whiskey Rebellion drew from the examples of both the American and the French revolutions. Liberty poles, for example, bearing slogans such as "liberty and equality," were in common use.[115] Hugh Henry Brackenridge, the first historian of the rebellion, noted the prevalence of "the revolutionary language and the ideas of the French people."[116] Although Washington was certainly mistaken when he blamed the insurgence on the Democratic Societies forming in Philadelphia and elsewhere, the local Mingo Creek and Washington County Democratic Societies did play a strong leadership role after the movement was already underway.[117] The western Democratic Societies not only joined the eastern ones in protesting Hamilton's economic program and urging aid to France, but also added a strong element of western regionalism to their program.

The western radicalism of the Whiskey Rebellion occasionally found expression in religious as well as strictly secular terms. An address from the Kentucky Democratic Society that was officially approved by the Washington County society and printed in the *Pittsburgh Gazette* in August 1794, for example, envisioned the American west becoming the agent of God, spreading the principles of true liberty to the oppressed parts of the world. The United States, the author objected, had initially been formed on behalf of the entire people's "aggregate happiness" or "general good," but now "corrupt men and British influence" in the east and south threatened to sink the west "to the most profound obscurity & poverty," to reduce the republic "to discord and contempt with a rapidity that nothing but the spirit of 1775 can counteract." Calling for vigorous action against the federal government in order to secure navigation rights on the Mississippi, he argued that increased trade with Louisiana would not only elevate the virtuous westerners to their rightful position of wealth and dignity, but would, by extending their influence throughout the benighted Spanish Empire, make them "the glorious instruments in the hands of Providence, of relieving the galling chains of Louisiana and South America."[118]

This fusion of Protestant and classical republican outlooks, a legacy of American revolutionary ideology, often took place in western Pennsylvania during the period of the Whiskey Rebellion. Just as the radical state constitution of Pennsylvania in 1776 had required voters to swear to their belief in Protestant Christianity, the local Mingo Creek Democratic Society included in its founding resolutions a plank calling for Bible education in the schools.[119] Local enthusiasm for the French Revolution expressed itself in biblical millennial terms, as it so often did elsewhere in America in these years. In the summer of 1793 the *Pittsburgh Gazette* presented the widespread opinion that the French were fulfilling the glorious prophecies of the Book of Revelation by finally defeating the Pope.[120] Biblical images of the Antichrist evidently also pervaded the rhetoric of the Rebellion itself. According to Brackenridge, as the rural rebels contemplated their invasion of the relatively more urbane, wealthy, and conservative town of Pittsburgh, they commonly referred to it as the "second Sodom."[121] Two of the remaining pieces of propaganda written against the whiskey tax associated it with satanic forces. One of these, a local newspaper article signed with the pseudonym "Sidney," closed an otherwise secular radical whig argument against the encroaching power of "minister" Hamilton by drawing an analogy between the tax and the terrible Beast in Daniel, which would, according to the prophecy, be smashed to pieces in the end.[122]

According to a recent student of the rebellion, many of the rebels themselves were active members of the dominant Presbyterian Church despite the fact that the leading clergymen of the area were strongly opposed to the insurrection and refused to give communion to unrepentant rebels as late as the summer of 1795.[123] One Baptist minister named David Phillips was reputed to be one of the "violent party" in the insurrection.[124] Another local lay preacher, the same Herman Husband who defended the North Carolina Regulation in 1770 and who later supported the Pennsylvania state constitution and the Anti-Federalist attack on the Constitution, also played a minor leadership role in the Whiskey Rebellion. He served as the representative of his county on the leading Committee of Conference set up by the militant Parkinson's Ferry meeting of August 1794, and at another mass meeting at Brownsville later the same month he was appointed a member of a committee to negotiate with the United States Commissioners. His actual role in the rebellion is otherwise obscure, especially in comparison with either the leading radical, David Bradford, or the leading moderate sympathizers, Brackenridge and William Findley. He was, however, evidently regarded as part of the radical wing since he was one of four rebels singled out for arrest by Washington's troops.[125]

Of the few active participants who left a record of their thought, Husband emerges as an especially intriguing figure, for he provides the most direct evidence of a link between speculations on biblical prophecy and the radical ideology of the Whiskey Rebellion. Already in the early 1780's, after his flight from North Carolina to the Pennsylvania frontier, Husband had begun to develop an elaborate millennial theory about the American west. According to Hugh Henry Brackenridge, who visited Husband in 1781 and later ironically recalled his eccentric interpretation of Ezekiel:

It was the vision of the temple, the walls, the gates, the sea of glass, &c. Logger-head divines, heretofore, had interpreted it of the New Jerusalem; but he conceived it to apply to the western country; and the walls were the mountains, the gates the gaps in them, by which the roads come, and the sea of glass, the lake on the west of us.[126]

The German traveler Johann David Schoepf, who happened to stop at Husband's home in the Pennsylvania backwoods in 1783, reported that Husband was working on a map that charted the Alleghenies and imaginatively extended the range into a vast rectangular system of mountains patterned after Ezekiel's description of the walls of the New Jerusalem, running north to the Hudson, west almost to the Pacific, and south to Mexico.[127] When asked whether he believed that the combined American states were the twelve ruling tribes of the Chosen People, Husband reportedly replied with great western pride that the eastern states "would have nothing to do with the New Jerusalem, which will form a kingdom to itself and will bring into

182

vassalage all provinces and peoples from the Allegheny, or eastern wall, to the Atlantic Ocean."[128] In a series of published and unpublished pamphlets written in the late 1780's and early 1790's, Husband spelled out the details of his western millennial vision. Between 1788 and 1789, in the midst of his disillusionment over the passage of the federal Constitution, he moved even farther towards excluding the eastern United States from his millennial order. Whereas he had previously presented plans for a united confeder- ation of empires in America, including both the east and the west, he later concentrated on the western New Jerusalem alone. His pro- posals included a complicated description of a new form of decen- tralized government, structured in ascending levels of power from the local towns to a central supreme council (anachronistically labeled the "privy council"). Husband's scheme also contained guidelines for the extensive reform of the court system and called for a more equal distribution of land. Summing up the populist and militant thrust of his millennial message, he promised that "in the last days, the labouring, industrious people, the militia of freemen, shall prevail over the standing armies of kings and tyrants, that only rob them, and live upon their labour, in idleness and luxury."[129] According to Husband's understanding of the figures in Daniel, the "finall Accomplishment" of this millennial age would occur both by human and supernatural means sometime between 1814 and 1844.[130]

Brackenridge and Schoepf both viewed Husband with amused condescension. For Brackenridge, despite the fact that he himself had indulged in millennial speculation during the 1770's, the frontier preacher's fantastic vision was recorded only as the butt of a joke. For Schoepf, ever on the lookout for American curiosities, Husband's ideas could best be explained by the "loneliness of his mountain sojourning-place, lively powers of imagination, a certain degree of erudition, [and] a restless and enterprising spirit."[131] If these urbane informants viewed Husband as a backwoods eccentric, however, it is doubtful that the people who continued to elect him to positions of leadership and to listen to his preaching would have concurred in their judgment. According to Brackenridge, in 1781 Husband complained that, aside from his wife, others refused to accept his unorthodox view that the "western country" was the true realization of Ezekiel's vision – presumably because they (in Brackenridge's words "the ignorant and the dissembling") adhered to a more traditional millennial interpretation. Nonetheless, other prophetic speculations of his received circulation in almanacs, and, despite his probably idiosyncratic positions on Ezekiel and Daniel, Husband quite clearly retained influence in the local community. Given the militant separatist tendencies within the Whiskey Rebellion, it is certainly plausible, if unprovable, that Husband's exalted vision of the region as the New Jerusalem enhanced his leadership role.

Ranging from Herman Husband's intriguing vision of an autonomous western paradise to the more pervasive image of a universal republic extending from France, the biblical millennial tradition permeated American radicalism in the 1790's. Even occasional voices from the fledgling American antislavery movement, which cut across denominational, political party, and regional lines, invoked the threats and the promises of scriptural prophecy. A group of Universalists printed a Circular Letter in the *Kentucky Gazette* describing the millennium as the time when "slavery of every kind shall cease, and no more clank her iron chains in the hearing of the sons of LIBERTY."[132] Speaking before the Abolition Society of Hartford, Zephaniah Swift interpreted the spread of liberty to France as a sign that Providence was establishing "a new order of things" in which Africans along with the rest of the world would at last be happy and free.[133] This vision of the millennium as the age of liberty for black slaves was shared as well by the Philadelphia liberal physician Benjamin Rush and by the Baptist ministers John Leland and David Barrow.[134] Urging slaves to look ahead to the millennial day of their liberation, Barrow, who was also an ardent Republican, proclaimed his belief in "the natural equality of man" and expressed his wish that "all the oppressed, in all countries, may enjoy the sweets of liberty, and *every man*, of all complexions, *return to his inheritance.*"[135]

For the most part, however, religious critics of slavery in the late eighteenth century did not engage in millennial speculation about future racial equality. Instead they concentrated on the sinfulness of slavery and at most drew consolation from the ultimate promise of divine justice. Like Jefferson and others earlier, several antislavery spokesmen in the 1790's struck an apocalyptic note as they warned of the inevitability of providential judgment.[136] Others similarly relied on the workings of Providence as they invested millennial hopes in the propagation of the gospel and encouraged blacks to participate in evangelical activities. Proponents of free black colonization in Africa, including such leading American antislavery Protestants as the Congregationalist Samuel Hopkins and the Methodist Bishop Thomas Coke, based millennial expectations on the possibility of christianized ex-slaves serving as missionaries spreading the gospel to the heathen overseas.[137] For others it was enough simply to urge

184

American blacks to persist in the faith and thereby encourage its expansion. The black Free African Society in Philadelphia actually took issue with the colonization scheme advocated by Hopkins and his free black associates in Newport, arguing that the best means of bringing on the millennium was not emigration to Africa but a collective "fasting from sin and iniquity... that the Lord thereby may be pleased to break every yoke, and let the oppressed go free."[138] In a discourse delivered before the newly founded African Church in Philadelphia in 1794, the Anglican rector Samuel Magaw held a similar prospect of gradual evangelical progress towards the millennium. Urging his black audience to be humble, sober, peaceful, and circumspect, he consoled them with the prediction that "the general cause of justice and of freedom, and of peace on earth, will at last prevail."[139]

Given the unlikelihood and general fear of complete emancipation, it is not surprising that these clerical and free black opponents of slavery regarded millennial prophecy more as consolation for the faithful than as a stimulus for direct institutional change. Even though many of the most active critics of slavery were Scripture-minded Protestants who were capable of issuing millennial statements on other occasions, their antislavery arguments tended not to refer to the promise of biblical prophecy. The small amount of published literature by black religious leaders of the period also generally avoided the subject of future millennial bliss. Perhaps because a millennial vision required not only a negative judgment of existing reality but the positive projection of a future ideal, the inability of virtually all white Americans in the late eighteenth century to imagine a harmonious interracial society precluded the development of millennial hopes in the antislavery movement. It was only decades later, among the radical abolitionists of the 1830's and 1840's, that millennial symbolism finally came to infuse arguments for total and immediate emancipation.

The later generation of millennial radical abolitionists generally inherited their millennialism not from late eighteenth-century radicals but from Federalist parents within the northeastern Congregationalist and Presbyterian ecclesiastical establishments. The fact that even these relatively conservative millennial ideas could be so transformed within a few decades attests, however, to the latent social criticsm contained within virtually any millennial vision of a radically new social order. Within the volatile political culture of the 1790's, the distinctively conservative, Federalist, and francophobic millennial literature produced in New England in such great quantity between 1798 and 1800 has gained a false reputation as the predominant political expression of millennial thought of the decade. Far from being the special province of the Federalist clergy, millennial speculation in the 1790's appears initially to have suited religious Republicans far more. Under the combined stimulus of the French Revolution and domestic political conflicts, the renewed politicization of millennial thought in the mid-1790's occurred primarily along francophilic and often even radical-Republican lines.

Speculations about the meaning of prophecy in the 1790's took a bewildering variety of forms: premillennial and postmillennial, quietistic and activistic, antimonarchical and antipapist, provincial and universalistic. Yet within this variety there remained certain irreducible ingredients of Protestant millennial theory. All asserted the possibility of this worldly perfection, all believed in its divine ordination, and all expected it to be realized in the future course of history. Even the most politically passive and spiritualized varieties of millennial thought held out the prospect of a fundamentally restructured, just, and harmonious world. In America in the eighteenth century virtually all millennialists, moreover, predicted that this transformation would occur, somehow, within the next two hundred years. Inasmuch as the nonpolitical prophetic exegesis of the period developed in reaction against loose political readings, these two tendencies existed in tension. But they also complemented each other, with one providing the theological legitimacy, the other the political immediacy, for an ongoing American preoccupation with the coming of the Kingdom of God.

8

Biblical millennialism and radical Enlightened utopianism

>... many shall run to and fro, and knowledge shall be increased.
>
> Daniel 12:4

Alongside the resurgence of biblical millennialism in the 1790's arose a secular utopian vision. It too saw the French Revolution as promising an imminent and radical transformation of the world and looked forward to the universal establishment of peace, freedom, morality, and truth on the ruins of political tyranny and religious superstition. In contrast to biblical millennialism, however, secular utopian prophecy was not based on the authority of Scripture, nor did it assume the active role of a providential God. Its key terms were not those of revealed Christianity but more exclusively those of the radical republican Enlightenment: liberty, reason, and the rights of man.

The relationship between biblical millennialism and this radical Enlightened utopianism of the 1790's was at first not antagonistic but complementary. Gradually after the middle of the decade the boundaries between them became increasingly distinct as many leading orthodox Protestants gravitated towards Federalism and strongly disassociated themselves from the Deism of the French revolutionary government. During the initial phases of the French Revolution, however, when much of the clergy still regarded French republicans as the agents of God, biblical millennialism continued to be interwoven with varieties of radical Enlightenment thought. The sense of the incompatibility of revelation and reason, like the opposition of churches to political revolution, developed much more slowly and incompletely in America than in England or on the Continent, where the established clergy had long been firmly identified with the ancien régime. In America many established as well as other clergymen had been at the forefront of both the Enlightenment and the struggle for republican government. Until the end of the eighteenth century, moreover, there were scarcely any vocal Deists or religious skeptics in America to challenge the basic tenets and authority of the Protestant churches. Although intellectual clergymen had armchair knowledge of the debates over the truth of Christianity that had long developed in England and Europe, nothing, not even the Great Awakening, had seriously upset the comfortable balance between reason and revelation, liberty and order, characteristic of the moderate Protestant Enlightenment in America.[1]

In Europe there was a long history of secular utopian thought, but in America visions of future worldly perfection had almost always been framed in biblical millennial terms. When in the 1790's a nonbiblical Enlightened utopianism began to emerge, it still bore many affinities to biblical millennial thought. It was as much the direct offspring of this older, indigenous religious tradition as it was an import from revolutionary France. Millennialism in England and America had long encouraged a belief in positive historical transformation and social reform. The downplaying of miracles, the emphasis on human activity, the belief that secular political developments were auspicious signs – all had become widespread features of prophetic exegesis in the eighteenth century. Despite their obvious differences, biblical millennialism and secular utopianism remained intertwined in America until the very end of the eighteenth century.[2]

It was the hopeful Republican perspective on the French Revolution that most clearly brought together Enlightenment political radicalism and Protestant Christianity, fusing them into a surprisingly harmonious vision of an ideal future world. Like the biblical millennial enthusiasm over France, secular utopian radicalism rose to its highest pitch in the years 1793 and 1794. Its basic vision appeared above all in the speeches and toasts delivered on public ritual occasions such as Fourth of July ceremonies and periodic "civic festivals" called to celebrate the progress of the French. Conducted in several towns and cities throughout the United States, these public gatherings were usually often sponsored by local voluntary associations. The most active organizations were the newly formed Democratic societies, but others included organizations of mechanics, merchants, Freemasons, soldiers, and French immigrants. Together they represented a small, if socially diverse, minority of the population, one disproportionately concentrated in urban

areas. The demonstrations they sponsored often drew wider participation, however, and through the medium of the press – especially
the Democratic-Republican Party press – secular utopian statements
about the French Revolution gained considerable public exposure.[3]

Compared to the often intricate exegesis by biblical millennialists,
the secular utopian perspective on the French Revolution was, on the
whole, remarkably simple. Yet it often inspired impassioned and
extravagant oratory. According to the hopeful visions projected
repeatedly and with little variation, the French Revolution was the
decisive step in the expansion of liberty and enlightenment throughout the world. Republican speakers in various parts of the country
hailed the French Revolution as "a revolution, destined, at some
future period, to enlighten a benighted world," to spread "the
blessings of rational liberty," including universal love, to all the
oppressed, and to raise the world "from the gloomy abyss of Tyranny
to the bright summit of Liberty and equality."[4] This vision of France
bringing freedom, reason, and equality to the rest of the world also
resounded through the toasts commonly proposed at the end of
Republican civic ceremonies that were generally reported in full in
the newspaper coverage of the festivities.

Liberty, equality and fraternity – may they pervade the universe.[5]

The Rights of Man . . . May the light of philosophy irradiate the caverns of
superstition and despotism.[6]

Aristocracy, monarchy and despotism; may they be banished from the face of
the earth, and mankind resume their natural rights, under the only rightful
governments.[7]

The age of peace; its speedy arrival; its endless duration, and its ameliorating
effect on the human mind.[8]

Such secular utopian sentiments were so often declared by francophilic Americans that they quickly assumed the quality of platitudes.
What they lacked in originality, however, they more than made up
for in emotional fervor. For American Republicans who attended
these civic festivals the most simple, even superficial, visionary
statements about the French Revolution appear to have wielded an
impressive rhetorical power.

Like much of the biblical millennialism of the period, the secular
utopianism inspired by the French Revolution linked American
patriotism to a universalism reminiscent of the mid-1770's. In many
of these exclamations France appeared as the gateway through which
a glorified American example of peace, freedom, equality, and truth
would pass to the world. As with the similar biblical millennial view,

such a perception of events overseas both gratified the pride of francophilic Americans who otherwise might find themselves on the periphery of the momentous events abroad and at the same time helped to legitimate the greater radicalism of the French Revolution by presenting it as a simple continuation of the American cause. "The tree of liberty first planted here, and moistened with the blood of our brave allies, is now taking root in France," proclaimed "A Citizen" in the Republican *New York Journal* in 1794 who advocated war against England in the hope that this tree "may grow up and spread, until the whole world is covered with its branches."[9]

Just as francophilic biblical millennialists saw France as a gateway between America and the rest of the world, so too secular patriotic orators hailed the prospect of the global extension of what began in America. Americans should conceive it as their historic mission to disseminate liberty and "regenerate the old world," declared John Mercer in a speech before the faculty of William and Mary College in 1792. "Already may we welcome the happy aera, that now begins to dawn in the regions of Europe."[10] John Clay, Jr., a Georgian whose oration on France was printed in the *State Gazette of South-Carolina*, similarly congratulated his country for being the first "to raise the flaming beacon of freedom whose beams have pervaded the eastern hemisphere." He foresaw the happy day when "one unclouded blase [*sic*] of freedom, shall overflow the whole earth," and all humanity would finally join together "in expressing, with angelic rapture, 'Peace on earth and good will towards man.'"[11] Earlier revolutionary patriots had exploited Bishop Berkeley's poetic image of freedom and empire passing from east to west, but in the 1790's francophilic utopians saw the progressive movement of history traveling the opposite way, from America to the rest of the world. Thomas Paine summed up this grand historical process in *The Rights of Man*, the most important utopian Enlightenment text to appear in either England or America. As he perceived the thrust of recent events, the elevated principles of the American Revolution were "now revolving from West to East," and, sweeping forward through France at an irresistible pace, they promised "a new era to the human race."[12] Only rarely did Enlightened Republicans in America use the example of "the golden age" of French "philosophy and equality" to criticize American backsliding towards Britain, and then only after party polarization was well under way.[13] During the height of the enthusiasm for France in the first half of the decade, they generally viewed the French Revolution in highly patriotic fashion as the promising offspring of America.

Despite all the high hopes for France, surprisingly few American visionaries concerned themselves with the internal transformation of French society. Whether out of ignorance or actual knowledge about the unsettled situation in France, most confined their statements to vague and abstract exclamations about the dawn of reason, equality, and the rights of man. The only detailed commentary came from writers actually living in France, most notably Paine in *The Rights of Man* and the Connecticut radical Joel Barlow. Although both of these men wrote as much for Europeans as for Americans, their publications of the early 1790's received a warm welcome in America during the heyday of American optimism about France and before their personal reputations became tarnished by religious radicalism. In these works Paine and Barlow integrated secular utopian aspirations with specific arguments for economic and political reforms, especially in government fiscal policy and methods of taxation. Yet these more programmatic points in their writings were rarely incorporated into other, indigenous utopian writings about France of the period. Instead, it was for the most part simply assumed that the arrival of republicanism and reason would automatically solve social problems.

Secular utopians as well as biblical millennialists in the 1790's set their sights not upon the concrete workings of French society but upon a much more vast and abstract universe. The common course of imagination led from the present sight of liberty spreading across the Atlantic to the glorious prospect of its global expansion. The contagion of republican revolution would first infect neighboring Europe, some suggested, perhaps even resulting in a united republican confederation.[14] More commonly, however, these enthusiasts skipped over any such intermediary steps and linked the success of France directly to "the future happiness and prosperity . . . of the whole world of mankind."[15]

In accord with this image of the worldwide triumph of liberty, commentators on the French Revolution frequently challenged narrow nationalistic loyalties. The Savannah orator Joseph Clay contrasted the patriotism of the ancients and most moderns, which he described as only a limited virtue, with the real virtue or "disinterested love of mankind" animating the American and French revolutions. "It was reserved for this bright era of happy revolutions to behold the pulse of various nations, of discordant manners beating in unison."[16] This idea of the common pursuit of liberty occasionally gave rise to an even more radical vision of a universal community undivided by national allegiance. As a spokesman for the

Philadelphia Democratic Societies described the utopian future, "the Rights of Man shall become the supreme law of every land, and their separate fraternities be absorbed in one great Democratic society comprehending the human race."[17]

OVERLAPPING SECULAR AND BIBLICAL VISIONS

The secular utopian hopes for France corresponded closely to francophilic biblical millennialism. They had in common both a republican universalism and a tendency to accept the violence of the French Revolution as part of an inevitable historical process dictated by a higher infallible law. Of course, the biblicists, unlike the secularists, based their predictions on the authority of Scripture, and included the triumph of Christianity among their central millennial goals. But both opposed what was mutually regarded as Catholic superstition and both conceived of the Revolution as the carrier of truth to a benighted world. Francophilic secular utopians and biblical millennialists were, without distinction, patriotic in their pride in the American Revolution and universalistic in their broader aspiration for the spread of republicanism to the rest of the globe. Both associated liberty and republicanism with a transcendent moral order, whether divine or natural, and assumed an inherent connection to a new age of temporal prosperity, peace, justice, and general human happiness.

Few of the secular utopians of the 1790's openly challenged Christianity. The skeptics and Deists among them, including Joel Barlow, Philip Freneau, and even Paine in *The Rights of Man*, for the most part kept their religious radicalism off center stage. Even their anticlericalism was usually aimed at ecclesiastical legal establishments rather than at Christian religion per se. Despite the predominance of such essentially nonreligious concepts as reason and the rights of man, the secular utopian statements about the French Revolution are, indeed, often difficult to distinguish from the religious millennialism of the period.

So interwoven were the two that individuals could actually alternate between biblical millennial and secular utopian modes. Samuel Miller, the francophilic, moderately Enlightened but finally orthodox Presbyterian minister in New York, delivered sermons in the 1790's proclaiming his visionary hopes for France both inside and outside a biblical framework.[18] Benjamin Rush had only praise for Paine's *Rights of Man*, yet he himself continued to believe that "the Spirit of the Gospel" was what was most responsible for "rooting monarchy out of the world."[19] Ezra Stiles, the Congregationalist president of Yale, was in theology a confirmed biblical millennialist, but he wrote about the French Revolution in 1794 in a purely secular utopian vein. While denying that social perfection could be achieved in the "present state of man," he nonetheless predicted the establishment of liberty, equality, and universal peace as republican revolutions swept over the face of the world. "The amelioration of human society must and will take place," he declared, and then added an image from the Book of Revelation: "This war of Kings, like that of Gog and Magog, will be terrible."[20] At civic festivals organized in support of France, secular utopian and religious millennial statements often intermixed, presumably endorsed by the same crowd. Alongside toasts to reason, philosophy, and the rights of man came ones to the spread of "true religion" or even to the coming of "IMMANUEL'S reign," as well as sermons on millennial passages in Isaiah and Daniel, and lay speeches on such subjects as "the universal reign of righteousness and peace."[21]

Moreover, many of the "secular" utopian statements used biblical language or metaphor. Toasts at a Democratic-Republican Fourth of July celebration in New York in 1795 mixed paeans to the rights of man and the "flame of liberty" with the hope that the "God of Battles" would help France; even the founding *Principal Articles* of the Philadelphia Democratic Society gratefully acknowledged "the Blessings which Providence hath bestowed upon our Country" alongside its resolution to promote "Freedom and Equality" and "the Rights of Man."[22] Notwithstanding any possible inconsistencies, Enlightened secularists not only thus periodically invoked the concept of Providence in order to account for the great and mysterious benefits of the historical process but chose to articulate their visions in language straight from biblical prophecy. Drawing from millennial passages in Psalms and Revelation, an article in the *Virginia Gazette* predicted that France, "struggling in the cause of heaven and humanity," would beat her enemies "with a rod of iron, and dash them in pieces like a potter's vessel!"[23] William Willcocks of New York, later to become a virulent opponent of the Democratic Societies, published an open letter to Genêt in 1793 expressing the hope that the achievement of a stable republicanism would, in the millennial language of the biblical prophecy, "hasten the day, when the Lamb may in peace and security lay down with the Lyon [*sic*]."[24] The biblical text quoted most often in these otherwise secular utopian statements was the passage in Isaiah and Micah about the future time of peace when people "shall beat their swords into plowshares, and their spears into pruning hooks." Toasts at civic festivals and articles in the Republican press repeatedly looked ahead to the day when "every weapon of war shall become an instrument of agriculture" and "useless lances into scythes shall bend."[25] Some secular utopian literature went so far as to describe the happy future as "the true millennium," "the millennium of peace and perfectibility of man and nature," "the millennium of political happiness."[26]

Such rhetorical use of religious imagery was, of course, a far cry from the literal exegesis of the biblical millennialists. Instead of providing the explicit authority for historical speculation, the Bible merely added a kind of eloquence to statements otherwise presented in purely secular terms. Yet, however limited these metaphorical references may seem, the obvious appeal of the scriptural imagery attests to the enduring emotional power of the Protestant millennial tradition even in the most secularized political culture of the radical Enlightenment. The differences between bibilical millennialism and secular utopianism were in the long run to prove more significant than their similarities, but in America in the 1790's these differences were yet often obscure.

THE RISE OF REASON AND UTOPIAN DEISM

The theme that most clearly differentiated secular utopian from biblical millennial thought was the exaltation over the rise of reason. Although Protestant interpretations of Scripture often incorporated the growth of reason into their millennial schemes, they tended to tie reason to revelation as the twin pillars of true religion. In much the same way as the biblicists associated the expansion of liberty with that of Protestantism, they associated reason with faith. For secular utopians, however, who foresaw the future outside a biblical framework, reason became in itself the means to social perfection. The automatic equation of liberty and reason became virtually a cliché in their statements about France. Whether combined with a loose reference to Providence, an outright rejection of a supernatural God, or (as was common) no mention of religion whatsoever, this theme was continually reiterated in toasts, orations, newspaper columns, and influential political polemics alike. "The present age will hereafter merit to be called the Age of Reason," Paine proclaimed, "and the present generation will appear to the future as the Adam of a new world."[27]

Like Paine, a few American utopians of the 1790's took a further step towards Deism and looked forward to the triumph of unadulterated natural law. According to Paine in *The Rights of Man*, the American and French revolutions renovated "the natural order of things, a system of principles as universal as truth and the existence of man."[28] American radicals occasionally elaborated this perception of the French Revolution as the political realization of natural principles. An article that appeared in Freneau's Republican *National Gazette* in the summer of 1792 commended the Revolution for conforming to "that wisdom and due proportion of things" observable in "the world of nature around us."[29] Another newspaper piece printed in the *State Gazette of South-Carolina* of 1793, signed by "A Jacobin of Charleston," claimed that the French would "procure to the world a general peace and liberty . . . as constant and true, as the immutable laws of nature."[30]

This emphasis upon reason and natural law was taken to its farthest extreme by a small but vocal group of American Deists. Unlike the majority of secular utopians of the period, who simply avoided biblical argument or, like Jefferson, Barlow, and Freneau, kept their private rejection of Christianity distinct from their public political statements, these religious radicals launched a direct attack on revealed Christianity. The battle had begun already in 1784 with the publication of Ethan Allen's iconoclastic *Reason the Only Oracle of Man*, which turned a populist, commonsense Deism against the paradoxical teachings of biblical Christianity. Exposing the "fraudulence" of a wide variety of central Christian beliefs, Allen insisted that God is discoverable by reason alone and that "moral rectitude," rather than intangible faith, is properly "the sum of all religion' and the "greatest perfection that human nature is capable of."[31] But Allen's vision of the future had not been particularly optimistic or utopian. Despite his objections to the doctrine of original sin, he never took the position that human beings are innately good or that human society is morally perfectible. Indeed, in the course of its arguments against the veracity of biblical prophecy, *Reason the Only Oracle of Man* categorically dismissed Micah's vision of swords being beaten into plowshares as "very improbable or rather incompatible with human nature."[32]

It was only in the 1790's that American Deism began to invoke its own distinctive utopian vision. Inspired by both the politics and the religious views of the French revolutionaries, a few American radicals proclaimed newfound confidence in the future hegemony of the religion of nature. Led by the blind but tireless preacher Elihu Palmer, tiny groups of Deists concentrated in cosmopolitan Philadelphia and New York formed themselves into clubs conceived as spearheads of American religious change. Thomas Paine's *Age of Reason*, published a few years after *The Rights of Man*, provided a major text for the fledgling movement. Palmer's prodigious efforts also yielded numerous printed speeches and treatises and two shortlived Deist papers at the turn of the century.[33] For him and his followers the French Revolution represented the victory of scientific reason over religious superstition. Borrowing from Allen, Paine, earlier English Deists, and the French philosophes, Palmer perceived religious orthodoxy everywhere at the heart of political despotism. Unlike other francophilic Americans who seemed to mean Catholicism when they denounced superstition and priests, Palmer did not hesitate to direct at least as much venom against local Protestant ministers.Eagerly noting the mounting conservatism of American clergymen like Jedidiah Morse in 1793 (actually before many ministers had turned against France), he gleefully predicted that the "empire of reason will soon sweep off the earth this bundle of nonsense and oppression."[34]

For Palmer the rise of reason was always a more important agent of historical change than republican revolution. While assuming a general connection between science and liberty, between the defeat of "priest-craft" and the defeat of "king-craft," his writings typically described despotism as being replaced not by popular rule, or even by constitutional liberty, but by a "reign" or "empire" of reason abstracted from any tangible political or institutional framework. Perhaps because he was fundamentally indifferent to the concrete workings of politics, he, unlike the more ardently republican Paine, could sustain an uncritical enthusiasm for France through the phases of the Terror, the Directory, and the early Napoleonic conquests. It was only when Bonaparte sought to repair relations with the Catholic Church in 1802 that Palmer felt suddenly, and utterly, betrayed.[35]

Although the utopian Deists associated with Palmer were admirers of the French Revolution and at least nominally Republican, the Deist glorification of reason could combine with anti-French, conservative politics. Next to Palmer, the most active Deist proselytizer who wrote in America in the 1790's was the English immigrant and critic of France James Stewart. Thoroughly outraged by the popular violence of the French Revolution, Stewart praised the judicious balance of the English and American constitutions and objected to all demonstrations of democratic emotion including Paine's *Rights of Man* (he liked *The Age of Reason*), the American Democratic Societies, and the Whiskey Rebellion.[36] Despite his desire to spread his Deist principles among ordinary people, the mixture of

Stewart's politics and religious system was too idiosyncratic to attract much attention from even the most committed American Deists following Palmer. In 1805, however, after the French Revolution was no longer so polarizing an issue, Palmer recognized Stewart as enough of an ally to publish and advertise some of his writing in the official Deist paper *The Prospect*.[37]

Despite their political differences, Palmer and Stewart shared the basic conviction that the rise of reason, not political change, would be most responsible for transforming the world into a utopian state of perfection. The spread of Deism, or the religion of nature, was for them the means and the end of the world-historical process. Stewart envisioned his own Deistic theological system as passing first to an Enlightened intelligentsia and then gradually throughout the world. Palmer invested much more hope in republican revolutions, but far from emphasizing their concrete political programs, he too tended to see them on a highly elevated plane, as "the progressive movements of intellectual power."[38] Compared to other secular utopians of the period, they both were unusual in their emphasis on the transforming effects of ideas. Although it was common enough to celebrate the rise of reason, others tied it more closely to political change. Even Thomas Paine, despite his avowed Deism, never put the religion of nature at the heart of the historic transformation of the world. *The Rights of Man* described the French Revolution as the product of reason, but – refraining from an open espousal of Deism – stressed the role of republican government in giving rise to reason in turn and advocated a host of concrete structural reforms. Paine's later Deist tract *The Age of Reason*, more like Ethan Allen's *Oracles of Reason* than like the prophetic writings by Palmer, was not in itself a utopian work. It ridiculed belief in biblical revelation, insisting upon the veracity of natural reason instead, but never suggested that Deism itself would provide the basis for social perfection.

Like Paine, most American secular utopians phrased their arguments far more in political than in religious terms. Tunis Wortman, a New York radical with pronounced Deist convictions, took an even more extreme environmentalist position. Citing the British sense psychology of Locke, Hartley, Godwin, and others, he insisted that vice was caused by tyrannical "political establishments" and that only under a republican system would human character change so that "persecution and superstition, vice, prejudice and cruelty will take their eternal departure from the earth."[39] Wortman's oration contained echoes of Joel Barlow's *Advice to the Privileged Orders*, a political treatise written shortly before in revolutionary France. Barlow similarly maintained that only the material reorganization of external institutions into "a natural state of society," not internal individual reformation, could produce a just society. Now that societies were starting to change, man was only beginning to realize his vast moral potential. "He rises into light, astonished at what he is, ashamed of what he has been and unable to conjecture at what he may arrive." Barlow even speculated about the possibility that private property would eventually prove uncongenial to "the social nature of man."[40]

The visionaries of the 1790's who altogether rejected the concept of a providential God thus tended to view either reason or institutional change as the main force producing the new utopian age. In actual practice, however, these two perspectives were usually mixed together in joint celebrations of liberty and enlightenment that, like the biblical millennialism of the period, conveyed a vague causal indeterminacy. It is revealing that the most extreme and systematic positions on causality were taken by those who were among the most religiously radical. The utopian leader of organized Deism in America, Elihu Palmer, most consistently viewed the diffusion of reason and the religion of nature as the primary precondition of the new age. Joel Barlow, who had moved past Deism to private doubts about the very existence of God, developed, to the contrary, the most consistently materialist idea of causation of any American writer.[41]

Yet even these individuals, who pushed the secular utopian argument to its two farthest extremes, never wholly settled on either a thoroughly idealist or a thoroughly materialist historical theory. For all Barlow's emphasis on the moral transformation to be caused by "natural" social and political organization, he expected this organization to be discovered and implemented by Enlightened reason. Although this theme became less pronounced in the second part of *Advice to the Privileged Orders*, he never retracted his earlier conviction that society was moving into a new stage dominated by human intellect. Having passed successively from ancient "predatory spirit" through the feudal "spirit of Hierarchy" to the recent "spirit of Commerce," history had, he claimed, just arrived at a new stage characterized by the "spirit of inquiry." The recent effusion of knowledge was "leading the people to change the form of their governments that society may be restored to its proper foundation, the general happiness of the great community of men."[42]

Unlike the more concrete and politically minded Barlow and Paine, the utopian Deists Palmer and Stewart never attributed much of a role to the state in regulating the new moral order. Generally they blandly assumed that the exercise of natural reason would automatically give rise to a heightened social morality. On occasion, however, both took this problem a step farther and used a materialist utilitarian psychology to prove that in an Enlightened world no tension would exist between individual rational calculation and the good of society. If the ideas transmitted through the senses to the brain were consistently rational, natural, and true, they maintained, universal benevolence would arise spontaneously from the sheer pursuit of pleasure.[43] In taking this more materialist view of moral conditioning, according to which the sensate environment determines behavior, they sounded very much like Barlow despite their relative disregard of the role of the state.

Secular utopians thus laid varying amounts of emphasis on internal reason and external environment as the means to social transformation, but in the last analysis none of them devised a thoroughly consistent position. Most secular utopians simply assumed an overarching connection between physical conditions, social relations, and individual consciousness, avoiding any thoroughgoing causal analysis of the coming of the future age of perfection. They opted instead for a loose combination of the rise of reason and the spread of republican political institutions. In this pre-Marxist era no one suggested that class conflict would lead to a revolutionary reconstitution of the social order.

The strong materialist and even occasional communist tendencies within the late eighteenth-century European Enlightenment had only limited transmission onto American soil through the writings of radicals like Barlow, Paine, and Godwin. The economic assumptions underlying such thinking were primarily those of Adam Smith, who held that in a free market unhampered by an authoritarian state, self-interest would automatically serve the interests of the whole. As Paine phrased the benefits of commerce in *The Rights of Man*, "The most effectual process is that of improving the condition of man by means of his interest."[44] This was also the guiding theory underlying the use of utilitarian psychology by Stewart and Palmer, and Godwin similarly translated it into his anarchist theory of politics. Although liberal utilitarian theory left many questions open, it did help to solve certain moral problems facing secular utopians who did away with the just hand of a providential God. Utilitarianism provided a crucial if somewhat artificial link between individual rationality and collective happiness, thereby adding a social and political dimension to the Enlightenment view of a harmonious natural order.[45]

For these advanced secular utopians, the future utopian era would be entirely of this world. Inasmuch as there was a God (and the Deists strongly believed that there was), he ruled through nature. Both social and individual redemption were mediated not by supernatural grace but by the discovery and application of natural law. Despite these clear-cut differences between Enlightenment radicalism and millennial Protestantism, however, there remained significant points of connection between them. Both were profoundly critical of the present social order, which they regarded as largely corrupt and benighted. Both saw contemporary politics in terms of a fateful struggle between good and evil, the former identified with liberty and truth, the latter with tyranny and superstition. Both predicted the imminent triumph of the good, and the future establishment of a golden age of universal peace, comfort, benevolence, and understanding. Both tended to view this coming utopian era as at once the culmination of the entire course of human history and the restoration of a primitive natural order that antedated the introduction of evil. Both usually stressed the importance of human efforts in achieving this goal, and yet also conceived of the process as somehow predetermined by God – if not directly by an active Providence working in history, then indirectly by a divinely endowed human reason inevitably progressing towards truth. And, in the mid-1790's, moreover, both biblical millennialism and radical Enlightenment utopianism saw the French Revolution as a key agent in this glorious transformation. They shared the fervent expectation that France would deliver a mortal blow to European monarchism and Roman Catholicism, thereby opening the way to freedom and truth. It was only in the second half of the decade that Federalist Protestant millennialists condemned the revolution itself as antichristian and tyrannical, thereby parting ways with the radical Enlightened utopians much more clearly than before.

This striking congruence between francophilic biblical millennialism and Enlightenment utopianism in the mid-1790's arose in large part from the ancestral Protestantism of many of the major proponents of radical Enlightenment in America. Freneau, for all his speculation along Deist and even Epicurean lines, never entirely shed the vestiges of his earlier Presbyterian faith.[46] Barlow, a scion of Calvinist Yale College and a chaplain during the Revolutionary War, had in his youth written patriotic poetry within a biblical millennial framework before gravitating towards philosophic materialism while in revolutionary France. Palmer had received his education at New Light Dartmouth College and began his preaching career within the

Congregationalist religious establishment. Paine himself, although probably never as deeply affected by his religious upbringing as these native Americans, nevertheless did receive instruction from his Quaker father and kept long personal and political associations with many ardent (often intensely millennial) English Dissenters and American liberal and evangelical Protestants. For such people the wholesale rejection of Christianity was hardly an impersonal or dispassionate act. It is not so surprising, then, that some of the most radical millennial tendencies in Anglo-American Protestantism continued to resonate in their exaltations over the French Revolution. Similarly moralistic, sectarian, and convinced of the coming of social perfection, they fought fire with fire. Whatever the more remote historical connections between the Protestant Reformation and the radical Enlightenment may have been, the attraction of these particular Americans to the romantic utopian ideas of the French philosophes owed as much to their religious heritage as to their reaction against it.

9

Francophobic reaction and
evangelical activism

And the kingdom and dominion, and the greatness of the
kingdom under the whole heaven, shall be given to the
people of the saints of the Most High.

Daniel 7:27

In America before 1798 it was rare for either biblical millennialists or
secular utopians to take a hostile view of the French Revolution. The
few anti-Jacobin visionaries like Charles Crawford and James Stewart
tended to be recent immigrants to the United States. Most American
critics of France simply abstained from millennial or utopian analysis
of the French Revolution. For the vast majority of American utopians
and millennialists, the revolution's joint attack on monarchy and
papal superstition seemed sufficient to outweigh, even to justify,
evidence of its violence and infidelity. A few radical Deists went so far
as to applaud openly the French government's wholesale rejection of
Christianity. For Protestant millennialists, of course, the French civil
religion posed greater interpretative problems. But in the mid-1790's
they too usually viewed the French as divine instruments crushing the
papal Antichrist and thereby indirectly advancing the interests of the
true faith.

THE INFIDEL ANTICHRIST AND THE PERILOUS LAST DAYS

In the second half of the decade, however, increasing numbers of
American Protestants were no longer compelled by this logic. The
threats posed by French Deism and atheism now seemed to counter-
balance, indeed even to outweigh, French anti-Catholicism. Few
remained sanguine about the possibilities of a Protestant France.
However much most American millennialists still welcomed the
collapse of the Papacy, those who published their views on the world
tended to see infidelity as an equally pernicious force. The line

dividing the legions of Satan and the legions of Christ was thus significantly redrawn. American Protestants were still far from sympathizing with the Catholic Church of the ancien régime, yet quite suddenly they identified a new, even more dangerous enemy outside the ranks of organized Christianity.

The shift from francophilic millennialism in the mid-1790's to francophobic millennialism at the end of the decade can be traced most clearly in the changing attitudes of the northeastern Presbyterian and Congregationalist ministries. In the late 1790's many clergymen who had earlier welcomed the French Revolution became alarmed by a combination of domestic and foreign developments and threw themselves behind the Federalist Party. The proliferation of Deist literature like Paine's *Age of Reason*, the emergence of small but vocal Deist organizations in America, and the threat of social upheaval posed by the Whiskey Rebellion – all contributed to the clerical backlash. In addition, although in 1793 and 1794 many Protestant leaders had been able to excuse the Terror and even the French civil religion, they had done so in the faith that the republic would soon find its proper Protestant and libertarian, religious and political bearings. Shortly after the outbreak of the European war, however, Federalist propaganda escalated its attacks against French infidelity. Even more damaging to the earlier millennial hopes for the revolution was the growing recognition that the French revolutionary state continued to be unstable and repressive, even if less so after 1795 than under the Jacobins. It also conquered such venerated and historically Protestant republics as Switzerland and the Netherlands and created disturbing diplomatic altercations within the United States. In the face of such events, the initial francophilic euphoria of even such ardent Republican and generally pro-French Deists as Jefferson and Paine was no longer sustained.[1]

By the end of the decade few Protestant Republicans were still comfortable conceiving of the French Revolution in millennial terms. The most avidly francophilic millennialists of the mid-1790's generally did not themselves switch sides and become leading Federalist spokesmen – in fact a number, particularly Baptists and Presbyterians, apparently remained within the Republican fold – but they tended to cease publishing on political millennial themes.[2] Their francophilic eschatology had given a boost to the Republican Party in its formative years, but the aura of their revolutionary millennial visions faded in the second half of the decade. In the late 1790's the dominant political millennial outlook was Federalist, not Republican. Most Federalist writers on prophecy had themselves earlier supported the French Revolution, especially in its attack on Catholicism, but few had embraced the egalitarian politics of the revolution with the millennial fervor of the Republicans.[3] Once their moderate approval had given way to antipathy, the Manichaean dualism of the millennial perspective suited them better than it did the disillusioned Republicans. The revolution could now appear as the representative of cosmic evil if not of cosmic good.

For them, the rationalist creed of the French state constituted a fundamental evil comparable to Catholicism itself. This emerging perspective found particularly dramatic expression in the specious theory of the Bavarian Illuminati that swept through Federalist circles in 1798.[4] Originally proposed in an inflammatory book by the Edinburgh theologian John Robison, this theory purported to explain the French Revolution as the work of a secret order of Masons conspiring to subvert both Christianity and government throughout the world. The influential Massachusetts minister and geographer Jedidiah Morse first seized upon it in 1798 to substantiate his fears of anticlericalism and Jacobin clubs in America, and soon this idea of a Masonic conspiracy against religion and political order reverberated throughout Federalist millennial writings.[5] Timothy Dwight, president of Yale College, delivered a sermon on the Book of Revelation that interpreted the French philosophes and the Order of the Illuminati as the unclean spirits prophesied as coming out of the mouth of the papal Beast.[6] Like Dwight, others showed that whereas the symbol of the Beast stood for Catholicism and the Harlot was Rome, the man of sin and the three unclean spirits were French infidelity.[7] One tract of 1798 published by an anonymous American in New York challenged the traditional Protestant interpretation of the Beast's "little horn" as the Pope, arguing that it must mean the French Revolution instead.[8] The western Massachusetts minister Joseph Lathrop, who in 1793 had been enthusiastic about the fall of the papal Beast at the hands of the French republicans, reluctantly came to the conclusion that the devil had merely changed his facade. First clothed in ancient paganism and then in popery, Satan had, according to Lathrop, reappeared with the French Revolution dressed in "deism, materialism, atheism and every species of infidelity."[9] As one minister expressed the prevailing New England clerical opinion of the shift from Catholicism to the Enlightened civil religion, "The French power is not the less antichristian for the revolution."[10]

Just as earlier francophilic millennialists had fused Protestantism with republicanism and Catholicism with tyranny, Federalist millennialists identified religious infidelity with both the tyranny and the disorder of French revolutionary politics. France seemed not only hopelessly infidel but a threat to stable republican government. The Antichrist, whether Catholic or infidel, had, according to this view, remained consistently tyrannical. Nathan Strong, one of Connecticut's leading Congregational clergymen, wrote a sermon accusing the French infidels of wishing to replace the Papacy with "another universal tyrannical dominion."[11] Timothy Dwight warned about the possibility of a French invasion that would deprive Americans of their liberty and subject them to the arbitrary power of satanic agents as the world approached the final days.[12]

Only rarely, however, did these millennialist Federalist diatribes link the Antichrist to revolutionary republican values as such. An exception was a relatively early sermon preached against the Jacobin Terror and the Whiskey Rebellion in 1795 by the Harvard divinity professor David Tappan. Tappan sought to expose the dangers of "pursuing the splendid phantom of an undefined, romantic liberty and equality, which would at once clash with social order, moral justice, and the present fame and condition of man."[13] He insisted on the supremacy of Christian morality over social and political equality, yet even he concluded with the millennial promise of universal "temporal freedom and happiness."[14] By the end of the decade other New England Federalists, including the Baptist Abraham Cummings, repudiated "the false doctrines of liberty and equality, which have contaminated millions of mankind."[15] Cummings took this antipolitical thrust of Federalist millennialism still further by insisting that true Christians should prepare for the Last Days only by tending their souls. They should, in his view, "never appear the first in political revolutions."[16]

For these conservative New Englanders, egalitarian revolutionary values seemed essentially at odds with the religious imperatives of Christian faith. They offered no alternative political ideal whatsoever, asserting simply that the road to the millennium lay not in liberty and equality but in piety. But it still took a more virulent conservative than most Protestant Federalists to identify republican ideals themselves with the Antichrist. The English immigrant poet Charles Crawford, unusually antagonistic to the Jacobin state as early as 1793, stepped up his attack on political equality in 1796. He cited not only the French Revolution but the Whiskey Rebellion and the American Democratic Societies as illustrations for the claim that the "modern spirit of democracy may be as fatal to mankind, and people hell as fast, as the spirit of Popery."[17] In 1800 he published *An Essay upon the Eleventh Chapter of the Revelation of St. John*, which specifically challenged the earlier francophilic readings of the text. Denying that the prophesied destruction of the city referred to either the French monarchy or Rome, he presented a detailed refutation of the various republican interpretations current in the mid-1790's – including those by Jurieu, Love, James Bicheno, and even Richard Brothers.

> ... the interpretations of those men are false, who would pervert this book to encourage a pernicious spirit of democracy. There is nothing in this book, or in any part of scripture, which is favourable to the wanton murder of kings and nobility, from an erroneous idea of equality.[18]

One index to the fundamental shift in political mood in the late 1790's was the emergence, for the first time since the 1750's, of a strongly catastrophic apocalyptical perspective on future events. To Federalist Protestants contemplating the French Revolution, the rise of infidelity, the false promise of political salvation, and the terrible bloodshed in Europe all seemed obvious signs of expanding satanic power. In the light of these apparent conditions, the previously common theory of gradual social and spiritual progress towards the millennium no longer aroused much conviction. Disillusioned former French enthusiasts such as the Boston Baptist Samuel Stillman and the New York Dutch Reformed clergyman William Linn altogether abandoned their millennial interpretation of the French Revolution. Instead they preached jeremiads interpreting the danger of war with France, domestic party strife, and the yellow fever epidemic as divine chastisements for infidelity and other sins.[19] Federalist ministers who did regard events in France as signs of the approaching millennium – generally not the same individuals who had earlier supported the revolution in millennial terms – gravitated towards an eschatology that emphasized the great cataclysms of the last days and the final supernatural intervention by God. A common theme of sermons preached by leading New England clergymen in 1798 and 1799 was that God was beginning to pour out his last wrath upon the sinful world and that the sole hope for millennial salvation lay in spiritual and moral reform.[20] Timothy Dwight, who claimed that the world was currently undergoing the horrors of the sixth vial just before the millennium, even inclined towards premillennialism with his dramatic warning, "the advent of Christ is at least at our doors."[21] Yet, despite all the fear and foreboding, the technical premillennialist view that Christ would physically descend before (rather than after) the millennium never became a dominant feature of Congregationalist Federalist eschatology. The New England established clergy raised the spectre of impending judgment and insisted on the necessity of supernatural salvation without departing from postmillennial exegesis.

It was outside the northeastern ministerial establishment that a more literal premillennialism continued to take hold in the late 1790's – among both Federalist and Republican commentators on prophecy. Premillennial exegesis had attracted increasing numbers of adherents in America since the late 1780's, and in the mid-1790's several premillennialists began to refer to the French Revolution and the European war as signs of the approaching conflagration. One anonymous premillennial work that appeared in Boston in 1800 saw the French Revolution – with its fulfillment of the prophecy of "nation rising against nation," its destruction of the papal Beast, and its leadership of the "false prophets" of infidelity – as the main sign of the impending Second Coming and Last Judgment.[22] The minutes of the New York Baptist Association in 1799 interpreted the war between France and England as divine wrath against "antichrist, whether Papal or Protestant," and urged the faithful to prepare their souls for "the coming of the Lord" while abstaining from political involvement.[23] As the French Revolution gained its reputation for violence and became widely discredited towards the end of the decade, the cataclysmic premillennialist perspective became incorporated into even more explicitly political points of view.

It was only a small theological step from the apocalyptical sermons of the Federalist clerical establishment to a full-fledged premillennial indictment of the French. The New England Baptist Abraham Cummings, author of an earlier premillennial tract that contained no political commentary, published a fast-day sermon in Maine in 1799 that integrated his eschatology with his now strenuous, and for a Baptist atypical, Federalism. In his view Christ would appear suddenly to judge the world regardless of human action. Efforts to bring on the millennium by revolution would prove futile, even sinful, he warned those sympathetic to France: "There will be no fifth monarchy before Christ appears. It is not the reign of monarchy, but of anarchy, which is now approaching, and already begun."[24] An anonymous New York commentary on prophecy similarly imbedded a Federalist interpretation of the "Terrible Republic" as the Antichrist within an explicitly premillennial framework. The author challenged not only supporters of France but postmillennialists with the spectre of imminent supernatural judgment: "Go on ye figurative constructors, preach up enigmas, figure and absurdity; your time is short, and your field is contracted and contracting."[25] Another publication that carried apocalyptical conservatism over into full-scale premillennialism was an English exegetical work reprinted in Philadelphia in 1800. Written by a wealthy amateur archaeologist and theologian named Edward King, this volume used both the Bible and the apocryphal Book of Esdras to prove that the French Revolution was the last great woe under the final, seventh vial. Predicting the imminent Second Coming and Last Judgment, he told his readers "nothing remains, but for us to wait, with awful apprehensions, for the End."[26]

An even more conservative critic of King, the anglophilic Philadelphian Charles Crawford, objected not to King's premillennialism but to his granting the "Atheistical Democracy of France" any millennial role whatsoever.[27] Indeed, as these francophobic premillennialists feared, an apocalyptical interpretation of the French Revolution could prove at least as appealing to political radicals. The premillennial idea of a sudden, miraculous upheaval that would destroy the present world of sin and usher in a new age of perfection was always laden with revolutionary implications. Although most American francophilic millennialists writing in the mid-1790's had assumed a more gradualistic theory of change, towards the end of the decade, after revolutionary France had lost its initial aura of perfection, a type of radical premillennialism emerged. A few American millennialists actually glorified the violence of the French Revolution and interpreted it as God's wrath immediately before the Second Coming.

In 1799 Simon Hough, the excommunicated premillennialist from Stockbridge, Massachusetts, described the French revolutionary struggle for liberty and equality as the fire in the tenth chapter of Revelation. He acknowledged that the French were "devil-like creatures," "a most abominable wicked people," but insisted that God would use them to carry on his terrible judgment against tyranny and popery "until other nations make peace with them." He accused the Federalist clergy of being sacrilegiously "displeased at Providence," noting that "because God has made uses of an instrument they disapprove, they are now praying as hard for the overthrow of that power." Noting the unequal distribution of wealth, "even in America," this disaffected New Englander attacked the established clergy for profiting from the taxes imposed on less fortunate people. "Woe unto you who have exclaimed against tyranny, and are tyrants yourselfs," he threatened, proclaiming that the world was presently in the midst of the last days and that Christ would shortly return to judge.[28] Another work that combined a premillennial interpretation of the French Revolution with singularly radical social criticism was an anonymous publication that appeared in Boston and Portsmouth in 1798. Regarding the destructiveness of the French Revolution as a preview of the forthcoming Last Judgment, the author warned that only the Elect who forsake the things of this world would be granted a place in the Kingdom of Christ. God planned the French Revolution to give the wealthy a last chance to share their riches with the poor and the established clergy a chance to renounce their worldly connections.[29]

Other Republicans who inclined towards a premillennial eschatology did not join in the radical criticism of American social and ecclesiastical inequalities. Both the Connecticut school inspector Benjamin Farnham and the New York farmer who wrote the anonymous treatise *A Northern Light*, however, did still support the French attack on popery and monarchy as late as 1800. Their basically positive evaluation of France, in spite of its acknowledged sins, was joined with a tendency to stress spectacular supernatural transformations. Understandably, they anticipated a miraculous divine intervention that would supersede the flawed revolution and bring millennial perfection after all.[30]

Given the marginal quality of these publications by obscure and anonymous writers, it is impossible to know how deeply this radical premillennialism penetrated into the view of ordinary religious Republicans at the turn of the century. There is, however, evidence of a persistent millennialism among influential, more moderate Republicans who had grown disillusioned with the promise of the French Revolution but who nonetheless continued, as did the Federalists, to harbor hopes for a new age. Over the course of the decade several leading Republicans came to attack France as the tyrannical Antichrist, as a traitor to the true moral and libertarian principles of Christian republicanism, without forsaking their pro-Jeffersonian political principles. Many moved towards a kind of apolitical premillennialism in their disillusionment with the effects of the republican revolution. The prominent Philadelphia physician Benjamin Rush, for example, already soured on radical political experiments during his earlier battle against the Pennsylvania Constitution of 1776, found Elhanan Winchester's Universalist premillennialism congenial in the 1790's. Rush considered the French Revolution a perversion of true, Christian republicanism, and increasingly invested his millennial hopes in the supernatural coming of Christ rather than in political change.[31] Joseph Priestley, the English scientist who had fled from Tory terrorism to the United

States, likewise drew upon Winchester's work as he shifted from his earlier francophilic millennialism to a gloomier premillennialist view of the revolution during the Jacobin period. Appalled by its irreligion and cruelty, he came to regard the revolution not as a fulfillment of millennial promise but, as Winchester did, as part of the great conflagration before the sudden and miraculous physical coming of Christ. The Messiah's kingdom of truth and righteousness, he explained, "will not be established without the general convulsions, and the violent overthrow of other kingdoms." However reprehensible the actions of the French revolutionaries, he told anti-Jacobin conservatives, it was futile to oppose them; true Christians should trust in Providence and wait patiently for the End.[32] In their combination of nonpolitical premillennialism and Republican politics, both Priestley and Rush were true to the perspective of Winchester himself, who, while always insisting that political activism could do little to prepare for the millennial future nonetheless adhered to a basically Republican view of the American government.[33]

Samuel Miller, a Republican Presbyterian minister of New York, similarly inclined towards an increasingly apocalyptical, if not technically premillennial, outlook on France towards the end of the decade. Unlike many of his formerly francophilic colleagues, Miller continued to incorporate the French Revolution into his Republican eschatology despite his disillusionment with France. In his fast-day sermon of 1798 he joined the New England Federalist ministry in interpreting current developments in Europe and America as the increasing darkness of the last days before the sudden new dawn. Citing scriptural texts on the perilous nature of the Last Days, he noted that "irreligion, disorder, and violence, will be more extensively and dreadfully prevalent than they have appeared since man was an inhabitant of the earth." As for the French Revolution, it had probably succeeded in drawing "systems of unnatural domination" to an end, but he lamented that "the evil has gone too far to be remedied without means as grievous as the disease."[34]

By 1802 Miller no longer expected the imminent arrival of the millennial day, having concluded that this hope was as yet "premature."[35] But he continued to stress the essential difference between Christianity and the Enlightenment theories of human perfectibility that had arisen in France. He criticized Helvétius, Condorcet, Godwin, and their disciples for vainly expecting "every thing to be accomplished by the progress of knowledge" alone. The Scriptures, he insisted, teach that the peace and happiness of the millennium will come only by means by "divine illumination" and "evangelical holiness."[36]

Miller's critique of the revolutionary Enlightenment, and his insistence on the necessity of spiritual grace, was part of a widespread clerical reaction against American as well as foreign Deism and religious skepticism. For the reaction against France was intimately joined to a domestic crisis of faith. Federalist clergymen, especially, repeatedly warned that French "atheistical" ideas were currently spreading onto American soil. In 1798 Jedidiah Morse claimed that the Bavarian Illuminati had already established several societies in America, while Timothy Dwight luridly contemplated the spectre of America's sons becoming "the disciples of Voltaire," and her daughters "the concubines of the Illuminati."[37] Elias Boudinot, the Presbyterian New Jersey Federalist congressman, published a lengthy refutation of Paine's *Age of Reason* designed for the young and the poor because, as he perceived it, "some unknown persons in this country [are] fixing on the rising generation, and the lowest order of the people, as the chief objects of an attack, for spreading the principles of infidelity."[38] According to such orthodox conservative Protestants, the threat posed by irreligion at home as well as abroad had reached crisis proportions. As an essay published in the Congregationalist *Connecticut Evangelical Magazine* in 1802 extravagantly warned its readers, "Never, never were the gates of hell more moved, never were the enemies of religion more thoroughly awake and active, than at the present time, while the unclean spirits like frogs are going out to the kings of the earth, and the whole world."[39]

This perception of infidelity surging over the earth and threatening the very basis of American Christianity was only partly produced by fears of the revolutionary turmoil abroad. The importation of radical Enlightenment ideas from France certainly alarmed conservative Protestants, but far larger and more concrete a danger came from within America itself. In addition to the rise of political party conflict in the late 1790's, which, at least for Federalist ministers, seemed largely the result of foreign atheist influence, the swelling domestic migration into the new territories posed a fundamental challenge to the traditional ecclesiastical order. The leading Congregationalist and Presbyterian churches, in particular, found themselves unable to keep pace with the westward movement, and they became increasingly preoccupied with the threat of irreligion on the frontier. For them, just as ominous as radical Enlightenment ideas were the various "false teachers," "deluded religionists," and "self-stiled preachers of the gospel" – by whom they usually meant Methodists and Universalists – who were active in the unchurched settlements along the frontier.[40] Analyzing the religious situation in the northern backcountry, the *Connecticut Evangelical Magazine* reported that "in those settlements, from all that we can learn, the people are fainting, and scattered abroad, as sheep having no shepherd."[41] In 1797 the Congregationalist minister Levi Hart described settlements he had recently visited in Vermont as posed at a critical spiritual crossroads. Were respectable New England ministers to cease evangelizing on the frontier, he warned, "it is much to be feared, that those settlements in general will either continue destitute of public teachers, or fall under the influence of ignorant and evil-minded leaders."[42] An appeal for public support of Congregationalist missionaries on the frontier described the settlers in 1801 as "exposed to the seduction of infidelity on one hand, and the enthusiasm of ignorant pretenders to religion on the other; they are gradually forgetting the religious habits and truths received in their youth."[43] Another such piece published the following year dramatically predicted that the "people in our new settlements will, doubtless, gradually lose sight of the gospel, and sink into heathenism, if they, for a long time, remain destitute of faithful preachers."[44]

The forces of darkness seemed to be closing in on American Protestantism from both Europe and the American wilderness. At the same time as the French Revolution bred widespread dissatisfaction with the promise of revolutionary change, the leading clergy began to turn inward, away from events in Europe and towards the internal state of American religion. This shift reflected both a mounting pessimism about the possibilities of political action and an increasing apprehension about the national, as compared to the international, future. But by no means all the hope of the faithful was lost. Despite the highly demonstrative cries of doomsday, the American religious establishment simultaneously turned vigorously towards the mobilization of the forces of Zion. The keen sense of urgency so common among orthodox leaders around the turn of the century became rapidly translated into an ambitious program of domestic evangelical action. As the prominent Massachusetts divine Nathaniel Emmons typically mixed sentiments of hope and alarm in a sermon of 1800,

. . . it is not yet too late to attempt the propagation of the gospel through this extensive country. Though we have lost much time, . . . though the enemies of religion have, within a very few years, greatly increased in numbers and strength; though they have set every engine in motion, to spread error, deism, and even atheism, through every corner of our land . . . yet it may not be too late.[45]

REGENERATION AND AMERICAN DESTINY

In the traditional manner of the jeremiad, the warning of disaster was delivered in conjunction with a countervailing promise. Even in the gloomiest moments of the late 1790's, ministers held out the hope that the antichristian powers of Europe would destroy one another, that a regenerated Protestant America might yet escape the horrors of the conflagration, and that the remaining people of God would make their own way towards millennial bliss. For divine scripture clearly indicated that "in the last days perilous times shall come," and ministers repeatedly offered the optimistic prediction that the very progress of infidelity would serve to prepare the way for the millennial day. Interest in the prophetic passages of Scripture had been high throughout the 1790's, and continued to soar around the turn of the century in this heated atmosphere of crisis. Whatever the short-run perils to the faithful posed by the French Revolution and religious decline, prophetic commentators found reason to believe that in the grand scheme of things even the escalating evil portended great good.

Far from always assuming a pessimistic attitude, orthodox Federalist clergymen commonly took heart in the terrible calamities visited upon papist "philosophical" France. These calamities "assure us," proclaimed David Osgood in 1799, "that over all this disorder and confusion, this carnage and desolation, these sallies of the wrath of man, and malignant efforts of infernal spirits, an Almighty ruler presides, who will . . . secure the accomplishment of his own decrees in the final overthrow of all Anti-christian powers," and the establishment of his glorious kingdom "among all the nations on earth."[46] The New York Dutch Reformed minister John Henry Livingston similarly derived encouragement from the "vials of wrath now pouring upon those nations which gave their aid and comfort to the man of sin."[47] The rise of revolutionary violence and religious infidelity could be interpreted as the last desperate convulsions of an already severely wounded Antichrist. Timothy Dwight, who saw these developments as the work of the "three unclean spirits" of prophecy, explained that their appearance, alongside the decline of the Roman Beast, signaled the approach of the millennial age.[48] "It is the dying pangs of the . . . beast which now convulse the world," proclaimed the Connecticut Congregationalist leader Nathan Strong in 1798, adding that infidelity would soon fall under the hand of God.[49] His cousin and colleague Cyprian Strong concurred, arguing in his election sermon of 1799 that all the contemporary assaults on God's kingdom were merely temporary, for they would only serve in the end to pave the way for divine victory.[50] Other New England clergymen who in 1801 delivered "century sermons" that reflected on the opening of the nineteenth century further developed this theme, interpreting the French Revolution and the spread of irreligion as signs of the forthcoming collapse of the Antichrist.[51]

According to the common interpretation of scriptural prophecy, both sides would gather their forces during the last days preceding the millennium. Just as Satan would rise up in mighty anger before his final demise, so too Zion would expand its domain and thereby lay the foundations for Christ's Kingdom on earth. At the same time as these conservative Protestant leaders voiced alarm over the evidence of religious decay, they pointed to contrary signs of the advancement of the Kingdom of God. As the Papacy was crumbling, they repeatedly observed, Protestant missionary societies were being founded in America and England. In the expectation that warring Europe would be the principal site of the final conflagration, Nathan Strong cautioned Americans to support Federalist policies and evangelical activism so that the United States might proceed to the final days as a Christian nation unscathed by divine wrath.[52]

For all the Federalist sympathies imbedded in the scenario, it is significant that the mounting conservatism of these ministers most often found expression in a religious rather than a political attack on the French. The revolutionaries were more strongly indicted as infidels than as either tyrants or anarchists. In a marked shift away from the highly political and francophilic Republican millennialism of the mid-1790's, Federalist clergymen typically invested their millennial hopes in the promotion of true Christianity in America by evangelical rather than political means. According to a Connecticut preacher propagating the gospel in western New York, the main lesson taught by the French Revolution was "that Republicanism will not itself fraternize the world."[53] The only proper antidote to such political unrest was aggressive Christian piety. As the New England Congregationalist missionary Alexander Gillet phrased this analysis in 1797, "the gospel is the only plan of safety," the only "preservative of the world from speedy destruction."[54] "Where religion prevails," Timothy Dwight enthusiastically agreed, "Illuminatism cannot make disciples, a French directory cannot govern, a nation cannot be made slaves, nor villains, nor atheists, nor beasts."[55]

The Federalism of leading Congregationalist clergymen thus often involved the devaluation of political action. Although these ministers rarely repudiated the revolutionary republican values of either the 1770's or the mid-1790's, they kept them from the center of their millennial vision. They conceived of their divine mission not in terms of a republican struggle against tyranny but in terms of an evangelical campaign against religious decline. Nathan Strong counseled that the principal duty of Christians as the Last Days drew near was "to grow in the Christian temper and practice" and to "strive to spread a knowledge of this salvation to the ends of the earth."[56] The millennium would come "not by might nor power, but by the divine spirit," Jeremy Belknap expressed the antipolitical eschatological message in 1798, "By such means, and by none else, will true religion prevail, till the kingdom of Christ shall become universal."[57] Outside New England, in Charleston, South Carolina, the Congregationalist clergyman William Hollinshead also urged American Protestants to dedicate themselves to the promotion of "Christian knowledge in our own land," for by "such means we may contribute more to the national virtue, improvement, and happiness, than ever will be effected by the sword of the hero, or the policy of the statesmen."[58]

Nor were Federalist Congregationalists the only religious leaders to insist on the futility of political transformation. By 1802 the still steadfast Republican Samuel Miller had joined in the antipolitical evangelical chorus. To think of purifying society "by literature – by science – by the prevalence of political orthodoxy – by any thing but Christianity," he now insisted, "is an expectation which all experience has shown to be a vain dream."[59] In Connecticut an 1805 meeting of Baptists, also most likely Republicans, likewise warned against excessive engagement in "Political disputes, and State politics," explaining that more could be done to bring about the millennium "in a few moments with God through Jesus Christ than all the vain disputes: – all the laborious Assembles [*sic*] of States and Empires without him."[60] Republican religious leaders as well as Federalist clergymen ceased to engage in millennial celebrations of the French Revolution and republican government, investing their hopes for the future in the propagation of the gospel instead.

Compared to the prorevolutionary republican millennialism of the 1770's and mid-1790's, the evangelical millennialism that began to take hold around the turn of the century lost its earlier association with institutional social and political change. The dominant form of millennialism was still patriotically American, but it emphasized the spread of American Christianity rather than the establishment of republican forms of government. In certain respects the shift away

215

from political to evangelical millennialism in the late 1790's resembled the transition in millennial thought between the 1770's and 1780's, when moral and spiritual issues similarly came to replace earlier revolutionary political goals. Both the 1780's and the late 1790's were characterized by widespread disillusionment with the transforming effects of republican government. But whereas in the 1780's millennialism in general reached a low ebb, at the turn of the century eschatological hopes remained high: Disenchantment with the French Revolution did not so much dampen American millennial expectations as redirect them towards evangelical aims. Quite unlike the 1780's, moreover, the late 1790's and early 1800's marked the beginning of the long period of religious revivals known as the Second Great Awakening, during which there was not only widespread millennial fervor but an upsurge in organized religious activism. Rather than simply call for the regeneration of national virtue and piety, evangelical Protestants mobilized their forces and aggressively moved to propagate the faith.

American Protestants were repeatedly told that they could not simply passively await the destruction of the Antichrist but must exert themselves to spread the gospel over the face of the earth. In a missionary sermon delivered in 1797 before the Scots Presbyterian Church in New York, John Mason impressed on his listeners that "the means" to the conversion of the world "are in your hands." "We are called not merely to condolence, but to action."[61] The Baptist Morgan John Rhees, preaching to Army officers in the Northwest Territory on the subject of Indian missions, warned the zealous not to "imagine that we are to be idle spectators" while God brought on the millennium alone.[62] Samuel Miller similarly encouraged the work of the New York Missionary Society in 1802, pointing out that "the Church on earth has been, and, until the universal reign of righteousness and peace shall commence, always will be in a militant state."[63] Reflecting on the numerous signs that the millennium was drawing near, a lead article in the *Connecticut Evangelical Magazine* in 1801 pointedly drew the conclusion that the "present is not a period of indolence or indifference [but] for the most vigorous exertions."[64] "We are not to expect any miraculous preparation for this event," Nathan Strong advised, and he recommended "natural means of extensive operation": "First, unfettering the human mind from superstition, and from the power of religious oppression; and secondly, the general spread of doctrinal knowledge through the earth."[65]

In accord with this evangelical program, most American clergymen

216

looked forward to the gradual expansion of God's Kingdom rather than to sudden, apocalyptical change. For all the feeling of crisis surrounding the European war and domestic political conflict in the late 1790's, by the early 1800's the premillennial overtones in earlier sermons by orthodox clergymen largely faded away. Samuel Miller acknowledged in 1802 that the recent belief of "many Protestant believers" that the Pope had already fallen and the millennium "was *nigh, even at the door*" was mistaken, that the accomplishment of divine prophecy would still take time to occur.[66] Several clergymen combined the excited conviction that "the day approaches," that the present was already in "what the scriptures call, *the last days*," with the view that change would be "gradual" and would probably take more than a century to fully achieve.[67] William F. Miller, Congregationalist minister in Windsor, Connecticut, published in 1803 a detailed exegetical work entitled *Signs of the Times*, which argued that the downfall of the Beast would occur in three protracted stages ending only in the year 2000.[68] Even Timothy Dwight's widely shared opinion that the present time fell in the midst of "the pouring of the sixth vial" left room in the future for the conversion of the world by Protestant saints.[69] After the crushing of the Antichristian powers in Europe, Jeremy Belknap explained, "the gentle, peaceful kingdom of the Son of David will be gradually, but universally established."[70] This emerging consensus among Congregationalist and Presbyterian clergymen established the basis for nineteenth-century orthodox postmillennialism, despite the fact that few dwelt specifically on the matter of Christ's return. Although postmillennialism as a technical exegetical theory had already aroused opposition from dissident premillennialists, it was only in the context of the evolving evangelical movement of the early nineteenth century that a more broadly progressive, activistic postmillennialism came to be the standard prophetic theory of the leading American churches.[71]

Before the foundation of the vast "benevolent empire" of educational, moral, and social reform organizations in the 1810's and 1820's, evangelicals relied on Protestant missions as the principal means by which God's agents would accomplish the final conversion of the world.[72] Presbyterian, Reformed, Congregationalist, and Baptist clergymen in the northeast formed several missionary societies in the late 1790's and early 1800's in order to propagate the gospel among the Indians and unconverted settlers along the frontier. Designed partly to combat the growing influence of Methodist and other itinerant preachers in the new territories, this burst of proselytizing activity also brought forth a conspicuous millennial impulse. When assessing the state of religion in the late 1790's, these ministers frequently interpreted the widespread foundation of missionary societies, along with the recent resurgence of the revival, as especially promising signs that the millennium indeed was at hand. The opening statement of the constitution of the Missionary Society of Connecticut in 1800, for example, expressed the hope that the evident "zealous exertions" of the "sundry Christian bodies" signified that "the time is near in which God will spread his truth through the earth."[73] A sermon preached before the Northern Missionary Society in upstate New York in 1797 similarly cited recent missionary activity as compelling evidence that the millennial prophecies "are hastening to their fulfillment."[74] The Republican Presbyterian John McKnight, one of the rare ministers who as late as 1802 still expressed sympathy for the French Revolution, saw both the extension of liberty in France and the rise of the missionary spirit in Britain and America as reasons to believe that the millennium was about to begin.[75] More commonly, the usually Federalist Congregationalist and Presbyterian evangelical ministers regarded the missionary effort as counterbalancing the baneful effects of the French Revolution. Just as the rise of infidelity could be interpreted as the last desperate strategy of a wounded Antichrist, the proliferation of missions seemed a decisive step towards the eventual triumph of the forces of Zion.[76]

Often the very inevitability of the millennium was taken specifically as a promise of success to the mission movement. Citing the scriptural prophecies of the Kingdom of God spreading through the earth, clerical leaders exhorted the faithful to persevere in the evangelical work. John Henry Livingston reassured the members of the New York Missionary Society that "whatever" the immediate results of their missions to the Indians, "it will not be long before the morning will break, and with its rising lustre dispel the shades of night."[77] In a sermon entitled *Missionary-Encouragement*, delivered in Philadelphia, the Baptist William Staughton likewise stressed the certainty of the eventual conversion of the world.[78] Referring to numerous signs that "the time is not very distant, when God shall arise, and have mercy upon Zion," John Mason's *Hope for the Heathen* implored Christian missionaries to "rouse each latent energy, and brave opposition like good soldiers of Jesus Christ."[79]

By working to propagate the gospel through the world, missionary societies were seen to serve as fellow workers with God, bringing on the latter-day glory. From New England to South Carolina, clergymen of various denominations and political persuasions used the language of millennial prophecy to describe the ultimate blessings of the missionary endeavor.[80] John Rodgers, the Republican Presbyterian president of the New York Missionary Society, concluded a sermon marking the departure of an Indian missionary with the hope that he be "an instrument of hastening on the glorious period, when *the desert shall rejoice and blossom as the rose, etc.*"[81] The millennium would come, according to these visions, by means of aggressive evangelical action. "Under the influence of a blaze of light from the fulfillment of prophecy, and a powerfully, [*sic*] preached gospel," proclaimed Federalist Connecticut missionary leader Moses Welch in 1801, "infidelity will sink, deism vanish, and the cause of Jesus triumph and prevail. Righteousness and peace will then overspread the earth."[82]

The dominant Congregationalist and Presbyterian missionary societies of the northeast were composed primarily of Federalist clergymen, but they typically subordinated partisan politics to a broader evangelical world view. Literature advocating missions occasionally contended in vague terms that "the civil and political as well as the religious welfare of our brethren in the New Settlements require that the gospel should be preached to them."[83] These evangelical activists do not, however, appear to have had any specific party objectives in mind. Even though the settlers on the frontier to whom they offered the gospel often were Republican, there is surprisingly little evidence that the Federalist preachers aimed to effect concrete political change. Missionaries for the Connecticut Missionary Society, for example, rarely commented on the political composition of the regions through which they passed. Missionary Thomas Robbins's caustic observation that "infidels in religion are apt to be Democrats," entered in his diary while he was on tour in Vermont in 1799, is the exception rather than the rule.[84] In fact, even when so partisan a clergyman as he visited some settlements in northern Pennsylvania four years later, he generously conceded that "most of the ministers and serious people in this part of the country, and of all classes, are Democrats."[85] Rather than attacking the Jeffersonians, Federalist evangelicals at most voiced resentment of electioneering in general for being an unseemly distraction from religious concerns.[86]

Although for New England Congregationalists such an abhorrence of party politics formed an essential ingredient of their Old School Federalist creed, even the generally Republican Baptist missionaries shared this antipolitical stance.[87] In an open letter published in 1803, the trustees of the Massachusetts Baptist Missionary Society counseled their missionaries to "solicitously avoid all interference and allusion to those political topics which divide the opinions, and too much irritate the passions of our fellow citizens."[88] This fastidious avoidance of political issues enabled the burgeoning evangelical movement, despite its Federalist domination, to include growing numbers of Republicans in its ranks. For all the momentary hysteria among conservative clergymen immediately before the election of Jefferson, by the early 1800's they formed a united front against the religious ignorance and apathy they regarded as the true counterpart of French Jacobinism in America.

Far from provincial in their outlook, American evangelical leaders derived special encouragement from the work of missionary societies overseas. The emergent sense of world crisis that sparked their own millennial aspirations made them particularly eager to associate with an international Protestant missionary movement that encompassed far more than their mere local concerns. When British Methodists, Presbyterians, Independents, and Episcopalians founded the London Missionary Society in 1795 and began to undertake missions in distant parts of the empire, the news made an immediate impact on American religious circles. As ministers in the northern United States, especially, formed their own missionary societies beginning in 1796, they conspicuously drew from the English precedent. Even though these organizations were usually run by Congregationalists and Presbyterians, they stressed the importance of interdenominational unity. In 1797 the Northern Missionary Society in upstate New York, for example, rejoiced that "a coalition has been recently formed amongst Christians of various denominations, both in Europe, and America, to propagate the Gospel."[89] The very titles of the American societies – the New York Missionary Society, the Connecticut Missionary Society, the Massachusetts Missionary Society – reflected their sense of alliance with the British agency. When the General Association of the Connecticut Congregationalist Church presented its public case for the establishment of a missionary society in 1797, its "Address" contained long extracts from London Missionary Society publications and specifically cited the major incentive provided by "the uncommon success God has been graciously pleased to grant to late undertakings of this kind, both in Great Britain and the United States."[90] American missionary literature frequently played on the cooperative theme. According to the preface to the constitution of the Massachusetts Baptists' society, they too were "animated by the laudable exertions which our Christian

220

friends . . . on both sides of the Atlantic are making.''[91] Periodicals published on behalf of the missionary societies, such as the *Connecticut Evangelical Magazine*, the *Massachusetts Missionary Magazine*, and the *Massachusetts Baptist Missionary Magazine*, contained regular coverage of British foreign missionary activities.[92] Whereas the Congregationalists covered the missions of the London Missionary Society, the Baptists concentrated on those of the English Baptist Missionary Society. For both denominations, however, the consciousness of being part of an international movement was vital to their own sense of purpose.

For American Protestant leaders, long accustomed to measuring their experience in global terms, the launching of domestic missions was closely interlocked with events unfolding abroad. With one eye on the French Revolution and the growth of radical Enlightenment ideas, the other on the Indians and the unchurched white settlements on the frontier, it appeared to them that the emerging threat to Christianity in America was simply one more manifestation of a universal phenomenon. At a time when the fledgling American republic seemed in danger of slipping into the backwaters of history, moreover, the strong sense of identification with the British evangelicals helped to sustain worldwide millennial aspirations. The growing disenchantment with France among both Federalist and Republican Protestants by the late 1790's had inevitably revived a latent anglophilia among many divines, one nurtured by the memory of prerevolutionary Anglo-American victories over France. Since Protestant England had now, once again, declared war on the satanic forces amassed on the Continent, it was obvious that the British would play a key role in accomplishing the defeat of the Antichrist. Especially high hopes were aroused when, during the brief Peace of Amiens, the London Missionary Society launched a preliminary campaign to convert the French and Italians to the Protestant faith.[93]

Impressed with Britain's uniquely pivotal position in relation to France, the Americans even more deeply admired the sheer scope of the British missionary activity. Insofar as their broad historical analysis called for the conversion of the entire world, only by close identification with the British missionaries in heathen lands could they hope to satisfy these global ambitions. The constitution of the Missionary Society of Connecticut, for example, cited the success of the British missions in Africa, India, and the South Seas – along with the domestic American revivals – as "strong grounds to hope that

God, in fulfillment of ancient prophecies, is about to give to his Son the Heathen for his inheritance, and the uttermost parts of the earth for his possession."[94]

Thus gaining reinforcement from the work of missionaries overseas, American evangelicals felt assured that they were engaged in an international, cooperative mission to bring Protestantism to the world. In fact, however, these Americans' assumption that their own domestic endeavors were essentially akin to British missions to the heathen was largely illusory. For whereas the British missionaries dramatically undertook to spread the gospel in pagan lands, their American brethren concentrated most of their frontier missions, as the *Connecticut Evangelical Magazine* put it, "among new and scattered settlements of those born from Christian parents," and sent only relatively small numbers of preachers to evangelize among the American Indians.[95] The few Indian missions that were established in these years gained considerable publicity as steps towards the universal conversion of the heathen foretold in millennial prophecy, but the actual priority given to the so-called home missions in white settlements reveal a greater preoccupation with the future course of Anglo-American society.

In the minds of the New England Federalist clergy, in particular, many centrifugal forces were threatening to pull their traditional society apart and cause widespread defections from their faith. The spread of irreligion and sectarianism along the frontier, the internal challenges to the local ecclesiastical establishments, the erosion of national political unity, and the dangers of foreign infidelity were, for them, all of a piece. They sought to curb the forces of fragmentation by aiming their evangelical activity towards unchurched Americans in the new settlements. Frontier settlers were, in the words of the Connecticut General Association, "without the stated preaching of the word – without the ordinances of the gospel – without sanctified sabbaths, or regular religious instruction; many of them, though called Christians, are Heathen in reality."[96] In the face of basic problems of social and religious disorganization posed by westward migration, they claimed that Christian faith offered the best guarantee of a stable, cohesive community. Describing the purpose of their missions, the trustees of the Connecticut Missionary Society explained that "the civil and political welfare of societies no less than the present and future happiness of individuals depends much on religious institutions."[97] Once the settlers began to receive "the occasional ministration of proper missionaries," evangelical leaders predicted that "their civil order, every advantage of social life, and all their temporal interests, will be advanced by family order, and the public observation of the sabbath."[98] Openly committed to the promotion of "good order," missionary societies aimed to propagate certain social values along with their gospel faith. They denied that religious and social concerns could be separated, claiming that the Bible "teaches whatever is essential to the common weal."[99]

In accord with the Federalist politics of many Congregationalist and Presbyterian evangelicals, their statements about society were generally conservative, in both content and tone. They firmly believed, for example, that social happiness depended on a stable and hierarchical class structure. A pamphlet entitled *A Summary of Christian Doctrine and Practice: Designed Especially for the Use of People in the New Settlements* issued under the auspices of the Connecticut Missionary Society, for example, elaborated on the importance of preserving traditional patterns of authority in society. It devoted several pages to a discussion of social roles in which relationships were broken down into a series of unequal pairs. These included husbands and wives, parents and children, masters and servants, and other impersonal "superiors" and "inferiors" as well.[100]

Yet while these conservative promoters of missions assumed that good societies have fixed and layered structures, they also firmly believed that status should accrue to virtue as well as to wealth. In their view, prestige should reward the discreet, steadfast, pious, and socially responsible. In accord with this traditional notion of an honorable and dependable elite, they despised acquisitiveness and generally mistrusted new wealth. In 1798, Joseph Lathrop went so far as to regret the "singular prosperity of this country," for it gave incentive to the financial fraud and speculation that, along with the spread of Deism and atheism, threatened to unravel the moral fabric of the nation.[101] Samuel Miller, who combined his critique of materialistic values with his Jeffersonian Republican politics, regarded the "spirit of commerce and speculation" as a modern vice kin to infidelity itself.[102] Evangelicals especially deplored the fact that economic opportunity in the west often brought men of doubtful character into positions of leadership – such as "the great land dealers" who refused to support a ministry in the new settlements.[103] The qualities they admired the most in individuals were "chastity, temperance, and sobriety."[104] They proudly characterized their own supporters on the frontier – the influential and the more modest alike – as "respectable," "judicious, steady and serious."[105]

223

The infidels, by contrast, they typically claimed were "licentious," interested only in the unrestrained "gratification of their lusts and passions."[106] In the view of such degenerate characters "self-love is to be indulged to the highest degree; covetousness also is to reign uncontrolled; boasting is to be free in everyone's mouth; pride is to have its full run." The goal of these unrestrained individualists was, in the words of the *Connecticut Evangelical Magazine*, "to subvert all the foundations of society, to break every human tie and let every man act as he pleases."[107] Once "you drive religion from a people," the former missionary William Lyman ominously observed, "you present to the view of degraded man the groveling scene of a lustful paradise."[108] Society needed Christian religion to curb such destructive individual inpulses and to instill a spirit of mutual responsibility.

According to this perspective, religion and communitarian values closely intertwined. The social dimension of the missionary endeavor thus involved far more than simply the conservation of deferential attitudes. For, in the minds of these ministers, good order depended not only on the hierarchical ordering principle but, even more importantly, on that sense of reciprocal moral obligation that came alongside religious faith. As Connecticut Missionary Society trustee Nathan Perkins once elaborated on Lockean theory, "it is apparent that the blessings sought by the social compact, cannot be attained, without piety and morality – a sense of moral obligations – a belief of a divine existence – of man's accountability – and the ties of justice and humanity."[109] Only such rigorous Christian faith could counteract the destructive forces pushing towards anarchic individualism. Fearful that frontier society might never properly congeal, evangelical ministers stressed "the salutary tendency of the Missionary Societies to reform selfish man."[110]

For all their concern about the preservation of social bonds, however, it is significant that evangelicals at the turn of the century oriented themselves to the task of individual conversion rather than directly towards social reform. In their view personal piety and morality remained the key to the wider societal well-being. Frequently they stressed the importance of families, in particular, as the connecting link between private virtue and public happiness. "Will that man be kind, generous and faithful to his neighbor, who neglects and abuses his own parents and family?" asked the South Carolina Baptist Richard Furman in 1802.[111] Abraham Cummings cited the disobeying of parents and the dissolution of kin ties, both of

224

which he blamed at least partly on the doctrines of the Illuminati, as signs that the Last Days were near.[112]

Alongside the increasing emphasis on family life, a development that would continue within American evangelical Protestantism for many decades to come, clergymen in this period began to place special value on the redemptive qualities of women.[113] The view that women played a dominant role in the regeneration of the world had already arisen among the Shakers and Universal Friends, the small radical sects led by prophetesses who altogether repudiated wider social and political involvement. Another figure on the religious fringe who stressed the millennial agency of women, the Loyalist Dutch immigrant William Gerar DeBrahm, outlined a continuing conflict through history between a masculine, tyrannical, anti-christian "reason" and a feminine, republican, Christian "under-standing."[114] By the turn of the century less eccentric Protestant commentators also began to play on this theme. Noting that "individuals form families, and families form communities," the Connecticut minister William Lyman called on mothers, in par-ticular, to "exert all their influence to drive discord, infidelity and licentiousness from our land – to train our sons and daughters for virtue and happiness, and, with the aid of all the pious in the more vigorous sex, labour to reform the world and ripen this earth for a paradise."[115] By striking vice and promoting virtue within the family, women would lay the foundations for the personal faith of indi-viduals who would then form the advancing legions of Christ.

This evangelical emphasis on the importance of individual piety and morality found its consummate expression in the religious revivals of the early part of the Second Great Awakening. First sweeping through various parts of the country at the turn of the century, the wave of ecstatic conversions greatly bolstered the morale of evangelical organizers, who were quick to interpret it as a divine sign of the certain success of their cause. Missionaries especially appreciated the positive impact of religious revivals on the new settlements, for the contagious workings of the spirit proved by far the greatest unifying force among Protestants on the frontier. As soon as the flood of revivals began to pass over New England in the late 1790's, Methodists, Baptists, and Congregationalists alike sought to spread the revival impulse over the new territory. Un-doubtedly the most powerful means of overcoming infidelity, spiritual deadness, and religious apathy, these awakenings shortly became the chief index of success for the missionaries preaching in the new settlements. They generally remained longest in those areas receiving the spiritual outpourings, and often kept close records of the progress of the revival that were subsequently publicized in the missionary literature.[116] Almost from the onset of the Awakening, these clergymen heralded it as the great turning point in the history of frontier missions. Inspired by "the great effusions of the divine spirit in the wilderness within a year and a half past," a Connecticut missionary writing from western New York in 1800, for example, joyously proclaimed, "the year of redemption is come, when the prison doors are open to the captive and Jerusalem breaks forth in songs, and deserts learn the joy."[117]

Accounts of revivals in various denominations and parts of the country were frequently punctuated by millennial wishes that the gospel spread "till the glory of the Lord covers the earth as the water does the sea," "till the earth shall become a mountain of holiness and a habitation of righteousness," "until all nations and all orders and degrees of men shall submit to the sceptre of King Immanuel, and peace and truth pervade the world."[118] In the early years of the nineteenth century evangelical ministers often cited the revivals in New England, New York, Pennsylvania, Kentucky, North Carolina, and elsewhere as grounds for confidence that history was leading towards the triumph of the Kingdom of Christ.[119] "May we not conclude" upon observing God's hand in the spiritual outpouring, asked a member of the New York Baptist Society in May 1799, "that the approaching crisis of some signal display of his power is near? Is he not about rescuing his abused truth and the glory of his name from the sacrilegious hands of Antichrist, whether Papal or Protestant?"[120] Another anonymous Baptist in Hartford, Connecticut, issued a broadside calling ministers of all denominations to join in the propagation of religious revivals because the millennial "Desire of all Nations, is at hand."[121] The eschatological excitement generated by the revivals spread along the path of the spirit into the west itself. In western Pennsylvania an observer of the awakening remarked in 1799 that the revival enthusiasm "is often as a fresh spring to prayer for, and expectation of, the fulfillment of the promises respecting the later day Glory."[122] The "Great Revival" in Kentucky should be considered "as a prelude" to the millennium, suggested David Thomas in his spirited defense of the spectacular upsurge of grace in the southwest.[123] Thomas actually wondered whether the millennial prophecies had "not been already fulfilled," and other evangelical clergymen often preached that the millennium was then under way.[124] The prominent Lexington minister David Rice was evidently countering widespread opinion when he denied that the revivals signified the millennium was "very near."[125] He regarded the revivalists' constant preoccupation with the coming of the millennium as an example of their unfortunate excesses.[126]

Nevertheless, for all his caution, Rice agreed that the Kentucky revival had greatly improved the moral standards of the region.[127] Apprehensive that the spiritual effusion would overcome all restraint and spill over into irresponsible antinomian fervor – as it had, briefly, in the 1740's – evangelicals at the turn of the century generally agreed that the ultimate test of any revival was its long-range moral effect. An essay entitled "Remarks on the late religious revivals and on the use of means" that appeared in an 1801 issue of the *Connecticut Evangelical Magazine*, for example, reminded its readers that although regeneration is "the *beginning* of salvation, yet it is not the *whole* of salvation," and underscored the continuing necessity of a sanctified life.[128] *The Summary of Christian Doctrine* prepared for the inhabitants of the new settlements even inadvertently leaned towards an Arminian position in its stress on the voluntary, moral aspects of the religious life.[129]

In the aftermath of the first wave of revivals, evangelical leaders began to measure their substantial gain. Preachers were pleased to report that many regions formerly known for their "divided people, neglect of religion, profaned sabbaths, corrupt sentiments, forgetfulness of God, and a general unconcern about the salvation of the soul" had been virtually transformed by the combined work of the missionaries and the spirit.[130] During the opening years of the century a victorious note reverberated throughout the evangelical literature. The Presbyterian General Assembly's "Report on the state of religion" issued in 1803 observed that wherever the revivals had occurred "the general aspect of society changed from dissoluteness and profanity, to sobriety, order and comparative purity."[131] Defenders of the western revival likewise placed special emphasis on the "good fruits" of the Awakening. People were "now as distinguished for sobriety as they had formerly been for dissoluteness," reported one observer of the Kentucky revival.[132] Another pointed out that it "had done good in many families, made better husbands and wives, parents and children, masters and servants, and every domestic relation."[133] Recipients of the divine spirit typically demonstrated their greater "honesty, sobriety, fidelity, philanthropy, benevolence, meekness, charity, peace and tranquility, &c. &c. &c."[134]

Indeed, according to John McKnight in 1802, the revivals indicated that infidelity had already "spent its force" and was now in a process of worldwide decline.[135] "The mouth of deism is at present stopped," announced another minister, reporting on revivals in Maine; "O may the Lord go on from conquering to conquer, till the whole earth shall be filled with his glory."[136] The Presbyterian Assembly of 1803 celebrated the fact that throughout the nation the forces of irreligion were "less bold, and active, than formerly" and stated, "On the whole, the Assembly, cannot but declare, with joy, . . . that the state and prospects of vital religion, in our country *are more favorable and encouraging than at any period within the last forty years.*"[137]

With infidelity apparently on the run and the frontier settlements falling under the spell of the revivals, evangelical ministers increasingly turned to contemplate the prospect of a triumphant American Christianity. No longer preoccupied with the threat of irreligion from abroad, they focused once again on exalted ideas of the future destiny of America. In addition to the encouraging onset of revivalism, the most pressing reason for this altered perspective was that the French Revolution never came to the apocalyptical head so widely prophesied by the conservative clergy in the late 1790's. It neither seized hold of the Jefferson administration in Washington nor suffered a resounding defeat at the hands of the British but, instead, anticlimactically dragged out into the protracted Napoleonic Wars. Particularly after the resumption of European warfare in 1803, the American evangelicals perceived less of an organic connection between the conflict overseas and their own domestic endeavors. The annual "New Year's" essay in the *Connecticut Evangelical Magazine*, for example, gave progressively less attention to world political events. In 1805 the editors actually drew an explicit distinction between the European and American situations, complacently comparing the "politics, broils, and wars" on the far side of the Atlantic to "our peace, our distinguished civil and religious privileges and enjoyments."[138]

This sense of regained confidence often found expression in heady visions of the gospel spreading westward across the American continent, sweeping aside Indian heathenism and carrying along the civilized settlements of the American legions of God. While continuing to believe that they, like the British missionaries, were advancing Christ's Kingdom into benighted regions of the earth, American clergymen often attached an increasingly physical, rather than a spiritual, significance to this idea. Whereas missionaries to the Indians and to foreign lands aimed to teach gospel truths to heathens, it was suggested that among Americans the kingdom would spread by means of the actual territorial expansion of Zion across the continent. In his century sermon *On the Universal Spread of the Gospel* the Hartford evangelical leader Nathan Strong described how Christianity would progress throughout the globe, overcoming Turks, Heathens, and Jews, but gave special attention to the American migration west.

In all the eastern shores of America, from north to south, Christianity is planted; and that tide of men, which is rolling westward, with an unparralleled [sic] velocity of population, long before the present century is finished, will carry the gospel of Christ across to the Pacific ocean and the eastern shores of Asia.[139]

When the Ohio missionary Joseph Badger encountered "professing Christians mourning the loss of their former privileges," he consoled them with the thought "that they had been moved here by the hand of God, to plant the church in the wilderness."[140] Ashbel Hosmer, a Baptist of western New York, interpreted the cultivation of "golden fields and spacious meads" in the new territory, which promised "a rich reward to the industrious husbandmen," as evidence of "the increasing glory of the Redeemer's Kingdom, exhibited, in this spacious theatre."[141] The Connecticut missionary Thomas Robbins, in a sermon at the ordination of a fellow western evangelist, took this analysis one step farther. Even those pioneers who recklessly "go forth, thinking thereby to become extricated from those restraints which the gospel imposes wherever it is received" inevitably become "used in the providence of God, as harbingers of the Prince of peace." For, he confidently observed, God was sending civilization through the west precisely in order "to advance the glorious kingdom of the Redeemer."[142]

American evangelical literature often resounded with the biblical refrain "the desert and solitary place bud and blossom as the rose," a theme with decidedly nationalistic as well as spiritual implications. While early nineteenth-century Protestant activists were perhaps less certain than their revolutionary predecessors that America alone would inaugurate the millennium – and far less inclined to view republican politics as its principal means – they nevertheless continued to believe that the new nation would play a leading role in advancing the Kingdom of God. This originally Puritan idea, now largely stripped of the revolutionary implications it had assumed in the 1770's, would later become an integral part of the nineteenth-century creed of American manifest destiny.[143]

The nationalistic evangelical millennialism that arose at the very end of the eighteenth century would remain the dominant type of American millennialism for many decades to come. Protestant leaders of almost all major religious persuasions, including even some who were not evangelical, came to imbibe and deliver its basic message of transcendent national promise. Possessed of a keen sense of divine mission and sustained by high eschatological expectations, the dozens of missionary, moral reform, and benevolent associations formed by a wide range of denominations in the early nineteenth century carried this message through the new nation. Zealous, patriotic, expansionistic, and generally optimistic about the future, this type of millennialism would continue to hold sway over a large part of American religious culture through the crisis of the Civil War and into the late nineteenth century.[144]

No sooner had this nationalistic evangelical millennialism become virtually hegemonic within many Protestant churches, however, when other kinds of millennial currents arose, again, to compete with it. In the 1830's and 1840's various radical movements – abolitionism, health reform, early socialism – drew inspiration from millennial prophecy both in their attacks on the institutions and values of contemporary society and in their promise of a better world. Although many figures in these movements had evangelical backgrounds, they rejected the nonpolitical (often implicitly conservative) tenor of evangelicalism and pushed the millennial tradition again towards basic social and political criticism.[145] Still other kinds of radical millennialists rejected both social reform and optimistic evangelical religion, embracing instead the catastrophic outlook on the immediate future of the Millerites and other early nineteenth-century premillennialists. In time this originally eccentric and sectarian perspective would permeate many churches and become an important feature of modern American fundamentalism. By the middle of the twentieth century fundamentalist premillennialism probably had become the dominant type of explicitly biblical millennial thought in America. But millennial traditions within liberal and evangelical Protestantism and within the history of American social reform have also persisted, if usually in a less literal form, into the present day.[146]

Millennial themes have thus continued to reverberate through American thought since the end of the eighteenth century. Changing in accord with shifting historical circumstances, they have embodied a variety of cultural tensions and expressed a series of collective ideals. Yet, for all the adaptiveness of American millennial thought, its continuity is at least as important as its variations. Until the late nineteenth century, and in many cases even beyond, millennialism provided a major intellectual framework through which Americans understood the general course of history and defined their national purpose. Although the ultimate origins of this pattern of thought can be traced back to ancient Israel, it was during the late eighteenth century that millennialism fully merged with American secular republican ideology and became an essential ingredient of the national culture. During a period defined more by its political than its religious enthusiasm, American millennialism lost most of its former identification with specific religious movements and became a general and diffuse cultural orientation. Inspiring Americans of many different regions, religious denominations, and political points of view, the heady vision of a future age of worldly perfection gave transcendent meaning to the experience of the American Revolution and imbued the American republic, for both better and worse, with a remarkably enduring sense of world-historical mission. At once a source and a legacy of the revolutionary spirit of the 1770's, millennialism in its various forms had by 1800 become deeply imbedded in the thought and the character of the American people.

Notes

Introduction

1. Eric Voegelin, *Order and History: Israel and Revelation* (Baton Rouge: Louisiana University Press, 1956); Shirley Jackson Case, *The Millennial Hope* (Chicago: University of Chicago Press, 1918); Mircea Eliade, *The Myth of the Eternal Return, or, Cosmos and History*, trans. Willard R. Trask (Princeton: Princeton University Press, 1954); Yonina Talmon, "Millenarian Movements," *European Journal of Sociology* 7 (1966): 159-200.

2. Major representative examples of scholarly works that take one or more of these perspectives include Norman Cohn, *The Pursuit of the Millennium*, rev. ed. (New York: Oxford University Press, 1970); Gershom Scholem, *Sabbatai Sevi*, trans. R. J. Zwi Werblowsky (Princeton: Princeton University Press, 1973); E. J. Hobsbawm, *Primitive Rebels* (New York: Norton, 1959); Peter Worsley, *The Trumpet Shall Sound*, 2nd ed. (New York: Schocken, 1968); Sylvia L. Thrupp, ed. *Millennial Dreams on Action* (The Hague: Mouton, 1962); Marjorie Reeves, *Prophecy in the Later Middle Ages* (Oxford: Clarendon Press, 1969); Donald Weinstein, *Savonarola and Florence* (Princeton: Princeton University Press, 1970); Clarke Garrett, *Respectable Folly* (Baltimore: Johns Hopkins University Press, 1975). For a useful review essay, see Hillel Schwartz, "The End of the Beginning: Millenarian Studies, 1969-1975," *Religious Studies Review* 2 (1976): 1-15.

3. See especially Carl Becker, *The Declaration of Independence* (New York: Knopf, 1922); Vernon Parrington, *Main Currents in American Thought* (New York: Harcourt, Brace, 1930); Edmund S. and Helen M. Morgan, *The Stamp Act Crisis* (Chapel Hill: University of North Carolina Press, 1953); Louis Hartz, *The Liberal Tradition in America* (New York: Harcourt, Brace and World, 1955); and Daniel Boorstin, *The Genius of American Politics* (Chicago: University of Chicago Press, 1953).

4. Bernard Bailyn, *The Ideological Origins of the American Revolution* (Cambridge, Mass.: Harvard University Press, 1968); Bernard Bailyn, "Religion and Revolution: Three Biographical Studies," *Perspectives in American History* 4 (1970): 85-169; J. G. A. Pocock, *The Machiavellian Moment* (Princeton: Princeton University Press, 1975).

5. See, for example, Perry Miller, "From the Covenant to the Revival," in *Nature's Nation* (Cambridge, Mass.: Harvard University Press, 1967);

233

Edmund S. Morgan, "The Puritan Ethic and the American Revolution," *William and Mary Quarterly*, 3d ser. 24 (1967): 3-43; Robert Middlekauff, "The Ritualizaton of the American Revolution," in *The National Temper*, ed. Lawrence W. Levine and Robert Middlekauff (New York: Harcourt Brace Jovanovich, 1972), pp. 100-10; John F. Berens, *Providence and Patriotism in Early America, 1640-1815* (Charlottesville: University Press of Virginia, 1978); Rhys Isaac, *The Transformation of Virginia* (Chapel Hill: University of North Carolina Press, 1982).

6. The two major works stressing the importance of millennial thought in the American Revolution and setting the terms for subsequent historiographical debate are Alan Heimert, *Religion and the American Mind* (Cambridge, Mass.: Harvard University Press, 1966), and Ernest Lee Tuveson, *Redeemer Nation* (Chicago: University of Chicago Press, 1968). Both draw upon C. C. Goen, "Jonathan Edwards: A New Departure in Eschatology," *Church History* 38 (1959): 25-40. Other recent works that touch on this theme in the course of developing more general arguments are Gordon S. Wood, "Rhetoric and Reality in the American Revolution," *William and Mary Quarterly*, 3d ser. 23 (1966): 3-32; J. F. Maclear, "The Republic and the Millennium," in *The Religion of the Republic*, ed. Elwyn A. Smith (Philadelphia: Fortress Press, 1971), pp. 183-216; William G. McLoughlin, *New England Dissent, 1630-1833*, 2 vols. (Cambridge, Mass.: Harvard University Press, 1971); Cushing Strout, *The New Heavens and New Earth* (New York: Harper and Row, 1974); Sacvan Bercovitch, *The American Jeremiad* (Madison: University of Wisconsin Press, 1978); and Charles Royster, *A Revolutionary People at War* (Chapel Hill: University of North Carolina Press, 1979).

7. Nathan O. Hatch, *The Sacred Cause of Liberty* (New Haven: Yale University Press, 1977); James West Davidson, *The Logic of Millennial Thought* (New Haven: Yale University Press, 1977).

8. Most of my research has been in the Readex microprint collection compiled from Charles Evans's *American Bibliography*, 14 vols. (Chicago: Blakely Press and Columbia Press, 1903-34, and Worcester, Mass.: American Antiquarian Society, 1955), and *Supplement to Charles Evans' American Bibliography*, ed. Roger P. Bristol (Charlottesville: University Press of Virginia, 1970). I have also used newspapers and magazines not included in this collection.

9. *Atlas of Early American History: The Revolutionary Era, 1760-1790*, ed. Lester J. Cappon (Princeton: Princeton University Press, 1976), pp. 25, 36; Edwin Scott Gaustad, *Historical Atlas of Religion in America* (New York: Harper and Row, 1962), p. 4. About 60 percent of the white religious population in 1775 appears to have been Congregationalist, Presbyterian, or Baptist. All but a small fraction of the white population was at least informally churched. See Patricia U. Bonomi and Peter R. Eisenstadt, "Church Adherence in the Eighteenth-Century British American Colonies," *William and Mary Quarterly*, 3d ser. 39 (April 1982): 245-86.

10. *Atlas*, ed. Cappon, p. 36.

11. Kenneth A. Lockridge, *Literacy in Colonial New England* (New York: Norton, 1974), pp. 72-101.

1. Millennialism and the origins of Anglo-American radicalism

1. For a recent survey of the historical literature on the civic republican tradition, see Robert E. Shalhope, "Republicanism and Early American Historiography," *William and Mary Quarterly*, 3d ser. 39 (April 1982): 334-56.
2. This discussion draws primarily from J. G. A. Pocock, *The Machiavellian Moment* (Princeton: Princeton University Press, 1975). For whig theories of history, also see H. Trevor Colbourne, *The Lamp of Experience* (Chapel Hill: University of North Carolina Press, 1965).
3. On medieval and early Renaissance Continental millennialism, see Norman Cohn, *The Pursuit of the Millennium*, rev. ed. (New York: Oxford University Press, 1970); Marjorie Reeves, *Prophecy in the Later Middle Ages* (Oxford: Clarendon Press, 1969); Howard Kaminsky, *A History of the Hussite Revolution* (Berkeley: University of California Press, 1967); Donald Weinstein, *Savonarola and Florence* (Princeton: Princeton University Press, 1970).
4. William Haller, *Foxe's Book of Martyrs and the Elect Nation* (London: Jonathan Cape, 1963); William Lamont, *Godly Rule* (London: Macmillan, 1969); Christopher Hill, *Antichrist in Seventeenth-Century England* (New York: Oxford University Press, 1971), pp. 1-40; and *Puritans, the Millennium and the Future of Israel*, ed. Peter Toon (Cambridge: James Clarke, 1970).
5. Peter Toon, "The Latter-Day Glory," and R. G. Clouse, "The Rebirth of Millenarianism," in *Puritans, the Millennium*, ed. Toon, pp. 23-65.
6. This development is traced in Christopher Hill, *The World Turned Upside Down* (New York: Viking, 1972), Michael Walzer, *The Revolution of the Saints* (Cambridge, Mass.: Harvard University Press, 1965), and the various works on revolutionary England cited above.
7. B. S. Capp, "Extreme Millenarianism," in *Puritans, the Millennium*, ed. Toon, p. 86; Bernard S. Capp, *The Fifth Monarchy Men* (London: Faber, 1972), p. 152.
8. Michael Fixler, *Milton and the Kingdom of God* (Chicago: Northwestern University Press, 1964), pp. 205-6, 221-71.
9. J. G. A. Pocock's *Machiavellian Moment* stresses this connection. See especially James Harrington, *Oceana*, ed. S. B. Liljegren (Heidelberg: Carl Winters Universitätsbuchhandlung, 1924), pp. 187-8, 194.
10. Hill, *Antichrist*, p. 151; Margaret C. Jacob, *The Newtonians and the English Revolution 1689-1720* (Ithaca: Cornell University Press, 1976), pp. 151-2.
11. Jacob, *Newtonians*, and Ernest Lee Tuveson, *Millennium and Utopia* (Berkeley: University of California Press, 1949). There is also a little evidence of apocalyptical ideas among Restoration conservatives. See J. G. A. Pocock, "Time, History and Eschatology in the Thought of Thomas Hobbes," in *Politics, Language and Time* (New York: Atheneum, 1973), and William Lamont, "Richard Baxter, the Apocalypse and the Mad Major," *Past and Present* 52 (May 1971): 106-17. But Lamont and Jacob make it clear that millennialism was still publicly associated with radicalism, and that conservative millennialists tended not to publicize their ideas.

12. On Whitby and Lowman, see Ernest Lee Tuveson, *Redeemer Nation* (Chicago: University of Chicago Press, 1968), pp. 39-46, and James West Davidson, *The Logic of Millennial Thought* (New Haven: Yale University Press, 1977), pp. 141-9. These discussions concentrate on the doctrinal issue of postmillennialism, offering opposite views.

13. Hillel Schwartz, *The French Prophets* (Berkeley: University of California Press, 1980). On the resurgence of English millennialism at the turn of the eighteenth century, see the varying interpretations of Clarke Garrett, *Respectable Folly* (Baltimore: Johns Hopkins University Press, 1975); J. F. C. Harrison, *The Second Coming* (London: Routledge and Kegan Paul, 1979); E. P. Thompson, *The Making of the English Working Class* (New York: Knopf, 1963), pp. 375-400. John Wesley, the Methodist leader, did briefly apply himself to prophetic speculation, borrowing from the elaborate apolitical schema of the German Johann Albrecht Bengel, who predicted that a purely spiritual millennium would begin in the mid-nineteenth century. See John Wesley, *Explanatory Notes upon the New Testament*, orig. ed. 1754 (Philadelphia, 1791), pp. 220-342. And, according to Schwartz, Methodism drew some of its sustenance from the French prophets. But Methodism as a movement concentrated on individual conversion and, partly because of its cautious social and political conservatism, never proclaimed a millennial message in the manner of either the earlier English Puritans and sectaries or the contemporary Calvinist evangelicals in America.

14. Perry Miller's seminal studies of the New England mind, which have long remained definitive, largely ignore this theme – perhaps because, as Robert Middlekauff and J. F. Maclear have observed, Miller was especially concerned to underscore the extent of Puritan rationalism. Major recent works emphasizing the importance of millennialism in seventeenth-century American Puritanism are Robert Middlekauff, *The Mathers: Three Generations of Puritan Intellectuals, 1596-1728* (New York: Oxford University Press, 1971), pp. 20-4; J. F. Maclear, "New England and the Fifth Monarchy: The Quest for the Millennium in Early American Puritanism," *William and Mary Quarterly*, 3d ser. 32 (1975): 223-60; Sacvan Bercovitch, *The Puritan Origins of the American Self* (New Haven: Yale University Press, 1975), pp. 35-108; and Sacvan Bercovitch, *The American Jeremiad* (Madison: University of Wisconsin Press, 1978), pp. 3-92.

15. As quoted in Hill, *Antichrist*, p. 100.

16. Increase Mather, "Preface," *A Discourse Concerning Faith and Fervency in Prayer, and the Glorious Kingdom of the Lord Jesus Christ, on Earth, Now Approaching* (Boston, 1710), p. i.

17. Middlekauff, *Mathers*, pp. 323-4.

18. Davidson, *Logic*, pp. 63-75.

19. Joseph Morgan, *The History of the Kingdom of Barasuah*, ed. Richard Schlatter (Cambridge, Mass.: Harvard University Press, 1946).

20. On this anti-Catholic apocalyptical rhetoric, see Thomas More Brown, "The Images of the Beast: Anti-Papal Rhetoric in Colonial America," in *Conspiracy: The Fear of Subversion in American History*, ed. Richard O. Curry and Thomas M. Brown (New York: Holt, Rinehart and Winston, 1972), pp. 1-20.

21. Davidson, *Logic*, p. 102.
22. Jonathan Edwards, "Notes on the Apocalypse," in *The Works of Jonathan Edwards* (New Haven: Yale University Press, 1977), V, 136.
23. As quoted in Davidson, *Logic*, p. 40. Davidson suggests the connection to Mather.
24. Arthur Bestor, *Backwoods Utopias*, 2nd ed. (Philadelphia: University of Pennsylvania Press, 1970), pp. 20-31.
25. Perry Miller, "Religion and Society in the Early Literature of Virginia," in *Errand into the Wilderness* (New York: Harper and Row, 1956), pp. 115-18. There has been considerable scholarly work done on the "utopian" themes in southern promotional literature, but whether (and how often) they appeared in a specifically eschatological context remains unclear. See Louis B. Wright, *The Colonial Search for a Southern Eden* (Birmingham: University of Alabama Press, 1953); Charles L. Sanford, *The Quest for Paradise* (Urbana: University of Illinois Press, 1961).
26. [William Burnet], *An Essay on Scripture-Prophecy* ([New York], 1724), especially pp. 85, 92-109.
27. Jonathan Edwards, *Some Thoughts Concerning the Present Revival of Religion in New England*, orig. ed. 1742, in *Works of Jonathan Edwards*, IV, 513.
28. Josiah Smith, *The Character, Preaching, &c. of the Reverend Mr. George Whitefield . . . a Sermon Preach'd in Charlestown, South-Carolina* (Boston, 1740), pp. 19-20. This sermon was also printed in Philadelphia in 1740 and in Charlestown in 1765. In addition to the other examples cited below, see the letter of John Moorhead to John Willison, July 30, 1742, in Jules H. Tuttle, "The Glasgow-Weekly-History, 1743," *Proceedings of the Massachusetts Historical Society* 53 (1919-20): 213. As cited by Stephen J. Stein, "Introduction," in *Works of Jonathan Edwards*, V, 26. Also see *The Testimony and Advice of an Assembly of Pastors of Churches in New-England, At a Meeting in Boston July 7, 1743 . . .* (Boston, 1743); excerpted in *The Great Awakening*, ed. Richard L. Bushman (New York: Atheneum, 1970), pp. 129-32.
29. Samuel Finley, *Christ Triumphing, and Satan Raging* (Philadelphia, 1741), in *The Great Awakening*, ed. Alan Heimert and Perry Miller (New York: Bobbs-Merrill, 1967), p. 154.
30. Davidson, *Logic*, pp. 124-5; Nathan O. Hatch, *The Sacred Cause of Liberty* (New Haven: Yale University Press, 1977), p. 29.
31. Perry Miller, "The End of the World," in *Errand*, p. 233.
32. Stephen Stein, "Introduction," in *Works of Jonathan Edwards*, V, 19.
33. Isaac Watts and John Guyse, "Preface to the First Edition (London, 1737)," in *Works of Jonathan Edwards*, IV, 130-7; Joseph Sewall, Thomas Prince, John Webb, and William Cooper, "Preface to the Third Edition (Boston, 1738)," *Works*, IV, 141.
34. Jonathan Edwards, *A History of the Work of Redemption*, in *The Works of President Edwards* (New York, 1849), 1, 462, 469-70, 480-506.
35. Henry Abelove, "Jonathan Edwards' Letter of Invitation to George Whitefield," *William and Mary Quarterly*, 3d ser. 29 (1972): 488-9.
36. Jonathan Edwards, *Some Thoughts Concerning the Present Revival*, in *Works of Jonathan Edwards*, IV, 353-8.
37. See especially Charles Chauncy, *Seasonable Thoughts on the State of Religion* (Boston, 1742); excerpted in *The Great Awakening*, ed. Heimert and

Miller, pp. 302-44. For Edwards's defensive reaction, see Stein, "Introduction," *Works of Jonathan Edwards*, V, 29.

38. Jonathan Edwards, *An Humble Attempt to Promote Explicit Agreement and Visible Union of God's People in Extraordinary Prayer*, orig. ed. 1747, in *Works of Jonathan Edwards*, V, 316-20, 361-4, 378-427.

39. Scholars assessing the relationship of the Great Awakening to the Revolution have arrived at decidedly opposite conclusions. The most important work stressing the protorevolutionary character of the revivals is Alan Heimert, *Religion and the American Mind* (Cambridge, Mass: Harvard University Press, 1966). More recent scholars have reviewed the Awakening as fundamentally apolitical. See Davidson, *Logic*, especially pp. 216-32, and Hatch, *Sacred Cause*, especially pp. 24-36.

40. C. C. Goen, "Jonathan Edwards: A New Departure in Eschatology," *Church History* 38 (1959): 25-40; Tuveson, *Redeemer Nation*, especially pp. 26-51; Heimert, *Religion and the American Mind*, especially pp. 59-94.

41. The case against the importance of the postmillennial-premillennial distinction is made in Davidson, *Logic*.

42. Edwards, *Humble Attempt*, in *Works of Jonathan Edwards*, V, 361-2; for Thomas Prince and Joseph Sewall, see Heimert, *Religion*, p. 82, and Hatch, *Sacred*, p. 37.

43. Edwards, *History of the Work of Redemption*, in *Works of President Edwards*, I, 303. For his description of the great apocalyptic warfare under the sixth and seventh vial, see pp. 483-5.

44. Edwards, *History of the Work of Redemption*, in *Works of President Edwards*, I, 466-8, 483. Also, "Notes on the Apocalypse," in *Works of Jonathan Edwards*, V, 469.

45. Edwards, *Humble Attempt*, in *Works of Jonathan Edwards*, V, 357-8.

46. Edwards, *History of the Work of Redemption*, in *Works of President Edwards*, I, 493. In "Notes on the Apocalypse," Edwards once wrote that kings would be saints in the millennium and that after the millennium and the Last Judgment, in the new heavens and earth, the saints would reign as kings. See "Notes," in *Works of Jonathan Edwards*, V, 155.

47. Edwards, *Some Thoughts Concerning the Recent Revival*, in *Works of Jonathan Edwards*, IV, 371.

48. Edwards, *Some Thoughts Concerning the Recent Revival*, in *Works of Jonathan Edwards*, IV, 373.

49. Edwards, *History of the Work of Redemption, in Works of President Edwards*, I, 428-9, 458.

50. Edwards, *Humble Attempt*, in *Works of Jonathan Edwards*, V, 344-6, 359.

51. See, for example, how the term is used in the selections from Gilbert Tennent, *The Danger of an Unconverted Ministry* (1741) and *Remarks upon a Protestation* (1741); Elisha Williams, *The Essential Rights and Liberties of Protestants* (1744); and Solomon Paine, *A Short View of the Church of Christ* (1752), in *The Great Awakening*, ed. Heimert and Miller, pp. 80, 89, 174, 323-39, 418. Also see Isaac Backus, *A Short Description of the Difference Between the Bondwoman and the Free* (Boston, 1756), in *Isaac Backus on Church, State, and Calvinism*, ed. William G. McLoughlin (Cambridge, Mass.: Harvard University Press, 1968), pp. 129-66.

52. This comparison was drawn, for example, by the Virginia Anglican Alexander Garden and the Old Light Congregationalists Charles Chauncy and Harvard professor Michael Wigglesworth. See Heimert, *Religion and the American Mind*, p. 92; Chauncy, *Seasonable Thoughts on the State of Religion* (1743), in *The Great Awakening*, ed. Heimert and Miller, pp. 303-4.

2. Colonial millennialism on the eve of the revolutionary crisis

1. The interpretation presented in this chapter addresses a debate among American religious historians about the influence of the millennialism of the Great Awakening on subsequent political or revolutionary millennialism. See Alan Heimert, *Religion and the American Mind* (Cambridge, Mass.: Harvard University Press, 1966); James West Davidson, *The Logic of Millennial Thought* (New Haven: Yale University Press, 1977); Nathan O. Hatch, *The Sacred Cause of Liberty* (New Haven: Yale University Press, 1977).
2. David Ramsay, *History of South Carolina*, orig. ed. 1809 (Charleston, 1858), II, 252.
3. Richard Clarke, *The Prophetic Numbers of Daniel and John Calculated* (Philadelphia, 1759), p. 22.
4. On Love's prophetic reputation in England, see Clarke Garrett, *Respectable Folly* (Baltimore: Johns Hopkins University Press, 1975), pp. 171-2. In America, as in England, his "prophecy" was revived on a much larger scale (in an updated version) in the 1790's (see Chapter 7 below).
5. I have found no evidence that the work actually existed before the American edition of 1759. I am grateful to J. F. Maclear for suggesting this possibility. On the ancient origins of the uncanonical Book of Enoch and its repeated use by Jews and Christians, see Shirley Jackson Case, *The Revelation of John* (Chicago: University of Chicago Press, 1919), pp. 75-86; and Case, *The Millennial Hope* (Chicago: University of Chicago Press, 1918), pp. 88-93.
6. *The Strange and Wonderful Predictions of Mr. Christopher Love* (Boston, 1759).
7. David Imrie, *A Letter from the Reverend Mr. David Imrie* (Boston, 1756), pp. 6-9, 15, 17. On Burnet, see Davidson, *Logic*, pp. 86-93.
8. *A Most Remarkable Prophecy Concerning Wars and Political Events* (Philadelphia, 1760). The eagle-lily symbolism that predominates in this piece was a major motif in late medieval Central European popular prophecy. See Marjorie Reeves, *The Influence of Prophecy in the Latter Middle Ages* (Oxford: Clarendon Press, 1969), pp. 293-392.
9. *Zwölf Sibyllen* (Philadelphia, [1762]).
10. *A Prophecy, Lately Discovered* ([Philadelphia], 1763).
11. John Nathan Hutchins, *Hutchins's Improved. Being an Almanack . . . for the Year of Our Lord, 1762* (New York, [1761]), pp. 17-27.
12. *From a Folio Manuscript* (Boston, 1759).
13. *Some Thoughts on the Duration of the Torments of the Wicked, and the Time When the Day of Judgment May be Expected* (Charleston, S.C., 1759), p. 33.

14. *Some Thoughts on the Duration of Torments*, pp. 18-21.
15. *Some Thoughts on the Duration of Torments*, p. 34.
16. Joseph Bellamy, *The Millennium* (orig. ed. Boston, 1758), in *Sermons Upon the Following Subjects . . .* (Northampton, England, 1787).
17. Bellamy, *Millennium*, p. vi.
18. Bellamy, *Millennium*, p. 55.
19. This theme reappears, for example, in millennial speculations by the moderate Calvinist Ezra Stiles and the later Baptist universalist Elhanan Winchester, both of whom I will discuss in subsequent chapters.
20. Bellamy, *Millennium*, p. 57.
21. Bellamy, *Millennium*, p. 41.
22. It is possible, as James Davidson has suggested, that Thomas Prince sponsored the publication of Cheever's work as well. See *Logic*, p. 108, n.52.
23. Ezekiel Cheever, *Scripture Prophecies Explained* (Boston, 1757).
24. William Torrey, *A Brief Discourse Concerning Futurities or Things to Come* (Boston, 1757), pp. iv, 1-27, 55-60. As James Davidson's painstaking analysis of an overwhelming variety of exegetical positions shows, disputes over this and related matters did not automatically reflect broader theological alignments or world views. See his *Logic*.
25. The difference between the millennialism of the 1750's and that of the Awakening was subtle, for even Edwards had balanced his optimism with the belief that progress would be uneven. Aaron Burr, who objected to Edward's view that the slaying of the witnesses was over, acknowledged in a footnote that Edwards in the *Humble Attempt* also foresaw the possibility of further decline. See Aaron Burr, *Sermon Before the Synod of New-York, Convened at Newark, in New-Jersey* (New York, 1756), p. 26. Indeed, Edwards usually saw history in a fairly dialectical fashion, as containing the seeds both of destruction and of renewal. See, for example, *A History of the Work of Redemption*, orig. ed. 1776, in *Works of President Edwards* (New York, 1848), I, especially 428, 463-72; and *An Humble Attempt*, orig. ed. 1747, in *Works of Jonathan Edwards* (New Haven: Yale University Press, 1977), V, 357-64. On balance, however, he emphasized a long-range pattern of gradual amelioration. See *History*, passim, especially pp. 472-7, 481-3; *Humble*, pp. 378-94, 407-27. There is no doubt that the difference between Edwards and Burr over the slaying of the witnesses was that between a relatively more progressive and a relatively more cataclysmic view.
26. John Gill, *Three Sermons: On the Present and Future State of the Church*, orig. London eds. 1751, 1753 (Boston, 1756), pp. 26-35, 70-95.
27. Historians assessing the impact of the Awakening upon American millennialism have been too mechanistic in searching for a strict correlation between New Light Calvinism and later millennial ideas. Alan Heimert, in *Religion and the American Mind*, has shown that millennialism was an integral part of New Light Calvinist theology, but he mistakenly contends that millennialism (or at least "optimistic" postmillennialism) was a *uniquely* revivalist pattern of thought. Conversely, Davidson, in *Logic*, and Hatch, in *Sacred Cause*, present numerous cases of Old Light Arminians who similarly professed millennial ideas,

and (following Heimert's logic if not his conclusions) deny that the Great Awakening had much to do with later millennialism at all.

28. Charles Chauncy, "Seasonable Thoughts on the State of Religion," in *The Great Awakening*, ed. Alan Heimert and Perry Miller (Indianapolis: Bobbs-Merrill, 1967), p. 304.

29. See, for example, *Blazing Stars: Messengers of God's Wrath* (Boston, 1759); A. F., *A Poem on the Rebuke of God's Hand in the Awful Desolation Made by Fire* (Boston, 1760); *An Account of a Surprising Phenomenon . . .* (Philadelphia, 1765). On the early American understanding of earthquakes, see Michael N. Shute, "Earthquakes and Early American Imagination: Decline and Renewal in Eighteenth-Century Puritan Culture" (Ph.D. dissertation, University of California, 1977).

30. Davidson has demonstrated that wishful and fearful tendencies typically intermixed in earthquake sermons and did so virtually regardless of variations in technical millennial theories. See *Logic*, pp. 103-21.

31. Charles Chauncy, *The Earth Delivered from the Curse* (Boston, 1756), pp. 18, 26. James Davidson, in *Logic*, pp. 108-11, stresses the unorthodoxy of Chauncy's exegesis. It is uncertain whether, in the 1750's, Chauncy believed there would be a millennium on earth, although later he did incorporate such a belief into his universalist eschatology.

32. This work, published anonymously in England in 1784, is discussed in Davidson, *Logic*, pp. 110-11.

33. Jonathan Mayhew, *The Expected Dissolution of All Things, a Motive to Universal Holiness* (Boston, 1755). James Davidson's *Logic* contains an interesting and more detailed exegetical analysis of this and the following sermon, as well as the sermon by Chauncy cited in note 31, although Davidson evidently was not aware of the later sermon by Mayhew, which significantly differs in interpretation. Nor does he present these liberal sermons in the context of the recent Awakening. See *Logic*, pp. 108-13.

34. Jonathan Mayhew, *A Discourse on Rev. IV. 3ᵈ 4ᵗʰ Occasioned by the Earthquakes in November 1755* (Boston, 1755), pp. 20-1, 36-7, 44.

35. Jonathan Mayhew, *Practical Discourses Delivered on Occasion of the Earthquakes in November, 1755* (Boston, 1760), pp. 369-70.

36. Mayhew, *Practical Discourses*, pp. 369-70.

37. Mayhew, *Practical Discourses*, p. 371.

38. William Smith, *A Discourse Concerning the Conversion of the Heathen American* (Philadelphia, 1760), p. 12.

39. Thomas Barnard, *A Sermon Preached to the Ancient and Honourable Artillery Company* (Boston, 1758), pp. 17, 7; Amos Adams, *The Expediency and Utility of War* (Boston, 1759), p. 29.

40. Samuel Cooper, *A Sermon Preached Before His Excellency Thomas Pownall, . . . October 16th, 1759* (Boston, 1759), p. 53.

41. East Apthorp, *The Felicity of the Times* (Boston, 1763), p. 29.

42. Ebenezer Prime, *The Importance of the Divine Presence with the Armies of God's People* (New York, 1759), p. 13.

43. Joseph Fisk, *Anti-Christ Discovered or the True Church Sought For* ([New Haven?], 1762), pp. 2, 23.

44. Heimert, *Religion*, p. 128.

45. Gilbert Tennent, *The Good Man's Character and Reward* (Philadelphia, 1756), p. 23; Jonathan Parsons, *Good News from a Far Country. In Seven Discourses* (Portsmouth, N.H., 1756), p. 168.
46. Samuel Finley, *The Curse of Meroz* (Philadelphia, 1757), p. 31.
47. Burr, *Sermon Before the Synod*, pp. 20-1, 32.
48. Samuel Davies, "The Crisis: Or, the Uncertain Doom of Kingdoms at Particular Times," in *Sermons on Important Subjects* (New York, 1792), pp. 403-4.
49. Davies, "The Crisis," in *Sermons*, p. 404.
50. Robert Smith, *A Wheel in the Middle of a Wheel* (Philadelphia, 1759), p. 55.
51. Samuel Langdon, *Joy and Gratitude to God for the Long Life of a Good King and the Conquest of Quebec* (Portsmouth, N.H., 1760), pp. 16-17, 42-3.
52. Jonathan Mayhew, *Two Discourses Delivered October 5th, 1759* (Boston, 1759), p. 49.
53. Aaron Burr, perhaps the only commentator on the war who addressed such exegetical issues at all, combined a very bleak and catastrophic outlook on the immediate future – conventionally associated with premillennialism – with a technical postmillennialism still faithful to his mentor Jonathan Edwards. Burr, *Sermon Before the Synod*, pp. 21-6, 31. Many historians have stressed the connection between postmillennialism and a progressive, activistic, and optimistic historical outlook. See, for example: C. C. Goen, "Jonathan Edwards: A New Departure in Eschatology," *Church History* 28 (1959): 25-40; Ernest Lee Tuveson, *Redeemer Nation* (Chicago: University of Chicago Press, 1968); and Heimert, *Religion and the American Mind*. James Davidson has more recently denied the accuracy of this set of correlations for the eighteenth century in his *Logic*. My own findings agree more with Davidson on the *technical* point of pre- versus postmillennialism, but, unlike him, I think other useful distinctions between types of millennialism can be made.
54. For an interpretation that instead stresses continuities between the 1750's and the 1770's, see Hatch, *Sacred Cause*, especially pp. 23, 55-96.
55. John Mellen, *A Sermon Preached at the West Parish in Lancaster, October 9, 1760* (Boston, 1760), p. 30; Burr, *Sermon Before the Synod*, p. 36; Gilbert Tennent, *The Happiness of Rewarding the Enemies of our Religion and Liberty* (Philadelphia, 1756), p. 20.
56. Davies, "The Crisis," in *Sermons*, p. 401.
57. Langdon, *Joy and Gratitude*, p. 42.
58. Jonathan Mayhew, *Two Discourses Delivered October 9th, 1760* (Boston, 1760), p. 55.
59. Nathaniel Appleton, *Sermon Preached October 9* (Boston, 1760), p. 25.
60. Mayhew, *Two Discourses Delivered . . . 1760*, p. 54.
61. *Canada Subjected. A New Song* (n.p. 1759?).
62. Peter Shaw, *American Patriots and the Rituals of Revolution* (Cambridge, Mass.: Harvard University Press, 1981), pp. 207, 229-31.
63. Christopher Hill, *Antichrist in Seventeenth-Century England* (New York: Oxford University Press, 1971); William Haller, *Liberty and Reformation in the Puritan Revolution* (New York: Columbia University Press, 1955). Also see Chapter 1 above. For interpretations that contrast in different ways

with my own, see Heimert, *Religion and the American Mind*, pp. 85-8, and Hatch, *Sacred Cause*, pp. 38-9, 45-51.

64. Langdon, *Joy and Gratitude*, p. 9; also Andrew Eliot, *A Sermon Preached October 25th 1759* (Boston, 1759), p. 18.
65. William Hobby, *The Happiness of a People* (Boston, 1758), p. 19.
66. Samuel Haven, *Joy and Salvation by Christ* (Portsmouth, N.H., 1763), p. 20.
67. Burr, *Sermon Before the Synod*, p. 36.
68. Langdon, *Joy and Gratitude*, p. 41.
69. Joshua Tufts, *The Believers Most Sure Freedom Purchased by Jesus Christ* (Portsmouth, N.H., 1757), p. 10.
70. Tufts, *Believers*, p. 12.
71. See Chapter 1 above.
72. Langdon, *Joy and Gratitude*, pp. 16, 17.
73. William Smith, *Discourse Concerning Conversion*, pp. 26-7; Apthorp, *Felicity*, p. 19; Cooper, *Sermon Preached Before His Excellency*, p. 53.
74. Clarke, *Prophetic Numbers*, p. 22.
75. Joseph Bellamy, *A Sermon Delivered Before the General Assembly of the Colony of Connecticut* (New London, 1762), p. 20.
76. Bellamy, *Sermon Delivered Before General Assembly*, pp. 25-30.
77. Jonathan Edwards, *Some Thoughts Concerning the Present Revival of Religion in America*, orig. ed. 1742, in *The Works of Jonathan Edwards* (New Haven: Yale University Press, 1972), IV, 353.
78. See, for example, Nathaniel Appleton, *Sermon Preached October 9 . . . 1760*, p. 36; Robert Smith, *Wheel in Middle of Wheel*, p. 46; Samuel Woodward, *A Sermon Preached October 9, 1760* (Boston, [1760]), p. 27.
79. Smith, *Discourse Concerning Conversion*.
80. Thomas Barnard, *A Sermon Preached Before his Excellent Francis Bernard* (Boston, 1763), p. 44.
81. Mayhew, *Two Discourses Delivered . . . 1759*, p. 61.
82. Eli Forbes, *God the Strength, and Salvation of His People* (Boston 1761), p. 33; Ezra Stiles, *A Discourse on the Christian Union* (Boston, 1761), pp. 121-3, 109-10.
83. See Eliot, *Sermon Preached October 25th 1759*, pp. 42-3; Mayhew, *Two Discourses Delivered . . . 1759*, pp. 50-1; Mayhew, *Two Discourses Delivered . . . 1760*, pp. 37, 53-60, 63; John Mellen, *The Duty of All to Be Ready for Future Impending Events* (Boston, 1756), pp. 21-2; Mellen, *Sermon Preached . . . 1760*, pp. 31-3; Langdon, *Joy and Gratitude*, p. 43; Solomon Williams, *The Relations of God's People to him* (New London, Conn., 1760), pp. 27-8; Haven, *Joy and Salvation*, p. 39; Apthorp, *Felicity*, pp. 14-15; William Smith, *Discourse Concerning Conversion*, pp. 12–13; Robert Smith, *Wheel in Middle of Wheel*, pp. 54–5. With the exception of the New Light Presbyterian Robert Smith (who hoped the gospel would spread by the means of both renewed revivals and Indian missions) and the moderate Calvinist Samuel Langdon, all of these ministers were Anglican and Congregationalist liberals.
84. An exception is Robert Smith, cited in note 83. For an evangelical call to missionary activity in the late 1750's that had millennial overtones, see Samuel Hopkins, *An Address to the People of New-England. Representing The Very Great Importance of Attaching the Indians to Their Interest* (Philadelphia,

1757), p. 27. David Brainerd and Eleazar Wheelock were devoted New Light missionaries to the Indians, and there was definitely a millennial dimension to their involvement. See Heimert, *Religion and the American Mind*, p. 82. For Edwards's hopes about Indian conversions, see *History of the Work of Redemption*, in *Works* (New York ed.), I, 468-9; and *Humble Attempt*, in *Works* (New Haven ed.), V, 363. This theme goes all the way back to John Eliot and other first-generation American Puritans.

85. Bellamy, *Sermon Delivered Before General Assembly*.
86. Mayhew, *Two Discourses Delivered . . . 1759*, p. 51; *Two Discourses Delivered . . . 1760*, pp. 60-2. His opponent, East Apthorp, used similar millennial imagery in the SPG's defense. See East Apthorp, *Considerations on the Institution and Conduct of the Society of the Propagation of the Gospel in Foreign Parts* (Boston, 1763), p. 24.

3. Whig resistance and apocalyptical Manichaeanism

1. *A Discourse, Addressed to the Sons of Liberty, At a Solemn Assembly, near Liberty-Tree, in Boston, February 14, 1766* (Providence, 1766), p. 3.
2. *Discourse to Sons of Liberty*, pp. 4-5.
3. *Discourse to Sons of Liberty*, pp. 5-6.
4. *Discourse to Sons of Liberty*, p. 7.
5. For example: *Liberty, Property, and No Excise. A Poem . . . the 14th of August, 1765* (Boston, 1765); *Oppression. A Poem. By an American* (New York, 1765), pp. 6, 9, 11; [Thomas Plant], *Joyful News for America; And the Downfall of the Stamp-Act* (Philadelphia, 1766); "Taxation of America" (1765), in *Songs and Ballads of the American Revolution*, ed. Frank Moore (New York, 1855), pp. 3-4.
6. On this feature of patriot ritual and its connection to Pope's Day, see Peter Shaw, *American Patriots and the Rituals of Revolution* (Cambridge, Mass.: Harvard University Press, 1981), especially pp. 15-18, 177-83, 197-9, 204-26.
7. Lawrence Henry Gipson, *Jared Ingersoll: A Study of American Loyalism* (New Haven: Yale University Press, 1920), p. 169; Samuel Peters, *General History of Connecticut*, orig. ed. 1781 (New York, 1877), p. 238.
8. Peter Oliver, *Origin and Progress of the American Revolution: A Tory View*, orig. ed. 1781, ed. Douglass Adair and John A. Schultz (San Marino, Calif.: Huntington Library, 1961), p. 65.
9. Paul Revere, "A Warm Place – Hell" (1768), with accompanying lyrics by Benjamin Church, in Elbridge H. Goss, *The Life of Colonel Paul Revere*, 5th edition (Boston: Howard W. Spurr, 1902), p. 60; *Description of the Pope, 1769* (Boston, 1769); Ezra Gleason, *The Massachusetts Calendar; or an Almanack for the Year of Our Lord Christ 1774* (Boston, 1773), the cover.
10. *South-Carolina Gazette*, November 21, 1774. News of these ritual events carried far. See, for example, the description of one in New York in the *Virginia Gazette* (Rind), July 7, 1774.
11. For example: *The Watchman's Alarm to Lord N ** h* (Salem, Mass., 1774); *The Crisis. Number II* (New York, 1775), pp. 9-10; John Hancock, *An Oration Delivered March 5, 1774* (Boston, 1774), p. 9; "The Times" (1776) and "Off from Boston" (1776), in *Songs and Ballads of the American Revolution*, ed. Moore, pp.110, 125; *A Poem upon the Present Times*

... ([New Haven?], 1775); *The Speech of William Tr** n, Esq.* (New York, 1776); *New-York Journal*, August 8, 1774.

12. *The First Book of the American Chronicles of the Times. Chap. II* (Philadelphia, 1774), pp. 17-18. A more esoteric reference to millennial prophecy in the *American Chronicles* appears in the subplot introduced in Chapter 3 of the old witch "Mother Carey," who is commissioned by the American priestly hero "Jedidiah" to resurrect Oliver Cromwell. This is probably meant to refer to Mary Cary, a radical revolutionary millennialist in England in the 1640's and 1650's.

13. As quoted in Eric Foner, *Tom Paine and Revolutionary America* (New York: Oxford University Press, 1976), pp. 115, 293 n.3.

14. [Nathan Daboll], *Freebetter's Connecticut Almanach ... For 1774*, 2nd ed. (New London, Conn. [1773]).

15. *The Crisis. Number XXIII* (New York, 1775), pp. 189-96.

16. As reported in the *Maryland Journal and Baltimore Advertiser*, July 17, 1776.

17. J. P., *Concerning the Number of the Beast Rev. XIII. 18* (n.p., [1777]).

18. There were, of course, many sermons (as well as secular pamphlets) printed in the 1760's and early 1770's that defended the colonial cause on both religious and legal grounds. But before 1773 scarcely any employed this satanic imagery. Significant exceptions were Daniel Shute, *A Sermon Preached To the Ancient and Honorable Artillery Company in Boston, New-England June 1, 1767* (Boston, 1767), p. 22; Nathaniel Appleton, *The Right Method of Addressing the Divine Majesty in Prayer* (Boston, 1770), p. 10. But even these were still quite mild insinuations.

19. Richard Bland, *A Letter to the Clergy of Virginia* (Williamsburg, 1760), p. 20.

20. Bland, *Letter to Clergy*, p. 18.

21. Jonathan Mayhew, *Popish Idolatry: A Discourse Delivered in the Chapel of Harvard-College ... May 8, 1765* (Boston, 1765), p. 50.

22. For example: Enoch Huntington, *A Sermon, Delivered at Middletown, July 20th, A.D. 1775* (Hartford, 1775), p. 21; and the Appendix "By another Hand," in Samuel Sherwood, *Church's Flight into the Wilderness* (New York, 1776), pp. 51-4.

23. Joseph Lyman, *A Sermon Preached at Hatfield December 15th, 1774* (Boston, 1775), p. 30.

24. *The First Book of the American Chronicles of the Times. Chap. VI* (Philadelphia, 1775), p. 63; [Philip Freneau], *American Liberty, A Poem* (New York, 1775), p. 9.

25. Alexander Hamilton, *A Full Vindication of the Members of the Congress, from the Calumnies of Their Enemies* (1775), in *The Papers of Alexander Hamilton*, ed. Harold C. Syrett and Jacob E. Cooke (New York: Columbia University Press, 1961), I, 69.

26. *South-Carolina Gazette*, November 21, 1774.

27. Elhanan Winchester, *Thirteen Hymns Suited to the Present Times* (Baltimore, 1776), p. 6.

28. Samuel Langdon, *Government Corrupted by Vice and Recovered by Righteousness* (Watertown, Mass., 1775), p. 29. His earlier exegetical exercise was *A Rational Explication of St. John's Vision of the Two Beasts* (Portsmouth, N.H., 1774).

29. *The Crisis. Number XII* (New York, 1775), p. 102; Judah Champion, *Christian and Civil Liberty* (Hartford, 1776), p. 18; *The First Book of the American Chronicles of the Times. Chap. IV* (Philadelphia, 1775), p. 40.

30. *Maryland Journal and Baltimore Advertiser*, May 3, 1775; *A Poem upon the Present Times* ([New Haven?], 1775).

31. Between 1765 and 1775 several ministers explicating the symbols of prophecy noted the tyranny of the Antichrist, in accord with standard exegetical convention, without drawing any relationship to British imperial policy. See Mayhew, *Popish Idolatry*, pp. 48-9; Samuel Cooper, *A Discourse on the Man of Sin* (Boston, 1774), pp. 65-6; Langdon, *Rational Explication*, pp. 3–4, 11; Elisha Rich, *The Number of the Beast Found Out by Spiritual Arithmetic* (Chelmsford, Mass., 1775), pp. 10–12.

32. [Jacob Green], *A Vision of Hell* (New London, Conn., 1770). The same illustration appears in the 1772 New London edition, and it has been used as the frontispiece in this book.

33. For example: Amos Adams, *A Concise Historical View of the Perils, Hardship, and Discouragements* (Boston, 1769), p. 5; John Tucker, *A Sermon Preached at Cambridge, Before his Excellency Thomas Hutchinson* (Boston, 1771), p. 62; John Joachim Zubly, *The Law of Liberty* (Philadelphia, 1775), p. 28; William Foster, *True Fortitude Delineated* (Philadelphia, 1776), p. 20.

34. John Adams, *A Dissertation on the Canon and Feudal Law*, in *The Works of John Adams*, ed. Charles Francis Adams (Boston, 1865), III, 453.

35. Jonathan Mayhew, *The Snare Broken* (Boston, 1766), p. 36.

36. Gad Hitchcock, *A Sermon Preached at Plymouth December 22d, 1774* (Boston, 1775), p. 23; Samuel West, *A Sermon Preached Before the Honorable Council . . . May 26, 1776*, in *The Pulpit of the American Revolution*, ed. John Wingate Thornton (Boston, 1860), p. 319.

37. *New-York Journal*, November 2, 1775.

38. Wesley Frank Craven, *The Legend of the Founding Fathers* (New York: New York University Press, 1956), pp. 1-55. On the use of this myth by the revolutionary clergy, also see Nathan O. Hatch, *The Sacred Cause of Liberty* (New Haven: Yale University Press, 1977), pp. 76-9.

39. The preoccupation with the need for virtue became more pronounced in the 1780's, but the idea that religion supplied its underpinnings was already an imbedded feature of American Protestantism. See, for example: Samuel Davies, *Religion and Public Spirit* (New York, 1761); Isaac Story, *The Love of Our Country Recommended and Enforced* (Boston, 1774), especially p. 10; Jacob Duché, *The American Vine* (Philadelphia, 1775), pp. 27-33; John Witherspoon, *Dominion of Providence* (Philadelphia, 1776), pp. 50-1.

40. [John Allen], *An Oration upon the Beauties of Liberty* (Boston, 1773), p. 28.

41. *Boston Gazette*, May 30, 1774.

42. *The Crisis. Number XX* (New York, 1775), p. 169.

43. For example: Mayhew, *Snare Broken*, p. 2; Judah Champion, *A Brief View of the Distresses, Hardships and Dangers Our Ancestors Encounter'd* (Hartford, 1770), p. 44; Jacob Duché, *The Duty of Standing Fast in Our Spiritual and Temporal Liberties* (Philadelphia, 1775); [Silas Downer], *A Discourse Delivered in Providence, . . . upon the 25th Day of July, 1768*, (Providence, 1768), p. 14; *New York Journal*, January 5, 1775.

44. For example: Amos Adams, *Religious Liberty an Invaluable Blessing* (Boston, 1768), pp. 6-8; Zubly, *Law of Liberty*, especially pp. 6, 23; Sherwood, *Church's Flight*, introduction.
45. Jacob Duché, *The Duty of Standing Fast*, p. 7.
46. Levi Hart, *Liberty Described and Recommended* (Hartford, 1775), p. 8.
47. [Stephen Johnson], *Some Important Observations . . . December 18, A.D. 1765* (Newport, R.I., 1766), p. 60; Hugh Alison, *Spiritual Liberty* (Charleston, S.C., 1769), p. 8.
48. Isaac Backus, *True Faith Will Produce Good Works* (Boston, 1767), p. 89.
49. On the revolutionary jeremiad, see especially Perry Miller, "From the Covenant to the Revival," in *Nature's Nation* (Cambridge, Mass.: Harvard University Press, 1967), pp. 90-120. Also Sacvan Bercovitch, *The American Jeremiad* (Madison: University of Wisconsin Press, 1978). Bercovitch, however, does not clearly distinguish jeremiads that were millennial from those that were not. Hatch, *Sacred Cause*, pp. 76-7, 94-6, also notes affinities between the jeremiad and radical whig historical theory but does not present revolutionary millennialism as a departure from this retrospective framework.
50. Nathaniel Appleton, *Right Method of Addressing the Divine Majesty*, p. 30.
51. Timothy Hilliard, *The Duty of a People Under the Oppression of Man* (Boston, 1774), pp. 23, 25-6.
52. Alexander Martin, *America. A Poem* (Philadelphia, [1769?]), especially p. 7.
53. For example: Henry Cumings, *A Thanksgiving Sermon Preached at Billerica November 27, 1766* (Boston, 1767), p. 11; Amos Adams, *A Concise Historical View*, p. 17-8; Judah Champion, *A Brief View of the Distresses*, p. 25.
54. Benjamin Church, *An Oration, Delivered March Fifth, 1773* (Boston, 1773), p. 18.
55. Charles Chauncy, *A Discourse on "The Good News from a Far Country"*, in *Pulpit of the American Revolution*, ed. Thornton, p. 135.
56. William Bates, *Christ in the Clouds Coming to Judgment* (Hartford, 1767). This work had already appeared three times previously in Boston, in 1729, 1742, and 1752.
57. John Murray, *The Last Solemn Scene* (Boston, 1768); John Peck, *A Description of the Last Judgment*, 2nd ed. (Boston, 1773).
58. *A Prophecy, or a Warning to All Sinners* (Philadelphia, 1765).
59. *Blazing Stars: The Messengers of God's Wrath* (Boston, 1769), p. 4.; [Samuel Clarke], *A Short Relation, Concerning a Dream* (Boston, [1769]), p. 7. This dream, with variations including *Blazing Stars*, above, went into six New England editions between 1769 and 1776.
60. Clarke, *Short Relation*, pp. 12-13.
61. Allen, *Oration upon the Beauties of Liberty*, pp. 17, xiii.
62. William Tennent, *An Address Occasioned by the Late Invasion of the Liberties of the American Colonies* (Philadelphia, 1774), pp. 10-11.
63. Jacob Johnson, *Zion's Memorial: of the Present Work of God* (n.p., 1765), pp. 3, 12, 44, 47, 64-5; Samuel Buell, *A Faithful Narrative of the Remarkable Revival of Religion, in . . . East Hampton, on Long-Island* (New York, 1766), pp. 2, 23-5, 77, 87.
64. James Dana, *A Century Discourse Delivered at the Anniversary Meeting of the Freemen of . . . Wallingford, April 9, 1770* (New Haven, 1770), especially pp.

20-1; Samuel Cooper, *A Discourse on the Man of Sin*; Andrew Eliot, *Twenty Sermons* (Boston, 1774), pp. 79-82.

65. *An Account of a Surprising Phenomenon* (Philadelphia, 1765), p. 3. Also see the new, revised millennial prophecies by Richard Clarke in John Tobler, *The South-Carolina and Georgia Almanack, For . . . 1772* (Charleston, [1771]), pp. 33-4.

66. Joseph Emerson, *Thanksgiving Sermon Preached at Pepperell, July 24th. 1766* (Boston, 1766), pp. 36-7.

67. John Joachim Zubly, *The Stamp Act Repealed* (Savannah, Ga., 1766), p. 30.

68. *A Sermon, Preached at the Anniversary Meeting of the Planter's Society* (Charleston, S.C., 1769), p. 13.

69. James Otis, *The Rights of the British Colonies Asserted and Proved* (Boston, 1764), p. 459.

70. Jason Haven, *A Sermon Preached Before His Excellency . . . May 31st. 1769* (Boston, 1769), p. 52.

71. Haven, *Sermon . . . May 31st. 1769*, pp. 52-3; Peter Whitney, *The Transgression of a Land Punished by a Multitude of Rulers* (Boston, 1774), p. 65.

72. Daniel Shute, *A Sermon Preached Before his Excellency . . . May 25th. 1768* (Boston, 1768), pp. 51, 63. Also see Jonathan Shipley's view of the past as the "true golden age of America" in his *Sermon Preached Before the Incorporated Society for the Propagation of the Gospel in Foreign Parts* (Philadelphia, 1773), p. 14.

73. William Smith, *An Oration Delivered, January 22, 1773, Before . . . the American Philosophical Society* (Philadelphia, 1773), pp. 5-6.

74. John Adams, *Dissertation*, in *Works*, ed. C. F. Adams, III, 452.

75. Philip Freneau and Hugh Henry Brackenridge, *A Poem on the Rising Glory of America* (Philadelphia, 1772), p. 25; also Timothy Dwight, *America; or, A Poem on the Settlement of the British Colonies*, orig. ed. 1770 (New Haven, [1780]), p. 12.

76. John Tobler, *The Georgia and South-Carolina Almanack for . . . 1774* (Charleston, 1773), p. 29.

77. [Samuel Mather], *An Attempt to Shew, that America Must be Known to the Ancients* (Boston, 1773), pp. 17-18.

78. [Hugh Henry Brackenridge], *A Poem on Divine Revelation* (Philadelphia, 1774), p. 17.

79. Marvin L. Michael Kay, "The North Carolina Regulation, 1766-1776: A Class Conflict," in *The American Revolution: Explorations in the History of American Radicalism*, ed. Alfred E. Young (DeKalb: Northern Illinois University Press, 1976), especially pp. 105-7; James Penn Whittenburg, "Planters, Merchants and Lawyers: Social Change and the Origins of the North Carolina Regulation," *William and Mary Quarterly*, 3d ser. 34 (1977): 215-38; A. Roger Ekirch, "North Carolina Regulators on Liberty and Corruption, 1766-1771," *Perspectives in American History* 11 (1977-8): 199-256.

80. [Herman Husband], *Continuation of the Impartial Relation of the First Rise and Cause of the Recent Differences in Publick Affairs* [New Bern, N.C., 1770], p. 15.

81. [Herman Husband], *An Impartial Relation of the First Rise and Cause of the*

Recent Differences (n.p., 1770), pp. 23, 78-102, 309-12, 322-3; *A Continuation of the Impartial Relation*, pp. 20, 63-4.

82. Mary Elinor Lazenby, *Herman Husband: A Story of His Life* (Washington, D.C.: Old Neighborhoods Press, 1940); [Herman Husband], *Some Remarks on Religion, with Author's Experience in Pursuit Thereof* (Philadelphia, 1761). Much of my information about Husband's life and millennial ideas also comes from the excellent work of Mark H. Jones, "Herman Husband: Millenarian, Carolina Regulator, and Whiskey Rebel" (Ph.D. dissertation, Northern Illinois University, 1982).
83. As quoted in Jones, "Herman Husband," p. 95.

4. The revolutionary millennialism of the 1770's

1. Izrahiah Wetmore, *A Sermon Preached Before the Honorable Assembly . . . on the Day of Their Anniversary Election, May 13th, 1773* (Hartford, 1773), p. 19; Thomas Coombe, *A Sermon, Preached Before the Congregations of Christ Church and St. Peter's . . . July 20, 1775* (Philadelphia, 1775); Ebenezer Baldwin, *The Duty of Rejoicing under Calamities and Afflictions* (New York, 1776), pp. 38-9.
2. *The Triumph of the Whigs: or, T'Other Congress Convened* (New York, 1775), p. 8.
3. "Suffolk Resolves" (September 1774) and "Address to the People of Ireland" (July 1775), *Journals of Congress* (Philadelphia, 1800), I, 15, 172.
4. *Boston Gazette*, January 23, 1775; also January 3, 1774, July 18, 1774; *New-York Journal*, August 24, 1775; also October 26, 1775; *Virginia Gazette* (Dixon and Hunter), September 30, 1775; *New-England Chronicle*, May 5, 1776.
5. Thomas Paine, "Common Sense," in *Common Sense and the Crisis* (New York: Anchor Books, 1973), p. 59.
6. For example: *Maryland Journal and Baltimore Advertiser*, January 16, 1777; Elijah Fitch, *A Discourse, The Substance of Which Was Delivered at Hopkinton . . . March 24th, 1776* (Boston, 1776); Hugh Henry Brackenridge, *Six Political Discourses Founded on the Scripture* (Lancaster, Pa., 1778), p. 50; John Murray, *Nehemiah, or the Struggle for Liberty Never in Vain* (Newburyport, Mass., 1779), p. 9; *New-York Journal*, October 26, 1775.
7. Jonas Clarke, *The Fate of Blood-thirsty Oppressors* (Boston, 1776), pp. 29-30; Andrew Lee, *Sin Destructive of Temporal and Eternal Happiness* (Norwich, Conn., 1776), p. 27; *Maryland Journal and Baltimore Advertiser*, January 1, 1777; [Continental Congress] *An Address of the Congress to the Inhabitants of the United States* (Williamsburg, 1778), p. 1.
8. John Joachim Zubly, *The Law of Liberty* (Philadelphia, 1775), p. ix.
9. [Samuel Clarke], *The Strange and Remarkable Swanzey Vision* (Salem, Mass., 1776), pp. 8-9; Samuel Clarke, *The American Wonder: Or, the Strange and Remarkable Cape-Ann Dream* (Salem, Mass., 1776), especially pp. 17-18.
10. *Maryland Journal and Baltimore Advertiser*, January 16, 1777.
11. [David Rittenhouse], *The Continental Almanac, for the Year of Our Lord, 1780* (Philadelphia, 1779), p. 17.

12. Husband's authorship is indicated by several pieces of evidence. First of all, he appears as the subject of one of the prophecies (see [Rittenhouse], *Continental Almanac, For . . . 1780*, p. 22). Secondly, similar prophecies claimed to be by the same mysterious recluse appeared in Rittenhouse's, Goddard's, and other almanacs in the 1780's under the pseudonyms "Outrim Houtrim" and "the Allegany Philosopher." According to the memoirs of a German traveler who met Husband at that time, these were his pen names. See Johann David Schoepf, *Travels in the Confederation 1783-4*, trans. and ed. Alfred J. Morrison (Philadelphia: William J. Campbell, 1911), I, 296.

13. Elisha Fish, *A Discourse Delivered at Worcester, March 28th. 1775*, (Worcester, Mass., 1775), p. 17.

14. For example: Samuel Sherwood, *Church's Flight into the Wilderness* (New York, 1776); William Foster, *True Fortitude Delineated* (Philadelphia, 1776), p. 17; [Wheeler Case], *Poems, Occasioned by Several Circumstances . . . in the Present Grand Contest of America for Liberty* (New Haven, 1778), p. 21.

15. M. W., "A Breviate of Scriptural Prophecies," *United States Magazine* 1 (July 1779): 304, 307.

16. For example: *State of Massachusetts-Bay. Proclamation for a Day [of] Public Thanksgiving . . . December 12, 1776* (Boston, 1776); *State of New-Hampshire . . . A Proclamation for a General Fast . . . August 7, 1777* (Exeter, N.H., 1777); *By the Honorable Jonathan Trumbull . . . of the State of Connecticut: A Proclamation . . . [for a fast day] January 29, 1777* (Hartford, 1777).

17. *A Solemn Warning by the Associated Presbytery* (Lancaster, Pa., 1778), p. 27.

18. Richard Price, *Observations on the Nature of Civil Liberty, The Principles of Government, and The Justice and Policy of the War with America*, 6th ed. (Philadelphia, 1776), p. 37; David Ramsay, *An Oration on the Advantages of American Independence* (Charlestown, S.C., 1778), p. 1; Nathan Strong, *The Agency and Providence of God Acknowledged, in the Preservation of the American States* (Hartford, 1780), pp. 11-12; Peter Whitney, *American Independence Vindicated* (Boston, 1777), pp. 53-4; David Avery, *The Lord Is to Be Praised for the Triumphs of His Power* (Norwich, Conn., 1778), pp. 45-7.

19. Elhanan Winchester, *Thirteen Hymns Suited to the Present Times* (Baltimore, 1776), p. 15; Joel Barlow, *Prospect of Peace* (New Haven, 1778), p. 11.

20. Ebenezer Baldwin, *The Duty of Rejoicing under Calamities and Afflictions* (New York, 1779), pp. 38-9. The standard periodization was that of the earlier English theologian Moses Lowman, who held that the present was between the fifth and sixth "vials" of the Book of Revelation and the millennium would begin after the seventh, around the year 2000.

21. M. W., "A Breviate of Scriptural Prophecies," pp. 306-7; Thomas Wells Bray, *A Dissertation upon the Sixth Vial* (Hartford, 1780), pp. 93, 98, 106.

22. Brackenridge, *Six Political Discourses*, p. 87.

23. Samuel Magaw, *A Sermon Preached in Christ-Church, Dover, On Monday, December 17th, 1779* (Philadelphia, 1779), p. 15.

24. Sherwood, *Church's Flight*, p. 49.

25. Chauncey Whittelsey, *The Importance of Religion in a Civil Ruler, Considered* (New Haven, 1778), p. 19.
26. Ebenezer Parkman, *The Diary of Rev. Ebenezer Parkman*, ed. Harriette M. Forbes (Westborough, Mass., 1899), p. 94. *Sibley's Harvard Graduates* contains an even more extreme version of West's millennial theories, according to which he thought the millennium had begun in 1775 and the Pope would be reduced in 1813. Parkman's diary, the source cited as documentation, does not, however, provide these details. See *Sibley's Harvard Graduates*, ed. Clifford Kenyon Shipton, 17 vols. (Boston: Massachusetts Historical Society, 1873–1975), XIII, 503.
27. Samuel West, *An Anniversary Sermon Preached at Plymouth, December 22d. 1777* (Boston, 1778), p. 50.
28. *New-England Chronicle*, May 2, 1776.
29. Paine, "Common Sense," p. 35; John Adams, "Thoughts on Government" (1776), in *The Works of John Adams*, ed. Charles Francis Adams (Boston, 1865), IV, 200.
30. Whitney, *American Independence*, p. 54; *By the Honorable John Trumbull [for a fast day] January 29, 1777*; Sherwood, *Church's Triumph*, p. 39; Gad Hitchcock, *A Sermon Preached at Plymouth December 22d, 1774* (Boston, 1775), *Prayer . . . April 16, 1778* (Exeter, Mass., 1778).
31. Abraham Keteltas, *God Arising and Pleading His People's Cause* (Newburyport, Mass., 1777), p. 32; Franklin Bowditch Dexter, *Biographical Sketches of the Graduates of Yale College* (New York, 1885–1911), II, 289–90.
32. *Boston Gazette*, January 23, 1775; January 1, 1774.
33. *New-York Journal*, September 1, 1774; *Virginia Gazette* (Rind), August 4, 1774.
34. For example: Samuel Cooper, *A Sermon Preached Before His Excellency John Hancock* (Boston, 1780), p. 53; Avery, *Lord Praised*, pp. 46–7. This image often appeared in a visionary context, which, while not technically millennial, may have suggested millennial possibilities. For a few of many such examples, see: "A Soldier," in *The Maryland Journal and Baltimore Advertiser*, December 18, 1776; Price, *Observations on Civil Liberty*, p. 39; Samuel Williams, *A Discourse on the Love of Our Country* (Salem, 1775), p. 22.
35. It has been argued instead that this increased emphasis on liberty in the millennialism of the New England clergy displaced an earlier stress upon religion, introducing a new "civil" or "political" millennialism. See Nathan O. Hatch, *The Sacred Cause of Liberty* (New Haven: Yale University Press, 1977). The sociologist Robert N. Bellah and others have used the term "American civil religion" to refer, more specifically, to the transcendent beliefs imbedded in the collective understanding of the American republic during and after the American Revolution – not to "political religion" in general, which long preceded the late eighteenth century. Robert N. Bellah, "Civil Religion in America," in *Beyond Belief* (New York: Harper and Row, 1970), pp. 168–89.
36. Murray, *Nehemia*, p. 56; Avery, *Lord Praised*, p. 46; Timothy Dwight, *A Valedictory Address to the Young Gentlemen Who Commenced Bachelors of Arts, July 25th. 1776* (New Haven, 1776), p. 14.
37. Avery, *Lord Praised*, p. 46.

38. Winchester, *Thirteen Hymns*, p. 15.
39. Avery, *Lord Praised*, pp. 46-7; Hitchcock, *Sermon Preached at Plymouth*, p. 23; Whitney, *American Independence,* p. 53; Brackenridge, *Six Political Discourses*, p. 88; Dwight, *Valedictory*, p. 14.
40. Hitchcock, *Sermon Preached at Plymouth*, p. 44; West, *Anniversary Sermon*, p. 49; Cooper, *Sermon Preached Before . . . John Hancock*, p. 52; Whitney, *American Independence*, p. 53.
41. For example: Cooper, *Sermon Preached Before . . . John Hancock*, p. 52; Hitchcock, *Sermon Preached at Plymouth*, p. 44; Brackenridge, *Six Political Discourses*, pp. 38-9; Barlow, *Prospect of Peace*, pp. 5-6. Alan Heimert has, I think, rightly emphasized that the liberal millennialists were still somewhat more materialistic and commercially minded than the Calvinists, although some of the latter were also becoming so in the revolutionary period. See Heimert, *Religion and the American Mind* (Cambridge, Mass.: Harvard University Press, 1966), especially pp. 438-9, 289-90.
42. Avery, *Lord Praised*, p. 47.
43. Winchester, *Thirteen Hymns*, pp. 14-15; Edward Martin Stone, *Biography of Rev. Elhanan Winchester*, orig. ed. 1836 (New York: Arno Press, 1972), pp. 25-7, 35-7.
44. Baldwin, *Duty of Rejoicing*, p. 38.
45. Foster, *True Fortitude Delineated*, p. 17.
46. Barlow, *Prospect of Peace*, pp. 7–8.
47. For example, for a liberal view, see Whitney, *American Independence*, p. 53; for an evangelical one, see Dwight, *Valedictory*, pp. 12, 18, 19–20.
48. For example: Henry Cumings, *A Sermon Preached in Billerica on the 3rd of November, 1775* (Worcester, Mass., 1775), p. 9; Fitch, *Discourse . . . March 24th, 1776*, p. 17.
49. Ramsay, *Oration on American Independence*, p. 17.
50. John Trumbull, *An Elegy on the Times* (New Haven, 1775), p. 12; Philip Freneau, "American Independence, an Everlasting Deliverance from British Tyranny," *Miscellanies for Sentimentalists* (Philadelphia, 1778), pp. 124-5; [David Rittenhouse], *The Lancaster Almanack, for the Year of Our Lord, 1779 . . . By Anthony Sharp, Philom.* (Lancaster, Pa., 1778).
51. The metaphors "each man sitting under his own vine" (Micah 4:4), "land flowing with milk and honey" (Exodus 3:8), "desert blossoming as the rose" (Isaiah 35:1), for example, appear in Philip Freneau, *American Liberty, A Poem* (New York, 1775), p. 12; Case, *Poems*, p. 24; *An Address of the Congress to the Inhabitants of the United States of America* (Williamsburg, 1778), p. 2.
52. Keteltas, *God Arising*, pp. 19-20.
53. For example: West, *Anniversary Sermon*, p. 49; Sherwood, *Church's Flight*, pp. 38-9; Bray, *Dissertation*, pp. vii, 75-6, 102-3; [Connecticut], *By the Honorable Jonathan Trumbull . . . A Proclamation [for Jan. 29, 1777]*; [Massachusetts], *A Proclamation for a Day of Public Humiliation, Fasting, and Prayer . . . May 1, 1777* (Boston, 1777).
54. Barlow, *Prospect of Peace*, pp. 10-11.
55. For example: Cushing, *Divine Judgment*, p. 18; Samuel Buell, *Best New-Year's Gift for Young People* (New London, 1775), pp. 53-4.

56. Dwight, *Valedictory*, pp. 14, 16. See also Paine, "Common Sense," pp. 11, 27.
57. Baldwin, *Duty of Rejoicing*, p. 4.
58. Bray, *Dissertation*, p. 101.
59. *New-York Journal*, August 24, 1775.
60. Case, *Poems*, p. 21. This volume went into three Connecticut editions in 1778, and more in Philadelphia, Chatham, Massachusetts, and Trenton, New Jersey, in 1779.
61. Stephen A. Marini, *Radical Sects of Revolutionary New England* (Cambridge, Mass.: Harvard University Press, 1982).
62. On these groups I have relied heavily on Edward Deming Andrews, *The People Called Shakers* (New York: Oxford University Press, 1953), and Herbert Andrew Wisbey, *Pioneer Prophetess: Jemima Wilkinson, the Publick Universal Friend* (Ithaca: Cornell University Press, 1964).
63. See Andrews, *People Called Shakers*, pp. 18-19. Previously in England, in 1772, Lee had called herself "Mother of the new creation," but this did not translate into a clear millennial theory until after several years in America and the exposure to millennial revivalism. That the Shakers were soon known for their millennialism, as well as for their celibacy and emotional rituals, is evident from the first official Shaker publication, Joseph Meacham's *Concise Statement of the Principles of the Only True Church* . . . (Bennington, Vt., 1790), pp. 13, 15-16, and from the popular exposé by Valentine Rathbun, *An Account of the Matter, Form, and Manner of a New and Strange Religion* (Providence, R.I., 1781), pp. 4-6, 22.
64. As quoted in Wisbey, *Pioneer Prophetess*, pp. 18-19.
65. Abner Brownell, *Enthusiastical Errors, Transcribed and Detected* (New London, Conn., 1783), pp. 7-8.
66. Brownell, *Enthusiastical*, pp. 3-4.
67. Wisbey, *Pioneer Prophetess*, p. 82. For expressions of ardent revolutionary millennialism in Marshall's letter books between September 1774 and January 1776, see Eric Foner, *Tom Paine and Revolutionary America* (New York: Oxford University Press, 1976), p. 114. On the decline of Quaker millennialism in the late seventeenth century, see T. L. Underwood, "Early Quaker Eschatology," in *Puritans, the Millennium and the Future of Israel*, ed. Peter Toon (Cambridge: James Clarke, 1970), pp. 91-103.
68. On Lee's use of this image, see Andrews, *People Called Shakers*, p. 27, and Daniel Rathbun, *A Letter from Daniel Rathbun . . . to James Whittacor, Chief Elder of the Church Called Shakers* (Springfield, Mass., 1785), p. 6; on Wilkinson's, see Brownell, *Enthusiastical*, pp. 12-13.
69. Brownell, *Enthusiastical*, p. 13; Daniel Rathbun, *Letter*, p. 21. See the contemporary scientific observations of Harvard professor Samuel Williams in the *Annals of the American Academy of Arts and Sciences* I (1785).
70. Samuel Gatchel, *The Signs of the Times* (Danvers, Mass., 1781).
71. For example: *Some Remarks on the Great and Unusual Darkness* (Danvers, Mass., 1780); John Kennedy, *A Scriptural Account of the Uncommon Darkness* (Boston, 1781); *Bold Conscience and Old Self. A Warning Piece* (n.p., 1781); Elam Potter, *A Second Warning to America* (Hartford, 1777), p. 7.
72. In the 1770's a man in Harvard, Massachusetts, named Shadrack

Ireland, for example, also claimed to be the second messiah. See Andrews, *People Called Shakers*, p. 36. For other examples of millennial pacifism, see the earlier work of Isaac Childs, *The Visio of Isaac Childs* (Philadelphia, 1766), and William Scales, *The Confusion of Babel Discovered* (n.p., 1780).

5. Visions of progress and ruin in the Critical Period

1. Robert Smith, *The Obligations of the Confederate States of North America to Praise God* (Philadelphia, 1782), p. 27n.
2. David Tappan, *A Discourse Delivered At the Third Parish in Newbury, on the First of May, 1783* (Salem, Mass., 1783), pp. 12-13.
3. Thomas Welsh, *An Oration Delivered March 5th. 1783* (Boston, 1783), p. 18; *Maryland Journal and Baltimore Advertiser*, July 8, 1783.
4. *The Virginia Gazette or American Advertiser*, March 23, 1782.
5. John Adams, *Letters of John Adams Addressed to His Wife*, ed. Charles Francis Adams (Boston, 1841), pp. 82-3. Although written as a letter to Abigail, this statement by Adams received wider circulation. It was printed in full in Ezra Stiles's *United States Elevated to Glory and Honor* (New Haven, 1783).
6. Smith, *Obligations*, p. 35; Phillips Payson, *A Memorial of Lexington Battle, and of Some Signal Interpositions of Providence in the American Revolution* (Boston, 1782), p. 12; Levi Frisbie, *An Oration Delivered at Ipswich, at the Request of a Number of the Inhabitants. On the Twenty-ninth of April. 1783* (Boston, 1783), p. 13.
7. David Humphreys, *The Glory of America: or Peace Triumphant over War: A Poem* (Philadelphia, 1783), p. 16.
8. Frisbie, *Oration*, p. 16.
9. Joseph Buckminster, *A Discourse Delivered in the First Church of Christ at Portsmouth. On Tuesday December 11, 1783* (Portsmouth, N.H., 1784), pp. 22-3; Benjamin Trumbull, *God Is to Be praised for the Glory of His Majesty* (New Haven, 1784), pp. 22-3; Ezra Stiles, "The United States Elevated to Glory and Honor," in *The Pulpit of the American Revolution*, ed. John Wingate Thornton (Boston, 1860), p. 454; David Osgood, *Reflections on the Goodness of God in Supporting the People of the United States* (Boston, 1784), p. 29.
10. *The Virginia Gazette and the Weekly Advertiser*, November 29, 1783.
11. George Duffield, *A Sermon Preached in the Third Presbyterian Church in the City of Philadelphia* (Philadelphia, 1784), p. 16.
12. Frisbie, *Oration*, p. 15; Buckminster, *Discourse*, p. 20; Duffield, *Sermon*; John Rodgers, *The Divine Goodness Displayed, in the American Revolution* (New York, 1784), p. 30; Israel Evans, *A Discourse Delivered in New-York* (New York, 1783), p. 8.
13. Felix Gilbert discusses this theme in relation to the ideal of the "model treaty," in *To the Farewell Address: Ideas of American Foreign Policy* (Princeton: Princeton University Press, 1961). Also see Drew R. McCoy, *The Elusive Republic* (Chapel Hill: University of North Carolina Press, 1980), pp. 86-104.
14. Tappan, *Discourse*, pp. 11-12; Buckminster, *Discourse*, pp. 21-2.

15. Joel Barlow, *The Vision of Columbus* (Hartford, 1787), pp. 242n., 243n., 244n.
16. Smith, *Obligations*, p. 29; Samuel MacClintock, *A Sermon Preached Before the Honorable Council, and the Honorable Senate, and House of Representatives, of the State of New-Hampshire, June 3, 1784* (Portsmouth, 1784), p. 26.
17. Timothy Matlack, *An Oration, Delivered March 16, 1780* (Philadelphia, 1780), p. 25.
18. Samuel West, *An Anniversary Sermon Preached at Plymouth, December 22d, 1777* (Boston, 1778), pp. 55-6.
19. John Murray, *Nehemiah, or the Struggle for Liberty Never in Vain, When Managed with Virtue and Perseverence* (Newburyport, Mass., 1779), p. 53.
20. Murray, *Nehemiah*, pp. 53-6; David Avery, *The Lord Is to Be Praised for the Triumphs of His Power* (Norwich, Conn., 1778), p. 46; Elisha Rich, *On the Bloody Engagement that Was Fought on Bunker's Hill* (Chelmsford, Mass., 1775); Samuel Clarke, *The American Wonder* (Salem, Mass., 1776), p. 18; *A Discourse on the Times* (Norwich, Conn., 1776), pp. 5, 14-15.
21. West, *Anniversary Sermon*, p. 57.
22. Thomas Jefferson, "Notes on the State of Virginia," *The Writings of Thomas Jefferson*, ed. Paul Leicester Ford (New York, 1892-1899), 3: 268.
23. *Rudiments of Law and Government, Deduced from The Law of Nature* (Charleston, S.C., 1783).
24. Richard Price, *Observations on the Importance of the American Revolution* (Boston, 1784), pp. 57-8.
25. Duffield, *Sermon Preached in Third Presbyterian Church*, p. 16.
26. [Herman Husband], *Proposals to Amend and Perfect the Policy of the Government of the United States of America* ([Baltimore or Philadelphia], 1782), p. 11. Mark H. Jones, who informed me that Husband was the author of this pamphlet, discusses it in "Herman Husband: Millenarian, Carolina Regulator, and Whiskey Rebel" (Ph.D. dissertation, Northern Illinois University, 1982).
27. *Maryland Journal and Baltimore Advertiser*, June 3, 1783.
28. Alan Heimert to the contrary, the frequent homage paid to "religious liberty" on the part of most evangelical Congregationalists did not imply an anti-establishment position akin to the Baptists'. Congregationalists, whether evangelical or liberal, generally believed that their ecclesiastical establishment was already part of a system of "religious liberty." A notable exception was David Avery, *Lord Praised*, p. 47n. See Alan Heimert, *Religion and the American Mind* (Cambridge, Mass.: Harvard University Press, 1966), pp. 395-6.
29. Elisha Rich, *The Number of the Beast Found Out by Spiritual Arithmetic* (Chelmsford, Mass., 1775), especially pp. 8-12, 19. Rich's broadside poem of 1775, *On the Bloody Engagement*, was more overtly revolutionary millennialist. On Rich's life, see *The Vermont Historical Gazetteer*, ed. Abby Maria Hemenway (Claremont, N.H., 1877), 3: 955. For another example of a Baptist attacking "religious tyranny" as an obstacle in the way of the millennium, see Elhanan Winchester, *Thirteen Hymns Suited to the Present Times* (Baltimore, 1776), p. 14.

30. John Leland, "The Rights of Conscience Inalienable," in *The Writings of John Leland*, ed. L. F. Greene (New York, 1845), p. 192.
31. Isaac Backus, "An Appeal to the Public for Religious Liberty" (1773), "Truth Is Great and Will Prevail" (1781), "A Door Opened for Christian Liberty" (1783), in *Isaac Backus on Church, State, and Calvinism*, ed. William G. McLoughlin (Cambridge Mass.: Harvard University Press, 1968), pp. 342, 414, 438.
32. Benjamin Rush, *Considerations upon the Present Test-Law of Pennsylvania* (Philadelphia, 1784), pp. 19-20.
33. Rush, *Considerations upon the Present Test-Law*, pp. 19-20.
34. Samuel Hopkins, *A Dialogue Concerning the Slavery of the Africans* (Norwich, Conn., 1776), p. 14.
35. Rich, *On the Bloody Engagement*; Avery, *Lord Praised*, p. 46n.; Joel Barlow, *Prospect of Peace* (New Haven, 1778), p. 6. Also, by implication, the millennial works by Murray, *Nehemiah*, p. 9, and Thomas Bray, *A Dissertation upon the Sixth Vial* (Hartford, 1780), p. 64.
36. *Discourse on the Times*, pp. 4, 5, 14-15. Other antislavery statements of the 1770's also rang with the prophetic words from Isaiah. For example: Avery, *Lord Praised*, pp. 45-6; Barlow, *Prospect of Peace*, p. 6; Daniel Byrnes, *A Short Address to the English Colonies in North America* [Wilmington, Del., 1775]; "A New-Englandman," *The Boston Chronicle*, February 27 to March 2, 1769.
37. See Chapter 7 below.
38. Benjamin Rush, "Of the Mode of Education Proper in a Republic," in *Essays, Literary, Moral and Philosophical*, 2nd ed. (Philadelphia, 1806), p. 20.
39. Charles Turner, *Due Glory to Be Given to God* (Boston, 1783), p. 29.
40. [David Hoar], *The Natural Principles of Liberty, Moral Virtue, Learning, Society, Good Manners, and Human Happiness* (Boston, 1782), especially pp. 6-10.
41. Buckminster, *Discourse*, p. 33; Tappan, *Discourse*, p. 18; Samuel Cooper, *A Sermon Preached Before His Excellency John Hancock* (Boston, 1780), pp. 50-5; MacClintock, *Sermon*, pp. 27-31, 35-6, 40-7.
42. Timothy Dwight, *A Sermon Preached at Northampton, on the Twenty-Eighth of November, 1781* (Hartford, 1781), p. 27, 28-9.
43. Stiles, "The United States Elevated to Glory and Honor" (1783), in *Pulpit*, ed. Thornton, p. 472.
44. *Minutes of the Warren Association, at Their Meeting, in Middleboro', Sept. 7 and 8, 1784* (n.p., n.d.), p. 6.
45. *A Theological System of Government. Adapted to the Immediate Final Salvation of Mankind* (Boston, 1784), p. 5.
46. On the Shakers, see Edward Deming Andrews, *The People Called Shakers* (New York: Oxford University Press, 1953), pp. 35-53, 61. On the Universal Friends, see Herbert Andrew Wisbey, *Pioneer Prophetess* (Ithaca: Cornell University Press, 1964), pp. 50-1, 57-96. Jemima Wilkinson's own *Universal Friend's Advice, to Those of the Same Religious Society* (Philadelphia, [1784]) also illustrates the sect's greater preoccupation with remaining apart from the world.
47. Dwight, *Sermon Preached at Northampton*, p. 27; David Tappan, *The*

Question Answered, "Watchman, What of the Night?" (Salem, 1783), p. 9; Thomas Brockway, *America Saved or Divine Glory Displayed, in the Late War with Great Britain* (Hartford, 1784), pp. 23–4; Benjamin Gale, *A Brief Essay* (New Haven, [1788]), pp. 55–6. The Delaware Baptist Morgan Edwards insisted on the originality of his own computations, but he came up with the similar date of 1993. See Morgan Edwards, *Two Academical Exercises on Subjects Bearing the Following Titles: Millennium. Last-Novelities* (Philadelphia, 1788), pp. 33-4.

48. Stiles, in *Pulpit*, ed. Thornton, p. 485. My knowledge of this unpublished work is from Richard Popkin, "Millenarianism in England, Holland, and America: Jewish and Christian Relations in England, Holland, and Newport," unpublished paper, 1982.

49. Brockway, *America Saved*, p. 22; Dwight, *Sermon*, p. 27.

50. Barlow, *Vision of Columbus*, pp. 241n., 244n.

51. Price, *Observations*, pp. 5, 8.

52. Dwight, *Sermon*, p. 31.

53. Samuel Magaw, *A Sermon Delivered in St. Paul's Church. On the 4th of July, 1786* (Philadelphia, 1786), pp. 13-14.

54. For examples along the Calvinist theological spectrum, see Stiles, in *Pulpit*, ed. Thornton, p. 467; Dwight, *Sermon*, pp. 33-4; and Nathanael Emmons, *The Dignity of Man* (Providence, 1787), p. 13.

55. On Priestley and Price, see Jack Fruchtman, Jr., *The Apocalyptic Politics of Richard Price and Joseph Priestley* (Philadelphia: American Philosophical Society, 1983).

56. Benjamin Rush, "The Influence of Physical Causes upon the Moral Faculty" (1786), in *The Selected Writings of Benjamin Rush*, ed. Dagobert D. Runes (New York: Philosophical Library, 1947), p. 209.

57. Quoted in Henry F. May, *The Enlightenment in America* (New York: Oxford University Press, 1976), p. 215.

58. *Maryland Journal and Baltimore Advertiser*, June 3, 1783.

59. MacClintock, *Sermon*, pp. 27-31, 41.

60. Price, *Observations*, p. 70.

61. Henry Cumings, *A Sermon Preached in Billerica on the 3rd of November, 1775* (Worcester, Mass., 1775), pp. 26-7; William Foster, *True Fortitude Delineated* (Philadelphia, 1776), p. 13; Phillips Payson, *A Sermon Preached Before the Honourable Council, and the honourable House of Representatives, of . . . Massachusetts . . . May 27, 1778* (Boston, 1778), pp. 15-17, 35; Jacob Duché, *The American Vine* (Philadelphia, 1775), pp. 27-8, 30-1.

62. Perry Miller notes the perfunctory character of the revolutionary jeremiads in "From the Covenant to the Revival," in *Natures's Nation* (Cambridge, Mass.: Harvard University Press, 1967), pp. 90-120.

63. On the rise of the jeremiad in the 1780's, also see Nathan O. Hatch, *The Sacred Cause of Liberty* (New Haven: Yale University Press, 1977), pp. 160-3.

64. Charles Royster highlights this wartime transition in his *Revolutionary People at War* (Chapel Hill: University of North Carolina Press, 1979).

65. West, *Anniversary Sermon*, p. 57.

66. For example, Samuel Hopkins, *A Dialogue*, pp. 56, 58; Elam Potter, *A Second Warning to America* (Hartford, [1777]), p. 13; *Extract from an Address in the Virginia Gazette, of March 19, 1767* [Philadelphia, 1780].
67. Jacob Green, *A Sermon Delivered at Hanover (in New-Jersey) April 22d, 1778* (Chatham, N.J., 1779), p. 16.
68. The growth of the antislavery movement during the Revolution has been attributed to the "contagion" of the radical whig ideas of liberty that underlay the political rebellion. See especially Bernard Bailyn, *The Ideological Origins of the American Revolution* (Cambridge, Mass.: Harvard University Press, 1967), pp. 230-46. It is also apparent, however, that several leading opponents of slavery, such as Jacob Green, Samuel Hopkins, and Levi Hart, as well as many of the more obscure figures cited above, were New Light Calvinists moved by religious conviction as well as by political ideology. On this point, see Mark A. Noll, "Observations on the Reconciliation of Politics and Revolution in Revolutionary New Jersey: The Case of Jacob Green," *Journal of Presbyterian History* 54 (Summer 1976): 228-33, and David S. Lovejoy, "Samuel Hopkins: Religion, Slavery, and the Revolution," *The New England Quarterly* 40 (June 1967): 227-43. Mark Noll emphasizes that Jacob Green was not a millennialist in his theology. Samuel Hopkins and Levi Hart did, however, express millennial ideas upon other occasions – but not in relation to the antislavery cause.
69. John Woolman, *Considerations on the True Harmony of Mankind* (Philadelphia, 1770).
70. *The Virginia Gazette or American Advertiser*, September 13, 1783.
71. Tappan, *Question*, pp. 11, 15-16; Turner, *Due Glory*, p. 17. Tappan also introjected a similar note of warning into his generally more optimistic sermon *Discourse*, p. 17.
72. [Hannah Adams], *Women Invited to War* (Boston, 1787), pp. 11–12, 30.
73. *The Prophet Nathan, or, Plain Friend* (Hudson, N.Y., 1788).
74. Isaac Backus, "Truth Is Great," in *Isaac Backus*, ed. McLoughlin, p. 425. McLoughlin, in his introductory remarks, p. 400, notes that Backus preached a "more ambivalent millennialism" in the 1780's than in the 1770's. Elhanan Winchester, *The Outcasts Comforted* (Philadelphia, 1782).
75. I discuss this trend at length in Chapter 6. For examples, see Benjamin Gale, *A Brief Essay, or, An Attempt to Prove, from the Prophetic Writings of the Old and New Testament, What Period of Prophecy the Church of God Is Now Under* (New Haven, 1788), pp. 23-6, and Charles Crawford, *Observations upon the Fall of Anti-Christ on the Seventy weeks of Daniel* (Newport, R.I., 1787), pp. 13-17, 30-2.
76. *The Virginia Gazette and Weekly Advertiser*, January 19, 1782.
77. Samuel Wales, *The Dangers of Our National Prosperity* (Hartford, 1785), p. 27.
78. Charles Backus, *A Sermon preached at Long Meadow, at the Publick Fast, April 17th. 1788* (Springfield, Mass., 1788), pp. 8, 9, 24.
79. For example, *Maryland Journal and Baltimore Advertiser*, June 3, 1783; MacClintock, *Sermon*; Tappan, *Question*. Nathan Hatch has also noted this thematic convergence in sermons by New England clergymen. See *Sacred Cause*, especially pp. 105-7.

80. A thorough exposition of civic republican theory is contained in J. G. A. Pocock, *The Machiavellian Moment* (Princeton: Princeton University Press, 1975). On the theme of virtue in the American literature of the revolutionary period, see also Gordon Wood, *The Creation of the American Republic* (New York: Norton, 1969); Lance Banning, *The Jeffersonian Persuasion* (Ithaca: Cornell University Press, 1978); McCoy, *Elusive Republic*. Although all these works point to the importance of the concept of virtue, they do not entirely agree in their definition of it. None, moreover, stresses its religious dimension.

81. In the theology of the leading evangelical Calvinist Jonathan Edwards, for example, disinterested virtue was understood directly in relation to saving grace, scarcely possessing a political meaning at all. When Edwards's southern colleague Samuel Davies delivered a sermon entitled *Religion and Public Spirit* ([New York], in 1760), he, too, stressed that the true source of virtue and benevolence was a primary dedication to God. Patriot ministers of both liberal and Calvinist persuasions returned to this theme in the 1770's. I discuss this briefly in Chapter 3. For examples, see Isaac Story, *The Love of our Country Recommended and Enforced* (Boston, 1774), p. 10; Samuel Magaw, *A Discourse Preached at Christ-Church* (Philadelphia, 1775), pp. 13-14; John Witherspoon, *Dominion of Providence* (Philadelphia, 1776), pp. 50-1; Israel Evans, *A Discourse Delivered at Easton, on the 17th of October, 1779* (Philadelphia, 1779), p. 26.

82. For example: *The Virginia Gazette or American Advertiser*, December 21, 1782; *Prophet Nathan*, pp. 27-30; Joseph Huntington, *A Discourse, Adapted to the Present Day* (Hartford, 1781), p. 28; Rodgers, *Divine Goodness*, p. 41; Magaw, *Sermon in St. Paul's Church; A Concert of Prayer Propounded to the Citizens of the United States of America* (Exeter, N.H., 1787), p. 4; Thomas Reese, *An Essay on the Influence of Religion* (Charleston, S.C., 1788).

83. George Richards Minot, *The History of the Insurrections, in Massachusetts, in the Year MDCCLXXXVI, and the Rebellion Consequent Thereon* (Worcester, Mass., 1788), pp. 72-3; also see pp. 34-7.

84. *Hampshire Gazette*, October 4, 1786.

85. Marion Starkey, *A Little Rebellion* (New York: Knopf, 1955), pp. 13, 108, 28, 224. There are no footnotes citing the primary sources.

86. Robert Taylor, *Western Massachusetts, in the Revolution* (Providence: Brown University Press, 1954), pp. 147-50; Starkey, *A Little Rebellion*, pp. 94, 135; David P. Szatmary, *Shays' Rebellion* (Amherst: University of Massachusetts Press, 1980), pp. 89, 165 n.87.

87. "Spectator," in the *Independent Chronicle*, August 8, 1786; James Bowdoin, *A Proclamation* (Boston, 1786).

88. Reprinted in the *Pittsburgh Gazette*, January 13, 1787. Also see: *Independent Chronicle*, August 31, 1786; "The Warner," in the *Independent Chronicle*, October 19, 1786; Amicus Republicae, *Address to the Public* (Exeter, N.H., 1786), pp. 7-8.

89. Leon Howard, *The Connecticut Wits* (Chicago: University of Chicago Press, 1943), pp. 180-200.

90. "Cassius" for the *Massachusetts Gazette*, in *Essays on the Constitution of the United States*, ed. Paul Leicester Ford (Brooklyn, 1892), p. 15; [James

Iredell], "Answers to Mr. Mason's Objections to the New Constitution," in *Pamphlets on the Constitution of the United States*, ed. Paul Leicester Ford (Brooklyn, 1888), p. 370; *Pittsburgh Gazette*, March 29, 1788.

91. *State Gazette of South-Carolina*, November 12, 1787.
92. From the Boston *Independent Chronicle*, reprinted in the *State Gazette of South-Carolina*, January 1, 1788.
93. [William Findley], *Address from an Officer of the Late Continental Army* (Philadelphia, 1787), pp. 7-8.
94. For example: *Pittsburgh Gazette*, September 6, 1788; Enos Hitchcock, *An Oration: Delivered July 4. 1788* (Providence, 1788), pp. 16-18; Benjamin Rush, in "American Intelligence," *State Gazette of South-Carolina*, December 24, 1787; [John Dickenson], "Letters of Fabius," in *Pamphlets*, ed. Ford, pp. 208-9; James Wilson, in *The Columbian Magazine* II (July 1788), pp. 399-400.
95. Reprinted from the Boston *Independent Chronicle* in the *State Gazette of South-Carolina*, April 14, 1788. Also see "Sermon," *Pittsburgh Gazette*, March 22, 1788.
96. See "Aristocrotis," "A Farmer," and "Brutus," in *The Antifederalist Papers*, ed. Morton Borden (East Lansing, Mich.: Michigan State University Press, 1965), pp. 148, 6-7, 58-9.
97. "Letters of a Federal Farmer," in *Pamphlets*, ed. Ford, p. 281.
98. In *Antifederalist Papers*, ed. Borden, p. 248.
99. In *Pamphlets*, ed. Ford, p. 285.
100. In *Antifederalist Papers*, ed. Borden, p. 214.
101. "Concerning Dangers from War Between the States," in *The Federalist Papers*, ed. Clinton Rossiter (New York: Mentor, 1961), pp. 54, 59.
102. Pelatiah Webster, in *Pamphlets*, ed. Ford, p. 123.
103. Ellsworth, in *Essays*, ed. Ford, p. 167. Also see Noah Webster, in *Pamphlets*, ed. Ford, p. 63; Hamilton, in *Federalist Papers*, ed. Rossiter, p. 253.
104. *Pittsburgh Gazette*, January 30, 1790. Also see Noah Webster in *Pamphlets*, ed. Ford, p. 59.
105. [Herman Husband], *XIV Sermons on the Characters of Jacob's Fourteen Sons* (Philadelphia, 1789). The 1788 "Sermon to Bucks and Hinds" is described in the preface. Mark Jones's "Herman Husband" highlights the shift to an exclusively western New Jerusalem.
106. In *The Debates in the Several State Conventions on the Adoption of the Federal Constitution*, ed. Jonathan Elliot (Philadelphia: J. B. Lippincott, 1901), 2: 529.
107. Joel Barlow, *An Oration, Delivered at the North Church in Hartford, at the Meeting of the Connecticut Society of the Cincinnati, July 4th, 1787* (Hartford, 1787), p. 20.
108. For example, Hitchcock, *Oration*, p. 22; Samuel Stillman, *An Oration, Delivered July 4th, 1789* (Boston, 1789), pp. 20, 29.
109. John Woodhull, *A Sermon, for the Day of Publick Thanksgiving. Appointed by the President, on Account of the Establishment of the New Constitution* (Trenton, 1790), pp. 22-3.

6. Exegesis

1. Glenn T. Miller, "'Fashionable to Prophesy': Presbyterians, the Millennium and the Revolution," *Amerikastudien/American Studies* 21 (1976): 246.
2. Thomas Newton, *Dissertations on the Prophecies*, 3 vols. (London, 1766), especially Volume 3.
3. Charles Crawford, *Observations upon the Fall of Anti-Christ, and the Concomitant Events* (Philadelphia, 1786), pp. 5-6, 9-10.
4. Benjamin Gale, *A Brief Essay*.
5. Benjamin Foster, *Dissertation on the Seventy Weeks of Daniel* (Newport, 1787), pp. 37-8.
6. Morgan Edwards, *Two Academical Exercises on Subjects Bearing the Following Titles: Millennium. Last-Novelities* (Philadelphia, 1788), p. 24.
7. Edwards, *Two Academical Exercises*, pp. 43-4; *The Baptist Encyclopedia*, ed. William Cathcart (Philadelphia, 1881), p. 362.
8. Samuel Langdon, *Observations on the Revelation of Jesus Christ to St. John* (Worcester, Mass., 1791).
9. This numerical estimate is based on the number of entries under the topics "prophecy" and "millennium" in the subject indexes of Charles Evans's *American Bibliography*, 13 vols. (Chicago and Worcester, Mass.: Blakely Press, Columbia Press, and American Antiquarian Society, 1903-55). Because many of these entries are repeated editions of one or two exceptionally popular works (most notably *The Prophecies of Christopher Love* and Richard Brothers's *Revealed Knowledge* – both discussed in Chapter 7), I have considerably scaled down the number and settled on a conservative estimate.
10. *The Millennium*, ed. David Austin (Elizabethtown, N.J., 1794).
11. *Isaiah. A New Translation* (Albany, 1794). For references to future fulfillment, see pp. 15, 119, 123, 163-4, 173, 184, 210, 218, 227.
12. Joseph A. Conforti, *Samuel Hopkins and the New Divinity Movement* (Grand Rapids: Christian University Press, 1981); Edward Martin Stone, *Biography of Rev. Elhanan Winchester* (Boston, 1836).
13. Samuel Hopkins, *A Treatise on the Millennium* (Boston, 1793), p. 115.
14. Hopkins, *Treatise*, p. 41.
15. Hopkins, *Treatise*, p. 151
16. Hopkins, *Treatise*, p. 97.
17. Hopkins, *Treatise*, p. 152.
18. Hopkins, *Treatise*, p. 6.
19. Stone, *Biography of Winchester*, p. 36.
20. "Events in the Life of John Leland: Written by Himself," in *The Writings of John Leland*, ed. L. F. Greene (New York, 1845), p. 11.
21. Publications on millennial themes by American universalists include: *Evangelical Psalms, Hymns and Spiritual Songs* (Philadelphia, 1792); James Bolton, *Treatise of Universal Restoration* (Ephrata, 1793); "A Circular Letter," *Kentucky Gazette*, August 31, 1973, p. 3. Winchester's book was advertised in the *Kentucky Gazette*. See, for example, June 17, 1795, p. 5. Priestley acknowledges Winchester in "The Present State of Europe

Compared to Antient Prophecies," in *Two Sermons* (Philadelphia, 1794), p. 35. Rush does in his correspondence with Winchester, in *Letters of Benjamin Rush*, ed. L. H. Butterfield (Princeton: Princeton University Press, 1951), 1: 581-2, 611-12. Also Donald J. d'Elia, *Benjamin Rush: Philosopher of the American Revolution* (Philadelphia: American Philosophical Society, 1974), pp. 69, 88.

22. [Charles Chauncy], *Mystery Hid from Ages and Generations* (London, 1784). James West Davidson, in *The Logic of Millennial Thought* (New Haven: Yale University Press, 1977), pp. 110-11, summarizes Chauncy's position in relation to that of previous Universalists.

23. Elhanan Winchester, *Lectures on the Prophecies That Remain to be Fulfilled* (Norwich, Conn., 1795) 2: 285.

24. Winchester, *Lectures* 2: 59.

25. Winchester, *Lectures* 2: 92-3.

26. Elhanan Winchester, *The Three Woe Trumpets* (Boston, 1794), p. 44.

27. Hopkins, *Treatise*, p. 72. Also Winchester, *Lectures* 2: 35-7.

28. Winchester, *Three Woe Trumpets*, p. 77. Also Hopkins, *Treatise*, pp. 73-5.

29. Hopkins, *Treatise*, pp 67-70; Winchester, *Lectures* 2: 31, 97.

30. Hopkins, *Treatise*, p. 57.

31. Hopkins, *Treatise*, p. 78; Winchester, *Lectures* 2: 235-45.

32. Winchester, *Lectures* 2: 205-6.

33. Winchester, *Lectures* (1975 ed.) 2: 31, 38-47, 159-73.

34. Hopkins, *Treatise*, pp. 70, 74.

35. Hopkins, *Treatise*, p. 72.

36. Hopkins, *Treatise*, p. 71.

37. Winchester, *Lectures* 2: 47-56.

38. For Winchester's decidedly Republican (if anti-infidel) political views, see Elhanan Winchester, *A Plain Political Catechism* (Philadelphia, 1796), especially p. 52.

39. Hopkins, *Treatise*, p. 79.

40. Winchester, *Lectures* 2: 249, 24, 95-6.

41. Hopkins, *Treatise*, p. 67.

42. Hopkins, *Treatise*, p. 73.

43. Hopkins, *Treatise*, p. 56.

44. Hopkins, *Treatise*, p. 48-9, 55.

45. Winchester (much like Thomas Newton) saw the present as at the end of the sixth trumpet and reserved for the future the sounding of the seventh and the pouring of the vials, whereas Hopkins (following Moses Lowman) held that six vials had already poured and only the seventh remained. See especially Winchester, *Three Woe Trumpets*, pp. 40-79; Hopkins, *Treatise*, pp. 98-120.

46. Davidson, *Logic*, especially pp. 27-76. Davidson, however, does not address the question of why this issue became a matter of polarization at all.

47. Ebenezer Baldwin, *The Duty of Rejoicing under Calamities and Afflictions* (New York, 1776), pp. 38-40; Thomas Bray, *A Dissertation upon the Sixth Vial* (Hartford, 1780), pp. ix-x; Levi Hart, *The War between Michael and the Dragon Briefly Considered* (Providence, 1790), pp. 22-3; Langdon,

Observations, pp. 293-308. The ministers within the New Divinity movement are identified in Conforti, *Samuel Hopkins*, 227-32.

48. Eliphaz Chapman, *Discourse on the Prophecies* (Portland, Maine, 1797), pp. 2, 35, 37-8.

49. Winchester, *Lectures* 2: 15.

50. Winchester, *Lectures* 2: 292.

51. Stephen A. Marini, *Radical Sects of Revolutionary New England* (Cambridge, Mass.: Harvard University Press, 1982), pp. 46-7.

52. William Cowper, *The Task* (Boston, 1791), especially pp. 179-85; Edward Young, *The Last Day. A Poem* (Elizabethtown, 1797). For editions see Evans, *American Bibliography*. Other such devotional poems include R. Perry, *A Poem on the Destruction of Sodom by Fire; or the Day of Judgment* (Middletown, Conn., 1790); Benjamin Francis, *Conflagration: A Poem on the Last Day* (New York, 1789).

53. See, for example, Isaac Watts, *Hymn and Scriptural Songs* (Salem, Mass., 1794), pp. 7, 10-11, 17, 20-2, 25-7, 34-7, 39, 44-5, 56-7, 109, 174-5, 180, 192, 213, 244-5. Other examples of hymns on these themes include those by the Baptist Lucy Allen, *Hymns on Various Subjects* (Windsor, Conn., 1795), especially pp. 11-12, 18-19.

54. *The History of the Holy Jesus* (Boston, 1792), p. 35; *Christian Oeconomy. Translated from the Original Greek* (Albany, 1790), pp. 35-6. For editions, see Evans, *American Bibliography*.

55. *Independent Chronicle*, April 7, 1786.

56. John Smith, *The Coming of the Son of Man* (Concord, 1797). Another apocalyptical work drew on William Whiston's earlier geophysical theories, as well as on the scientific authority of Isaac Newton and the astronomer Halley, arguing that the end of the world would be caused by a colliding comet (it did not, however, mention the Second Coming). See John Watkins, *An Essay on the End of the World* (Worcester, Mass., 1795).

57. B. J., *Four Sermons* (Philadelphia, 1797), p. 64.

58. For example: Devereux Jarratt, "The Danger of Surprize at Death or Judgment," in *Sermons on Various and Important Subjects* (Philadelphia, 1794) 3: 64-92; Joseph Pilmore, *The Journal of Joseph Pilmore, Methodist Itinerant, for the Years August 1, 1769 to January 2, 1774*, ed. Frederick E. Maser and Howard T. Maag (Philadelphia: Message Publishing, 1969), pp. 29, 57, 82, 108; Francis Asbury, *The Heart of Asbury's Journal*, ed. Ezra Squier Tipple (New York: Eaton and Mains, 1904), p. 29; Thomas Coke, *The Substance of a Sermon on the Godhead of Christ Preached at Baltimore* (New York, 1785), pp. 20, 22; *The Arminian Magazine* I (March 1789): 142-3; II (November 1790): 585-94; *A Pocket Hymn-Book, Designed as a Constant Companion for the Pious*, 13th ed. (Philadelphia, 1791), pp. 17, 18, 256.

59. Ezekiel Cooper, *Beams of Light on Early Methodism in America*, ed. George A. Phoebus (New York, 1887), p. 244.

60. Cooper, *Beams*, p. 244. John Wesley drew his theory of the double millennium from the German exegete Johann Albrecht Bengel. See Wesley, *Explanatory Notes upon the New Testament. Volume the Third* (Philadelphia, 1791), pp. 329-38.

61. Ernest E. Sandeen, *The Roots of Fundamentalism* (Chicago: University of Chicago Press, 1970); Timothy P. Weber, *Living in the Shadow of the Second Coming* (New York: Oxford University Press, 1979); George M. Marsden, *Fundamentalism and American Culture* (New York: Oxford University Press, 1980).

62. Foster, *Dissertation*, especially pp. 37-8; Edwards, *Two Academical Exercises*, p. 24. As a Baptist, moreover, Edwards suggested that Antichrist had branched out from papal Rome to Protestant church establishments. See p. 20.

63. *Minutes of the Ketocton Baptist Association, Held at Goose Creek, Loudon County, Virginia, August, 1795* (Dumfries, Va., 1795); *Minutes of the Danbury Association, Holden at Pawlingstown, [New York] September . . . 1795* (Newfield, Conn., [1795]), p. 8; *Minutes of the New-York Baptist Association . . . May . . . 1799* ([New York], 1799), p. 8.

64. Abraham Cummings, *A Dissertation on the Introduction and Glory of the Millennium* (Boston, 1797), pp. 31, 16-36, 99-104.

65. Crawford, *Observations*, pp. 26-7.

66. Samuel Osgood, *Remarks on the Book of Daniel, and on the Revelations* (New York, 1794), especially pp. 372-414.

67. Osgood, *Remarks*, p. 298.

68. Osgood, *Remarks*, p. 264.

69. Osgood, *Remarks*, pp. 423-6. This same doctrinal question occupied the attention of another premillennial, anonymous work that, since it was also published by Greenleaf's press in New York in the mid-1790's and espoused a similar (if not identical) chronological scheme, may have been written by Osgood as well. See *Observations on 1st the Chronology of Scripture. 2d. Strictures on the Age of Reason* (New York, 1795).

70. Samuel Fish, *Discourse. Shewing the Certainty of Christ's Personal Appearance* (Windham, Conn., 1793); Fish, *An Humble Address to Every Christian of Every Nation* (Norwich, Conn., 1793); Fish, *A Discourse, Shewing the Certainty of Christ's Spiritual Reign* (Windham, Conn., 1793).

71. Gale, *Brief Essay*, pp. 12-13.

72. Gale, *Brief Essay*, p. 20.

73. Simon Hough, *An Alarm to the World* (Stockbridge, Mass., 1792), p. 20. Also his later *The Sign of the Present Time* (Stockbridge, Mass., 1799).

74. David Austin, "The Downfall of Mystical Babylon," in *The Millennium*, ed. David Austin (Elizabethtown, N.J., 1794), pp. 392-3.

75. Nicholas Murray, in William Sprague, *Annals of the Americal Pulpit* (New York, 1859-69) 2: 195.

76. Sprague, *Annals* 2: 196.

77. Sprague, *Annals* 2: 196.

78. *The New-Jersey Journal* (Elizabethtown), June 8, 1796. This item was reprinted from the *New-York Gazette*. It was responding to a critical article that had appeared in the *New-York Gazette*, reprinted from the *Minerva*, on May 21.

79. Sprague, *Annals* 2: 200. In 1800, Austin proposed a similar venture in Washington, D.C., which he had come to think of as the New Jerusalem. David Austin, *The Dawn of Day* (New Haven, 1800), p. 21.

80. Abel McEwen, in Sprague, *Annals* 2: 200.
81. David Austin, *The Dance of Herodias* (East Windsor, Conn., 1799), p. 44; *A Discourse on the Occasion of the Death of Washington* (New York, 1800), pp. 25, 35; *The National "Barley Cake"* (Washington, D.C., 1802), pp. 25, 47.
82. Austin, *Dance of Herodias*, especially pp. 19-33, and *The First Vibration of the Jubilee Trump!* (Elizabethtown, N.J., 1799).
83. David Austin, *Masonry in Its Glory* (East Windsor, Conn., 1799), p. 14.
84. The best discussion of Austin's politics, which corrects previous misconceptions, is James Davidson, "Searching for the Millennium," *New England Quarterly* 45 (1972): 241-61.
85. Joshua Spaulding, *Sentiments Concerning the Coming and Kingdom of Christ* (Salem, Mass., 1796), p. 244.
86. Spaulding, *Sentiments*, pp. 264-6.
87. Spaulding, *Sentiments*, pp. 241-2.
88. Spaulding, *Sentiments*, p. 46.
89. Hopkins, *Treatise*, especially pp. 143-4.
90. Le Roy Edwin Froom, *The Prophetic Faith of Our Fathers*, 4 vols. (Washington, D.C.: Review and Herald, 1946-54), 3: 230.
91. Osgood, *Remarks*, pp. 255-9.
92. Langdon, *Observations*, pp. 266-7.
93. Crawford, *Observations*, pp. 17-19; Gale, *Brief Essay*, pp. 10, 17.
94. Osgood, *Remarks*, pp. 266-7.
95. J. F. Maclear, "New England and the Fifth Monarchy: The Quest for the Millennium in Early American Puritanism," *William and Mary Quarterly*, 3d ser. 32 (1975): 229.
96. For editions of Flavius Josephus, see Evans, *American Bibliography*; Timothy Telescope, pseud., *The Philadelphia Newest Almanac for the Year 1776* (Philadelphia, 1775); Abraham Keteltas, *God Arising and Pleading His People's Cause* (Newburyport, Mass., 1777), p. 32; Jacob Cushing, *Divine Judgements upon Tyrants and Compassion to the Oppressed* (Boston, 1778), p. 18; Bray, *Dissertation*, pp. 66-73.
97. I owe my knowledge of this unpublished manuscript by Stiles to Richard Popkin, "Millenarianism in England, Holland, and America: Jewish and Christian Relations in England, Holland and Newport," unpublished paper, 1982.
98. Hopkins, *Treatise*, pp. 199-200.
99. *Minutes of the New-York Baptist Association Held in New-York, May 23rd, 1794* [New York, 1794?], pp. 7-8.
100. Winchester, *Lectures* 2: 12-13, 202-17.
101. Crawford, *Observations*, pp. 4, 21-3; also Gale, *Brief Essay*, pp. 4, 29-31.
102. *A Divine Call to That Highly Favoured People the Jews. By a Watchman* (Annapolis, Md., [1790]), p. 30.
103. Joseph Priestley, *Letters to the Jews*, and David Levi, *Letters to Dr. Priestley, in Answer to Those He Addressed to the Jews* (New York, 1794); James Bicheno, *A Friendly Address to the Jews* (Providence, 1795).
104. Priestley, *Letters*, p. 50. Also see Priestley, "The Present State of Europe Compared with Antient Prophecies," in *Two Sermons*, pp. 40-4.

105. William Cooper, *The Promised Seed* (Boston, 1796), p. 28. This went into eleven editions in America, primarily in New England, between 1796 and 1798.
106. Cooper, *Promised*, p. 4. Perhaps regarded as another promising sign of the joining of Christians and Jews was an originally French rabbinical rebuttal of Voltaire published in Philadelphia in 1795, which defended the authenticity of the Old Testament, explained Jewish rites such as circumcision, and protested the traditional anti-Semitic charges of bestiality and cannibalism. See Antoine Guénée, *Letters of Certain Jews to Monsieur Voltaire Containing an Apology*, 2 vols. (Philadelphia, 1795).
107. Samuel Brett, *A True Relation of the Proceedings of the Great Council of the Jews* (Keene, N.H., 1795); [Nathaniel Crouch, pseud.], *A Journey to Jerusalem* (Hartford, 1796). This latter, containing Brett's piece, went into another 1796 edition in New Hampshire. A summary of Brett was also appended to Rycaut, cited below.
108. Brett, *True Relation*, pp. 3, 11.
109. Paul Rycaut, *The Counterfeit Messiah; or False Christ* (Keene, N.H., 1795), p. 32. Extracts from Rycaut also appeared in the editions of *A Journal to Jerusalem*, cited above. On Rycaut, see Gershom Scholem, *Sabbatai Sevi: The Mystical Messiah*, trans. R. J. Zwi Werclowsky (Princeton: Princeton University Press, 1973), especially pp. 615-16, 824.
110. Hopkins, *Treatise*, p. 97; Winchester, *Three Woe Trumpets*, p. 44; Langdon, *Observations*, pp. 84, 267; Osgood, *Remarks*, p. 254; Fish, *Humble Address*, pp. 36-8; Hough, *Alarm*, pp. 16-17. Also Gale, *Brief Essay*, pp. 22-4.

7. Francophilic millennialism and partisan Republican ideology

1. James Winthrop, *An Attempt to Translate the Prophetic Part of the Apocalypse of Saint John into Familiar Language* (Boston, 1794), p. 3.
2. Winthrop, *Attempt*, pp. 9-10.
3. Winthrop, *Attempt*, pp. 13, 74-6.
4. James Winthrop, *A Systematic Arrangement of Several Scripture Prophecies Relating to Antichrist* (Boston, 1795), pp. 14, 33.
5. Winthrop, *Systematic*, p. 16, alludes to criticism of his former "translation" of the Book of Revelation. James West Davidson notes the disapproval of Winthrop's fellow liberal (but nonmillennial) clerical correspondent William Bentley in *The Logic of Millennial Thought* (New Haven: Yale University Press, 1977), pp. 268-9.
6. For example: Gustav Adolf Koch, *Republican Religion* (New York: Henry Holt, 1933); Lance Banning, *The Jeffersonian Persuasion* (Ithaca: Cornell University Press, 1978); Drew R. McCoy, *The Elusive Republic* (Chapel Hill: University of North Carolina Press, 1980).
7. On the political affiliations of denominations, see Richard E. Ellis, *The Jeffersonian Crisis* (New York: Oxford University Press, 1971), and Sidney Mead, *The Lively Experiment* (New York: Harper and Row, 1963).
8. Samuel Langdon, *Observations on the Revelation of Jesus Christ to St. John* (Worcester, 1791), pp. 265-7. Langdon dated the beginning of the fall

of Antichrist at 1760 and expected the process to take fifty or sixty years. See p. 266n.

9. Charles Crawford, *Observations upon the Revolution in France* (Boston, 1793). On Crawford's life, see Lewis Leary, "Charles Crawford: A Forgotten Poet of Early Philadelphia," *Pennsylvania Magazine of History and Biography* (1959): 293-306.
10. *Boston Gazette*, April 29, 1793, p. 2. Also see the other extract from a letter from Liverpool on the same page.
11. *New-Jersey Journal*, March 23, 1796, p. 2.
12. *Columbian Centinel*, April 13, 1793, p. 4.
13. *Greeenleaf's New York Journal and Patriotic Register*, February 1, 1794, p. 2.
14. *State Gazette of South-Carolina*, January 10, 1794, p. 3.
15. For example: Chandler Robbins, *An Address, Delivered at Plymouth . . . to Celebrate the Victories of the French Republic, over Their Invaders (Boston, 1793), p. 7; Joseph Lathrop, The Happiness of a Free Government* (Springfield, 1794), pp. 22-3; Joseph Lyman, *The Administration of Providence Full of Goodness and Mercy* (Northampton, Mass., 1794), p. 20.
16. Samuel Stillman, *Thoughts on the French Revolution* (Boston, 1795), p. 27.
17. Samuel Adams's speech before the Massachusetts legislature on January 17, 1794, in Greenleaf's *New York Journal and Patriotic Register*, January 29, 1794, p. 2.
18. Elias Lee, *The Dissolution of Earthly Monarchies; the Downfall of Antichrist; and the Full Display of Zion's King* (Danbury, Conn., 1794), p. 22.
19. Simon Hough, *The Sign of the Present Time* (Stockbridge, Mass., 1799), p. 6.
20. The main examples of non-New England clergymen who made this ideological transition are William Linn, the Dutch Reformed president of Queen's College in New Jersey, and Samuel McCorkle, the Presbyterian cofounder of the University of North Carolina. Linn was an early supporter of the French Revolution and of the Republican Tammany and Humane societies in New York City. In 1794 he published a work on prophecy that was decidedly sympathetic to the French republican cause, but by 1798 he had come to support the Federalists against Jefferson. McCorkle, too, published a millennial sermon in praise of the French Revolution in 1795, yet later became known for his vituperative attacks on French infidelity. Whether McCorkle ever sided with either the Republican or the Federalist Party is, however, unclear. On Linn, see his *Discourses on the Signs of the Times* (New York, 1794). There is some debate among scholars about whether and when Linn shifted from the Republican to the Federalist side, but according to my reading, the *Discourses* are still decidedly pro-French. Compare Alfred Young, *The Democratic Republicans of New York* (Chapel Hill: University of North Carolina Press, 1967), pp. 400, 418, with Richard A. Harrison, *Princetonians, 1769-1775: A Biographical Dictionary* (Princeton: Princeton University Press, 1980), pp. 231-5. On McCorkle, see Samuel E. M'Corkle, *A Sermon, on the comparative Happiness and Duty of the United States of America* (Halifax, N.C., 1795).

Biographical works about McCorkle (neither of which mention his political affiliations) are: James F. Hurley and Julia Goode Eagan, *The Prophet of Zion-Parnassus: Samuel Eusebius McCorkle* (Richmond: Presbyterian Committee of Publication, 1934), and William Sprague, *Annals of the American Pulpit* (New York, 1859) 3: 346-9.

21. Samuel Miller, *A Sermon Preached in New-York, July 4th 1793* (New York, 1793), p. 32. On the Tammany Society, see Eugene Perry Link, *Democratic-Republican Societies 1790-1800* (New York: Columbia University Press, 1942).

22. *Greenleaf's New York Journal*, July 5, 1796.

23. *Greenleaf's New York Journal*, July 5, 1796; Joseph Pilmore, *The Journal of Joseph Pilmore, Methodist Itinerant, for the Years August 1, 1769 to January 2, 1774*, ed. Frederick E. Maser and Howard T. Maag (Philadelphia: Message Publishing, 1969).

24. William Staughton, *Missionary-Encouragement* (Philadelphia, 1798), pp. 32, 37.

25. William Sprague, *Annals of the American Pulpit* (New York, 1860) 6: 344-6.

26. Morgan John Rhees, *An Oration Delivered at Greenville . . . July 4th, 1795* (Philadelphia, 1795), pp. 3, 6-7.

27. John Blair Smith, *The Enlargement of Christ's Kingdom* (Schenectady, N.Y., 1797), pp. 32-3.

28. *A Northern Light; or New Index to the Bible* (Troy, N.Y., 1800), pp. 71, 76, 78, 81, 83-9, Appendix, pp. i-ii.

29. James Malcomson, *A Sermon, Preached on the 14th of July, 1794* (Charleston, S.C., 1795), pp. 26, 42.

30. James Madison, *Manifestations of the Beneficence of Divine Providence Towards America* (Richmond, 1795), pp. 7-8, 10.

31. *Twilight's Orations, or Revelations of Politics* (Norfolk, Va.: Willett and O'Connnor, 1796), p. 33. The author's possible Baptist affiliation is ambiguously indicated on p. 8.

32. *Twilight's Orations*, p. 18.

33. Bicheno's work, also published under the title *Signs of the Times*, appeared in West Springfield, Massachusetts, Providence, Rhode Island, Albany, Philadelphia, Baltimore, and possibly Richmond, Virginia (see Charles Evans, *American Bibliography* [14 vols. (Chicago: Blakely Press and Columbia Press, 1903-34, and Worcester, Mass.: American Antiquarian Society, 1955)]). It also appeared in extract in at least one almanac: Robin Goodfellow, *Poor Robin's Almanac for the Year 1796* (Philadelphia, 1795), pp. 18-21.

34. James Bicheno, *Explanation of Scriptural Prophecy* (West Springfield, Mass., 1796), pp. 18, 23, 74.

35. Stillman, *Thoughts*, pp. 13-15, 17.

36. Benjamin Farnham, *Dissertations on the Prophecies* (East Windsor, Conn., 1800), pp. 27-30, 75-7.

37. Christopher Love, *Prophecies of the Reverend Christopher Love* (Boston, 1793), p. 8.

38. Separate editions are listed in Evans's *American Bibliography*. For

almanacs containing Love's prophecy, see: Nehemiah Strong, *An Astronomical Diary, Calendar, or Almanack, for the Year of Our Lord, 1794* (Hartford, 1793); *Phillip's United States Diary, or an Almanack, for the Year of Our Lord 1794* (Warren, R.I., 1793); John Nathan Hutchins, *Hutchins Improved, Being an Almanack . . . for the Year of Our Lord 1794* (New York, 1793); David Hale, *Father Abraham's Almanac for the Year of Our Lord, 1794* (Philadelphia, 1793); *Haswell's Almanack, and Register for the State of Vermont: for the Year of Our Lord 1796* (Bennington, Vt., 1795); Isaac Bickerstaff [pseudonym of Benjamin West], *Webster's Calendar; or the Albany Almanack, for the Year of Our Lord 1796* (Albany, 1795). On Love's revival in England, see Clarke Garrett, *Respectable Folly* (Baltimore: Johns Hopkins University Press, 1975), pp. 171-2.

39. *The Kentucky Gazette*, April 21, 1792.
40. *The New York Magazine* 4 (July 1793): 400-1; *Father Hutchins Revived; Being an Almanac* (New York, 1793); Robert Fleming, *A Discourse on the Rise and Fall of the Papacy* (Boston, 1794). On Fleming and the revival of his prophecy in England, see Garrett, *Respectable Folly*, p. 8.
41. Thomas Williams, *The Age of Infidelity: In Answer to Thomas Paine's Age of Reason* (Boston, 1794), pp. 40-1. Williams's work was also reprinted in Worcester, Salem, New York, and Philadelphia in 1794.
42. For editions, see Evans, *American Bibliography*. The German one had the following title: *Prophetische Muthassungen über die Franzoische Staatsveranderung* (Philadelphia, 1794). This was one of two texts discussed in this chapter that were translated into German (the other was Richard Brothers's *Revealed Knowledge*).
43. *Prophetic Conjectures on the French Revolution* (Philadelphia, 1794), especially pp. 4, 70-84.
44. According to Clarke Garrett, despite the persistence of some English Dissenters and radicals (like Bicheno) who saw the French Revolution as harbinger of the millennium, by the end of 1792 most English prophecies about the French Revolution became negative, casting the revolution in the role of the Antichrist. See Garrett, *Respectable Folly*, pp. 164-72. In America this shift did not occur decisively until 1798, when the New England Federalist clergy began to issue large numbers of publications designating the French as the Antichrist.
45. *Prophetic Conjectures*, p. 78.
46. "Remarkable Prophecy," in David Hale, *The Pennsylvania, New-Jersey, Delaware, Maryland, and Virginia Almanac for . . . 1796* (Philadelphia, 1795), p. 14.
47. *Remarkable Prophecy* (Exeter, N.H., 1794), p. 11.
48. There were three separate editions: two in 1794 in Portsmouth and Exeter, and one again in Portsmouth in 1798. It appeared in at least the following almanacs: David Hale, *Pennsylvania, New-Jersey, Delaware, Maryland, and Virginia Almanac for the Year of Our Lord, 1796* (Philadelphia, 1795); Robert Andrews, *The Virginia Almanack, for the Year of Our Lord, 1796* (Richmond, 1795); Andrew Beers, *The Farmer's American Almanac, for the Year of Our Lord Christ, 1796* (Danbury, Conn., 1795). In my sampling of newspapers I came across a description of it

in *Greenleaf's New York Journal*, March 15, 1794, and an actual reprint in *The Kentucky Gazette*, March 29, 1794. The latter cited an unnamed New York paper as its source.

49. Eliphaz Chapman, *Discourse on the Prophecies* (Portland, Maine, 1797), pp. 2, 31.

50. For information about Brothers's career in London, I have relied most heavily on Clarke Garrett, *Respectable Folly*, pp. 179-208, and J. F. C. Harrison, *The Second Coming: Popular Millenarianism 1780-1850* (London: Routledge and Kegan Paul, 1979), pp. 57-85. Ronald Matthews, *English Messiah* (London: Methuen, 1936), pp. 85-126, and E. P. Thompson, *The Making of the English Working Class* (New York: Vintage, 1963), pp. 117-19, were also useful.

51. The quote is from Richard Brothers, *God's Awful Warnings to a Giddy, Careless, Sinful World. Being a Revealed Knowledge of the Prophecies and Times* (New London, 1795), p. 108. For the other prophecies that are noted here, see especially pp. 87-107, 117-19, 132, 185, 195-6, 200.

52. Evans, *American Bibliography*.

53. Halhed's *A Calculation on the Commencement of the Millennium* went into one edition, and his *Testimony of the Authenticity of the Prophecies of Richard Brothers* went into three. See Evans, *American Bibliography*.

54. Thomas Williams, *The Age of Credulity* (Philadelphia, 1796).

55. Almanacs containing these extracts include: *Banneker's Maryland, Pennsylvania, Delaware, Virginia, Kentucky, and North Carolina Allmanack and Ephemeris* (Baltimore, 1795); *Banneker's Virginia, Pennsylvania, Delaware, Maryland and Kentucky Almanack and Ephemeris for the Year of Our Lord 1797* (Baltimore, 1796); Mathias Day, *The New Jersey and Pennsylvania Almanac, for the Year of Our Lord 1796* (Trenton, 1795); Isaac Bickerstaff (pseudonym of Benjamin West), *Town and Country Almanack, for the Year of Our Lord 1796* (Norwich, Conn., 1795); Isaac Bickerstaff (pseudonym of Benjamin West), *Webster's Calendar: or the Albany Almanack, for the Year of Our Lord 1796* (Albany, 1795).

56. *Banneker's Maryland . . . Allmanack* (Baltimore, 1795); Mathias Day, *New Jersey and Pennsylvania Almanac*; Bickerstaff (pseudonym of West), *Town and Country Almanack*.

57. David Austin, "The Downfall of Mystical Babylon," in *The Millennium*, ed. David Austin (Elizabethtown, N.J., 1794), p. 392.

58. Austin, "Downfall, " especially pp. 392-4; David Austin, *The Millennial Door Thrown Open* (East Windsor, Conn., 1799), pp. 20-1 (though he adds a negative note on p. 26); David Austin, *The Dawn of Day* (New Haven, 1800), especially pp. 9, 11-12.

59. Austin, "Downfall," p. 368.

60. Austin, "Downfall," pp. 382-3.

61. Austin, *Millennial Door*, pp. 5, 23-6; David Austin, *The Dance of Herodias* (East Windsor, Conn., 1799); Austin, *Dawn of Day*, pp. 9-12.

62. On the two-stage theory, see Austin, "Downfall," especially pp. 393-4; Austin, *Dance of Herodias*, especially p. 14; Austin, *Millennial Door*, especially p. 13.

63. Austin, *Dawn of Day*, p. 21; Austin, *A Discourse on the Occasion of the Death*

of Washington (New York, 1800), especially p. 21; Austin, *The National "Barley Cake"* (Washington, D.C., 1802), especially pp. 20-1; Austin, *Republican Festival, Proclamation, and New Jerusalem* (New Haven, 1803), especially p. 16; Austin, *The First Vibration of the Jubilee Trump!* (Elizabethtown, N.J., 1799), especially p. 4.

64. Alan Heimert, *Religion and the American Mind* (Cambridge, Mass.: Harvard University Press, 1966); Nathan O. Hatch, *The Sacred Cause of Liberty* (New Haven: Yale University Press, 1977), pp. 149-53. The best treatment of Austin's politics is James W. Davidson, "Searching for the Millennium," *New England Quarterly* 95 (1972): 245-9.

65. Austin, *Dance of Herodias*, especially p. 48; *Dawn of Day*, pp. 14, 18; *National "Barley Cake"* pp. 22-3, 36-8; *Republican Festival*, pp. 3-10.

66. For basic information on these sects, see Stephen A. Marini, *Radical Sects of Revolutionary New England* (Cambridge, Mass.: Harvard University Press, 1982); Herbert Andrew Wisbey, *Pioneer Prophetess: Jemima Wilkinson, the Publick Universal Friend* (Ithaca: Cornell University Press, 1964); Edward Deming Andrews, *The People Called Shakers* (New York: Oxford University Press, 1953); Henri Desroches, *The American Shakers*, trans. John K. Savacool (Amherst: University of Massachusetts Press, 1971).

67. Duc de La Rochefoucauld-Liancourt, *Travels Through the United States of North America* (1799), I: 112; as cited in Wisbey, *Pioneer Prophetess*, p. 161.

68. For information on the Swedenborgians, see Marguerite Beck Block, *The New Church in the New World* (New Henry Holt, 1932), and their own numerous publications, including: *The Liturgy of the New Church Signified By the New Jerusalem in the Revelation* (Baltimore, 1792); James Jones Wilmer, *A Sermon, on the Doctrine of the New-Jerusalem Church* (Baltimore, 1792); [John Clowes], *Dialogues on the Nature, Design and Evidence of the Theological Writings of the Hon. Emanuel Swedenborg* (Boston, 1794).

69. See Robert Darnton, *Mesmerism and the End of the Enlightenment in France* (Cambridge, Mass.: Harvard University Press, 1968). For a new translation of Mesmer, see *Mesmerism*, trans. and comp. George Bloch (Los Altos, Calif.: William Kaufmann, 1980).

70. [John Clowes], *Remarks on the Assertions of the Author of the Memoirs of Jacobinism Respecting the Character of Emanuel Swedenborg* (Philadelphia, 1800).

71. Garrett, *Respectable Folly*, pp. 98-9, 110-13, 160-2, 188; Harrison, *Second Coming*, p. 72.

72. Lyman, *Administration*, especially p. 20.

73. For example: Bicheno, *Explanation of Scripture Prophecy*, pp. 45-51; *Northern Light*, pp. 1-11 and appendix; Benjamin Farnham, *Dissertations on the Prophecies*; Crawford, *Observations on French Revolution*. An article in the *Virginia Gazette and General Advertiser* reported that the French Revolution had raised millennial expectations among Jews and the belief among Greeks that the Ottoman Empire would shortly collapse. See the "Extra" issue for October 2, 1798. That millennial hopes for the Jews were even influential within Revolutionary France is shown in

Richard H. Popkin, "La Peyrère, the Abbé Grégoire, and the Jewish Question in the Eighteenth Century," *Studies in Eighteenth-Century Culture* 4 (1975): 209-22.

74. See Christopher Hill, *Antichrist in Seventeenth-Century England* (New York: Oxford University Press, 1971).
75. See, for example, the selections in *Prophetic Conjectures*.
76. *Columbian Centinel*, April 13, 1793, p. 4.
77. *Greenleaf's New York Journal*, September 3, 1794.
78. Lyman, *Administration*, p. 16.
79. Rhees, *Oration*, p. 4. Also see Lee, *Dissolution*; Linn, *Discourses*; Malcomson, *Sermon*.
80. *State Gazette of South-Carolina*, May 27, 1793, p. 4.
81. Isaac Backus, *Testimony of Two Witnesses*, 2nd ed. (Boston, 1793), p. 22.
82. Farnham, *Dissertations on the Prophecies*, p. 104.
83. *Northern Light*, pp. 70, 74, and Appendix, pp. i-ii.
84. *Prophetic Conjectures*, pp. 71, 82-3.
85. Joseph Priestley, "The Present State of Europe Compared with Antient Prophecies" in *Two Sermons* (Philadelphia, 1794), p. 48.
86. Bicheno, *Explanation of Scripture Prophecy*, p. 81.
87. Crawford, *Observations*, p. 14.
88. See, for example, Jedidiah Morse, *The Present Situation of Other Nations* (Boston, 1795), p. 14; Samuel Stanhope Smith, *Divine Goodness to the United States* (Philadelphia, 1795), p. 37; David Tappan, *Christian Thankfulness Explained and Enforced* (Boston, 1795).
89. *Columbian Centinel*, April 13, 1793, p. 4.
90. *Greenleaf's New York Journal*, February 1, 1794.
91. Miller, *Sermon Preached . . . July 4th 1793*, pp. 32-4.
92. Stillman, *Thoughts* (1795), p. 20.
93. Linn, *Discourses*, pp. 59, 16, 138, 17.
94. This was a standard feature of what Henry F. May has called "the Moderate Enlightenment" in his *Enlightenment in America* (New York: Oxford University Press, 1976).
95. *Columbian Centinel*, April 13, 1973; Robbins, *Address Victories French*, p. 17; William Jones, *An Oration, Pronounced at Concord . . .* (Concord, Mass., 1794), especially p. 19.
96. Adams's speech before the Massachusetts legislature, as quoted in *Greenleaf's New York Journal*, January 29, 1974, p. 4.
97. Lee, *Dissolution*, especially pp. 16-17; *Northern Light*.
98. May, *Enlightenment*.
99. See, for example, Joseph Lathrop, *Happiness of a Free Government*; William Staughton, *Missionary-Encouragement*.
100. David Austin most clearly took this position in his often repeated theory that there were two sequential steps leading towards the new age: "the *first* outward and political; the *second* inward and spiritual." (Austin, "Downfall," pp. 393-4). Scarcely a consistent or representative commentator on either current events or biblical prophecy, however, Austin himself undercut this analysis by welcoming the French attack on the Church more than its political reforms, and by doubting the

basic value of the revolution because of French infidelity. Here I am taking issue with Nathan Hatch, who, using Austin as a primary illustration, has emphasized the continuity of "civil" or "political" millennialism of the New England clergy between the 1770's and the 1790's and has argued that political tyranny *rather than* the Papacy and false religion had come to be seen as the Beast. See Hatch, *Sacred Cause*, especially pp. 145-56.

101. Miller, *A Sermon Preached . . . July 4th 1793*.
102. Linn, *Discourses*, pp. 142-3.
103. Joseph Pilmore, *The Blessings of Peace* (New York, 1794), especially pp. 18, 20-1.
104. *Twilight's Orations*, pp. 33-4.
105. *Columbian Centinel*, February 2, 1793, p. 2.
106. See, for example: Linn, *Discourses*, pp. 19, 63; *Prophetic Conjectures*, p. 80; Bicheno, *Explanation of Scripture Prophecy*, p. 8; Farnham, *Dissertations*, pp. 104-5.
107. *Minutes of the General Conference of the Methodist Episcopal Church . . . on the 20th of October. 1796* (Baltimore, 1796), p. 25. Also see the letter of Thomas Coke to Ezekiel Cooper, April 23, 1795, in Ezekiel Cooper, *Beams of Light on Early Methodism in America*, ed. George A. Phoebus (New York, 1887), p. 204; Staughton, *Missionary-Encouragement*, pp. 31-53; *Minutes of the Warren Association . . . September 10 and 11. 1799* (Boston, 1799).
108. Priestley, *Two Sermons*, especially pp. 48, 54.
109. For example: John Lathrop, *A Discourse on the Errors of Popery* (Boston, 1793); David Tappan, *Christian Thankfulness*, especially pp. 27-30. On Federalist millennialism in reaction against France, see Chapter 9 below.
110. For the view that Federalists and not Republicans were millennialists, see Ernest Tuveson, *The Redeemer Nation* (Chicago: University of Chicago Press, 1968), p. 120; J. G. A. Pocock picks this up in *The Machiavellian Moment* (Princeton: Princeton University Press, 1975), p. 532. Since both Nathan Hatch, in *The Sacred Cause of Liberty*, and James Davidson, in *Logic of Millennial Thought*, deal almost exclusively with New England Federalists, the comparative issue never gets raised. The one exception to this line of interpretation is Alan Heimert's *Religion and the American Mind*, but Heimert's disastrous choice of David Austin as his chief example has led to the discrediting of his argument. See Davidson, "Searching for the Millennium." I discuss Federalist millennialism in Chapter 9.
111. [Jedidiah Peck], *The Political Wars of Otsego: Or, Downfall of Jacobinism and Despotism* (Cooperstown, N.Y., 1796), p. 97. Also see pp. 100-1. For Peck's political biography I have relied on Alfred Young, *The Democratic Republicans of New York*, pp. 509-20.
112. Peck, *Political*, p. 10.
113. John Cox, *Rewards and Punishments; or, Satan's Kingdom Aristocratical* (Philadelphia, 1795); Simon Hough, *The Sign of the Present Time*; and *Notes upon Scripture Texts* (Boston, 1798).
114. For evidence of a separatist tendency within the rebellion, see "Papers

Relating to What Is Known as the Whiskey Insurrection in Western Pennsylvania, 1794," *Pennsylvania Archives*, Second Series, ed. John B. Linn and William H. Egle (Harrisburg, 1876), 4: 164, 217, 275, 390-1.

115. *Pennsylvania Archives* 4: 300; also Leland D. Baldwin, *Whiskey Rebels: The Story of a Frontier Uprising* (Pittsburgh: University of Pittsburgh Press, 1939), pp. 103, 169-70, 179, 187, 193, 207-8.

116. Hugh Henry Brackenridge, *Incidents of the Insurrection in the Western Parts of Pennsylvania in the Year 1794* (Philadelphia, 1795) 1: 54.

117. Harry Merlin Tinkcom, *The Republicans and Federalists in Pennsylvania* (Harrisburg: Pennsylvania Historical and Museum Commission, 1950), pp. 107-9; Eugene Perry Link, *Democratic-Republican Societies, 1790-1800* (New York: Columbia University Press, 1942), pp. 145-8.

118. *Pittsburgh Gazette*, August 2, 1794, pp. 1-2 (reprinted from the *Kentucky Gazette*).

119. Brackenridge, *Incidents* 3: 149.

120. *Pittsburgh Gazette*, July 6, 1793.

121. Brackenridge, *Incidents* 1: 43-4.

122. *Pittsburgh Gazette*, February 23, 1793, p. 2. Another, more humorous protest against the tax, a broadside poem in Scottish dialect, also portrayed the tax as the product of a conspiracy between the devil and the rising "aristocracy" to rob America's liberty. See *Petition and Remonstrance to the President and Congress of the United States* (Philadelphia, 1794). The author identified himself as a North Carolina planter.

123. Baldwin, *Whiskey Rebels*, pp. 81-2 (on Presbyterian rebels); pp. 49, 205, 210-11, 226, 264-5 (on ministerial opposition).

124. Link, *Democratic-Republican Societies*, p. 85.

125. My biographical information on Husband comes primarily from his own earlier published works; Mary Elinor Lazenby, *Herman Husband: A Story of His Life* (Washington, D.C.: Old Neighborhoods Press, 1940); and the excellent work by Mark H. Jones, "Herman Husband: Millenarian, Carolina Regulator, and Whiskey Rebel," (Ph.D. dissertation, Northern Illinois University, 1982). According to Baldwin, *Whiskey Rebels*, pp. 229-30, George Washington himself earmarked Husband along with Bradford for arrest. Jones, however, in "Husband," pp. 360-1, indicates merely that Washington was aware that his prisoners included Husband and Robert Philson.

126. Brackenridge, *Incidents* 1: 95.

127. Johann David Schoepf, *Travels in the Confederation, 1783-4*, trans. Alfred J. Morrison (Philadelphia: William J. Campbell, 1911) I, 294. Husband refers to several "plates," possibly including these maps, in his *XIV Sermons on the Characters of Jacob's Fourteen Sons* (Philadelphia, 1789), pp. viii-ix, but the edition I used did not contain them.

128. Schoepf, *Travels* I, 295.

129. Husband, *XIV Sermons*, p. 21.

130. Jones, "Herman Husband," p. 349.

131. Schoepf, *Travels* I, 295-6.

132. *Kentucky Gazette*, August 31, 1793, p. 3.

133. Zephaniah Swift, *An Oration on Domestic Slavery* (Hartford, 1791), pp. 21-3.
134. Benjamin Rush, *Letters of Benjamin Rush*, ed. L. H. Butterfield, 2 vols. (Princeton: Princeton University Press, 1951), 1: 620; John Leland, "An Oration Delivered at Cheshire, July 5, 1802," *The Writings of John Leland*, ed. L. F. Greene (New York, 1845), p. 269.
135. David Barrow, *Circular Letter* (Southampton County, Va., 1798), pp. 12-13.
136. See, for example, George Buchanan, *An Oration upon the Moral and Political Evil of Slavery* (Baltimore, 1793); Theodore Dwight, *An Oration, Spoken . . . the 8th day of May, A.D. 1794* (Hartford, 1794); Morgan John Rhees, *Letters of Liberty and Slavery* (New York, 1798); Granville Sharp, *Letter . . . to the Maryland Society for Promoting the Abolition of Slavery* (Baltimore, 1793).
137. Samuel Hopkins, *A Discourse on the Slave Trade, and the Slavery of the Africans* (Providence, 1793); Thomas Coke to Ezekiel Cooper, April 23, 1795, in Cooper, *Beams of Light*, pp. 204-5.
138. William Douglass, *Annals of the First African Church in the United States of America, Now Styled The African Episcopal Church of St. Thomas, Philadelphia* (Philadelphia, 1862), pp. 28-9.
139. Samuel Magaw, *A Discourse Delivered July 17, 1794 in the African Church of the City of Philadelphia* (Philadelphia, 1794), p. 20.

8. Biblical millennialism and radical Enlightened utopianism

1. I have borrowed the terms "moderate" and "radical" Enlightenment from Henry F. May, *The Enlightenment in America* (New York: Oxford University Press, 1976). May uses the term "secular millennialism" to refer to the type of radical Enlightened utopianism I discuss in this chapter.
2. Until recently, historians attributed the affinity between eighteenth-century millennialism and Enlightened ideas of historical progress to the rise of "postmillennial" exegesis. It has, however, been demonstrated that postmillennialism – the theory that Christ would return only after the millennium – was neither particularly important in theological circles before the nineteenth century nor automatically associated with optimistic and activistic attitudes towards historical change. As I suggest here, the truly significant contribution of millennialism to Enlightened utopianism arose not from any such technical exegetical shift but from more general intellectual currents within the millennial thought of the period. For an assessment of eighteenth-century postmillennialism, see James West Davidson, *The Logic of Millennial Thought* (New Haven: Yale University Press, 1977).
3. For a description of civic festivals, see Charles Hazen, *Contemporary American Opinion of the French Revolution* (Baltimore, 1897), pp. 164–88. On the social composition and program of the democratic societies, see Eugene Perry Link, *Democratic-Republican Societies, 1790–1800* (New York: Columbia University Press, 1942).

4. Archibald Buchanan, *An Oration, Composed and Delivered at the Request of the Republican Society of Baltimore* (Baltimore, 1795), p. 3; *An Oration, Commemorative of the Declaration of American Independence; Delivered Before the Ciceronian Society* (Philadelphia, 1794), p. 14; *The New-York Magazine* 5 (July 1794): 428-9.
5. *Greenleaf's New York Journal and Patriotic Register*, March 1, 1794, p. 3.
6. *Boston Gazette*, January 28, 1793.
7. *Kentucky Gazette*, January 31, 1800, p. 2.
8. *Greenleaf's New York Journal*, October 11, 1796, p. 3.
9. *Greenleaf's New York Journal*, May 28, 1794, p. 2.
10. John Mercer, *An Oration Delivered on the 4th of July 1792* (Richmond, 1792), p. 17.
11. *State Gazette of South-Carolina*, March 4, 1793, p. 4.
12. Thomas Paine, *The Complete Writings of Thomas Paine*, ed. Philip S. Foner, 2 vols. (New York: Citadel Press, 1945), 1: 356.
13. *South-Carolina State-Gazette*, November 24, 1796, p. 4.
14. For example: *State Gazette of South-Carolina*, March 4, 1793, p. 4; Paine, "Rights of Man," *Writings*, ed. Foner, 1: 344, 397.
15. *Greenleaf's New York Journal*, January 25, 1794, p. 2. Also see *Greenleaf's New York Journal*, August 5, 1796, p. 4, and November 24, 1798, p. 2; *The National Gazette*, May 4, 1793, p. 2; Buchanan, *Oration*, p. 3.
16. *State Gazette of South-Carolina*, March 1, 1793, p. 4.
17. *Greenleaf's New York Journal*, May 10, 1794, p. 2. Also: *State Gazette of South-Carolina*, December 17, 1793, p. 3; Joel Barlow, "Advice to the Privileged Orders," in *The Works of Joel Barlow*, ed. William K. Bottorff and Arthur L. Ford (Gainesville, Fla.: Scholars' Facsimilies and Reprints, 1970), 1: 169.
18. Compare, for example, Samuel Miller, *A Sermon Preached in New-York, July 4th 1793* (New York, 1793); Samuel Miller, *A Sermon Delivered in the New Presbyterian Church, New-York, July Fourth, 1795* (New York, 1795); and Samuel Miller, *A Sermon, Delivered May 9, 1798* (New York, 1798).
19. Benjamin Rush to Jeremy Belknap, June 21, 1792, *Letters of Benjamin Rush*, ed. L. H. Butterfield, 2 vols. (Princeton: American Philosophical Society, 1951), 1: 620.
20. Ezra Stiles, *A History of Three of the Judges of King Charles I* (Hartford, 1794), pp. 304, 282.
21. See, for example, newspaper reports of civic festivals: *Greenleaf's New York Journal*, March 15, 1794, p. 3; July 5, 1796; July 22, 1796, p. 1; *Columbian Centinel*, January 30, 1793, p. 3.
22. *Greenleaf's New York Journal*, July 8, 1795, p. 1; *Principal Articles, and Regulations . . . of the Democratic Society in Philadelphia, May 30th, 1793* (Philadelphia, 1793), p. 3.
23. "From the Virginia Gazetteer," *State Gazette of South-Carolina*, July 10, 1793, p. 4.
24. *State Gazette of South-Carolina*, July 7, 1793, p. 4.
25. *Boston Gazette*, January 28, 1793, p. 3; *State Gazette of South Carolina*, March 4, 1793, p. 4; *Greenleaf's New York Journal*, July 5, 1795, p. 2; *Greenleaf's New York Journal*, March 8, 1794, p. 3.
26. Elihu Palmer, *Principles of Nature*, 2nd ed. (New York, 1802), p. 334; [John Stewart], *The Revelation of Nature, With the Prophecy of Reason*, 2nd

ed. (New York, 1796), p. 96; *State Gazette of South-Carolina*, July 19, 1793, p. 4.

27. Paine, "Rights of Man," *Complete Writings*, ed. Foner, 1: 449.
28. Paine, "Rights of Man," *Complete Writings*, ed. Foner, 1: 342.
29. *National Gazette*, July 14, 1792, p. 3.
30. *State Gazette of South-Carolina*, December 7, 1793.
31. Ethan Allen, *Reason the Only Oracle of Man* (Bennington, Vt., 1784), pp. 468, 24-5.
32. Allen, *Reason*, p. 294.
33. On Palmer and organized Deism, see May, *Enlightenment*; Herbert M. Morais, *Deism in Eighteenth Century America* (New York: Columbia University Press, 1934); Gustav Koch, *Republican Religion* (Henry Holt, 1933).
34. Elihu Palmer, "Extract from an Oration, Delivered at Federal Point, near Philadelphia . . . ," *Political Miscellany* (New York, 1793), pp. 24-5.
35. Elihu Palmer, ed., *The Temple of Reason* 2 (1802): 145-6. Compare this with the fervently pro-French article "The New Year," *Temple of Reason* 1 (1801): 71.
36. See Stewart, *Revelation*, and Stewart, *Prospectus of a Series of Lectures* (Philadelphia, 1796).
37. Koch, *Republican Religion*, pp. 155-8.
38. Elihu Palmer, *An Enquiry Relative to the Moral and Political Improvement of the Human Species* (New York, 1797), pp. 3-4.
39. Tunis R. Wortman, *An Oration on the Influence of Social Institutions upon Human Morals and Happiness* (New York, 1796), pp. 24-5.
40. Joel Barlow, "Advice to the Privileged Orders," in *Works*, ed. Bottorff and Ford, 1: 266-8, 267-8, 223.
41. On Barlow's shift towards atheism and materialism, see Leon Howard, *The Connecticut Wits* (Chicago: University of Chicago Press, 1943), and May, *Enlightenment*, pp. 241-2.
42. Barlow, "Advice," in *Works* 1: 300-3.
43. Stewart, *Revelation*, especially pp. 47-56; Palmer, *Principles*, pp. 260-5, 281-93.
44. Paine, "Rights of Man," *Complete Writings*, ed. Foner, 1: 400.
45. Utilitarian theory did not, of course, necessarily lead in a secular utopian direction. In the thought of Joseph Priestley and Benjamin Rush it even partly fused with biblical millennialism. Usually it combined with incrementalist theories of progress rather than with outright utopian views. Nevertheless, it could be integrated with secular utopianism, smoothing the way between the exercise of reason, the demolition of authoritarian government, and the achievement of social perfection. On early utilitarian thought, see Elie Halévy, *The Growth of Philosophic Radicalism*, orig. ed. 1903-4 (New York: Kelley, 1972).
46. Nelson F. Adkins, *Philip Freneau and the Cosmic Enigma* (New York: New York University Press, 1949).

9. Francophobic reaction and evangelical activism

1. For the Context of the attitudinal shift, see Gary B. Nash, "The American Clergy and the French Revolution," *William and Mary Quarterly*, 3d ser.

22 (1965): 392-412; Henry F. May, *The Enlightenment in America* (New York: Oxford University Press, 1976), especially pp. 252-8.

2. This generalization is unfortunately based on impressionistic evidence because it is impossible to determine the later party affiliations of most of the francophilic millennialist writers of the mid-1790's. Only William Linn, Joseph Lathrop, and Samuel Stillman, however, shifted all the way from pro-French millennial enthusiasm to Federalist denunciations of France as Antichrist. The vast majority simply no longer published on the subject. Thomas Greenleaf's *New York Journal*, however, which published several of the pro-French millennial statements, remained staunchly Republican, as did the millennialist Presbyterians Samuel Miller, John Rodgers, and John MacKnight, the Baptist John Morgan Rhees, and the Anglican James Madison. The mildness of Baptist William Staughton's criticism of the French in 1798 suggests that he, too, was Republican.

3. Exceptions, again, are Samuel Stillman and Joseph Lathrop. William Linn attacked France and Jefferson at the end of the decade but not in millennial terms. Those Federalists who earlier went on record cautiously approving the Revolution for its attack on the Catholic Beast if not for its politics include David Tappan, John Lathrop, and Jedidiah Morse. Other leading Federalist clergymen such as Timothy Dwight, Nathan Strong, David Osgood, and Nathaniel Emmons had never printed favorable statements about the revolution even at the height of the French vogue.

4. On this episode, see Vernon Stauffer, *New England and the Bavarian Illuminati* (New York: Columbia University Press, 1918); May, *Enlightenment in America*, and Richard Hofstadter, *The Paranoid Style in American Politics and Other Essays* (New York: Knopf, 1965).

5. Jedidiah Morse, *A Sermon, Delivered at the New North Church . . . May 9th, 1798* (Boston, 1798).

6. Timothy Dwight, *The Duty of Americans, at the Present Crisis* (New Haven, 1798), pp. 11-14. Also see Dwight, *The Nature and Danger of Infidel Philosophy* (New Haven, 1798).

7. Nathan Strong, *Political Instruction from the Prophecies of God's Word* (Hartford, 1798), p. 23; Joseph Lathrop, *A Sermon on the Dangers of the Times* (Springfield, Mass., 1798), pp. 19-20; Abraham Cummings, *The Present Times Perilous* (Castine, Maine, 1799), p. 22.

8. *Characteristics in the Prophecies* (New York, 1798), especially p. 19.

9. Lathrop, *Sermon on Dangers*, p. 7.

10. Jeremy Belknap, *A Sermon, Delivered on the 9th of May, 1798* (Boston, 1798), p. 24. During the early years of the nineteenth century the identification of Napoleonic France with the Beast described as destroying the Whore, or the Catholic Church, became a standard feature of New England prophetic interpretation. See Nathan O. Hatch, *The Sacred Cause of Liberty* (New Haven: Yale University Press, 1977), pp. 155, 173-4n.

11. Strong, *Political Instruction*, p. 11.

12. Dwight, *Duty*.

13. David Tappan, *Christian Thankfulness Explained and Enforced* (Boston, 1795), pp. 21-2.

14. Tappan, *Christian Thankfulness*, pp. 27-9.
15. Cummings, *Present Times Perilous*, p. 13. Also see Lathrop, *Sermon on Dangers*, p. 13.
16. Cummings, *Present Times Perilous*, p. 14.
17. Charles Crawford, *The Progress of Liberty; A Pindaric Ode* (Philadelphia, 1796), p. 3.
18. Charles Crawford, *An Essay upon the Eleventh Chapter of the Revelation of St. John* (Philadelphia, 1800), p. 9. Also see pp. 22-42, 59, 69.
19. Samuel Stillman, *A Sermon Preached at Boston, April 25, 1799* (Boston, 1799); William Linn, *A Discourse on National Sins* (New York, 1798).
20. For example: Dwight, *Duty*; Strong, *Political Instruction*; David Osgood, *The Devil Let Loose, or the Woe Occasioned to the Inhabitants of the Earth* (Boston, 1799); Jedidiah Morse, *A Sermon, Exhibiting the Present Dangers* (Hartford, 1799).
21. Dwight, *Duty*, p. 31.
22. *Notes upon Luke xvii. 30. With Other Texts Respecting the Grand Epiphany, or the Second Appearing of Jesus Christ* (Boston, 1800).
23. *Minutes of the New-York Baptist Association, Holden in the City of New York, May 22d and 23d, 1799* ([New York]), 1799, p. 8.
24. Cummings, *Present Times Perilous*, p. 18.
25. *Characteristics in the Prophecies*, p. 25.
26. Edward King, *Remarks on the Signs of the Times* (Philadelphia, 1800), p. 21. For his belief in a literal Second Coming, see pp. 29, 62-3, 72.
27. Samuel Horsley, *Critical Disquisitions on the Eighteenth Chapter of Isaiah* (Philadelphia, 1800), pp. 21, 94.
28. Simon Hough, *The Sign of the Present Time* (Stockbridge, Mass., 1799), pp. 6, 7, 10, 11. On Hough, see James W. Davidson, "Searching for the Millennium," *New England Quarterly* 45 (June 1972): 241-61.
29. *Notes upon Scripture texts, No. I, viz. I. The Scripture Warning . . . II. Notes on the Parable of the Ten Virgins. III. Notes on Isaiah lxvi. 5.* (Boston, 1798). Two other editions, under the title *The Scripture Warning and Signs of the Last Times*, appeared in Portsmouth.
30. *A Northern Light* (Troy, N.Y., 1800), especially pp. 84-6. His account predicts numerous miraculous transformations. Farnham was not a technical premillennialist because he reserved the Second Coming for after the millennium, but he inclined towards the belief in a literal premillennial resurrection of the martyrs and also stressed other examples of supernatural intervention. See Benjamin Farnham, *Dissertations on the Prophecies* (East Windsor, Conn., 1800), pp. 124, 109-14, 101.
31. Benjamin Rush, *Letters of Benjamin Rush*, ed. L. H. Butterfield (Princeton: Princeton University Press, 1951), 1: 581-2, 611-12; 2: 779-80, 820-1, 935; Benjamin Rush, "The Correspondence of Benjamin Rush and Granville Sharp, 1773-1809," ed. John A. Woods, *Journal of American Studies* 1 (1967): 32-3. Also see Donald J. d'Elia, *Benjamin Rush: Philosopher of the American Revolution* (Philadelphia: American Philosophical Society, 1974), pp. 102-4.
32. Joseph Priestley, "The Present State of Europe Compared with Antient Prophecies," in *Two Sermons* (Philadelphia, 1794), pp. 31, 43, 50-1, 54. Also see "The Use of Christianity, especially in difficult Times," in *Two*

Sermons, especially p. 77. On Priestley's eschatology, see Clarke Garrett, *Respectable Folly* (Baltimore: Johns Hopkins University Press, 1975), and Jack Fruchtman, Jr., *The Apocalyptic Politics of Richard Price and Joseph Priestley* (Philadelphia: American Philosophical Society, 1983).

33. Winchester's political leanings are revealed not so much in his eschatological writings as in his *Plain Political Catechism* (Philadelphia, 1796), especially p. 59, where he attacks a typically Federalist moral position.

34. Samuel Miller, *Sermon, Delivered May 9, 1798* (New York, 1798), p. 29.

35. Samuel Miller, *A Sermon, Delivered Before the New York Missionary Society* (New York, 1802), p. 27.

36. Samuel Miller, *A Brief Retrospect of the Eighteenth Century* (New York, 1803), 2: 300.

37. Morse, *Sermon Delivered at the New North Church . . . May 9, 1798*, p. 23; Dwight, *Duty*, p. 21.

38. Elias Boudinot, *The Age of Revelation* (Philadelphia, 1801), p. xx.

39. *Connecticut Evangelical Magazine* 2 (June 1802): 451.

40. For a few examples of such language, see Timothy Dwight, *Travels in New England and New York* (Cambridge, Mass.: Harvard University Press, 1969), 2: 162-3; *Connecticut Evangelical Magazine* 2 (February 1802): 313; and the following publications by the Missionary Society of Connecticut: *Address to the People of Connecticut* (Hartford, 1801), pp. 5-6; *Narrative on the Subject of Missions* (Hartford, 1802), pp. 6-7; *Narrative on the Subject of Missions* (Hartford, 1809), pp. 7, 10, 11; *Narrative on the Subject of Missions* (Hartford, 1810), p. 10.

41. *Connecticut Evangelical Magazine* 3 (February 1803): 297.

42. Congregationalist Church in Connecticut, *A Continuation of the Narrative of the Missions to the New Settlements* (New Haven, 1797), p. 8.

43. *Connecticut Evangelical Magazine* 1 (March 1801): 324.

44. *Connecticut Evangelical Magazine* 3 (November 1802): 194-5.

45. Nathaniel Emmons, *A Sermon Delivered Before the Massachusetts Missionary Society . . . May 27, 1800* (Charlestown, Mass., 1800), p. 26.

46. Osgood, *Devil Let Loose*, pp. 14-15.

47. John Henry Livingston, "Glory of the Redeemer," in *Two Sermons Delivered Before the New-York Missionary Society* (New York, 1799), pp. 45-6.

48. Dwight, *Duty at the Present Crisis*, pp. 8-14.

49. Nathan Strong, *Political Instruction*, p. 11.

50. Cyprian Strong, *Connecticut Election Sermon, May 9, 1799: The Kingdom Is the Lord's* (Hartford, 1799), pp. 20, 33, 43.

51. Moses C. Welch, *A Century Sermon* (Hartford, 1801), pp. 23-4; Benjamin Trumbull, *A Century Sermon* (New Haven, 1801), p. 10.

52. Nathan Strong, *Political Instruction*, pp. 7, 25-9.

53. Seth Williston, "The Diaries of the Rev. Seth Williston, D.D. 1796-1800," ed. Rev. J. Q. Adams, *Journal of the Presbyterian Historical Society* 9 (1917-18): 34.

54. Alexander Gillet, "True Christianity the Safety of this World," in *Sermons on Important Subjects* (Hartford, 1797), p. 462.

55. Dwight, *Duty*, p. 18.
56. Nathan Strong, *A Sermon at the Ordination of the Rev. Thomas Robbins* (Hartford, 1803), p. 15.
57. Belknap, *A Sermon, Delivered on the 9th of May, 1798*, p. 28.
58. William Hollinshead, *The Gospel Preached to Every Creature* (Charleston, 1798), p. 18.
59. Miller, *Sermon Before the New York Missionary Society*, p. 52.
60. *Minutes of the Stonington Baptist [sic] Association, held at Montville, October 15 and 16, 1805* (Norwich, 1805), p. 5.
61. John M. Mason, *Hope for the Heathen* (New York, 1797), pp. 18, 29.
62. Morgan J. Rhees, *Altar of Peace* (Philadelphia, 1798), p. 10.
63. Miller, *Sermon Before the New York Missionary Society*, p. 34.
64. *Connecticut Evangelical Magazine* 2 (July 1801): 3.
65. Nathan Strong, *On the Universal Spread of the Gospel* (Hartford, 1801), p. 38.
66. Miller, *Sermon Before the New York Missionary Society*, pp. 26-7.
67. John McKnight, *A View of the Present State of the Political and Religious World* (New York, 1802), pp. 29, 16; Welch, *Century Sermon*, pp. 23, 34-5.
68. William F. Miller, *Signs of the Times, or the Sure Word of Prophecy* (Hartford, 1803).
69. Dwight, *Duty*, pp. 30-1. Also see Nathan Strong, *Political Instruction*, p. 23; Miller, *Signs of the Times; Connecticut Evangelical Magazine* 1 (January 1801): 241-50.
70. Belknap, *Sermon Delivered the 9th of May, 1798*, p. 26.
71. See James West Davidson, *The Logic of Millennial Thought* (New Haven: Yale University Press, 1977), pp. 275-6.
72. See Oliver Wendell Elsbree, *The Rise of the Missionary Spirit* (Williamsport, Pa.: Williamsport Printing, 1928); Colin B. Goody Koontz, *Home Missions on the American Frontier* (Caldwell, Ind.: Caxton Printers, 1939); J. A. de Jong, *As the Waters Cover the Sea* (Kampen, Netherlands: Kok, 1970).
73. *The Constitution of the Missionary Society of Connecticut* (Hartford, 1800).
74. *The Constitution of the Northern Missionary Society in the State of New-York* (Schenectady, 1797), p. 28.
75. McKnight, *View of the Present*, pp. 17-27. Also John McKnight, "Life to the Dead," in *Two Sermons Delivered Before the New-York Missionary Society* (New York, 1799), pp. 62-3.
76. See, for example, Dwight, *Duty*, pp. 8-14, 30-1; William Staughton, *Missionary Encouragement* (Philadelphia, 1798), pp. 31-8; *Connecticut Evangelical Magazine* 1 (January 1801): 241-50, and 2 (July 1801): 3.
77. Livingston, "Glory of the Redeemer," in *Two Sermons*, p. 47.
78. Staughton, *Missionary-Encouragement*. Also see Samuel Miller, *Sermon Before the New York Missionary Society*, p. 52; Eliphalet Nott, *A Sermon Preached Before the General Assembly of the Presbyterian Church* (Philadelphia, 1806), especially pp. 7-9.
79. Mason, *Hope*, p. 35.
80. In addition to the examples below, see *Massachusetts Baptist Missionary Magazine* 1 (January 1806): 175, and 2 (September 1808): 94; Hollins-

head, *Gospel Preached*, pp. 15-16; and Witherspoon, as quoted in *An Address of the General Association of Connecticut, to the District Association on the Subject of a Missionary Society* (Norwich, 1797), p. 32.

81. John Rodgers, "A Charge to the Rev. Mr. Joseph Bullen," in *Two Sermons Deliverd before the New-York Missionary Society* (New York, 1799), p. 83.
82. Welch, *Century*, p. 24.
83. *Connecticut Evangelical Magazine* 1 (September 1800): 119.
84. Thomas Robbins, *Diary of Thomas Robbins, D.D. 1796-1854* (Boston, 1886), l: 84.
85. Robbins, *Diary* 1: 211.
86. See, for example: Robbins, *Dairy* 1: 239; Seth Williston, "Diaries," p. 189; Hezekiah May, *A Thanksgiving Sermon, Preached at Bath, in the District of Maine* (Portland, 1802), p. 26.
87. For example, evidently none of the six officers of the Massachusetts Baptist Missionary Society sketched in William Sprague's *Annals of the American Pulpit* [9 vols. (New York, 1859-69)] had pronounced political views. Even Federalist trustee Samuel Stillman was "not what would be called a political partisan." See Sprague, *Annals* 6: 78.
88. *Massachusetts Baptist Missionary Magazine* 1 (September 1803): 8.
89. *Constitution of the Northern Missionary Society*, p. 14. Also see John Blair Smith, *The Enlargement of Christ's Kingdom* (Schenectady, N.Y., 1797), p. 34; Alexander Proudfit, *A Sermon Preached Before Northern Missionary Society in the State of New York* (Albany, 1798), p. 28; *Massachusetts Baptist Missionary Magazine* 1 (September 1804): 80-3.
90. *Address of the General Association*, p. 5.
91. *Massachusetts Baptist Missionary Magazine* 1 (September 1803): 5.
92. On the average, the *Connecticut Missionary Magazine*, the *Massachusetts Missionary Magazine*, and the *Massachusetts Baptist Missionary Magazine* published some news of British missions nearly every issue.
93. *Interesting Account of Religion in France* (New York, 1803); William Miller, *Signs of the Times*, pp. 35-6.
94. *Constitution of the Missionary Society of Connecticut*, p. 14.
95. *Connecticut Evangelical Magazine* 1 (July 1800): 5.
96. *Address of the General Association of Connecticut*, p. 30.
97. *An Address to the People of the State of Connecticut* (Hartford, 1801), pp. 13-14.
98. *A Continuation of the Narrative of the Missions to the New Settlements* (New Haven, 1797), pp. 13-14.
99. *A Summary of Christian Doctrine and Practice* (Hartford, 1804), p. 51.
100. *Summary of Christian Doctrine*, pp. 52-5.
101. Lathrop, *Sermon on the Dangers of the Times*, p. 13.
102. Miller, *Sermon Delivered May 9, 1798*, p. 20.
103. *Connecticut Evangelical Magazine* 1 (March 1801): 324. Also Timothy Dwight, *Travels in New England and New York* 2: 163.
104. *Summary of Christian Doctrine*, pp. 48-50.
105. *Connecticut Evangelical Magazine* 2 (September 1801): 118; *A Narrative on the Subject of Missions* (Hartford, 1801): 118; *A Narrative on the Subject of Missions* (Hartford, 1802), p. 12; *A Narrative on the Subject of Missions* (Hartford, 1806), p. 5.

106. "Thoughts on Infidelity," *Connecticut Evangelical Magazine* 1 (October 1800): 129-31.
107. *Connecticut Evangelical Magazine* 1 (February 1801): 295.
108. William Lyman, *The Happy Nation* (Hartford, 1806), p. 28.
109. Nathan Perkins, *The Benign Influence of Religion on Civil Government and National Happiness* (Hartford, 1808), p. 28.
110. *An Act to Incorporate the Trustees of the Missionary Society of Connecticut* (Hartford, 1803), p. 14.
111. Richard Furman, *America's Deliverance and Duty* (Charleston, S.C., 1802), p. 17.
112. Cummings, *Present Times Perilous*, p. 9.
113. See Nancy F. Cott, *The Bonds of Womanhood* (New Haven: Yale University Press, 1977); Ann Douglas, *The Feminization of American Culture* (New York: Knopf, 1977); Ruth H. Bloch, "American Feminine Ideals in Transition," *Feminist Studies* 4 (June 1978): 101-26.
114. [William Gerar DeBrahm], *Apocalyptical Gnomon Points out Eternity's Divisibility with Time* (Philadelphia, 1795), pp. 105-8.
115. William Lyman, *A Virtuous Woman the Bond of Domestic Union, and the Source of Domestic Happiness* (New London, Conn., 1802), p. 23.
116. Especially good examples from the Congregationalist-Presbyterian press are *Address to the People of Connecticut*, pp. 3-10; *Narrative on the Subject of Missions* (Hartford, 1802), pp. 3-11. Virtually every missionary report in the early years of the *Massachusetts Baptist Missionary Magazine* contains an account of a revival.
117. *Connecticut Evangelical Magazine* 1 (August 1800): 77.
118. Ashbel Hosmer and J. Lawton, *A View of the Rise and Increase of the Churches Composing the Otsego Baptist Association* (Whitestown, N.Y., 1800); *Minutes of the Warren Association Held at South Baptist Meeting-House in Middleborough* (Boston, 1799), p. 10; William W. Woodward, *Surprising Accounts of the Revival of Religion in the United States of America* (Philadelphia, 1800), p. 28.
119. Miller, *Sermon Before the New York Missionary Society*, p. 46; MacKnight, *View of the Present State*, pp. 26-7, 37; Welch, *Century Sermon*, pp. 22-3; *Connecticut Evangelical Magazine* 1 (July 1800): 6, and 2 (July 1801): 3.
120. *Minutes of New-York Baptist Association . . . May 22d and 23d, 1799*, p. 8.
121. *Millennial Orders, from the Throne of God and of the Lamb* [Hartford, 1799].
122. Woodward, *Surprising Accounts of the Revival*, p. 39.
123. David Thomas, *The Observer Trying the Great Reformation* (Lexington, 1802), pp. 33-4.
124. Thomas, *Observer*, p. 34. John B. Boles, *The Great Revival, 1787-1805* (Lexington: University of Kentucky Press, 1972), pp. 103-5.
125. David Rice, *A Sermon on the present revival of Religion* (Lexington, Ky., 1803), p. 37.
126. Boles, *Great Revival*, p. 100.
127. Rice, *Sermon on Revival*, p. 28.
128. *Connecticut Evangelical Magazine* 1 (February 1801): 286-91.
129. *Summary of Christian Doctrine*, especially pp. 62-3.
130. *Connecticut Evangelical Magazine* 2 (November 1801): 176-7.
131. As quoted in the *Connecticut Evangelical Magazine* 4 (August 1803): 69.

132. Woodward, *Surprising Accounts*, p. 106.
133. Thomas, *Observer*, p. 12.
134. Thomas, *Observer*, p. 13.
135. MacKnight, *View of Present State*, pp. 24-6, 37.
136. Woodward, *Surprising Accounts*, p. 16.
137. As quoted in *Connecticut Evangelical Magazine* 4 (August 1803): 69-70.
138. *Connecticut Evangelical Magazine* 5 (January 1805): 244.
139. Strong, *Universal Spread*, p. 40.
140. Joseph Badger, *A Memoir of Rev. Joseph Badger* (Hudson, Ohio, 1851), p. 26.
141. Hosmer and Lawton, *View of Churches Composing the Otsego Baptist Association*, p. 38.
142. Thomas Robbins, *A Sermon Delivered at the Ordination of the Rev. Samuel P. Robbins* (Marietta, Ohio, 1806), p. 14.
143. On this subject, see Ernest Lee Tuveson, *Redeemer Nation* (Chicago: University of Chicago Press, 1968).
144. For a few examples of the vast literature on nineteenth-century evangelicalism and evangelical millennialism, see: Charles I. Foster, *An Errand of Mercy; The Evangelical United Front, 1790-1837* (Chapel Hill: University of North Carolina Press, 1960); Clifford S. Griffin, *Their Brothers' Keepers: Moral Stewardship in the United States, 1800-1865* (New Brunswick: Rutgers University Press, 1960); de Jong, *Waters*; Paul E. Johnson, *A Shopkeeper's Millennium: Society and Revivals in Rochester, New York, 1815-1837* (New York: Hill and Wang, 1978); Timothy Smith, *Revivalism and Social Reform in Mid-Nineteenth Century America* (Nashville: Abingdon, 1958); James H. Moorhead, *American Apocalypse: Yankee Protestants and the Civil War, 1860-1869* (New Haven: Yale University Press, 1978).
145. See, in general: John F. C. Harrison, *Quest for the New Moral World: Robert Owen and the Owenites in Britain and America* (New York: Scribner, 1969); John L. Thomas, "Romantic Reform in America, 1815-1865," *American Quarterly* 17 (Winter 1965): 656-81; Anne C. Loveland, "Evangelicalism and 'Immediate Emancipation' in American Antislavery Thought," *Journal of Social History* 32 (May 1966): 172-88; Aileen S. Kraditor, *Means and Ends in American Abolitionism: Garrison and His Critics in Strategy and Tactics, 1834-1850* (New York: Pantheon, 1967); Robert H. Abzug, *Passionate Liberator: Theodor Dwight Weld and the Dilemma of Reform* (New York: Oxford University Press, 1980); Ronald G. Walters, *American Reformers, 1815-1860* (New York: Hill and Wang, 1978).
146. Ernest R. Sandeen, *The Roots of Fundamentalism: British and American Millenarianism, 1800-1930* (Chicago: University of Chicago Press, 1970); William G. McLoughlin, *Modern Revivalism: Charles Grandison Finney to Billy Graham* (New York: Ronald Press, 1959); George M. Marsden, *Fundamentalism and American Culture: The Shaping of Twentieth-Century Evangelicalism, 1870-1925* (New York: Oxford University Press, 1980); Timothy P. Weber, *Living in the Shadow of the Second Coming: American Premillennialism, 1875-1925* (New York: Oxford University Press, 1979).

Index

Index

Index

Dayton, Jonathan, 138
DeBrahm, William Gerar, 225
Declaration of Independence, 58, 76, 93, 159
Deism, 172–3, 187, 194–6, 198, 203, 211, 223
Deists, 120, 174, 178, 188, 192, 195–7, 200, 202–3
Democratic-Republican Party, see Republican Party
Democratic Societies, 180–1, 192–3; see also Republican Party
Diggers, 8
dissent, English, 3, 9, 10, 20, 103, 201
Duché, Jacob, 62, 168
Duffield, George, 96, 98
Dutch Reformed Church, xiv, 158; members, 14, 173, 206, 213, see also millennialism, denominational base of
Dwight, Theodore, 138
Dwight, Timothy, 71, 85, 101, 103, 140, 153, 174, 204–6, 211, 213–14, 217

earthquakes, 12, 22, 25–6, 32–6, 39, 50, 67, 127, 161, 164
Edwards, Jonathan, 12–14, 16–20, 22, 26, 29–34, 40, 47, 103, 119, 123–5, 128, 132, 135, 139, 141–2
Edwards, Jonathan, Jr., 138
Edwards, Morgan, 120–1
Eliot, John, 11
Ely, Samuel, 111
Emerson, Joseph, 68
Emmons, Nathaniel, 212
England, 7, 44, 53–4, 57–8, 69, 76, 86, 93, 145, 153, 163, 168; see also American Revolution; Antichrist, Britain as; Church of England; English Revolution of 1640's and 1650's
English Revolution of 1640's and 1650's, 3, 8–11, 20, 74, 87, 91, 125, 145; see also Glorious Revolution
Enlightenment, xii, 77, 85, 93, 103, 151, 168, 174, 187–8, 199–200, 211; see also liberalism; utopianism, secular
Ephrata community, 13
evangelicals, 16–17, 23, 33, 37, 39, 45, 67, 126, 214–17, 223–31; see also Great Awakening; New Lights; Second Great Awakening
Ezekial, see Book of Ezekial

Farnham, Benjamin, 160, 172, 209
Federalist Party, 112–14, 156, 179, 203

Federalists, 112–14, 129, 153–4, 156, 166, 173–4, 177–9, 186, 203, 205–7, 211, 213, 219
Fifth Monarchists, 9, 11, 71, 127, 207
Findley, William, 112, 182
Finley, Samuel, 16, 39
Fish, Elisha, 79
Fish, Samuel, 137, 148
Fisk, Joseph, 39
Fleming, Robert, 161–2, 170
Forbes, Eli, 48
Foster, Benjamin, 120, 135–6
Foster, William, 83
Foxe, John, 7–8
France, 150, 154, 158–9, 166, 171–4, 191; see also French and Indian War; French Revolution
Franklin, Benjamin, 31, 83, 103–4
Freemasons, 140, 164, 168, 188
Freewill Baptists, 88, 167; see also Baptists
French and Indian War, 23, 25–6, 28–9, 32–3, 36–7, 39, 40, 42, 57, 69, 83, 170
French Revolution, 121–2, 133, 141, 149, 151–62, 166–79, 186–93, 195–7, 200, 202, 206–9
Freneau, Philip, 59, 71, 84, 192, 195
Friends, Society of, see Quakers
Frisbie, Levi, 96
Furman, Richard, 224

Gale, Benjamin, 120, 137, 145
Gatchel, Samuel, 91–2
Genêt, Edmond, 193
George III, King of Great Britain and Ireland, 56, 59–60, 164–5
German Reformed Church, xiv, 14; see also millennialism, denominational base of
Germany, 26–7, 161
Gill, John, 32, 137
Gillet, Alexander, 214
Glorious Revolution, 3, 5, 9, 44, 69
Goddard, William, 99
Godwin, William, 197, 199, 210
Goodwin, Thomas, 160, 162, 170
Gordon, Thomas, 4
Great Awakening, 13–15, 19–21, 24; and American Revolution, 15, 17–18, 46, 56, 238n39; see also New Lights; Old Lights; revivals, religious
Great Britain, see England
Green, Jacob, 60, 106
Greenleaf, Thomas, 136, 156
Grenville, George, 54–5

287

Index